INSIGHT  GUIDES

LOS ANGELES
POCKET GUIDE

⊙ Walking Eye App

Your Insight Pocket Guide purchase includes a free download of the destination's corresponding eBook. It is available now from the free Walking Eye container app in the App Store and Google Play. Simply download the Walking Eye container app to access the eBook dedicated to your purchased book. The app also features free information on local events taking place and activities you can enjoy during your stay, with the option to book them. In addition, premium content for a wide range of other destinations is available to purchase in-app.

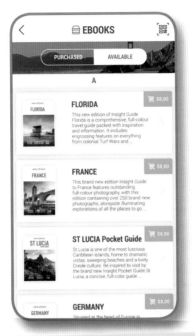

HOW TO D

Available on

1. Visit our
2. Download
   smartpho
   and the a
3. Select th
   container
4. Scan the
   a verification word from the book as proof of purchase
5. Download your free eBook* for travel information on the go

**ONLINE ACCESS
NOT AVAILABLE**

* Other destination apps and eBooks are available for purchase
separately or are free with the purchase of the Insight Guide book

TOP 10 ATTRACTIONS

THE GETTY CENTER
The museum has a great Western art collection. See page 44.

VENICE BEACH
There's always something going on here. See page 50.

DOWNTOWN LA
Historic streets and impressive landmark buildings. See page 53.

RODEO DRIVE
Shop alongside the rich and famous. See page 40.

TCL CHINESE THEATRE
A venerable Hollywood institution. See page 27.

UNIVERSAL STUDIOS
A window on the world of film. See page 65.

HUNTINGTON LIBRARY
Library, art and botanical gardens. See page 70.

GRIFFITH OBSERVATORY
Great views of the city day and night. See page 63.

THE HOLLYWOOD WALK OF FAME
Step out with the stars. See page 27.

SANTA MONICA PIER
Old-world arcades and that famous carousel. See page 47.

A PERFECT DAY

8.00am

Morning hike
Rise and shine early like an Angeleno and make your way to Hollywood's Runyon Canyon for a blood-pumping walk and some serious people-watching. If it's a clear day, you'll be able to see to the ocean from the top.

9.30am

Breakfast
Try a healthy Californian breakfast at your hotel or at Toast Bakery Cafe on West 3rd Street.

12 noon

Farmer's Market and lunch
Heading west down Third, you'll arrive at the historic Farmer's Market at the corner of Third and Fairfax, where you can check out the food stalls, and touristy shops. To work up an appetite before lunch, walk over first to the adjoining Grove outdoor shopping area and browse its upmarket chain stores.

10.30am

Shopping
Time for retail therapy – from Toast, stroll Third Street between La Cienega and Fairfax and explore the stylish clothing boutiques and gift stores.

1.30pm

Museum row
A five-minute drive south is Museum Row. Visit the Pavilion for Japanese Art; then spend hours at LACMA. For refreshment, head to Ray's & Stark Bar or across the street to the food trucks.

4.30pm

Hancock Park house tour

After leaving Museum Row, hop in the car and head to Hollywood. Take the scenic route by making a right on 4th Street off La Brea, and ogle the stunningly magnificent homes in LA's Hancock Park neighborhood.

Dinner

End the day by sliding into a leather booth and ordering a classic cocktail and steak at the famous Musso & Frank Grill (see page 106) on nearby Hollywood Boulevard. If an old-school menu doesn't appeal, head to the hipper Hungry Cat (see page 106) for a top-notch raw bar, beautifully cooked seafood, and equally excellent (though more modern) cocktails.

8.00pm

3.30pm

Tar Pits

From LACMA, take a stroll through adjacent Hancock Park to the La Brea Tar Pits. The Museum tells the story of the landmark site, but admission isn't necessary to see bubbling cauldrons of asphalt and life-size models of prehistoric animals excavated from the pits.

5.00pm

Early movie

Catch a movie at the state-of-the-art ArcLight theater in Hollywood. Advance reservations are advisable.

CONTENTS

INTRODUCTION

Los Angeles, perhaps more than any other place on earth, is preceded by its reputation. Here is a city teeming with movie stars, exorbitant wealth, sunny beaches, palm trees, and beautiful people. But LA is also linked with adventure and maybe even danger, complete with earthquakes, floods, crime, and scandals of global proportions. Because the world is watching, it's a town eternally destined to make a spectacle of itself, whether on-screen or in real life. The result is a modern-day 'Wild West' meshed with everyday life, where image is reality, poverty clashes with wealth, and fame is acquired overnight – all publicized to the hilt around the globe.

The world's perception, however, hardly reflects the real Los Angeles. The city is not merely beautiful coastlines, hit TV shows, opulent mansions in the hills, and the latest in celebrity gossip. Los Angeles County is a collection of 88 separate cities packed between the Pacific Ocean and Orange and San Bernardino counties. Many of these towns have their own city halls, police forces, and fire brigades. The result is that LA is a place without a geographic heart, but with lots of soul. If its soul is superficial, flighty, and playful – well, this is the entertainment capital of the world.

A VARIETY OF LIFESTYLES

Los Angeles encompasses a huge variety of American life within its borders. In fact, the cultural and economic lifestyles of some 10 million county residents vary so enormously from area to area that visiting Los Angeles is like visiting half a dozen destinations at once. You can go casual and carefree with the beach scene, blow the bank on a ritzy Beverly Hills shopping excursion, retreat to nature on a mountain hike, opt for the 'global' by touring the ethnic neighborhoods, flee to fantasy at any number of amusement parks, or simply entertain yourself

Downtown LA

with an exploration into the entertainment world and Hollywood exotica. Whatever you do, you'll experience in-your-face LA, because its eccentricities are abundant wherever you go.

The one attribute that suffuses everything in Los Angeles is its lively energy. Even on your first visit there's no denying the feeling that something – somewhere – is about to happen. It might be catching the eye of your favorite celebrity scurrying into a movie theater, watching a production company shoot a scene from the next big blockbuster movie, attempting to keep up with the freeway's pedal-to-the-metal drivers, or simply scanning the twinkling evening skyline from the heights of the Griffith Observatory. In a town where the fast lane is the norm and Hollywood isn't just a place but a state of being, you can't help feeling part of something exciting and unpredictable.

LARGE ETHNIC POPULATIONS

Much of this energy can be attributed to the residents. Few places on earth attract such a diverse population. The year-round sunshine appeals to all kinds and LA offers an ideal combination of urban and beach living. Add to this the entertainment industry folk and then LA's large groups of Americans of Chinese, African, Korean, Middle Eastern, and Japanese

The freeway

descent. Hispanic Americans comprise the largest ethnic group of all, numbering around 49 percent of the population.

With so many people packed into such a condensed area, Angelenos are constantly struggling to create unique identities for themselves, which would be more of a challenge if the town didn't have such an 'anything goes' attitude.

CITY OF FREEWAYS

What comes as no surprise is that the car is king. With nearly two vehicles per household, LA has one of the world's highest per-capita car populations. Visitors will have to join the masses traveling the streets and freeways to get a real feel for the city.

Tourist attractions are scattered from Malibu all the way to Disneyland but much of what you'll see will be through your car window because you'll likely be spending a lot of time driving. Used by over 12 million vehicles daily, the nation's 10 busiest freeways are all in the LA vicinity. Strict emission controls have considerably reduced the city's notorious smog, but air quality can still be poor. To combat highway congestion and pollution, LA is expanding its much-needed light rail network. The good news, however, is that freeway exits and visitor attractions are well marked, and you're bound to find an unexpected attraction to get you off the road and back to the excitement in no time.

A BRIEF HISTORY

Long before the arrival of Spanish colonists, this part of the West Coast was a pastoral home to 30,000 Native American Indians. In 1542, Juan Rodriguez Cabrillo, a Portuguese navigator in the service of Carlos I, king of Spain, was the first European to set foot in the area. But for the next two centuries LA remained nothing more than a pit stop on the trans-Pacific naval highway – a provisioning spot for Spanish galleons on their way back to Mexico from the Philippines. It wasn't until other nations cast their eyes towards California that Spain decided to strengthen its claim on the region through colonization.

FOUNDING COLONISTS

In 1769, Spanish colonists, led by two men, a 55-year-old Franciscan priest named Father Junípero Serra and Captain Gaspar de Portolá, arrived in San Diego and built the first of a string of missions up the coast to consolidate territories, extend borders, and bring Christianity to Native Americans. Natives didn't take well to the new lifestyle, and diseases that arrived with the colonists killed so many thousands that the Native American population of California never recovered from the initial encounter.

In 1771, Mission San Gabriel Arcangel was founded, marking the first major Spanish presence in the Los Angeles area. It was the fourth in the mission chain and still stands 9 miles (14.5km) east of LA. Within the next few years California's military governor Felipe de Neve decided the area needed a settlement and made plans to design a *pueblo*, or town. It took months to recruit any settlers, but in 1781, a group of 12 men, 11 women, and 21 children arrived at the mission from Mexico, and on September 4 they ceremoniously founded the new town 'El Pueblo de Nuestra Señora la Reina de Los Angeles de

Porciúncula' (Our Lady the Queen of the Angels of Porciúncula).
Today the site is better known as Downtown's Olvera Street.

Prosperity came slowly. In 1800, the population was 315.
The *pueblo* included 30 homes, a town hall and guardhouse,
granaries, a church, a central plaza, and 12,500 cows.

THE CALIFORNIA RANCHOS

De Neve's successor passed new laws enabling him to grant
vast tracts of land and grazing rights to settlers. He distributed tens of thousands of acres, largely to his friends and
comrades. It was not long before a dozen or so *patrones*
(landlords) owned nearly all of what is now coastal Los
Angeles County, with the exception of the mission lands and
the farms surrounding the *pueblo*.

Because colonial powers controlled all trade in their territories, Mexico and Spain at first received the wealth of goods

The Great Wall of Los Angeles

produced by the California *ranchos* (ranches or farms) and missions. But news soon made its way to the East Coast about cheap goods from the California settlements. With few Spanish ships or militia in the area to enforce colonial trading laws, Yankee ships began capitalizing on this lucrative market, ending California's isolation.

MEXICAN RULE AND AMERICAN ANNEXATION

After Mexico declared independence from Spain in 1822 and claimed California for itself in 1825, Spanish priests were ordered out of the region and missions lost their power. Commissioners were appointed to distribute 8 million acres (3 million hectares) of mission land and resources, most to powerful families and ranchers. The Native Americans, having lost their lands, either fled to the mountains or found themselves having to work for Mexican landlords.

Meanwhile, the *pueblo* of Los Angeles had become the largest settlement in the territory, with a population of nearly 1,250. A number of Americans had settled in California, joined the Catholic Church, and married into the area's leading families. Within a few years, these Americans became great landholders and wielded a monopoly on local commerce.

By the time war erupted between the United States and Mexico in 1846, agitators in Washington were already calling for the annexation of California. The Mexican settlers put up a good fight, against forces several times their number. Eventually, they were defeated, and in January 1847, General Andrés Pico relinquished Los Angeles to the Americans.

AFTER THE GOLD RUSH

Growth was still slow, but the discovery of gold in northern California in 1848 changed everything. Many Angelenos packed their bags and headed out to dig; those who stayed

Miners in the 1850s Gold Rush

found a lucrative market in supplying food and goods to miners. Meat replaced hides and tallow as the main industry of the ranches; cattle were herded north where they could be sold for ten times the going rate.

On April 4, 1850, the city of Los Angeles was incorporated and declared the county seat. Its first newspaper, *The Star*, began in the same year, published in both Spanish and English. Over the next 20 years, Los Angeles gained a reputation as a 'bad' town, with the largest number of gambling dens, brothels, and saloons per capita in the West. But new industries sprang up: wine became an important export; the first citrus trees were planted; and a water-supply system was installed. Los Angeles began to lose its frontier-town aspects.

THE BOOM YEARS

By 1870, Los Angeles' population numbered 5,614. Hotels and larger buildings were constructed; civic and cultural institutions such as a library, a dance academy, and a drama society were founded. Further prosperity followed the completion of the Southern Pacific Railroad line to Los Angeles in 1876, making the vital transcontinental link and sparking the biggest real-estate boom in the nation's history.

As the large *ranchos* were gradually divided, settlers planted orchards and gardens and introduced modern agricultural methods. Oranges became one of the major crops, when refrigerated rail cars arrived.

In late 1885, the Santa Fe Railroad line reached Los Angeles, competing with the Southern Pacific in a fierce price war that made cross-country travel virtually free. By 1887, trains had brought more than 120,000 to the town of 10,000 residents; most of the travelers settled in the area.

The real-estate boom collapsed three years after it began, but by the time the dust settled in 1890, Los Angeles had embarked on a new campaign designed to lure Midwestern farmers to the sunny state. California's prize agricultural produce was vigorously promoted, and people poured into the area believing the motto the city still promotes: 'LA is the place where fortunes are made and dreams come true.'

The discovery of petroleum in 1892, not far from the city center, prompted another flurry of development and added a few more names to the growing list of ultra-wealthy residents. The first well, drilled by Edward Doheny and Charles Canfield, yielded 45 barrels a day. Within five years nearly 2,500 wells had been sunk within the city limits, and the industry flourished. Led by Los Angeles, California produced a quarter

Small beginnings

With the rapidly expanding population, Los Angeles city lots were bought up quickly and new communities were founded. One of these, created by Horace and Daeida Wilcox when they subdivided their 120-acre (48-hectare) orchard, was named 'Hollywood.'

William Mulholland – the man who built the city's water infrastructure

of the world's oil supply right into the 20th century.

The 1890s marked further expansion with the construction of San Pedro's deep-water harbor. Port of Los Angeles, the largest man-made port in the world, opened in 1910.

THE 20TH CENTURY

During its first 120 years, Los Angeles had become a dynamic city with a population of more than 100,000. But with a new advertising venture that included the slogan 'Oranges for Health – California for Wealth,' the population of the city tripled in the first decade of the 20th century.

One concern stood in the way of further expansion: water – or, rather, the lack of it. As the population mushroomed, it became clear that the Los Angeles River, the sole source of water for the city, would not be able to support the city's needs. William Mulholland, chief engineer of the Municipal Water Bureau, planned to obtain water from the Owens River, which was fed by snow-melt from the High Sierra. In an amazing feat of determination, an aqueduct more than 233 miles (375km) long was constructed to deliver enough water to supply a city of 2 million. As an added benefit, a hydroelectric generating plant was completed along the aqueduct in 1917. In 1923, with the population rising by 100,000 each year, it was clear that an additional supply of water would soon be needed. Mulholland began to survey a route for a waterway from the Colorado River, 400 miles (644km) away in Arizona. The new aqueducts opened in 1939.

After World War I, LA became the fastest-growing city in the United States. The metropolis soon stretched from the southern harbor at San Pedro to the San Fernando Valley in the north. A streetcar system began operating in 1901, and by the late 1930s had become the largest in the US, servicing some 80 million passengers a year. Citrus crops accounted for a third of the county's produce. It was the nation's richest agricultural region. Large oil refineries were built, and with the coming of Firestone and Goodyear, LA also became a major rubber-producing center, which seems especially appropriate, considering its residents' already-established love affair with the car. Later, aircraft and car assembly plants were built. No single business, however, was – or is – as enduring in Los Angeles as the motion picture industry, which in 1919 was already making 80 percent of the world's supply of films. It has remained the city's chief industry.

In the 1920s Los Angeles was a boom town and a melting pot for immigrants, hustlers, adventurers, desperados, and dreamers. Institutions appropriate for a burgeoning city were built, including Downtown's historic Biltmore Hotel, the Central Library, City Hall, and the University of Southern California (which was founded in 1880).

Mulholland's drive

In 1924, LA honored water engineer William Mulholland by naming scenic Mulholland Drive after him. His work had given the city a reliable water supply. But 1928 brought disaster. A dam 40 miles (25km) north of Los Angeles collapsed only hours after he had inspected it, killing 450 people. Mulholland resigned in disgrace.

Hollywood Walk of Fame

When the Great Depression struck in 1929, southern California's growth slowed as dispossessed farmers of the Dust Bowl region (the south-central United States) and a long line of other not-so-welcome migrants headed west. But by 1935 the city was optimistic, recovering economically, and ranking fifth among the industrial counties of the US.

World War II brought further growth in industry and population, as workers flocked to LA to find jobs at aircraft plants and shipyards. Close to 200,000 African Americans moved into south-central LA to pursue job opportunities. Mexican residents, who had not been so welcome after the end of Mexican rule, were also accepted as laborers. But overcrowding, prejudice, and already obvious social ranking would continue to cause great tensions.

With the postwar population boom and the phaseout of LA's streetcars came the mass construction of today's freeway system, making possible the development of areas previously considered too remote. Along one of these freeway routes in Orange County was another major construction project, Disneyland, which was surrounded by orange groves when it opened in 1955.

THE WATTS RIOTS

By 1963, California had become America's most populous state. More water shortages, reduced services, and increased racial tensions resulted. In the summer of 1965, widespread rioting broke out in the black ghetto of Watts, in south-central LA, when a black motorist was accused of drink-driving. Six days of vandalism, looting, and fires left 34 dead and caused $40 million in damage. The scene was repeated in the spring of 1992, when the acquittal of four white policemen accused of beating black motorist Rodney King sparked 48 hours of riotous violence. The death toll reached 50, with thousands injured and property damage of over $1 billion. While other trials (O.J. Simpson's murder trial in 1995, for example) divided the city, others, including recovery from the 1994 Northridge earthquake, brought Angelenos together as a community. A strengthening economy in Southern California has helped as well.

FILMED IN HOLLYWOOD

Movies found a home in southern California because the sunny days and wide-open spaces were perfect for filmmaking. Cecil B. DeMille set up the town's first movie studio near Highland and Sunset in a horse barn and filmed *The Squaw Man*, the first feature-length film, in 1913. In the 1920s a box-office boom, led by such Hollywood stars as Douglas Fairbanks, Charlie Chaplin, and Mary Pickford, made movies a lucrative business. By 1939 cinemas out-numbered banks, and Americans spent twice as much time at the movies as they do today.

In the latter part of the 20th century, the Hollywood area's golden history was tarnished by decay as the studios and stars moved out and an ongoing parade of hustlers and lost souls, souvenir shops and touristy attractions moved in. But since the millennium, an extensive renovation program has brought shiny new attractions and enter-tainment venues that will ensure the city's encore performance.

City of Los Angeles Police

By the 1980s the growth of the metropolitan region forced city planners to begin rebuilding a system of public transport. A new light rail line, the Metro Blue Line, opened in 1990, connecting Downtown to Long Beach. The Red Line, the first subway, opened Downtown in 1993, and now stretches all the way to North Hollywood. The Green and Gold light rail lines, opened in 1995 and 2003 respectively, were joined in 2005 by the Orange Line, a dedicated bus transitway through the San Fernando Valley, and in 2006 by the Purple Line subway, serving west of Downtown. The latest addition is an extension to the Expo Line to the west with seven new stations linking Santa Monica with Downtown in under 50 minutes.

LA FOREVER

Los Angeles' sprawl has made creating a unified 'city' impossible. Though the entertainment industry and its revenues reach businesses and residents from Downtown to Malibu, in almost every other way each neighborhood is its own minicity struggling for a sense of itself. Los Angeles County with a population of over 10 million is facing the challenges of the 21st century as well as the perennial problems of soaring prices for energy and basic necessities. But that doesn't prevent Angelenos from looking on the bright side. Business is booming; the beach is packed; and movie stars and millionaires are still made overnight.

HISTORICAL LANDMARKS

1771 Founding of Mission San Gabriel Arcangel.

1781 Founding of El Pueblo de Nuestra Señora la Reina de Los Angeles de Porciúncula.

1825 California becomes a territory of Mexico.

1848 The treaty of Guadalupe Hidalgo ends the Mexican-American War. California annexed to the US, becoming a state in 1850.

1853 Don Matteo Keeler plants the first orange trees.

1876 First transcontinental railroad, the Southern Pacific, arrives.

1880 The University of Southern California is founded.

1881 The *Los Angeles Times* publishes its first issue.

1892 Oil is discovered in downtown Los Angeles.

1913 Cecil B. DeMille makes the first full-length feature film, *The Squaw Man*, in a barn near Highland and Sunset.

1923 The Hollywood sign is erected.

1927 Grauman's Chinese Theatre opens. The Academy of Motion Picture Arts and Sciences is founded at the Biltmore Hotel.

1928 LA's first airport, Mines Field, opens.

1932 The Summer Olympics take place in LA.

1947 Hollywood Freeway links Downtown with the Valley.

1955 Disneyland opens in Anaheim.

1961 The Hollywood Walk of Fame is launched.

1965 The Watts riots.

1984 The XXIII Olympiad is held in LA.

1992 Riots in reaction to the verdict in the Rodney King trial.

1993 LA's first subway line, the Red Line, opens in Downtown.

1994 The Northridge earthquake causes much destruction.

1995 The O.J. Simpson trial captures the world's attention.

2003 The Walt Disney Concert Hall opens at the Music Center.

2006 Getty Villa reopens in Malibu after a major restoration.

2011 'Carmageddon' strands Angelenos when the 405 freeway is shut down for two days.

2012 The Expo Line between Downtown and Culver City starts.

2015 The Broad, a new landmark contemporary art museum, opens.

WHERE TO GO

To savor the abundant flavors of LA, you need a taste for adventure, a car (ideally), and a good map. Add savvy plans that keep you off the freeways during rush hour, and you will discover why Angelenos consider their home the center of the universe. Visit Hollywood by day for its remnants of old-time movie-world glamour, or after dark for its theaters and nightclubs. Star-gazing in Beverly Hills or a night out on the Sunset Strip are also favorite LA experiences. For culture, head for the Wilshire District's Museum Row, the Westside's Getty Center and Hammer Museum, or Pasadena's superb art museums. Downtown has some of the city's finest architecture, historic sites, and vibrant neighbourhoods offering a mix of ethnicities. And no trip to LA is complete without at least one day on the beach and a visit to the Santa Monica pier. The surrounding mountains and valleys, along with Orange County to the south, offer theme parks, historic missions and wildlife reserves. For a longer excursion, you can escape to Palm Springs or Catalina Island.

HOLLYWOOD

'Hollywood' is not merely an actual place but, rather, a lifestyle unique to Los Angeles. While the city of Hollywood might once have had a glamorous reputation, during the past few decades the neighborhood, which stretches along

Tourist information

The city's main visitor information centers are located at the Hollywood & Highland Center and downtown at 685 South Figueroa Street, but many areas of the metro region also have their own tourist offices (see page 131).

Rooftop Bar at the Standard Hotel, Downtown

The iconic Hollywood sign

the base of the northern hills emblazoned with the land-mark Hollywood sign, deteriorated like a faded movie star. Now, it has been making a major comeback as one of the city's trendiest spots for shopping, dining, and night-time entertainment.

TINSELTOWN TRIUMPHS

The **Hollywood sign** over Beachwood Canyon is perhaps the most recognized landmark in LA and a favorite photo background. Originally constructed in 1923 to promote real-estate sales in the neighborhood then called 'Hollywoodland,' the 50ft (15m) letters were abbreviated in later years and replaced due to age in 1978. Even though you can't get close enough to the sign to touch it (it has a security system sur-rounding it, but a challenging hike via Griffith Park will bring you pretty close), it's still a powerful and beloved symbol, reminding visitors of Los Angeles' status as the center of the fast and glamorous world of movie making.

Equally famous is the **Hollywood Walk of Fame** ❶. The 'walk' refers to the legwork you'll need to do to check out the 2,300 or so bronze-and-terrazzo stars embedded in the pavement to honor celebrities in the music and entertainment industries. Stars stretch for a total of 3.5 miles (5.5km) along Hollywood Boulevard from La Brea Avenue to Gower Street, and along Vine Street from Yucca Street to Sunset Boulevard. Among the most sought-after are those of Marilyn Monroe (in front of McDonald's at 6774 Hollywood Boulevard), Charlie Chaplin (at 6751), and John Wayne (1541 Vine). To find the location of your favorite, visit www.walkoffame.com/star finder. What does it take to get one's name on a star? You must be nominated to the Hollywood Chamber of Commerce and, if selected, come up with $25,000 to pay for your star.

TCL Chinese Theatre ❷, still often referred to as Grauman's Chinese Theatre (6925 Hollywood Boulevard; tel: 323-463 9576 for tours; www.tclchinesetheatres.com), which you can't miss due to its flashy Chinese temple-style architecture and the swarms of tourists out front, is one of the other worthwhile stops on Hollywood Boulevard. While current films are still shown here, the real attraction is the exterior courtyard, where autographs, handprints and footprints in cement commemorate Hollywood's greatest celebrities. This Art-Deco picture palace, originally called The Grauman, was built by the great showman Sid Grauman in 1927. The courtyard tradition allegedly began at the opening, when actress Norma Talmadge accidentally stepped in wet cement. Among the famous signatures, you can also spot such unusual impressions as Jimmy Durante's nose and the hoof prints of Gene Autry's horse, Champion.

Adjacent to the TCL is the glamorous **Hollywood & Highland** shopping and entertainment complex (http://hollywoodandhighland.com; Mon–Sat 10am–10pm and Sun 10am–7pm), focal point of the city's renovation. It includes the

TCL Chinese Theatre at night

gorgeous Dolby Theatre (formerly known as the Kodak Theatre), permanent home of the Academy Awards; the Loews Hollywood Hotel; and Babylon Court, modeled after the set from the 1916 film *Intolerance*, with a grand staircase, 33ft (10m) pillars topped by a pair of elephants, and an archway that frames the Hollywood sign in the background. The Visitor Information Center (Mon–Sat 9am–10pm, Sun 10am–7pm) is the place to pick up half-price theater tickets to shows playing throughout the city. Tickets become available on Tuesdays for productions running that week, so you can book ahead as well as attend same-day shows.

While Grauman's is undoubtedly the hotspot for your 'That's-me-in-Hollywood!' snapshots, the area's other landmark cinemas deserve a peek as well. *Citizen Kane* premiered in 1941 at the Moorish-style **El Capitan Theatre** (6838 Hollywood Boulevard; https://elcapitantheatre.com), which today is a primary venue for Disney films. **The Egyptian Theatre** (6712 Hollywood Boulevard; tel: 323-466 3456; www.egyptiantheatre.com) was Hollywood's first movie palace, built by Grauman in 1922 after the discovery of Tutankhamen's tomb. Restored in 1998, it shows classic and independent films and has backstage tours once a month. Also noteworthy is the **Hollywood Roosevelt Hotel** (7000 Hollywood Boulevard;

tel: 323-856 1970; www.thehollywoodroosevelt.com), which established itself as the hotel of the film world when it opened in 1927. Just two years later, in 1929, the landmark building hosted the first public Oscar ceremony; it was also home to Marilyn Monroe for eight years. Its lobby features hand-painted ceilings and Spanish-revival décor of wrought-iron grillwork. On display on the mezzanine floor are historic Hollywood photographs and other memorabilia.

The former Max Factor Building, an Art-Deco gem, houses the **Hollywood Museum** (1660 N. Highland Avenue; tel: 323-464 7776; www.thehollywoodmuseum.com; Wed–Sun 10am–5pm). It contains some 5,000 artifacts of movie memorabilia, including costumes, props, posters, and photographs. Hollywood glamour is highlighted in the Max Factor exhibit of movie stars' dressing rooms and make-up cases.

STRICTLY TOURIST

Clustered together on Hollywood Boulevard is a range of cheesy but mildly entertaining attractions that are aimed

OSCARS

A gold-plated bronze figure standing on a reel of film holds a sword upright: this prestigious statuette has been awarded since 1928 for what the Academy of Motion Picture Arts and Sciences judge the year's best achievements in film, for everybody from actors and directors to scriptwriters, costume designers, and technical and effects artists. Why the name Oscar? Until 1931 the statuette had no name, until an obscure Academy librarian, Margaret Herrick (who eventually became its executive director), gave it the nickname because of its resemblance to her Uncle Oscar. The nickname stuck after it was reported in an article in a local newspaper.

squarely at relieving you of your tourist dollars. **Ripley's Believe It or Not!** offers lightweight entertainment, starting with the Tyrannosaurus rex towering above the entrance (6780 Hollywood Boulevard; tel: 323-466 6335; www.ripleys.com/hollywood; daily 10am–midnight). Robert Ripley was a cartoonist who traveled the far corners of the globe in the 1930s and 1940s, searching for examples of the bizarre. His first 'Odditorium' opened at the Chicago World's Fair in 1933, and the cartoon features based on his collection are still syndicated worldwide. Here you'll see a shrunken head, a two-headed goat, and a statue of Marilyn Monroe made of shredded money, among other curiosities.

Capitol Records Tower Building

Next door is the **Guinness World Records Museum** (6764 Hollywood Boulevard; tel: 323-463 6433; www.guinnessmuseumhollywood.com; daily 10am–midnight), which offers two floors of displays about bizarre facts, feats, and achievements. Across the street is the unimpressive **Hollywood Wax Museum** (6767 Hollywood Boulevard; tel: 323-462 5991; www.hollywoodwaxmuseum.com; daily 10am–midnight), featuring a collection of superstars from Jesus Christ to Sylvester Stallone.

Further along you'll spot the flashy pink exterior of **Frederick's of Hollywood**

(6751 Hollywood Boulevard), the shop best known for glamorizing trashy undergarments. Among the racks of feathery satin bras and panties are gallery presentations from their 'Lingerie Museum,' where you can peek at the apparel of celebrities such as Monroe and Madonna.

The intersection of Hollywood and Vine was once the heart of Tinseltown, but now it is rather nondescript, at least by day. A number of nearby theaters make it a busy spot for nightlife. A touch of the old glamour survives in the landmark **Capitol Records Building** ❸ (1750 N. Vine Street), which is shaped like a stack of records. The building's distinctive design is credited to recording stars Nat King Cole and Johnny Mercer. The Hollywood Jazz mural by Richard Wyatt on the south wall depicts Billie Holiday, Duke Ellington, and other music legends.

> **Hollywood Trolley**
>
> The Hollywood Trolley are three bus lines operating between Hollywood Beach and the Historic Downtown. One ride costs $1 per person, paid on-board. Trolleys depart approximately every 30 minutes every Wednesday, Thursday and Sunday 10am–10pm and every Friday and Saturday 10am–11pm. For further information and a route map, visit the website: www.visit hollywoodfl.org/trolley.aspx.

STUDIO TOURS

Paramount Studios ❹ (5555 Melrose Avenue; tel: 323-956 1777; www.paramountstudios.com; daily tours) is the only major motion-picture studio still located in Hollywood. If peeking in through the wrought-iron gates isn't enough shoulder-rubbing with stardom for you, you can view the back lot on a two-hour or even a four-and-a-half-hour walking tour through the studios, film sets (when not in use), sound stages, and props department, and catch a glimpse of other behind-the-scenes activities. It reveals a peek at such tricks of the trade as the B-tank, where Moses parted the waters in *The Ten Commandments*, and New York Street, a facade of brownstones made of fiberglass and aged to look like real brick. The After Dark Tours are by reservation only, for visitors aged 10 and over.

If you drive west on Melrose from Paramount Studios, you'll arrive at the trendy section of **Melrose Avenue** (between La Brea and Fairfax), where young tourists, local hipsters, and fashionable freaks populate the funky boutiques, restaurants, and cafés.

FAMOUS LAST RESTING PLACES

A few blocks from Paramount is the **Hollywood Forever Cemetery ❺** (6000 Santa Monica Boulevard at Gower; tel: 323-469 1181; gate hours: Mon–Fri 8.30am–5pm, summer until 5.30pm), where many stars are buried. The graves of Cecil B. DeMille and Douglas Fairbanks Sr. can be found in the lake area. The Cathedral Mausoleum holds Rudolph Valentino's crypt, which was visited by the mysterious Lady in Black each year on the anniversary of his death, until she died in 1989. For a true LA experience, check out one of the classic movie screenings or concerts the cemetery hosts on its grounds (seasonal; www.cinespia.org, www.hollywoodforever. com/culture).

Hollywood Hike

For breathtaking views of the city and people-watching at its finest, the 3-mile (5-km) loop at Runyon Canyon Park in the heart of Hollywood (2001 N. Fuller Avenue) is a favorite among tourists and Angelenos alike.

The Pierce Brothers Westwood Village Memorial Park (1218 Glendon Avenue; tel: 310-474 1579), a five-minute walk south of Westwood Village, boasts one of the most famous graves in all of Los Angeles, that of Marilyn Monroe. Her former husband, Joe DiMaggio, adorned her simple wall crypt with roses every week for 25 years after her death.

Marble statuary and mammoth artwork spread across both branches of **Forest Lawn Memorial Park** (tel: 800-204 3131; http://forestlawn.com; daily 8am–5pm, until 6pm during daylight savings time). Stan Laurel and Buster Keaton are among those buried in the Hollywood Hills branch, 4 miles (6km) north of Hollywood. Walt Disney, Humphrey Bogart, Spencer Tracy, Elizabeth Taylor and Michael Jackson are just a few of those buried in the Glendale branch, 7 miles (11km) north of Downtown.

La Brea Tar Pits

THE WILSHIRE DISTRICT

Wilshire Boulevard began as an Indian trail connecting the downtown area with the La Brea Tar Pits and later was developed as an upscale shopping and business district. Today it is one of the widest and longest boulevards in North America, showcasing the many faces of Los Angeles. Stretching 16 miles (25km) from Downtown to the sea, it passes through a variety of ethnic neighborhoods and financial brackets – from the very poor to the ridiculously wealthy.

The stretch of Wilshire between La Brea and Fairfax avenues is known as the Mid-Wilshire district or Miracle Mile. It boasts several cultural attractions along its 'Museum Row.'

A fascinating attraction is the **La Brea Tar Pits** ❻, one of the world's richest sources of Pleistocene fossils that date back 40,000 years. In the large pit in front of the Museum, life-size replicas of mastodons are shown trapped in the tar, which was formed by oil deposits collected in pools on the earth's surface. From viewing stations alongside other pits, you can watch the excavations and view the bones of the pre-historic beasts that perished here.

The adjacent **La Brea Tar Pits Museum** (5801 Wilshire Boulevard; tel: 213-763 3499; www.tarpits.org; daily 9.30am–5pm) provides fascinating insight into Ice Age life in southern California. The *Titans of the Ice Age* is an introductory 3D film illustrating how the animals became trapped in the asphalt as they edged down to a pool of water to drink. Skeletons of such extinct creatures as the saber-toothed cat, imperial mammoth, and giant ground sloth have been reconstructed from the fossils. The wall display of 400 wolf skulls brings a startling realization of just how many animals have been unearthed here.

Of the 420 animal species found in the area, only one human fossil has been discovered: the 9,000-year-old La Brea Woman. Killed by a blow to the head, she was perhaps LA's first murder victim. The museum also features a fishbowl laboratory where visitors can see fossils being cleaned and catalogued. The peaceful atrium nurtures primitive plants, several of which have evolved over a period of 100 million years.

After leaving the museum, take the scenic route by making a right on 4th Street off La Brea to admire the splendid homes in Hancock Park residential neighborhood.

MUSEUM ROW

The **Los Angeles County Museum of Art** ❼ (5905 Wilshire Boulevard; tel: 323-857 6000; www.lacma.org; Mon, Tue, Thu 11am–5pm, Fri 11am–8pm, Sat–Sun 10am–7pm), the city's

Farmer's Market and the Grove Shopping Mall

largest museum, is located next door. Among the treasures in this seven-building complex are a collection of pre-Columbian artifacts that were found in Mexico and Peru, European modern and contemporary art, American colonial art and furniture, Japanese masterpieces, and what is generally regarded as the finest Indian and Southeast Asian art collection in the West. The Broad Contemporary Art Museum at LACMA is the latest addition to the fold, with stunning display space for changing exhibitions of contemporary art (www.the broad.org). The museum is gearing up for a major makeover, which will see four of its old structures replaced by a state-of-the-art building in 2023. Before this, there are plans for a new neighbour onsite with The **Academy Museum of Motion Picture** (www.oscars.org), due to open in 2017. Designed by award-winning architect Renzo Piano, it's sure to become the world's premier movie museum.

The small but extremely significant **Craft and Folk Art Museum** (5814 Wilshire Boulevard; tel: 323-937 4230; www.

cafam.org; Tue–Fri 11am–5pm, Sat–Sun noon–6pm, 1st Tue of each month also 6.30–9.30pm; Sun "pay what you want") rotates exhibitions from around the world.

At 6060 Wilshire at Fairfax is the **Petersen Automotive Museum** (tel: 323-930 2277; www.petersen.org; Tue–Sun 10am–6pm). It celebrates the town's love affair with cars, showcasing over 160 distinctive motor vehicles in new innovative galleries, including interactive children's displays. At the time of writing the museum was preparing for its grand reopening in December 2015, following an extensive remodeling of its three floors and the exterior, which will now be wrapped in ribbons of stainless steel.

A few blocks north on Fairfax is the lively **Farmers' Market** ❽ (6333 West Third Street; tel: 323-933 9211; www.farmers marketla.com; Mon–Fri 9am–9pm, Sat 9am–8pm, Sun 10am–7pm). In the 1930s a small group of Depression-era farmers gathered in what was then a field at the edge of town, to sell produce directly to the people. Its popularity as a meeting place has kept it busy since then, with crowds perusing the fruit and vegetable stands for the best bargains, a maze of shops selling foodstuffs and gifts, and inexpensive food stalls. The upscale outdoor shopping center **The Grove** (323-900 8080; www.thegrovela.com) is directly adjacent, with boutiques and restaurants, a movie theater, choreographed fountains, and even a double-decker trolley for the kids.

THE WESTSIDE

Several communities make up the area collectively known as the 'Westside.' They are linked not only by geographical location but also by image: it is around here that some of the most beautiful people congregate. It's also where the upmarket and fashionable neighborhoods converge, with their affluent residential areas, trendy restaurants, and fabulous shopping areas.

Sunset and Hollywood Boulevard street signs

WEST HOLLYWOOD

While Hollywood is more remembered than experienced, its neighbor **West Hollywood** defines the cutting edge. Within its 2 square miles (5 sq km) are over 100 restaurants, many night-clubs, interior design shops and galleries, swanky hotels, and the offices of the entertainment and music industries.

Melrose Avenue and Beverly and Robertson Boulevards are known as the 'Avenues of Design.' The streets here are lined with design showrooms, fashion boutiques, and art galleries, including the **Pacific Design Center** ❾ (8687 Melrose Avenue; tel: 310-657 0800; www.pacificdesigncenter.com; Mon–Fri 9am–5pm), a gigantic, blue-glass building known as the Blue Whale, designed by Cesar Pelli in 1975. Some 130 showrooms are housed here and in the adjoining Green Center, which dis-plays an impressive range of traditional and contemporary home and office furniture created by famous designers. The latest addition, the Red Building, houses 400,000 sq ft/37,000 sqm of office and retail space and was completed in 2013. The showrooms are for trade only, meaning only interior designers and their clients can browse and buy. You can, however, visit the **MOCA Gallery** (tel: 213-626 6222; www.moca.org; Tue–Fri 11am–5pm, Sat–Sun 11am–6pm; free), a satellite of the Museum of Contemporary Art downtown, which presents temporary exhibitions on design and architecture.

Spanning the length of West Hollywood is **Santa Monica Boulevard** – the center of LA's gay and lesbian nightlife. Every year in June, the city holds LA Pride, a lively three-day festival and parade that has grown into the third largest in California. The street goes wild each Halloween, too.

Sunset Tower Hotel

SUNSET STRIP

West Hollywood's most famous thoroughfare is without a doubt the **Sunset Strip**, stretching from the 8200 block of Sunset Boulevard west to Doheny Drive. Since the 1920s it has been the stomping grounds for LA's partying celebrities. With many renovations dating from the 1990s economic boom, its hotels and clubs remained spectacularly impervious to the recent downturn. Many top comedians started here in clubs such as The Comedy Store (http://thecomedystore. com), while rock'n'roll legends were born in the dance halls of The Roxy (www.the

roxy.com) and Whisky-A-Go-Go (www.whiskyagogo.com). On weekends the Strip's traffic slows as the young and the hip traipse from one nightspot to the next. But even if you never leave your car, the huge billboards beaming with the faces of celebrities promoting their latest movie or recording (or simply themselves) announce this is the town's wild play palace.

Among the landmarks are the **Sunset Tower Hotel** ❿ (8358 Sunset Boulevard; www.sunsettowerhotel.com), a stately Art-Deco masterpiece. Built in 1931, it was the first all-electric apartment building in California, and has been featured in several films. Clark Gable, Errol Flynn, and Jean Harlow were three of the many stars who once lived here. Further west is the **Mondrian** hotel (8440 Sunset Boulevard), with modern décor by Philippe Starck, and a parade of celebrities who frequent the SkyBar cocktail lounge.

Sunset Plaza (8600–8700 Sunset Boulevard at Sunset Plaza Drive; www.sunsetplaza.com), an elite shopping area since 1934, is a cluster of Georgian-style buildings that were designed by Charles Selkirk. Once home to the Mocambo and Trocadero nightclubs, today the plaza is lined with upmarket, one-of-a-kind specialty shops and European-style sidewalk cafés – a top spot for people-watching.

BEVERLY HILLS

Hip gives way to chic at Doheny Drive, where the Strip ends and Sunset Boulevard enters **Beverly Hills**. Here, luxurious homes and landscaped lawns sit on some of the most expensive real estate in the world. It's worth sidetracking into the hills just to marvel at them. On this stretch of Sunset you're bound to find hawkers on street corners selling 'Maps to the Stars' to lead you to the homes of the rich and famous.

This millionaire mecca is a testament to the region's unparalleled success. At the turn of the 20th century the land was practically worthless, covered with failed oil wells and fields of lima beans. But in 1912, when developers built the **Beverly Hills Hotel** ⑪ (9641 Sunset Boulevard), everything changed. The Spanish Colonial-style building was soon dubbed the Pink Palace and fast became popular with the movie set. Its Polo Lounge is now a notorious watering hole for Hollywood's power brokers. Marilyn Monroe and John F. Kennedy were said to be among the celebrities who met secretly in the private bungalows. The hotel is now owned by one of the richest men in the world, the Sultan of Brunei, who restored it to its blatant grandeur for a whopping $100 million.

In 1920, silent-screen stars Mary Pickford and Douglas Fairbanks built their opulent estate, Pickfair, just up the hill (at 1143 Summit Drive). Charlie Chaplin, Gloria Swanson, Rudolph Valentino, and others also flocked in to establish one of the most concentrated celebrity enclaves in the world. (The homes 'in the hills' are regarded as somewhat more prestigious than those 'in the flats').

It's not surprising that the highest number of business licenses in Beverly Hills are issued to gardeners. Those who are not busy manicuring the residential lawns are often to be found working in the lovely **Beverly Gardens Park**, which borders Santa Monica Boulevard for 2 miles (3km) from Doheny to Wilshire.

Another stretch of beautiful gardens can be seen at **Greystone Mansion** ⑫, the spectacular neo-Gothic estate of oilman Edward Doheny. Now a city-owned property and frequent film set (eg *Witches of Eastwick, Big Lebowski*), the mansion is closed to visitors but the grounds are open daily (905 Loma Vista Drive; tel: 310-285 6830; www.greystonemansion. org; 10am–5pm, Mar–Oct until 6pm; free).

To see the most renowned section of Beverly Hills, take a walk through the elite shopping strip known as **Rodeo Drive** ⑬ (pronounced Ro-DAY-oh), where leading designers showcase their fashions to a rich, glamorous and sophisticated clientele. If the likes of Gucci, Hermès, Armani, and Tiffany are outside your budget, at least window-shopping is free. At its southern end, the street meets Wilshire Boulevard at Via Rodeo, a pretty cobblestone stretch designed to look like a European shopping street.

Opposite is the **Beverly Wilshire** (9500 Wilshire Boulevard), a landmark since 1928. The luxury hotel is still a favorite of celebrities and visiting royalty, some of whom rent entire floors for their stay. It's more publicly renowned as the setting where Julia Roberts' and Richard Gere's characters found love in the film *Pretty Woman*.

Nearby is the **Paley Center for Media**  (465 N. Beverly Drive; tel: 310-786 1000; www.paleycenter.org; Wed–Sun noon–5pm; donation suggested). Like its counterpart in New York, it

Rodeo Drive

contains a vast archive, with over 120,000 radio and television programs and commercials dating from the early days of broadcasting. Find your favorites and watch them in the screening room, or take in the special exhibits.

The **Beverly Hills Trolley** offers a 40-minute guided tour of landmarks and residential areas for $5 ($1 children 12 and under). Catch it at the southeast corner of Rodeo Drive and Dayton Way (year-round Sat–Sun 11am–4pm; July–Aug and Thanksgiving–Dec Tue–Sun 11am–4pm). For more information, call 310-285 1128 or visit www.beverlyhills.org.

CENTURY CITY

Though there is not much to see at **Century City**, it's worth noting that this complex of buildings was built on 180 acres (73 hectares) of what was once Twentieth Century Fox's enormous back-lot studio. The motion picture studio, now relegated to a huge compound on Pico Boulevard, is still active and churning out productions. But the surrounding area is a sleek Westside business center of high-rise office towers, high-flying corporations, theaters, and shops set around the striking, silver Century City Towers. If you find yourself with time to kill in this area, the **Westfield Century City** (10250 Santa Monica Boulevard; www.westfield.com/centurycity) outdoor shopping center offers department stores, upscale boutiques, an elegant food court, and a state-of-the-art movie theater. New to the area are the offices of the respected **Santa Monica Museum of Art** (www.smmoa.org), which no longer features a permamemt collection. As part of its SMMoA Unbound phase, pop-up exhibitions will take place at different sites through the city.

Opened in 1993, the **Museum of Tolerance** ❺ (9786 West Pico Boulevard; tel: 310-553 84032505; www.museumoftolerance. com; Mon–Fri 10am–5pm, Nov–Mar Fri until 3.30pm, Sun 10am–5pm, Thu until 9.30pm for "Anne"; last admission 1.5 hours

The University of California, Los Angeles

before closing, check website for closures on Jewish holidays; bring photo ID; advance reservations recommended) is a chilling and provocative experience, with impressive high-tech exhibits exploring racism and prejudice in America and elsewhere. A major part is devoted to *Hashoah*, the Holocaust. Visitors are given the 'passport' of a real person who experienced the concentration camps, which are depicted in film footage, sets, and interviews. This tour alone lasts a full hour, and at least equal time is necessary to appreciate the other collections, including a remarkable multimedia exhibit on the life and legacy of Anne Frank, and the learning center on the second floor.

WESTWOOD, BEL AIR, AND BRENTWOOD

The sprawling campus of the **University of California, Los Angeles** ⑯ (UCLA) dominates Westwood. The grounds, with lovely Royce Hall dating from 1929, Powell Library, Franklin Murphy Sculpture Garden (with works by Matisse, Rodin, and Miró), and the Mathias Botanical Gardens, offer a respite from the motor metropolis. Information is available from the kiosks in Westwood Boulevard, Westholme Avenue and Charles E. Young Drive; ask for the free 90-minute campus walking tours during the week (tel: 310-825 4321; www.ucla.edu/visit).

To the south of the campus, **Westwood Village** is an area that was once a hub of social activity but suffered a decline due to the revitalization of Santa Monica's Third Street Promenade. Today it's still a popular place to catch the latest film at any of the theaters or cruise the shops and restaurants. At the village's southern tip, the **Hammer Museum** (10899 Wilshire Boulevard; tel: 310-443 7000; www.hammer.ucla.edu; Tue–Fri 11am–8pm, Sat–Sun 11am–5pm; free) presents a small but exquisite collection of artwork gathered over a period of 50 years by the great industrialist Armand Hammer. Its galleries display masterpieces by painters from Rembrandt to Van Gogh, with an extensive collection of lithographs by Honoré Daumier. The museum regularly hosts special exhibitions.

To the north of UCLA, across Sunset Boulevard, is the exclusive neighborhood of **Bel Air**. As the tight-knit community is an enclave of old-money estates for such notables as the Reagans, you won't get to glimpse more than big front gates and lawns. You can, however, get a peek into the good life at **Hotel Bel-Air**'s **17** restaurant, lounge, and gardens (701 Stone Canyon Road), where celebs often linger.

The LA art world's star attraction is the **Getty Center 18**, the visual-arts complex designed by Richard Meier and perched on a bluff high above the 405 freeway in Brentwood, just west of UCLA. The cost: a whopping one billion dollars. Opened in 1998, the Center comprises the **J. Paul Getty Museum** (1200 Getty Center Drive; tel: 310-440 7300; www.getty.edu; Tue–Fri and Sun 10am–5.30pm, Sat 10am–9pm; free, parking fee) plus institutes for arts education, conservation, and research. The museum has a major collection of Western art from the

J. Paul Getty Museum

Middle Ages to the present day, with European paintings (by Rembrandt, Monet, Renoir, and Van Gogh, among others), drawings (including a few by Michelangelo, Leonardo da Vinci, and Raphael), illuminated medieval manuscripts, photographs, sculpture, and French decorative arts displayed within five two-story pavilions.

The impressive architecture, central gardens (designed by California artist Robert Irwin), and panoramic views of city, mountains, and ocean are awesome attractions in themselves. Take in the beautiful scenery by either dining in the museum's elegant restaurant, outdoor café, or by ordering a picnic lunch (tel: 310-440 6213) to enjoy alfresco on the beautiful grounds.

North of the Getty Center, the **Skirball Cultural Center** ⓮ (2701 N. Sepulveda Boulevard; tel: 310-440 4500; www.skirball. org; Tue–Fri noon–5pm, Sat–Sun 10am–5pm, check the website for closures on Jewish holidays; charge, free on Thu) depicts Jewish heritage and immigration, from ancient times to beginning life in America.

COASTAL LOS ANGELES

From Malibu in the north to Long Beach in the south, the shoreline communities of Los Angeles County stretch for 77 miles (115km) along the striking edge of the ocean.

Driving north on Pacific Coast Highway 1 (often marked 'PCH') from Santa Monica to Malibu is an excellent introduction to southern California's seductive beach life. Palos Verdes Drive is another eye-catching stretch, hugging the cliffs along the southern tip of Santa Monica Bay. But to really appreciate the allure of the California lifestyle, you must ditch the car and hit the sand and experience the natural beauty of the beaches first hand.

SANTA MONICA TO MARINA DEL REY

Ever since it was founded in the 1870s, **Santa Monica** has been thought of as the perfect seaside town. Nonetheless, in the

Overlooking the beach from Santa Monica Pier

1930s poker games, bingo parlors, and a casino barge anchored offshore brought such notoriety to the area that author Raymond Chandler used Santa Monica as the model for the freewheeling 'Bay City' of his detective novels. Today, with trendy boutiques, blue-chip art galleries, a buzzing nightlife scene, and some of the finest restaurants in the county,

Murals

Santa Monica and Venice Beach have dozens of murals, including 'Venice Reconstituted,' with Botticelli's Venus on roller skates. The half-mile long Great Wall of Los Angeles is another noteworthy site. For more information, contact the Social and Public Art Resource Center at 685 Venice Boulevard (tel: 310-822 9560; www.sparcmurals.org).

Santa Monica looks as if it is set to continue forever as LA's most popular playground.

Santa Monica Pier ㉔, site of the famous carousel as well as the former La Monica Ballroom, was built in 1908. Much of this historic structure was demolished by storms in 1983, prompting restoration to its original look. While the arcades and amusement park rides lining the pier lure tourists with their wonderfully tacky old-world ambiance, locals also come here to rent fishing tackle at the end of the pier or check out the festive free concerts held each summer. Beneath the pier and as far as the eye can see to the north and south you'll find beachgoers at play on the widest band of sand on the Pacific Coast. The busy path running alongside the beach to Venice is a coveted track for cyclists and rollerbladers, who either bring their own gear or rent from the numerous establishments nearby.

Above the sand is **Palisades Park**, a pretty, palm-lined stretch that runs for a mile (1.5km) along Ocean Avenue. Though it has become a notorious gathering place for the city's homeless population, it's worth strolling the broad walkway for its superb views of the ocean. Just inland you'll find onto Monica's **Main Street**, which is awash with unusual shops and excellent restaurants. Looming over its southern end at the intersection with Rose Avenue is a giant sculpture by Jonathan Borofsky known as *Ballerina Clown*. As the name implies, this is a giant clown's head on a tutu-clad body.

The **Edgemar complex**, located in the 2400 block, was designed by renowned postmodern architect Frank Gehry, a Santa Monica resident. Inside is a restaurant, retail shops, offices, and cinemas. Santa Monica artists also mount shows

BEST BEACHES

Angelenos converge all along the coast in a veritable beach party of surfers, volleyball players, families, skaters, bikers, bodybuilders, and bathing beauties.

Malibu's Surfrider Beach has some of the best surfing around.
Santa Monica Beach and **Venice Beach** are two of the most popular, with a wealth of activities on the boardwalk and pleasure pier.

South Bay beaches – Manhattan, Hermosa, and Redondo – are where California's beach culture started when George Freeth first caught the waves at Redondo Beach in 1907. The Beach Boys immortalized the surfer's life here in song in the 1960s.

Long Beach has an extensive 5.5 miles (9km) of beach, with numerous water sports and activities.

Orange County has some of the area's best beaches.
Bolsa Chica State Beach is a beautiful 6-mile (9.5km) stretch adjoining a wetlands reserve. Its gentle surf makes it good for families. Adjacent **Huntington Beach** is one of the world's great surfing spots.
Newport Beach and **Balboa Beach**, joined by a busy bike path, are the most popular spots on this part of the coast.

Main Beach lies smack in the middle of town in Laguna Beach, and the wooden boardwalk rivals few others as a vantage spot.

in the second-floor galleries of the **California Heritage Museum**  (2612 Main Street; tel: 310-392 8537; www.cali forniaheritagemuseum.org; Wed–Sun 11am–4pm). This former American Colonial home was moved to Main Street, and its lower floor has been restored to reflect a turn-of-the-20th-century lifestyle.

Beach volleyball is a popular sport

Dozens of prominent art galleries have set up shop in Santa Monica, with the result that it is now a major center of the contemporary art scene. Many shops are situated along a stretch of Colorado Avenue between 9th and 10th streets.

Aside from the beach, the **Third Street Promenade**  has become the most popular destination in Santa Monica. This three-block pedestrian mall, with its street performers, dinosaur topiaries, shops, movie houses, and restaurants, is perennially teeming with tourists and locals, especially on weekend evenings, when the pubs, pool halls, cafés, and shops guarantee an action-packed night out.

Curiously enough, Santa Monica has a large contingent of British residents, evident in the authentic pubs such as Ye Olde King's Head (complete with dart boards; www.yeolde kingshead.com), just off the Promenade. Roughly 10 percent of the city's residents are of British descent and there's an active expat community with organised events.

Further inland is the shopping street of **Montana Avenue**, where celebrities living in the coastal enclaves come to shop

A surfer cycles along Venice Beach

(see page 86). Santa Monica Airport's **Museum of Flying** ㉓, reopened in 2012 in a new building, displays vintage planes (tel: 310-398 2500; www.museumofflying.org; Wed–Sun 10am–5pm), and **Bergamot Station** (2525 Michigan Avenue), a converted trolley-car station, has an Art Center housing a number of commercial art galleries.

Just south of Rose Avenue, Main Street abruptly enters the bohemian community of **Venice Beach** ㉔. While cottages are scattered along small, quaint residential side streets, the Ocean Front Walk is an explosion of exuberance, with an ongoing parade of outrageous characters exhibiting their only-in-southern-California individualism. It's worth a stroll just to check out the freaks and the musclemen pumping iron at the open-air beachside gym known as Muscle Beach, but the sidewalk artists, snack shacks, T-shirt vendors, and Tarot readers also contribute to the local flavor. The show is at its best on weekend afternoons, with everything from beach boys on unicycles to rock musicians on roller blades. Make time for this California happening if you possibly can. Nearby boho-chic **Abbot Kinney Boulevard ㉕** (http://abbotkinneyblvd.com), with its hip boutiques, eclectic restaurants, and cutting-edge art galleries, is a worthwhile excursion as well.

Everything mellows out at Mother's Beach to the south, a lagoon specifically preferred by families, and becomes ultra-civilized at the vast man-made harbor of **Marina del Rey** (www.visitmarinadelrey.com), where harbor cruises and fishing trips can be arranged. Fisherman's Village on Fiji Way attracts tourists with gift shops and cafés. But if you just want to watch the yachts and other water craft, you should be able to find a shady spot along Mindanao Way at Burton Chase Park.

NORTH TO MALIBU

To the north of Santa Monica, PCH meets the western terminus of Sunset Boulevard. Follow this winding road into the hills and you will find yourself in the well-to-do residential enclave of the Pacific Palisades. Located a few miles farther on Sunset Boulevard is the turn-off for **Will Rogers State Historic Park** (1501 Will Rogers State Park Road; free, parking fee), a 186-acre (75-hectare) ranch that belonged to the late cowboy humorist. Tours of the ranch house (tel: 310-454 8212 ext.100; www.parks.ca.gov/willrogers; Thu–Fri 11am–3pm, Sat–Sun 10am–4pm on the hour) reveal some of Rogers' eccentricities, namely a porch swing in the living room and a raised ceiling that allowed him to practice rope tricks indoors. Rogers was an enthusiastic horseman and an experienced polo player. Weekend games are still held on the polo field in the front yard. A good system of hiking trails extends into the park.

A deeply centering experience comes free with a stroll through the **Self-Realization Fellowship Lake Shrine** (17190 Sunset Boulevard, a few blocks before PCH; www.lakeshrine.org; tours Fri and Sun at 3pm). Adjoining the temple (founded by Swami P. Yogananda) is a beautiful garden with gazebos, lakes, and waterfalls.

Malibu is best known for its exclusive beachfront colonies, home to movie stars since the 1930s. You'll get to see only the backs of these expensive bungalows as you travel its 21 miles (34km) on the ribbon of highway that lies between the mountains and the sea. Some homes have been destroyed by the brush fires and mudslides that periodically threaten this area. There are several beach access points where you can still admire the rolling surf and idyllic beach life that have made Malibu famous. One such is **Malibu Pier** (23000 Pacific Coast Highway), a popular spot for fishing. Constructed in 1905 and rebuilt several times since, this was the main connection with the south until the state highway was built in 1929. More recent additions include water-sports rentals and whale-watching and

The Getty Villa

harbor tours. Another is **Malibu Lagoon State Beach**, one of the few remaining wetlands in California. Several board-walks extend into the marsh, where you can see shorebirds such as the great blue heron and American avocet. A popular surfing beach adjoins the lagoon, as does the historic **Adamson House**, a Spanish-style mansion and museum decorated wall-to-wall with colorful ceramic tiles (23200 Pacific Coast Highway; tel: 310-456 8432; www.adamson house.org; Fri–Sat 11am–3pm, last tour at 2pm, Tue bus tour only).

The **Getty Villa**, with its classical architecture and stunning courtyard pool, is one of the coastline's most popular attractions (17985 Pacific Coast Highway; tel: 310-440 7300; www.getty.edu; Wed–Mon 10am–5pm; free, advanced timed tickets are required and can be reserved by phone or online; parking fee). Formerly known as the J. Paul Getty Museum (now at the Getty Center; see page 44), it opened in 1954 to house the billionaire's personal collection. The museum's 1974 addition was a re-creation of Villa dei Papiri, a Roman villa destroyed by the eruption of Mount Vesuvius in AD79. After a major nine-year restoration, the villa reopened in 2006 and is once more a fitting home for the outstanding collection of Greek, Roman, and Etruscan antiquities, dating back to 3000BC.

DOWNTOWN

For the majority of the residents of Los Angeles, 'Downtown' is not a hub but a distant skyline visited a few times a year when attending the opera or going to the Museum of Contemporary Art. But that's not to say the region east of Hollywood, which is defined by three freeways and the river, doesn't have its merits. A core of beautiful historic buildings, good restaurants, and colorful ethnic enclaves makes for excellent daytime

Strolling on Olvera Street

exploration. Several stellar performing arts venues and the centers of politics and finance also draw attention. This is a lively workaday business world, with hotels overflowing with conventioneers, and an atmosphere that is a refreshing diversion from the celluloid images to the west. Ten years ago, the place was all but a ghost town come night-time but thanks to an influx of hipster residents, hot bars, and trendy restaurants, these days it's is a hub of happening nightlife.

By day, Downtown is best explored on foot and on the DASH buses, which run through the area during the day for just 50 cents a ride (www.ladottransit.com/dash). By nightfall, when thousands of commuters return to the suburbs and the streets are more deserted (despite Downtown's recent revival, it's still no New York City), it's best to drive or take a cab. As in any large city, simple precautions are recommended.

One of the best ways to appreciate the area is to take one of the excellent walking tours given on Saturdays by the Los Angeles Conservancy. The Historic Downtown Tour is highly recommended. A variety of special-interest tours are also offered, including Art Deco or Downtown Renaissance. For information, call 213-623 2489 on weekdays between 9am and 5pm, or visit www.laconservancy.org.

LANDMARK BUILDINGS

At 5th and Figueroa, the five cylindrical towers of glass at the **Westin Bonaventure Hotel** form the city's most futuristic skyscraper (www.thebonaventure.com). Survey the area from the revolving restaurant and bar on the 35th floor. To the east at 630 West 5th Street, between Grand Avenue and Flower Street, is the pyramid-topped **Central Library** ㉖ (tel: 213-228 7000, tours: 213-228 7168; www.lapl.org/central; Mon–Thu 10am–8pm, Fri–Sat 9.30am–5.30pm, Sun 1–5pm). Built in 1926, it was devastated by fire 60 years later but was restored to its original design by 1993. On the second floor are murals of California history by Dean Cornwell and literary exhibits in the Getty Gallery. Free tours (no reservations necessary for groups of six or less) are given Mon–Fri at 12.30pm, Sat at 11am and 2pm, Sun at 2pm. On Saturdays at 12.30pm, there is also an art tour available of the library's Maguire Gardens.

Across from the library is the 73-story, 1,018ft (310m) **US Bank Tower** ㉗ (an office building formerly known as the Library Tower), the tallest building on the West Coast, designed by I.M. Pei. A rooftop observation deck is due to open to the public in 2016 as part of the building's $50 million makeover. Running alongside, the majestic **Bunker Hill Steps** lead to California Plaza, forming a symbolic link between the old Downtown and the new.

The **Millennium Biltmore** (506 South Grand Avenue; tel: 213-624 1011; www.thebiltmore.com), opened in 1923, is the *grande dame* of all the Downtown hotels. The Academy Awards were launched here in a private ceremony in the

Crystal Room in 1927. The majestic Rendezvous Court near Olive Street was originally the hotel lobby; from here, you can climb the Spanish baroque staircase leading up to the galleria, with its coffered ceiling.

On the other side of Olive Street, the landscaped **Pershing Square** is the city's oldest public park. Its history as a public commons dates back to 1781.

Art Deco is at its best in the nearby **Oviatt Building** (617 South Olive Street; http://oviatt.com). In 1927, merchant James Oviatt was entranced with the new architectural style that he saw in Paris. He subsequently commissioned René Lalique to design all the decorative glass for his building, which was home to his haberdashery and penthouse suite.

Some of Downtown's landmark buildings

From its terminal on 3rd and Hill streets, the **Angel's Flight** (http://angelsflight. com) inclined railway carried Downtowners up and down Bunker Hill beginning in 1901. After a fatal accident in 2001, the funicular railway was suspended, but it reopened in 2010. It's currently closed again, dealing with regulatory issues. So until it's back up and running, those wishing to get to **California Plaza**, a good spot to eat lunch outdoors, will need to tackle some steep steps.

BROADWAY AND THE CIVIC CENTER

The historic theater district on Broadway has evolved into a bustling Latino shopping street good for bridal gowns and electronic equipment. However, one monument to its past is the **Million Dollar Theater** (307 South Broadway; tel: 213-617 3600; www.milliondollar.la) with its wonderful, whimsical terracotta ornamentation. This famous 1917 vaudeville and movie theater, renovated, features classic film screenings and live Latino acts ('*variedades*').

Built in 1893, the lovely **Bradbury Building** 🄝 (at 304 South Broadway) is Los Angeles' oldest commercial building. It is also one of the grandest, with fancy Victorian wrought-iron balconies, marble staircases, and open-cage elevators surrounding a skylit atrium court. Both the Bradbury Building and the Million Dollar Theater, as well as the Angel's Flight and the Millennium Biltmore, are featured on the Historic Downtown tours run on Saturdays by the Los Angeles Conservancy (tel: 213-623 2489; www.laconservancy.org).

Since 1917, **Grand Central Market** (317 South Broadway; www.grandcentralmarket.com; daily 9am–6pm, Thu–Sat until 9pm; free) has provided the city with a daily cornucopia of enticing fresh produce, fish, poultry, meat, and exotic foodstuffs. Today, dozens of stalls display a wonderful ethnic diversity: you can sample everything from fresh tortillas to Chinese herbs. It's a great place for browsing and a quick snack or inexpensive lunch.

The streets around the Civic Center (the area bordered by First and Temple streets, and North Main Street and North Grand Avenue) are the heart of Los Angeles culture and politics. **City Hall** 🄞 (200 N. Spring Street; www.lacity.org/for-visitors), built in 1928, was the tallest building in the city until height restrictions were lifted in 1957. Best known as the *Daily Planet* building of the *Superman* TV series, its observation

Union Station

deck is open weekdays 8am–5pm; free; bring photo ID.

DOWNTOWN REVIVAL

Two more recent attractions form the centerpiece of Downtown's post-millennium revival. **The Cathedral of Our Lady of the Angels** (555 W. Temple Street; tel: 213-680 5200; www.olacathedral.org; Mon–Fri 6.30am–6pm, Sat 9am–6pm, Sun 7am–6pm; free) opened in 2002 with a controversial design by Spanish architect José Rafael Moneo. The sober façade of ochre-colored concrete is surrounded by gardens and a plaza. Bronze doors with multicultural art open into the airy interior lined with tapestries. Free guided tours are given at 1pm weekdays.

The **Music Center** (135 N. Grand Avenue; www.musiccenter. org) is the city's premier venue for the performing arts. Its four theaters (see page 94) were joined in 2003 by the **Walt Disney Concert Hall**, a magnificent stainless-steel building designed by Frank Gehry. There are tours available of its impressive interior (days and times vary, tel: 213-972 7483 or see website). Facing the concert hall is a brand new contemporary art museum called **the Broad** (tel: 213- 232 6220; www. thebroad.org). Two floors of gallery space bathed in diffuse light showcase nearly 2,000 works of art, and the state-of-the-art building is also home to the Broad Art Foundation, run by philanthropists Eli and Edythe Broad. Adjacent to the museum is a new outdoor public plaza. Part of the revitalization project of the area is also the **Grand Park** stretching between the City Hall and the Music Center which opened in 2012.

HISTORIC LOS ANGELES

LA's first settlement in 1781 was at **El Pueblo de Los Angeles**, a state historic park at North Main Street and Paseo de la Plaza. The district's heart is **Olvera Street ㉚**, a festive marketplace brimming with *piñatas* (hanging decorations filled with toys and candy), masks, and Mexican handicrafts, and surrounded by numerous Mexican restaurants and food stalls. The visitors' center (in Avila Adobe, Olvera Street E-25; www.olvera-street.com) provides information on the historical sites of the district, including the **Avila Adobe** (the first house in Los Angeles), the **Old Plaza Church**, and the shady plaza with its wrought-iron gazebo. Free tours are given Tue–Sat at 10am, 11am and noon. *Mariachi* singers and folk dance groups can usually be seen here on weekends.

In a region that long ago eschewed train travel, railway romance still permeates **Union Station** (800 N. Alameda Street). This handsome 1939 Spanish Mission-style building has a massive waiting room with arched corridors and a 52ft (16m) ceiling. The station once served nearly a million passengers a day; now, it is LA's new Metro Rail system hub.

LA'S ASIAN COMMUNITIES

Although Asian Americans live throughout Los Angeles County, there are several special cultural and shopping enclaves that deserve visitors' particular attention.

Chinatown is bounded by the 1000 block of North Broadway and bordered by Ord, Alameda, Bernard, and Yale streets. Here restaurants, souvenir shops, *dim sum* parlors, and

Chinese grocers fan out from the central pedestrian mall (Gin Ling Way). The **Chinese American Museum** (425 N. Los Angeles Street; tel: 213-485 8567; www.camla.org; Tue–Sun 10am–3pm; donation suggested) has exhibits ranging from historical photos to contemporary local artworks.

It's worth noting, however, that for truly authentic Chinese cuisine, Angelenos who are in the know head 10 miles northeast of Downtown to the **San Gabriel Valley**, home to the largest concentration of Chinese-Americans in the US.

The Japanese counterpart, **Little Tokyo**, is situated east of Downtown on the streets around 1st and Central. A medieval fire tower marks the entrance to the Japanese Village Plaza shopping mall (335 East 2nd Street; www.japanesevillageplaza.net). Other community highlights are a cultural center, a theater, and the **Japanese American National Museum** (100 North Central Avenue; tel: 213-625 0414; www.janm.org; Tue, Wed, Fri–Sun

Little Tokyo, Japanese cultural center

11am–5pm, Thu noon–8pm; free Thu after 5pm and 3rd Thu of each month all day), which presents changing exhibits in a Buddhist temple. A third Asian neighborhood, **Koreatown**, lies west of Downtown along Olympic Boulevard between Vermont and Western avenues. All the signs are in Korean, and there is a multitude of restaurants and a shopping mall of Korean stores at Koreatown Plaza (Western and San Marino).

DOWNTOWN MUSEUMS
The **Museum of Contemporary Art** ➌, known as MOCA (250 S. Grand Avenue; tel: 213-626 6222; www.moca.org; Mon and Fri 11am–5pm, Thu 11am–8pm, Sat–Sun 11am–6pm; free Thu after 5pm), is one of Los Angeles' most exciting museums, presenting major contemporary shows and a rotating permanent collection by such artists as Piet Mondrian, Mark Rothko, and Franz Kline. There's a superb gift shop on the premises. The museum's interesting annex, the Geffen Contemporary, is a few blocks away in Little Tokyo (at 152 North Central Avenue; same hours as MOCA) and features zany installations, multi-media, and the last 60 years of the museum's permanent collection.

Exposition Park, south of the central downtown area near the campus of the University of Southern California, is the site of several museums and attractions, including the Los Angeles Memorial Coliseum and Sports Arena (www.la coliseum.com).

Natural History Museum ➋ (900 Exposition Boulevard; tel: 213-763 3466; www.nhm.org; daily 9.30am–5pm; free on select Tues, see website) fans will enjoy its dinosaur skeletons and other fossils. Among the highlights of some three dozen galleries are dioramas of animals in their natural habitats, an impressive mounted megamouth shark, a collection of pre-Columbian artifacts, major exhibits on American history, and the Hall of Birds, with an animated rainforest. The museum's Discovery Center has excellent hands-on displays and activities for children.

The **California Science Center and IMAX Theater** (700 Exposition Park Drive; tel: 323-724 3623; www.california sciencecenter.org; daily 10am–5pm; free except IMAX and special exhibits, parking fee) presents technological exhibits from robotics and fiber optics to a miniature winery. Planes, rockets, and space probes are the focus of the center's Air and Space Gallery. Since 2012 the center has been home to the space shuttle Endeavour, which is now the museum's biggest draw.

Rotating exhibitions on the African-American experience in the United States are offered at the **California African-American Museum** (600 State Drive; tel: 213-744 7432; www. caamuseum.org; Tue–Sat 10am–5pm, Sun 11am–5pm; free, parking fee), which has become a showcase for black history and culture.

THE MOUNTAINS AND VALLEYS

When Angelenos refer to 'The Valley,' they are talking about the San Fernando Valley, a chain of communities north across the mountains from western and downtown Los Angeles. Although it's also home to such major film and television studios – in Burbank and Glendale – as Universal, Warner Brothers, and NBC, the Valley is forever battling its reputation as a boring and actionless suburbia. The nearby San Gabriel Valley is also separated from the Los Angeles basin by a range of mountains.

GRIFFITH PARK

An enticing reason to head to the hills is to visit one of the country's largest urban parks, **Griffith Park**, which separates Burbank and Glendale from Hollywood and covers over 4,000 acres (1,620 hectares). There are several entrances to the park; you can pick up a map at the visitors' center near the eastern

Overlooking Los Angeles from the Griffith Observatory

entrance (4730 Crystal Springs Drive; www.laparks.org/dos/parks/griffithpk), off the Golden State Freeway (Highway 5).

Perhaps the best view of LA can be seen on clear days and nights from the **Griffith Observatory** ㉝ (tel: 213-473 0800; http://griffithobservatory.org; Wed–Fri noon–10pm, Sat–Sun 10am–10pm; free, charge for shows in the planetarium) on Mount Hollywood, a location also featured in the classic James Dean movie *Rebel Without a Cause*. Evening visitors can usually look at the heavens through the Zeiss telescope, a 12-inch (30-cm) refracting telescope that more people have looked through than any other telescope in the world. The Planetarium Theater presents astronomical shows.

The **Los Angeles Zoo & Botanical Gardens** (5333 Zoo Drive, tel: 323-644 4200; www.lazoo.org; daily 10am–5pm), on the northeastern side of the park, harbors more than 400 different species of animals, birds, and reptiles, grouped according to their continental region. The zoo is known for its extensive breeding program for endangered species.

The park is also home to the **Autry National Center** (4700 Western Heritage Way; tel: 323-667 2000; https://theautry. org;Tue–Fri 10am–4pm, Sat–Sun 11am–5pm; free 2nd Tue of each month), a museum dedicated to the diversity and history of the people of the American West. Formerly known as the Autry Museum of Western Heritage, it was founded by Gene Autry, who rode the range in films from the 1930s to the 1950s. His tribute to the 'Wild West' features an impressive collection of historical artifacts, furniture, and art, as well as examples of how the West was romanticized in the arts, literature, film, and advertising. The museum also includes the former collection of the renowned **Southwest Museum of the American Indian**, which merged with the Autry in 2003. The collection represents Native American cultures from Alaska to South America and includes pre-Columbian pottery and textiles, making it one of the most important of its kind. Highlights of

Universal Studios

the collection are on view on Saturdays 10am–4pm in the Historic Southwest Museum Mt. Washington Campus (234 Museum Drive; tel: 323-221 2164; free).

In addition to the above attractions, the park also offers 53 miles (85km) of hiking and horseback riding trails. Perhaps the most popular (though challenging) trail

Mulholland Drive

One reason to head north is to do as the Harley Davidson motorcycle enthusiasts do: cruise Mulholland Drive, a scenic road that twists and turns through the mountains from Highway 101 to Ventura County. It is especially beautiful at night, when the lights of the city shimmer below.

is the one that leads right up to the famous 'Hollywood' sign on Mount Lee. The sign itself is fenced off to visitors, but the views from Mount Lee alone may make the trek worth it.

SAN FERNANDO VALLEY

In addition to seeing one of California's original missions, you'll want to visit this valley to see the movie studios.

The area's biggest draw is **Universal Studios Hollywood** ❸❹ (off the Hollywood 101 Freeway at either the Universal Center Drive or the Lankershim Boulevard exits; tel: 800-864 8377 or 800-UNIVERSAL; www.universalstudioshollywood.com; daily, hours vary by season). It combines a real working studio and behind-the-scenes tours with amusement park attractions. Visitors can board a tram that travels through famous film sets. Along the way you are attacked by the killer shark from *Jaws* and survive a collapsing bridge, a flash flood, and a bone-shaking simulated 8.3 earthquake. You are then free to explore the magic of Hollywood in attractions such as Jurassic Park: The Ride, a great log-flume ride that ends with a sudden drop; Shrek: 4-D, a cinematic fairytale adventure that puts you in the action; WaterWorld, where the movie comes to life in a wave of spectacular stunts and explosions; the horrifying Revenge of the Mummy ride; and King Kong 360 3-D, an intense immersive ride that puts you in the middle of a pack of carnivorous dinosaurs and the beast himself. The Wizarding World of Harry Potter theme park, which has been a smash hit in Orlando, is due to open in spring 2016. Although the queues for major attractions are often long, musical street shows are always close by to entertain.

Nearby is **CityWalk** (100 Universal City Plaza, Universal City; tel: 818-622 9841; www.citywalkhollywood.com; hours vary by season), a fantasy mall, where whimsical shops and fun, informal restaurants compete for tourist dollars.

Monument at Mission San Fernando Rey de España

Nothing is staged just for the guests at the **Warner Brothers Studios** (3400 Warner Blvd, Burbank; tel: 877-492 8687; www.wbstudio tour.com; daily 7.30am– 4pm, summer until 5.30pm). Here the two-hour Studio Tour changes every weekday, depending on shooting schedules, as small groups of guests over eight years of age walk through the back lot past TV and movie sets and tour production facilities. If scheduling allows, guests are permitted to watch rehearsals and the filming of TV shows.

One of California's finest missions lies in northern San

Fernando Valley. The **Mission San Fernando Rey de España** (15151 San Fernando Mission Boulevard, Mission Hills; tel: 818-361 0186 www.mission tour.org/sanfernando; daily 9am–4.30pm), built in 1797,

> ### WaterWorld
> With its set based on the film of the same name starring Kevin Costner, Universal's WaterWorld has plenty of thrills, spills, and pyrotechnics.

was named for King Ferdinand III of Spain. The complex includes the workshops, the convent with its Roman arches and painted Indian motifs, and the church with gold-leafed *reredos* (ornamental screens).

PASADENA AND THE SAN GABRIEL VALLEY

Northeast of Downtown you'll find that although the citrus groves that blossomed in the San Gabriel Valley 100 years ago have all but disappeared, this prosperous suburban area still has many botanical delights. The **Los Angeles County Arboretum & Botanic Garden** (301 North Baldwin Avenue, Arcadia; tel: 626-821 3222; www.arboretum.org; daily 9am–5pm; free on 3rd Tue of each month) nurtures plants from around the world. Stretching along the lower slopes of the San Gabriel Mountains, the **Descanso Gardens** (1418 Descanso Drive, La Cañada; tel: 818-949 4200; www.descansogardens. org; daily 9am–5pm) are known for their camellia displays and historic collections of roses.

The wealthiest of California's Spanish missions was the fourth to be built in the chain, **Mission San Gabriel Arcangel** (428 S. Mission Drive, San Gabriel; tel: 626-457 3035; www. sangabrielmissionchurch.org; Mon–Sat 9am–4.30pm, Sun 10am–4pm). The chapel, museum, winery, gardens, and cemetery are open to the public daily.

South of the often snowcapped San Gabriel Mountains is the charming city of **Pasadena**, which has remained true to

Pasadena City Hall at night

its Native American Indian name meaning 'Crown of the Valley. Attracted by its balmy weather and luscious orange groves, Midwesterners flocked here in the 1880s. Development was fast, and, by the turn of the 20th century, grand mansions and hotels had been built for those vacationing during the winter. Pasadena soon became a popular resort area.

This legacy is apparent in the handsome homes strung along the wide, shaded boulevards and in the grand dome of **Pasadena City Hall** (100 N. Garfield Avenue), built in 1927. The stretch of Colorado Boulevard nearby forms the heart of **Old Town Pasadena**. These 11 blocks are full of historic Victorian buildings that have been restored, and the area has been converted into a bustling shopping and dining district. Of Pasadena's highly reputed buildings, none is more famous than the **Gamble House** (4 Westmoreland Place; tel: 626-793 3334; www. gamblehouse.org; Thu–Sat 10am–3pm, Sun noon–3pm for 1-hour guided tours). Built in 1908 by Charles and Henry Greene, it is a masterpiece of the Arts and Crafts Movement that flourished at the turn of the 20th century. Every detail, from the hand-rubbed fine woods and original furniture to the Tiffany windows and light fixtures, was custom designed for David and Mary Gamble (of Proctor and Gamble fame).

Another architectural highlight is the **Fenyes Mansion** (470 W. Walnut Street; tel: 626-577 1660; www.pasadena history.org; tours Fri–Sun at 12.15pm), now part of the Pasadena museum of history. Built in 1905, it contains the mansion's original furniture and artwork, as well as historical exhibits.

PASADENA MUSEUMS

Some of LA's finest art museums are located in Pasadena. Several lie along Colorado Boulevard.

The highly reputable **Norton Simon Museum** (411 W. Colorado Boulevard; tel: 626-449 6840; www.nortonsimon. org; Mon, Wed–Thu noon–5pm, Fri–Sat 11am–8pm, Sun 11am–5pm; free 1st Fri of each month 5–8pm) is considered to have one of the world's finest European art collections, with masterpieces by Rembrandt, Goya, Picasso, and the Impressionists. In addition, there is an extensive collection of Degas sculptures, as well as works by Rodin. An outstanding selection of sculpture from India and Southeast Asia spanning a period of 2,000 years is a perfect complement to the Western art.

The **Pacific Asia Museum** (46 North Los Robles Avenue; tel: 626-449 2742; www.pacificasiamuseum.org; Wed–Sun 10am–6pm; free 2nd Sun of each month) has been designed to resemble a Chinese imperial residence. It houses galleries of traditional and contemporary Asian art as well as a Chinese courtyard garden.

Nearby is the latest addition to the city's art scene. The **Pasadena Museum of California Art** (490 E. Union Street; tel: 626-568 3665; www.pmcaonline.org; Wed–Sun noon–5pm, 3rd Thu also 5–8pm; free 1st Fri all day and 3rd Thu 5–8pm of each month) focuses on the state's artists and their works.

PASADENA AREA'S TREASURES

Pasadena is famous for the **Rose Bowl** stadium (Rose Bowl Drive; tel: 626-577 3100; www.rosebowlstadium.com), where, at full capacity, 103,000 spectators watch the annual college football game on New Year's Day. Prior to the game, one million people line Colorado Boulevard to see the **Tournament of Roses Parade** (www.tournamentofroses.com). The stadium also hosts the 'swapmeet,' or flea market, on the second Sunday of each month (9am–4.30pm, no admittance after 3pm). The headquarters for Pasadena's biggest event are located in **Tournament House**, previously the **Wrigley Mansion** (391 S. Orange Grove Boulevard; tel: 626-449 4100; tours Feb–Aug Thu at 2pm and 4pm; free). You can tour the former home of the chewing gum king to see its richly paneled rooms, marble staircases, and ornate ceilings.

Nearby San Marino is home to a few of the county's best museums. The **Huntington Library, Art Collections, and Botanical Gardens** (1151 Oxford Road, San Marino; tel: 626-405 2100; www.huntington.org; late May–early Sept Wed–Mon 10.30am–4.30pm, Sept–May Mon, Wed–Fri noon–4.30pm, Sat–Sun 10.30am–4.30pm; free 1st Thu of every month with advanced tickets) comprise a 207-acre (84-hectare) estate owned by railroad tycoon Henry E. Huntington. Its library is one of the most complete research facilities in the world. Among the rarities are a Gutenberg Bible and the illustrated Ellesmere manuscript of Chaucer's *Canterbury Tales*.

The three art galleries contain one of the most comprehensive collections of British and French 18th- and 19th-century art in the United States. Gainsborough's *Blue Boy* and Lawrence's *Pinkie* are the showpieces of the Huntington Gallery. In the Virginia Steele Scott Gallery you can view American paintings from the 1730s to 1930s, while the

Arabella Huntington Collection has Renaissance paintings and 18th-century French decorative arts.

The lovely Botanical Gardens offer 130 acres (50 hectares) of changing landscapes. Among the highlights are the Desert Garden, with a vast maze of mature cacti; the Japanese garden, with ponds, fish, and drum bridge; the sweet-smelling Rose Garden, showing the history and development of the rose over 2,000 years; and the new Chinese garden.

THE SOUTH COAST

PALOS VERDES TO SAN PEDRO

The coastal bluffs of the **Palos Verdes** peninsula offer some of the loveliest views of the ocean – best enjoyed from winding Palos Verdes Drive, which hugs the coast just south of Redondo Beach. The **Point Vicente Lighthouse** (31550 Palos

Point Vicente Lighthouse

Verdes Drive; www.vicentelight.org; closed for maintenance at the time of writing), with its adjacent Interpretive Center (daily 10am–5pm, summer longer hours), is a good place to stop and stretch your legs and admire the rugged beauty of the region. It's also a prime spot for whale-watching during the winter migrations, a popular activity for tourists and locals alike.

You'll find the pretty **Wayfarer's Chapel** (5755 Palos Verdes Drive South; www.wayfarerschapel.org) on the top of the southern cliffs. This intriguing glass structure nestled amidst the trees was created by architect Frank Lloyd Wright's son as a memorial to the Swedish philosopher Emanuel Swedenborg. It is open daily for meditation.

Amid a bevy of beach towns is **San Pedro**, a working seaport that borders Los Angeles Harbor. The shipyards, stretching for miles, are most impressive from the top of the soaring arch of the Vincent Thomas Bridge. You can watch the giant cranes as they unload the cargo ships.

An attractive waterfront promenade at San Pedro offers recreational boating, whale-watching and harbor cruises. Also along the shore is the **Cabrillo Marine Aquarium** (3720 Stephen White Drive; tel: 310-548 7562; www.cabrilloaq. org; Tue–Fri noon–5pm, Sat–Sun 10am–5pm; donation suggested). Housed in a building designed by Frank Gehry, it focuses on local sea life, and contains a touch tank where kids can pet sea creatures.

LONG BEACH

Long Beach established itself as a premier seaside resort by the early 1900s. Visitors took the old electric Red Car trolley from Los Angeles to spend a day at the beach, while silent film stars built lavish summer homes on the bluffs overlooking the Pacific. Long Beach's rebirth as a tourist destination started in 1967 when the city purchased the former luxury liner, the **Queen Mary**  (1126 Queens Highway; tel: 877-342 0738; www.queen mary.com; daily 10am–6pm). The world's largest cruise ship was docked in the harbor and converted into a hotel and tourist attraction. You can wander around the grand staterooms, promenade deck, bridge, and other exhibits that portray life in the working and living quarters of the ship. The ship is purportedly haunted; if you're not afraid of spirits, book a stay overnight and explore the ship's paranormal activity on a ghost tour. There are

The Queen Mary at Long Beach

plans to create a maritime museum aboard the ship.

Looking across the harbor from the ship, you'll see Wyland's **Planet Ocean**, a 10-story mural on the 16,000 sq ft (1,485 sq m) exterior wall of the Long Beach Arena depicting whales, dolphins, and sea lions. Long Beach has some 50 murals, many dating from the 1930s. Beside it is the Long Beach Convention and Entertainment Center.

The seven-block Promenade walkway (near Pine and Long Beach Boulevard and First and Third Streets) that leads from the business district to the marina is the heart of the city's revived downtown area, with new restaurants and jazz and comedy clubs.

A top Long Beach attraction is the **Aquarium of the Pacific** ㊱ (100 Aquarium Way; tel: 562-590 3100; www.aquariumofpacific.

org; daily 9am–6pm). With nearly 500 species, it is one of the largest aquariums in the country. Exhibits focusing on three Pacific Ocean regions range from sea lions to tropical fish in a shark lagoon. There is also an aviary full of Australian parrots.

The **Long Beach Museum of Art** (2300 E. Ocean Boulevard; tel: 562-439 2119; www.lbma.org; Thu 11am–8pm, Fri–Sun 11am–5pm; free every Fri) is housed in a historic 1912 house perched on a bluff overlooking the Pacific and Long Beach harbor. Its splendid ocean views compete with the changing exhibitions of contemporary California art.

The **Museum of Latin American Art** (628 Alamitos Avenue; tel: 562-437 1689; www.molaa.com; Wed–Sun 11am–5pm, Fri until 9pm; free every Sun and 4th Fri of each month 5–9pm) occupies a former roller-skating rink in the East Village Arts District. It has contemporary works from its permanent collection as well as temporary exhibitions.

With several miles of sandy beach, Long Beach is an excellent water-sports center (see page 92). Gondola Getaway (5437 East Ocean Boulevard; tel: 562-433 9595; www.gondola getawayinc.com) offers gondola cruises through the canals of Naples Island. The restaurant and gift shop complex at Shoreline Village is an attractive remake of a typical New England harbor town.

EXCURSIONS

With a car, you are no more than a couple of hours from deserts, beaches, mountains, and any number of outstanding southern California attractions. Here are some of the key sites a short distance from Los Angeles for that special day trip.

ORANGE COUNTY

Orange County adjoins Los Angeles County to the south, but it has developed an altogether different identity. In fact, some

Angelenos refer to the county as being 'behind the orange curtain,' due to its conservative lifestyle. Along with its 42 miles (67km) of sandy beaches and beach communities, it is best known as the home of two theme parks – Disneyland and Knott's Berry Farm – and one of the nation's top convention sites. The Anaheim Visitor and Convention Bureau has lots of information on the area (see page 131).

DISNEYLAND

Since 1955, when Walt Disney opened the doors of his Magic Kingdom, **Disneyland** ③ (1313 S. Harbor Boulevard, Anaheim; tel: 714-781 4565; www.disneyland.com; daily, hours vary by season) has become one of the world's most popular tourist attractions. The magic of Disney comes to life in its themed 'lands,' each of which offers rides and other entertainments. **Adventureland** recreates the exotic areas of Africa and the South Pacific on its Jungle Cruise. Here, you can try out one of Disneyland's best rides, the Indiana Jones Adventure, based on Steven Spielberg's popular films. **New Orleans Square** has two of the best attractions, Pirates of the Caribbean and the Haunted Mansion. At the backwoods

The Sleeping Beauty Castle, Disneyland

setting of **Critter Country** you'll find the exciting Splash Mountain log flume ride, while **Frontierland** takes you to the realm of the pioneers, along with steamships and runaway mine trains.

Fantasyland, entered via Sleeping Beauty's castle, is pure storybook enchantment. Don't miss *It's a Small World*, everyone's favorite cruise around the globe, and **Mickey's Toontown**, a cartoon world where children can explore Mickey Mouse's neighborhood. **Tomorrowland's** futuristic world of rocket jets, Star Tours, and Space Mountain (a terrifying roller-coaster ride in the dark) has been enhanced with such items as the Michael Jackson 3-D musical *Captain EO*.

The park's finest attractions, however, begin after dark. **Main Street's** parades are filled with magnificent floats and appearances by Disney characters. Later, Tinkerbell soars above the castle to ignite a splendid fireworks display. The most fantastic show of all is Fantasmic!, an interaction of special effects, animation, and performers. The unique technology projects film images onto giant water-mist screens that are 30ft (9m) tall and 50ft (15m) wide.

Disney California Adventure Park is a separate, adjacent 55-acre (22-hectare) theme park, celebrating the state in microcosm. Here you can try your hand at animation or be a TV star; 'hang-glide' over fabulous desert landscapes; sample wines, tortillas, and sourdough; visit the Muppets or a boardwalk; and ride a looping roller-coaster or thrilling river rapids.

Long lines

Disneyland can be crowded in summer. Expect waits of 30–90 minutes for popular attractions, and heavy crowds on Main Street two hours before the parade. During high season, arrive when the park opens and hit the popular attractions before lines get too long.

KNOTT'S BERRY FARM

The nation's oldest theme park, **Knott's Berry Farm** ❸, started as a berry farm on 20 acres (8 hectares) of rented land along a dusty road in Buena Park, just west of Anaheim (8039 Beach Boulevard, Buena Park; tel: 714-220 5200; www.knotts. com; daily, hours vary by season). In the 1930s Walter Knott began growing a new strain of berry, the boysenberry, and it soon became a booming enterprise. His wife, Cordelia, saw an opportunity to boost the family income and began serving chicken dinners on her

White-knuckle ride at Knott's Berry Farm

wedding china. Soon people waited for several hours for her delicious dinners and boysenberry pies. Walter had a keen interest in the old West and, in order to create a diversion for the ravenous patrons, began building a ghost town. Many of its buildings were brought piece by piece from abandoned desert towns. Eventually, a theme park was born.

Today the original park has expanded to several themed areas in an attempt to attract audiences of all ages and interests. The Ghost Town features a GhostRider roller coaster. The highlight of Wild Water Wilderness is Bigfoot Rapids, a whitewater river ride, while Indian Trails explores Native American legends, music, and dance. Fiesta Village is a tribute to California's early Spanish heritage, with The Jaguar!

(a roller coaster) and a very rare turn-of-the-20th-century Dentzel carousel with hand-carved animals. The Boardwalk, a re-creation of a California amusement park from the 1920s, features a buffalo nickel arcade. Camp Snoopy, home of the 'Peanuts' cartoon characters, has amusements for young children. There are also thrill rides for the older crowd, including 4D interactive rides. Entertainment, from music to old-time melodrama, is offered all around the park, and Mrs Knott's chicken dinners remain in great demand.

ATTRACTIONS NEAR ANAHEIM

If you decide to skip the chicken dinner come suppertime, you can join the crowds of families at nearby Medieval Times Dinner and Tournament (7662 Beach Boulevard; http://medievaltimes.com; see page 114), where diners eat with their hands in a castle-like dining room while actors fight with swords, joust, and do all they can to amuse.

Anaheim's **GardenWalk** (321 W. Katella Avenue; www.anaheimgardenwalk.com; daily 11am–9pm) is an outdoor shopping and dining center a few minutes' away from Disneyland Resort and the Anaheim Convention Center. Themed restaurants, movie theaters and a bowling and entertainment center are set amid manicured gardens.

At the **Richard Nixon Library and Museum** (18001 Yorba Linda Boulevard, Yorba Linda; tel: 714-993 5075; www.nixonlibrary.org; Mon–Sat 10am–5pm, Sun 11am–5pm), the life of the 37th president of the United States is showcased in detail. Displays allow you to listen to a Watergate tape or 'interview' Nixon.

The **Crystal Cathedral** (12141 Lewis Street, Garden Grove; tel: 714-620 7916; www.christcathedralcalifornia.org; campus tours Mon–Fri 10am–3pm and Sat 9am–4pm; free) is a monument to its time, built over the past quarter century by television evangelist Robert Schuller. This majestic structure is something like a four-pointed star, with 10,000 panes of glass forming translucent walls supported by a steel truss frame. Following the bankruptcy of Schuller's church, the cathedral was bought by the Roman Catholic Diocese of Orange in 2011 and at the time of writing was awaiting its reopening in 2016 as the Christ Cathedral.

Crystal Cathedral

The **Bowers Museum of Cultural Art** (2002 N. Main Street, Santa Ana; tel: 714-567 3600; www.bowers.org; Tue–Sun 10am–4pm) is another local gem. Displays focus on the discovery of cultures from around the world. Permanent exhibits include pre-Columbian art.

COASTAL ORANGE COUNTY

The coastline south of Los Angeles is the ultimate California dream: the beach is always a few steps away, the pace is slower, and dress is more casual. It's the kind of place where the big decision of the day will be where you go for sunset cocktails. Life is all about the beach here, but for those antsy for action there are also some worthwhile attractions on the side and even some 'high' culture performance venues.

Lying to the north of Huntington Beach is the **Bolsa Chica Conservancy**, a salt marsh that harbors more than 300 types

Laguna Beach

of birds, which you can see along a 1.5-mile (2.5km) loop trail (3842 Warner Avenue at PCH; tel: 714-846 1114; www.bolsachica.org; daily sunrise–sunset, interpretive center daily 9am–4pm; free).

Internationally known as Surf City, **Huntington Beach** has the largest stretch of uninterrupted beachfront on the West Coast (8 miles/13km). The focal point is the famous pier, which stretches more than 1,800ft (550m) into the Pacific, and provides a great vantage point for watching surfers in action.

Newport Beach, a fashionable beach community that surrounds Newport Harbor, hosts the upscale (and aptly named) Fashion Island shopping mall (www.shopfashionisland.com). Thousands of small boats are docked here, and on weekdays the dory fishermen still sell the morning catch on the beach at Newport Pier.

Separating the marina from the ocean is pretty **Balboa Peninsula**, where a paved walkway runs in front of beach-front homes. At the southern end of the marina is the

Victorian-style Balboa Pavilion; built as a bathhouse in 1902, it hosted big-band dances in the 1940s. It is now the center of a small arcade and shopping/dining area. Harbor cruises depart from here.

Here, too, is the **Orange County Museum of Art** (850 San Clemente Drive, Newport Beach; tel: 949-759 1122; www.ocma. net; Wed–Sun 11am–5pm, Fri 11am–8pm; free every Fri). Its well-regarded collection of modern and contemporary works by California-based artists ranges from Impressionism to Pop Art.

Laguna Beach is one of the coast's most attractive towns. Its history as an artists' colony in the 1950s and 1960s earned it the nickname 'SoHo by the Sea,' but, as usual, wealthy types follow hard on the heels of the artists, and today the beach is surrounded by fabulous homes perched along the hillsides and canyons. Its most famous arts festival is the **Pageant of the Masters** (www.foapom.com) in which local models enact striking tableaux of classic and modern paintings. The **Laguna Art Museum** (307 Cliff Drive; tel: 949-494 8971; www.laguna artmuseum.org; Fri–Tue 11am–5pm, Thu 11am–9pm; free 1st Thu of each month 5–9pm, see www.firstthursdaysartwalk. com) features changing exhibitions on California artists.

Mission San Juan Capistrano (tel: 949-234 1300; www. missionsjc.com; daily 9am–5pm), founded in 1776, lies inland near Dana Point, off the Ortega Highway. Although the Great Stone Church that earned it the nickname 'Jewel of the Missions' was destroyed in an earthquake in 1812 (just six years after it was completed), the beautiful grounds and adobe buildings have been restored. The Serra Chapel is the oldest building still in use in California, and the only remaining chapel where Father Junípero Serra, founder of the mission chain, celebrated Mass. The spot is perhaps best known, in legend and song, for the cliff swallows that return every spring on St Joseph's Day.

CATALINA ISLAND

One of the most popular excursions for both Angelenos and tourists is a trip to **Catalina Island**, the most developed of California's eight Channel Islands. Thousands of daytrippers come here each year to enjoy its beaches and water sports; there are also hotels for longer stays. It is easily reached by ferry from San Pedro or Long Beach, or the Catalina Flyer catamaran from Newport Beach. A helicopter service also runs to the island. Advance reservations should be made in summer.

The island's only town, **Avalon**, sits around the bay below stunning mountains that separate it from the rugged interior. Since no cars are allowed on the island, Avalon has the feel of an old-fashioned beach community. The beautiful landmark **Casino** building stands at one end of the harbor. It was built in 1929 by William Wrigley, the chewing gum magnate. For the next two decades boatloads of people came from San Pedro

Boats moored in the bay at Avalon on Catalina Island

to dance all night in the grand ballroom with its huge circular dance floor.

A number of boat trips leave from the pleasure pier. These include coastal cruises and a glass-bottomed boat trip to view the colorful fish and marine plant life. Catalina Island is a good location for scuba diving and snorkeling. The Wrigley Memorial and Botanical Garden is 2 miles (3km) inland. Most of Catalina's rugged interior is owned by the Santa Catalina Island Conservancy (www.catalinaconservancy.org), a nonprofit foundation that preserves the island's natural resources. A herd of buffalo brought here during the filming of a movie in 1924 now numbers around 150–200. Permits must be acquired for hiking or camping, but you can see the interior on an inland motor tour. The views climbing up the steep, narrow road are breathtaking.

LAKES, MOUNTAINS, AND DESERT

Los Angeles' closest mountain retreats are **Big Bear Lake** and **Lake Arrowhead**, which lie east of the city less than two hours away. They are connected by Rim of the World Drive, a scenic highway reaching elevations of 8,000ft (2,440m). These resorts are a welcome escape from the heat of the city in summer and offer many activities. In the winter, of course, Big Bear is an excellent downhill skiing area.

A fashionable way to experience the desert is by visiting one of the resort communities around **Palm Springs**, about two hours' drive east of LA. A haven for film stars and golf pros since the 1930s, it caters to a broad spectrum of visitors. You can relax at the pools or tennis courts, explore the desert landscape, take the aerial tramway for a view of sand and hills for miles, and dine at any number of fashionable restaurants. Palm Springs forms a major winter retreat for Angelenos as well as for visitors from the East Coast, but it is less popular in July and August, when temperatures soar well over 100°F (38°C).

WHAT TO DO

SHOPPING

If there was ever a shopping heaven, this is it. Everything you could possibly want is at your disposal with a flash of the credit card. With hundreds of shops located along charming streets, stacked in mega-malls, and tucked into nondescript neighborhood nooks, there's no doubt you'll find more than a few mementos to carry home.

SHOPPING DISTRICTS

Rodeo Drive in Beverly Hills is the first stop on every shopper's circuit (www.rodeodrive-bh.com). It's home to the pricey emporia Tiffany, Chanel, Louis Vuitton, and Giorgio Armani, but more affordable retailers such as Ralph Lauren and Guess vie for tourist dollars.

Funky and youthful attire is offered at every doorstep along **Melrose Avenue** between La Brea and Fairfax. Once the epicenter of hip Hollywood counterculture, this strip has become a strolling street for young tourists. Still, there are plenty of bargains to be found. Melrose Avenue carries on into West Hollywood, where, amid the art galleries and design showrooms, you'll find exorbitantly expensive Fred Segal, the best and most celebrity-frequented mini-department store in town. Another favorite is elite clothing store Maxfield (www.maxfieldla.com), which carries a range of top designers.

Third Street, between La Cienega and Fairfax, is the Melrose alternative, with a hipper and more stylish feel, along with antiques, clothing, shoe, and gift stores. Meanwhile, **La Brea** (the blocks between Wilshire and Melrose) and **Beverly Boulevard** (between La Brea and Stanley) are for the stylish locals too old for Melrose fashion and too hip for Rodeo. Along

The elusive Rodeo Drive

both streets are retro furnishings, vintage clothing, designer boutiques, and fun gift stores. **Robertson Boulevard** (between Beverly Boulevard and Third Street; www.robertsonboulevard-shop.com) is the best place to spot celebs as they dash into trendy boutiques like Kitson. Sunset Boulevard's **Sunset Plaza** (www.sunsetplaza.com) is another stretch of hip upmarket boutiques and Hollywood culture at its most flaunting and tawdry.

The city also has more than a dozen specialized **book-shops**, including the Bodhi Tree on Melrose (www.bodhitree.com), which carries metaphysical and New Age titles, and Book Soup on Sunset Boulevard (www.booksoup.com), which also carries international newspapers and periodicals.

The Grove shopping area

Since **Santa Monica** residents wouldn't think of driving so far east to spend their money, this chic seaside town has its own selection of comparable shopping streets. Very cool **Main Street** celebrates everything from thrift shops to chic boutiques. **Montana Avenue** (https://montanaave.com) is known for pricey upscale designer apparel and furnishings. The eternally crowded **Third Street Promenade** (www.downtownsm.com) caters to both tourist and local markets with an enormous choice of affordable chain clothing stores, jewelry shops, and gift boutiques.

Over the mountains to the northeast, **Old Town Pasadena** is a lovely place to browse the enticing clothing, lingerie, and gift stores. Just north of Los Angeles, the San Fernando Valley's main drag, **Ventura Boulevard**, is the place valley-dwellers go to buy virtually everything.

CityWalk

Universal Studios' CityWalk has a wide range of retail wonders, including magic shops, toy stores, and science-fiction memorabilia.

SHOPPING MALLS

In a town where time in traffic is to be avoided at all costs, one-stop shopping is essential. In shopping malls, everything you're looking for is available without moving your car. The Beverly Hills set usually bops over to **Westfield Century City** (www.westfield.com/centurycity), a pleasant open-air mall with a stadium-seating movie theater. Bordering West Hollywood and Beverly Hills is the 200-plus store **Beverly Center** (www.beverlycenter.com); Westwood has the **Westside Pavilion** (www.westsidepavilion.com); while in the Fairfax District the Farmers' Market has expanded into **The Grove** (www.thegrovela.com), a smart outdoor shopping area with upmarket chain stores. By the sea, head for **Santa Monica Place** mall (www.santamonicaplace.com) at the end of the Third Street Promenade.

On the periphery, there's the Valley's **Sherman Oaks Galleria** (www.shermanoaksgalleria.com) and nearby **Fashion Square** (www.westfield.com/fashionsquare). Orange County residents rejoice over Costa Mesa's **South Coast Plaza** (www.southcoastplaza.com), their classiest and most extensive mall with 300 stores, including designer outlets. **Fashion Island** (www.shopfashionisland.com) in Newport Beach is another good shopping enclave.

Department stores such as Macy's, Nordstrom, Blooming-
dale's, Neiman-Marcus, Saks Fifth Avenue, and Barneys New
York (the latter three with valet parking) are strategically
located around town, often in more than one location. Many
can be found along Wilshire Boulevard in Beverly Hills.

BARGAINS

LA's **Fashion District** (http://fashiondistrict.org) is the hub of the
West Coast garment industry. It covers 90 blocks southeast of
central Downtown, spreading out from a hub around Los Angeles
and 11th streets. Most of the designer showrooms are wholesale
businesses, but there are also hundreds of retail shops which
sell discounted clothing and accessories. On Saturdays many
wholesale-only stores sell to the general public. The **Jewelry
District** (http://the-jewelry-district.com) is also situated on
nearby Hill Street, between West Fifth and West Sixth streets.

Flea markets – usually called swap meets – sell antiques,
old Levi's, and every kind of vintage treasure you could imagine.

OUTDOOR MARKETS

Strolling the city's open-air markets is an excellent way to grab some
delicious and inexpensive grub and mingle with the locals. The famous
Farmers Market at Third and Fairfax is a mixture of old folks, tourists,
and hip Hollywood types who crowd the excellent food stands. Santa
Monica's outdoor farmers' market is held Wednesday and Saturday
8.30am–1pm along Arizona Avenue at the Third Street Promenade.
Smaller farmer's markets are held on every day of the week in different locations throughout the city.

Downtown's Grand Central Market on Broadway is LA's oldest and
largest open-air produce market. Also Downtown is the Flower Market, on Wall and 8th streets; the best selections are found before dawn.

They're held throughout the city, but an in-town favorite is the Melrose Trading Post held every Sunday 9am–5pm at Fairfax High School. One of the best is on the second Sunday of every month from 9am to 3pm at the Rose Bowl in Pasadena.

SPORTS

SPECTATOR SPORTS

You can experience America's *An LA farmers' market* favorite summer pastime by grabbing a hot dog and a beer and rooting for the Dodgers baseball team at **Dodger Stadium** (1000 Elysian Park Avenue; tel: 866-800 1275; www.dodgers.com), just north of Downtown in Chavez Ravine. In Anaheim you can cheer on the Angels at **Angel Stadium** (2000 Gene Autry Way, Anaheim; tel: 714-940 2000; www.angelsbaseball.com).

From October to April it's basketball season, when both the Lakers and the Clippers run the court at the Downtown **Staples Center** (1111 S. Figueroa Street; tel: 213-742 7100; www.staples center.com). College football games, played from August to December, are as entertaining as NFL and AFL games. UCLA plays at the **Rose Bowl** (see page 70), while USC games are at the **Los Angeles Memorial Coliseum** (3939 S. Figueroa Street; tel: 213-747 7111; www.lacoliseum.com). Ice hockey fans can watch the Los Angeles Kings play at the Staples Center (from November to March); Anaheim's Ducks play at the **Honda Center** (2695 E. Katella Avenue; tel: 714-704 2500; www.honda center.com) of Anaheim, across from Anaheim Stadium.

The **Toyota Grand Prix** auto race is held in Long Beach (www.gplb.com) every April. The **Northern Trust Open** finds world-class golf champions flocking to the city each February for the tournament at the Riviera Country Club, Pacific Palisades (www.northerntrustopen.com).

Santa Anita Park (285 W. Huntington Drive; tel: 626-574 7223; www.santaanita.com) in Arcadia offers two horse-racing seasons: fall and winter/spring. While **Hollywood Park Racetrack** in Inglewood was demolished in 2015 to make space for the 80,000-seat City of Champions Stadium scheduled for 2018, the Hollywood Park Casino remains a simulcast wagering facility (1050 S. Prairie Avenue; tel: 310-330-3514; www.hollywoodpark. com). **Los Alamitos** racecourse (4961 Katella Avenue; tel: 714-820 2800; www.losalamitos.com), near Disneyland, has quarterhorse racing and thoroughbred racing throughout the year.

With several yacht clubs based in Long Beach, the city hosts races, regattas and other yachting competitions.

OUTDOOR ACTIVITIES AND OTHER SPORTS

With exceptional year-round weather, over 72 miles (116km) of beaches, vast mountain ranges, and a hyperathletic community, Los Angeles has enough outdoor activities to keep you busy for the next 10 years.

Seaside fun is yours if you hit the coastal bike, skate, and jogging paths (for maps and guides, call the Visitor Information Line (tel: 310-305 9545) or stop off at the **Marina del Rey** Visitor Information Center (4701 Admiralty Way, Marina del Rey; www.visitmarinadelrey.com). The Los Angeles segment of the **Pacific Coast Bicentennial Bike Route** is a popular trail. For information and maps of LA bike routes, Los Angeles Bike Paths has a useful website, www.labikepaths.com.

More than 100 **golf courses** are open to the public. The City of Los Angeles operates seven 18-hole and five 9-hole courses; for information on these courses and reservations call 818-291 9980, or visit www.golf.lacity.org. Public courses are popular, so book in advance.

For information on **tennis** and other sports, see the LA Department of Recreation and Parks website at laparks.org or tel: 818-291 9980.Golf and tennis are also available in Orange County and in the desert communities in and around Palm Springs.

Hiking trails abound in the Santa Monica and San Gabriel mountains. For information on local hiking trails, contact the **Angeles National Forest** (tel: 626-574 1613; www.fs.usda.gov/angeles). For a closer spot to check out nature, visit **Griffith Park** or **Franklin Canyon**. The best place to jog is the **Hollywood Reservoir** in the Hollywood Hills.

For hiking in Pasadena's **Eaton Canyon** call the Nature Center (tel: 626-398 5420; www.ecnca.org). A series of

The Los Angeles area is ideal for cyclists

self-guided nature trails and some longer hiking trails wind through **Will Rogers State Historic Park** in the Pacific Palisades (tel: 310-454 8212; www.parks.ca.gov/willrogers, see page 51). Lake Arrowhead and Big Bear Lake, about two hours' drive east in the **San Bernardino National Forest** (www.fs.usda.gov/sbnf), consist of rugged mountain terrain. Contact either of the tourist offices in theseareas (see page 131).

For information about parks and activities in the Santa Monica Mountains, call the Visitor Center at tel: 805-370 2301 or head-quarters at tel: 805-370 2300 (www.nps.gov/samo). The **National Park Service** (www.nps.gov) can also give information about facilities and events in the West Coast's national park system.

Horseback riding is popular in the Los Angeles area. Diamond Bar Stables (tel: 818-242 8443; www.rockenpoutfitters.com) and the LA Equestrian Center (tel: 818-840 9063; www.la-equestrian center.com) use good bridle trails.

WATER SPORTS AND ACTIVITIES

The Pacific coast from Santa Barbara south through Orange County is one big water playground. Beaches from Long Beach to Malibu are perfect for surfing, boogie-boarding, wading, and swimming. Beachfront sports shops are willing to rent you a board and can usually direct you toward lessons as well.

Meanwhile, Long Beach is a major center for **boating**; you can rent sailboats, dinghies, canoes, and powerboats of all sizes. Marina del Rey is another, where you can also charter a yacht. In Orange County, Newport Beach is a major center for rentals, and so is Dana Point to the south. If you are hap-pier to leave the seamanship to someone else, take a harbor cruise at Marina del Rey, San Pedro, or the Balboa Peninsula. For a more romantic outing, try a gondola at Naples, near Long Beach. **Whale-watching** expeditions are organized during the winter migrations; they leave from Marina del Rey, San Pedro,

Newport Beach, and Long Beach. Jet skis can be rented in the above towns as well as in Malibu. Try parasailing at the Balboa Pavilion. You can rent kayaking or windsurfing equipment in Long Beach, Malibu, and Marina del Rey.

Other popular water sports include **scuba diving** and **snorkeling**. One of the best places to see underwater marine life is at Catalina Island, but equipment rental is also available in Long Beach, Redondo Beach, and Malibu. The best spot in Orange County is Laguna Beach, as the entire city beach area is a designated marine preserve.

Surfing at Zuma Beach, Malibu

WINTER SPORTS

Nearby mountain ranges make downhill skiing a popular winter sport. Further east is **Mt Baldy** (tel: 909-982 0800; www.mtbaldy skilifts.com). Ski areas usually sell out on weekends, and visitors are advised to buy lift tickets in advance by calling the resort directly. Larger ski resorts are under two hours away. The most popular is **Big Bear**. For information contact the Big Bear Lake Resort Association (tel: 800-424 4232; www.bigbearinfo.com).

ENTERTAINMENT

The entertainment capital of the world sure knows how to entertain. There are jazz clubs, world-class opera and symphony performances, comedy clubs, Broadway shows, concerts, strip clubs, transvestite reviews, and swing, country-western, and salsa clubs. You name it – LA's got it. To find out what's going on, pick up any of the city's free weekly papers (see page 125).

THE ARTS

LA's concert halls and theaters present some of the best music and drama in the country. The city's premier venue is Downtown's **Music Center** (tel: 213-972 7211; www.music center.org). It has several components: the **Dorothy Chandler Pavilion** presents classical music, opera, and ballet; the **Ahmanson Theater** hosts big musicals; and the **Mark Taper Forum** offers a more intimate setting for contemporary drama. The **Walt Disney Concert Hall** is the home of the Los Angeles Philharmonic and Los Angeles Master Chorale.

The **Geffen Playhouse** (10886 Le Conte Avenue, Westwood; tel: 310-208 5454; www.geffenplayhouse.com) stages musicals and comedies. The **Dolby Theatre**, formerly the Kodak Theatre, in Hollywood (6801 Hollywood Boulevard; tel: 323-308 6300; www.dolbytheatre.com) hosts music concerts and ballets. Visiting dance groups and bands perform at the **Shrine Auditorium** in downtown LA (665 W. Jefferson Boulevard; tel: 213-748 5116; www.shrineauditorium.com) and at the Center for the Art of Performance **at UCLA's Royce Hall** (340 Royce Drive, Westwood; http://cap.ucla.edu).

Opposite the Staples Center downtown, the new state-of-the-art **Microsoft Theatre**, formerly the NOKIA Theatre, (777 Chick Hearn Court and Figueroa Street; tel: 213-763

Tickets

Tickets to shows and concerts can be booked at the venue or by phone (with credit card) from ticket agencies such as Ticketmaster (tel: 213-480 3232; www.ticketmaster.com). For tickets to television recordings, see page 129.

6020; www.microsofttheater. com) presents concerts, performances and events on southern California's largest stage. Also downtown is the venerable **Orpheum Theatre** (842 S. Broadway, tel: 877-677 4386; www.laorpheum. com), which opened in 1926. It has played host to some of the most famous names in showbusiness and continues to present a wide range of performances.

The **Santa Monica Pier** is the coastal setting for the free summer Twilight Concert Series. Other free music and dance programs are held during the summer at the California Plaza **Watercourt** Downtown (www.grand performances.org).

Walt Disney Concert Hall

The **Segerstrom Center for the Arts** (600 Town Center Drive, Costa Mesa; tel: 714-556 2787; www.scfta.org) sponsors symphony, chamber music, and opera performances. The South Coast Repertory Theater is based here.

AMPHITHEATERS

Few experiences are as quintessentially southern Californian as entertainment under the stars. The **Hollywood Bowl** (2301 N. Highland Avenue; tel: 323-850 2000; www.hollywoodbowl. com), summer home of the Los Angeles Philharmonic and jazz and pop concerts by the Hollywood Bowl Orchestra, fills each

Hollywood Bowl

performance with Angelenos toting gourmet picnic baskets. The nearby **Ford Amphitheatre** (2580 Cahuenga Boulevard East; tel: 323-461 3673; www.fordamphitheater. org) is the historic setting for Shakespeare plays, summer music, and cabaret. The **Greek Theatre** (tel: 323-665 5857; www.greektheatrela. com) in Griffith Park is a favorite venue for rock and pop concerts.

FILM

Want to catch up on the hottest independent film or watch a blockbuster in the TCL Chinese Theatre (www.tclchinese theatres.com) or El Capitan (https://elcapitantheatre.com)? Just dial 323-777-FILM (3456) to find out what's playing. You might spot a celeb at the hip Arclight Cinemas on Sunset Boulevard (www.arclightcinemas.com). The Laemmle Theater chain (www.laemmle.com) shows top foreign releases. The Landmark (www.landmarktheatres.com) in West LA operates numerous state-of-the-art screens showing first-run and indie movies. The AMC Century City 15 Theaters (www. amctheatres.com) in the Westfield shopping center, the Pacific Theatres Stadium 14 at the Grove (www.pacifictheatres.com), and the AMC CityWalk Stadium 19 Cinemas next to Universal Studios are other big cinema complexes.

NIGHTLIFE

Some of the most famous **nightclubs** are found on Sunset Boulevard, including Whisky-a-Go-Go (www.whiskyagogo.

com) and The Roxy (www.theroxy.com). Another is the Troubadour (www.troubadour.com) on Santa Monica Boulevard. The hippest **bars** are scattered throughout Hollywood and western LA, including SkyBar, Bar 1200, Bar Marmont, and The Well. Good spots for **blues** are Harvelle's in Santa Monica (http://harvelles.com), and the House of Blues in West Hollywood (www.houseofblues.com/losangeles). Among the many **jazz** clubs are the famed Jazz Bakery (http://jazzbakery.org) which plans to move to a new permanent home designed by Frank Ghery next to the Kirk Douglas Theater in the heart of Culver City, the Catalina Bar and Grill in Hollywood (www.catalina jazzclub.com), and the Baked Potato in North Hollywood (www.thebakedpotato.com).

Cabaret entertainment can be found at the Center Stage Theater (http://centerstagefontana.com), which is home to Tibbies Great American Cabaret. Marty and Elayne, the husband-and-wife lounge duo performing for nearly 20 years at The Dresden in Los Feliz (www.thedresden.com), are Los Angeles legends.

Comedy clubs are big. Venues include The Comedy Store

COCKTAILS WITH A VIEW

Unless you're at the beach, there may be no better way to welcome a famous California sunset than perching yourself and a cocktail at one of the city's vista cocktail rooms.

You can watch the city light up the night from a number of unique spots: the landmark Yamashiro restaurant, the Penthouse lounge at the Huntley Santa Monica Beach, the Mondrian Hotel's SkyBar, the balcony at The Sunset Tower hotel's restaurant, or the bar in the Sky penthouse at the exclusive club Soho House (if you're lucky enough to know someone who's a member).

(http://thecomedystore.com) and The Laugh Factory (www.laughfactory.com) on Sunset Boulevard, and the Hollywood Improv (http://improv.com) on Melrose Avenue.

Coffeehouses are everywhere, many offering live entertainment and poetry readings. Some of the best are clustered in Santa Monica and in West Hollywood.

Billiards is another fun night-time option. Try Q's Billiard Club (http://qsbilliardclub.com) in Brentwood.

CHILDREN'S LOS ANGELES

This is certainly one city where you will never run out of things to do or places to go to keep the kids amused. Topping the list are the region's theme parks: Disneyland, Knott's Berry Farm, and Universal Studios. Farther away is Valencia's **Six Flags Magic Mountain** (tel: 661-255 4100; www.sixflags.com/magicmountain), renowned for high-speed roller coasters, and **Raging Waters** (tel: 909-802 2200; www.ragingwaters.com) in San Dimas, a fun water park.

Kidspace Children's Museum (tel: 626-449 9144; www.kidspacemuseum.org) in Pasadena lets kids direct TV shows and don astronaut outfits (up to age 12). The excellent **Natural History Museum** of Los Angeles County (see page 61) and its Burbank branch are great for the whole family. The highly rated **California Science Center and IMAX Theater** (see page 62) has interactive exhibits. The **La Brea Tar Pits Museum** is a local favorite.

The Los Angeles Zoo (see page 63) is in Griffith Park, and other attractions in Griffith Park include train, pony, and stagecoach rides, and a carousel. **Santa Monica Pier** is fun-filled with a carousel and other rides, arcade games, and inexpensive carnival food.

There's no better way to wear out kids than a day at the well-equipped beaches.

CALENDAR OF EVENTS

Whatever the time of year, there'll be a party somewhere in LA.

January Tournament of Roses Parade (Rose Bowl Parade), Pasadena, New Year's Day.

January/February Chinese New Year Celebration, Chinatown.

March Fiesta de las Golondrinas (Return of the Swallows) – month-long festivities at Mission San Juan Capistrano, St Joseph's Day March 19.

April Los Angeles Times Festival of Books, the largest book festival in the country.

May Cinco de Mayo, Mexican Independence Day, Olvera Street. Venice Art Walk – open studios, galleries, and homes in Venice artists' colony. The music and entertainment festival WorldFest has transformed itself into the VegFest, commencing in 2016.

June Playboy Jazz Festival, Hollywood Bowl. Los Angeles Pride – two-day LGBT festival with parade, West Hollywood. Los Angeles Film Festival – over 10 days in Westwood Village and other venues. Mariachi USA Festival – Latin music at the Hollywood Bowl.

July Orange County Fair, Costa Mesa. Pageant of the Masters live models re-create classical works of art, Laguna Canyon, through August, plus the Sawdust Art Festival across the road through August.

August Long Beach Jazz Festival – three days of world-class jazz overlooking the marina. Los Angeles African Marketplace and Cultural Faire – over three weekends, downtown LA. Nisei Week Japanese Festival, Little Tokyo.

September LA County Fair, County Fair & Exposition Center, Pomona.

October West Hollywood celebrates Halloween with the week-long Halloween Carnival ending in a wild costume party on October 31.

November Hollywood Christmas Parade – celebrities, floats, and marching bands, Sunday after Thanksgiving. Pasadena Doo-Dah Parade – spoof of the Tournament of Roses Parade.

December Light Festival – lighted displays with holiday themes at the ZOO, Griffith Park. Marina Del Rey Holiday Boat Parade – decorated brightly lit boats parade around the marina.

EATING OUT

Like the entertainment industry, LA's restaurants are often as much about image as they are about cuisine. The most popular restaurants attract a steady clientele, inspire the hip and famous to clamor for a reservation, and try to provide a special something that can't be found at the next place.

With nearly 20,000 dining options, that 'special something' comes in the form of everything from fast-food shacks to four-star formal affairs, which are invariably garnished with colorful Angelenos doing their thing. In fact, waiting for a chili dog and fries with a virtual people zoo at Pink's sidewalk grubbery is as glamorous an experience as dining alfresco next to Angelina Jolie at glitzy Spago. Wherever you dine, it's bound to be fun.

Although restaurant decor and glitz are often appetizing enough to keep diners coming back, in recent years

Dining alfresco at The Ivy

the dining experience has focused more on the food itself. With fantastic farm-fresh produce and superior fish and meats widely available throughout the state, today's 'California cuisine' reflects whatever's in season. The results are vibrant and creative preparations that are generously infused with influences from across the globe. Whether you crave sushi, French, Mexican, Burmese, Italian, vegetarian, or anything else imaginable, this town's got it and got it good.

Street food in Southern California

You can get away with spending next to nothing at ethnic eateries, or you can pay premium prices at any of the high-end haunts. But even eating at the top of the food chain doesn't have to break your budget. There's almost always something relatively affordable on the menu. If your pocketbook doesn't permit full-blown indulgence and you still want to check out one of the finer dining rooms, eat light (appetizers, salads) or consider going at lunchtime, when the prices are lower.

As for the ancillaries, desserts are decadent and splurge-worthy everywhere, which makes you wonder how everyone stays so fit. Wine lists highlight the state's best vintages.

Most areas have a range of restaurants to suit all budgets. Three of the most popular areas for dining out are West Hollywood, Beverly Hills, and Santa Monica; these are also the places where you will find the widest range of choices.

American breakfast of pancakes, bacon and eggs

Reservations are generally not required except in very prestigious or popular establishments.

BREAKFAST

In this town breakfast is not a meal – it's an event. At hotels like the Bel-Air and Four Seasons, the power breakfast has replaced the business lunch for making deals between handshakes and cell phone calls. Meanwhile, morning coffee culture and people-watching are at their best at the hundreds of cafés scattered from Downtown to the beaches.

As for the fare, you'll usually find everything from traditional pancakes or eggs Benedict to Mexican-style *huevos rancheros* (fried eggs smothered in salsa, served on corn tortillas with a side of refried beans). Menus are always rounded out with healthier and lighter options such as fresh fruit, yogurt, and a selection of muffins, pastries, and bagels. Fresh-squeezed juices (and combinations of them, in iced 'smoothies') are a particular delight in southern California.

Practically every restaurant accommodates special off-the-menu requests.

VARIED CUISINE

LA's large ethnic populations are reflected in the wonderful diversity of the city's restaurants, with practically every kind of international cuisine available somewhere nearby.

LA's sushi is the best in the state, exquisitely presented in Japanese restaurants from Downtown to the Westside; don't forget to check out the Little Tokyo district for the atmosphere as well as the food.

Chinese restaurants specializing in regional variations – Peking, Szechwan, Shanghai, Hunan, Cantonese – range from elegant establishments in Beverly Hills to simple dining rooms in Chinatown. And if you've never had spicy Korean cuisine, there are good restaurants on every block in Koreatown.

DINING DO'S

The most popular meals to dine out in LA are arguably breakfast and lunch, when you can dine alfresco in the Southern Calfornia sunshine. Angelenos are up early: Breakfast is served from around 6.30 until 11am, although many diners and cafés serve breakfast all day, especially on the weekends. Lunch hours are from 11.30am until 2.30pm, though hob-nobbing Hollywood types like to lunch late. Dinner is served from 5.30 until around 10.30pm, although there are plenty of late-night dining spots.

If you're going to grab a cocktail after dinner, don't forget ID: The legal drinking age in California is 21, but proof of age is frequently required for those older. Cocktail lounges and nightclubs do not admit people under the age of 21. Alcohol cannot be bought or consumed in public establishments between 2 and 6am.

Jewish delicatessens are located in many areas, especially along Fairfax Avenue and on Beverly Boulevard, where you can order up corned beef or pastrami sandwiches, matzo ball soup, cheese blintzes, as well as yummy potato pancakes.

Stalls selling Mexican food abound at Grand Central Market on Broadway or along Olvera Street, where zesty tacos, burritos, and other regional specialties are served streetside. Come nightfall, mobile taco trucks can be spotted all over the city and are a great place to grab a snack post bar-hopping. In fact, food trucks in general have become something of a craze in the city; gourmet ones now troll the streets offering everything from Korean barbecue burritos to *dim sum*, *schnitzel*, and Vietnamese sandwiches called *banh mi*.

California rolls

DRINKS

The morning, afternoon, and evening ritual of coffee-drinking takes on a humorous dimension in Los Angeles, where a java comes in enough sizes, variations, flavors, and calorific levels to confuse even the most sophisticated connoisseur. Whether you want yours with steamed milk, soy milk, vanilla, decaf espresso, or a lemon twist, all you need to do is be savvy enough to order it. An added bonus is excellent people-watching, which comes free of charge at most cafés.

Meanwhile, libations have developed a culture of their own. After the roaring 1990s, the champagne flow has slowed down a little bit but cocktails are still a popular way to toast the town. Creative concoctions boasting market-fresh ingredients have become as important to some restaurants as the dinner menu itself. Of course, the classic Mexican margarita is a local favourite made of tequila, triple sec, and (at the good establishments) fresh lime juice and simple syrup.

Celebrity hotspots

For the best shot at being seated next to someone famous, reserve a table at Mr Chow, Madeo, or The Ivy on Robertson. Or drop in for cocktails at the Four Seasons, a celebrity home-away-from-home, or the poolside Tropicana Bar at The Roosevelt Hotel, a frequent social spot for local celebs and visiting rock stars. Arrive before 8pm if you're not staying at the hotel; the guest list is often exclusive and everyone else is turned away.

At the dinner table, however, the most popular beverage is still California wine, which is showcased in virtually every dining establishment. With Napa Valley, Sonoma Valley, and, more recently, Central Coast varietals contending with France's finest, it's truly difficult to order a bad wine, whether by the glass or bottle.

The main red wines you'll find are Cabernet Sauvignon, Pinot Noir, and red Zinfandel. With whites, Chardonnay is often served as house wine, but it's become popular to experiment with Sauvignon Blancs, Pinot Grigios, and other lesser-known varietals.

Along with a good wine selection, many of LA's bars specialize in offering a wide range of local and West Coast beers and ales, though there are also English-style pubs in Santa Monica where you can find a pint of bitter.

PLACES TO EAT

As a guide, we have used the following symbols to give an indication of the price of a two-course meal for one (excluding drinks, tax, or tip), based on the average cost of main courses.

$$$$ = $50 and up   **$$$** = $25–$50
$$ = $$15–$25   **$** = under $15

ANAHEIM

McCormick and Schmick's Grille $$–$$$ *321 West Katella Avenue, Anaheim, tel: 714-535 9000,* www.mccormickandschmicks. com. Traditional seafood restaurant that also serves steaks and fresh salads. Convenient location near Disneyland and the Anaheim Convention Center. Sun–Thu 11.30am–10pm, Fri–Sat 11.30am–11pm.

HOLLYWOOD

The Hungry Cat $$–$$$ *1535 North Vine Street, tel: 323-462 2155,* www.thehungrycat.com. An outstanding raw bar with creatively cooked seafood dishes in a sleek and modern (but lively) setting, with top-notch cocktails to boot. Mon–Wed noon–10pm, Thu–Fri noon–11pm, Sat 11am–11pm, Sun 11am–10pm.

Musso and Frank Grill $$$ *6667 Hollywood Boulevard, tel: 323-467 7788,* http://mussoandfrank.com. Hollywood's oldest restaurant (established in 1919) has dark paneling, leather booths, seasoned waiters, and great Martinis. Famous customers have included Charlie Chaplin (who sat at table no 1 in the west room), Ernest Hemingway, Raymond Chandler, Orson Welles, Humphrey Bogart, Al Pacino, and Sean Penn. American-style dishes such as steaks, chops, clams, and macaroni and cheese come à la carte. The crepe-thin pancakes are hugely popular. Tue–Sat 11am–11pm.

Providence $$$–$$$$ *5955 Melrose Avenue, tel: 323-460 4170,* www.providencela.com. Elegant restaurant with sleek, modern décor, specializing in premium wild seafood and shellfish, simply prepared and presented. Lunch Fri noon–2pm, dinner Mon–Fri 6–10pm, Sat 5.30–10pm and Sun 5.30–9pm.

MID-WILSHIRE

A.O.C. $$–$$$ *8700 West Third Street, tel: 310-859 9859,* www.aoc winebar.com. An elegant cross between a wine bar and tapas-style restaurant, with a delectable range of small plates ranging from charcuterie to oven-roasted fish and vegetables to fine cheeses, with dozens of wines by the glass. Reservations recommended. Mon 11.30am–10pm, Tue–Fri 11.30am–11pm, Sat 10am–11pm, Sun 10am–10pm.

Toast Bakery Cafe $$ *8221 West Third Street, tel: 323-655 5018,* http://toastbakerycafe.net. An excellent American menu of all-day breakfast (including a number of healthy and vegetarian options), sandwiches, pastas, other specialties, and fabulous baked goods. Daily 7.30am–6pm.

Matsuhisa $$$–$$$$ *129 North La Cienega Boulevard, Beverly Hills, tel: 310-659 9639,* www.nobumatsuhisa.com. Considered the best Asian-inspired seafood in town, chef Nobu Matsuhisa's novel menu features top-notch sushi and pages of entrées. Always crowded and noisy. Reservations necessary. Mon–Fri 11.45am–2.15pm, dinner daily 5.45–10.15pm.

WEST HOLLYWOOD

Barney's Beanery $–$$ *8447 Santa Monica Boulevard, tel: 323-654 2287,* www.barneysbeanery.com. Known for burgers, giant hot dogs, famous chili, Mexican fare, and around 200 bottled beers. Funky bar décor, pool tables, and late-night dining for LA's bar-hoppers. Mon–Fri 11am–2am, Sat–Sun 9am–2am.

Chin Chin $$ *8618 W. Sunset Boulevard (in Sunset Plaza), tel: 310-652 1818,* www.chinchin.com. Great for people-watching and relatively healthy dim sum and noodle dishes within full Chinese menu. Indoor and outdoor dining. Sun–Thu 11am–10pm, Fri–Sat 11am–11pm.

Dan Tana's $$–$$$ *9071 Santa Monica Boulevard, tel: 310-275 9444,* www.dantanasrestaurant.com. A classic old-style Hollywood restaurant with northern Italian cuisine featuring veal, chicken, seafood, and the best cut of New York steak in town. Mon–Sat 5pm–1am, Sun 5pm–12.30am.

Urth Caffe $$ *8565 Melrose Avenue, tel: 310-659 0628,* www.urthcaffe.com. A popular café and casual lunch spot with organic coffee and tea. Healthy meals are on offer and there is a selection of delicious desserts which are made in house. The outdoor patio is a well-known spot for celeb-spotting. Daily 6am–11.30pm.

Pink's Famous Hot Dogs $ *709 North La Brea Avenue, tel: 323-931 4223,* www.pinkshollywood.com. The place to go when you're dying for a greasy quick bite. Hot dogs, burgers, sinful chili, and renowned fries are devoured at outdoor picnic tables. Sun–Thu 9.30am–2am, Fri–Sat 9.30am–3am. Cash only.

Versailles $–$$ *1415 South La Cienega Boulevard, tel: 310-289 0392,* www.versaillescuban.com. Locals frequent this inexpensive, delicious Cuban diner. Noteworthy garlic chicken as well as excellent pork and shrimp dishes are served in the ultra-casual dining room. Sun–Thu 11am–10pm, Fri–Sat 11am–11pm.

BEVERLY HILLS

Bouchon Bistro $$$–$$$$ *235 North Canon Drive, tel: 310-271 9910,* www.thomaskeller.com. Thomas Keller's third location of his famous restaurant packs in movie stars and foodies who come for outstanding French bistro cuisine. The adjoining bakery is a must-visit. Lunch Mon–Fri 11.30am–10.30pm, Sat 11am–10.30pm and Sun 11am–9pm.

Il Fornaio $$$ *301 North Beverly Drive, tel: 310-550 8330,* www.ilfornaio.com. A bustling and bright Italian trattoria with excellent breads, soups, pizzas, pastas, and rotisserie dishes and lively, crowded atmosphere. Wood stove; mesquite grill. Patio dining. There's also a bakery café. Reservations recommended. Mon–Thu 7am–10pm, Fri 7am–11pm, Sat 7.30am–11pm, Sun 7.30am–10pm.

Lawry's Prime Rib $$$ *100 North La Cienega Boulevard, tel: 310-652 2827,* www.lawrysonline.com. A venerable temple of prime ribs, also featuring lobster, fresh fish and their dramatic and delectable 'spinning bowl' salad. Mon–Fri 5–10pm, Sat 4.30–11pm, Sun 4–9.30pm. Reservations recommended.

Mr Chow $$$–$$$$ *344 North Camden Drive, tel: 310-278 9911,* www.mrchow.com. Celebrity spotting generally accompanies excellent Beijing-style (multiple-dish) Chinese fare including duck, dumplings, lobster, and house-made garlic noodles. A modern, see-and-be-seen setting. Reservations recommended. Lunch Mon–Fri noon–2.30pm, dinner daily 6–11.30pm.

THE WESTSIDE

La Serenata Gourmet $–$$ *10924 West Pico Boulevard, tel: 310-441 9667,* www.laserenataonline.com. It's not the bare-bones atmosphere but the excellent fish, tacos, moles, enchiladas, and zesty sauces that bring crowds to this bustling Mexican restaurant. Mon–Fri 11am–3pm and 5–10pm, Fri until 11pm, Sat 11am–11pm, Sun 10am–10pm.

Father's Office $$ *3229 Helms Avenue, tel: 310-736 2224,* www.fathersoffice.com. The gourmet blue cheese burgers served at at this upscale gastropub are famous, but equally deserving are the locavore small plates and the seasonally rotating selection of 36 craft beers on tap. ID is required. Mon–Thur 5pm–11pm, Fri–Sat noon–midnight, Sun noon–10pm, bar open later.

Shaherzad Restaurant $$ *1422 Westwood Boulevard, tel: 310-470-3242,* www.shaherzadrestaurant.com. In an area known as Little Persia, this casual restaurant serves up some of the most authentic Iranian cuisine around, with grilled kabobs, savory rice dishes, and an open oven that produces freshly-baked flatbread. Daily 11.30am–11pm.

Wolfgang Puck at Hotel Bel-Air $$$–$$$$ *701 Stone Canyon Road (at Hotel Bel Air), tel: 310-909 1644,* www.dorchestercollection.com. Celebrity Chef Wolfgang Puck's delicious, creative California-

Mediterranean menu served in the glamorous dining room or on the beautiful Spanish-style terrace. Reached by crossing a bridge over a swan-filled stream and tropical gardens. Reservations necessary. Breakfast daily 7am–10.30am, lunch Mon–Sat 11.30am–2.30pm, brunch Sun 11am–3pm, dinner Sun–Thu 6–10pm, Fri–Sat 6–10.30pm, afternoon tea and all-day menu also available.

SANTA MONICA/BEACH COMMUNITIES

Border Grill $$–$$$ *1445 4th Street, Santa Monica, tel: 310-451 1655,* www.bordergrill.com. Upscale Mexican fare with a Yucatán influence and festive atmosphere. Mon–Fri 11.30am–10pm, Fri until 11pm, Sat–Sun 10am–10pm, Sat until 11pm.

Cafe del Rey $$$ *4451 Admiralty Way, Marina del Rey, tel: 310-823 6395,* www.cafedelreymarina.com. One of the area's better restaurants overlooks the marina and serves Pacific Rim 'new wave' cuisine in a modern and airy dining room. Lunch Mon–Fri 11.30am–2.30pm, dinner Mon–Thu 5.30–10pm, Fri–Sat 5.30–10.30pm, Sun 5–9.30pm; brunch Sat 11.30am–2.30pm, Sun 10.30am–2.30pm.

Chinois on Main $$$$ *2709 Main Street, Santa Monica, tel: 310-392 9025,* www.wolfgangpuck.com. Renowned chef Wolfgang Puck's chic, trendy restaurant serves a creative blend of Chinese, French, and California cuisines in a bright, loud dining room. Lunch Wed–Fri 11.30am–2pm, dinner Mon–Thu 6–10pm, Fri–Sat 6–10.30pm, Sun 5.30–10pm.

Gladstone's 4 Fish $$–$$$ *17300 Pacific Coast Highway, Pacific Palisades, tel: 310-454 3474,* http://gladstones.com. This seafood restaurant's popularity is largely due to its enormous and fun deck seating overlooking the sea. Not affiliated with the one at Universal CityWalk. Mon–Thu 11am–9pm, Fri 11am–10pm, Sat 9am–10pm, Sun 9am–9pm.

Hillstone $$$ *202 Wilshire Boulevard, tel: 310-576 7558;* www.hillstone.com. The appealing menu features prime steaks, seafood, burgers, salads as well as handcrafted sushi. In other words: this place appeals to all tastes. The warm ambience and stylish interior make for a superb experience. Sun–Tue 11.30am–10pm and Wed–Sat 11.30am–11pm.

Ivy at the Shore $$$ *1535 Ocean Avenue, Santa Monica, tel: 310-393 3113;* www.theivyrestaurants.com. Excellent California-fresh fare with a Southern accent, such as Cajun pizza or fried chicken. Especially renowned for crab cakes, grilled-vegetable salad, and healthy menu items. Daily 9.30am–10pm.

Michael's $$$–$$$$ *1147 3rd Street, Santa Monica, tel: 310-451 0843,* www.michaelssantamonica.com. One of the original examples of California cuisine and a top spot in the area. Peaceful and beautiful, with an extraordinary art collection and a lovely garden patio. Reservations advised. Mon–Sat 6pm–10.30pm.

Rose Café and Market $–$$ *220 Rose Avenue, Venice, tel: 310-399 0711,* www.rosecafe.com. This casual café offers enticing bakery and deli fare plus various pizzas and inexpensive entrées. Mon–Fri 8am–3pm (counter 7am–5pm), Sat–Sun 8am–5pm.

Rustic Canyon $$$ *1119 Wilshire Boulevard, Santa Monica, tel: 310-393 7050,* www.rusticcanyonwinebar.com. This lovely and intimate wine bar and restaurant features a regularly changing menu of market-fresh dishes that use local and sustainable ingredients. Sun–Thu 5.30–10.30pm, Fri–Sat 5.30–11.30pm.

Valentino $$$–$$$$ *3115 Pico Boulevard, Santa Monica, tel: 310-829 4313,* www.valentinosantamonica.com. Expensive but worth every penny, this renowned Italian restaurant has an amazing wine list and top-notch food served in a formal dining room. Reservations recommended. Fri for lunch 11.30am–2.30pm, dinner Tue–Thu 5–10pm, Fri–Sat 5–10.30pm.

DOWNTOWN

Church & State Bistro $$–$$$ *1850 Industrial Street #100, tel: 213-405 1434,* www.churchandstatebistro.com. This lively and hip French bistro features nearly two dozen types of wine and reputedly one of the best raw bars in town. Lunch Mon–Fri 11.30am–2.30pm, dinner Mon–Thu 6–10pm, Fri 6–11pm, Sat 5.30–11pm, Sun 5.30–9pm.

Engine Company No. 28 $$–$$$ *644 South Figueroa, tel: 213-624 6996,* www.engineco.com. All-American food (firehouse chili, grilled fish and steaks, corn chowder, and lemon meringue pie) in an historic firehouse favored by lunching lawyers. Daily 11am–10pm.

The Palm $$$–$$$$ *1100 S. Flower Street tel: 213-763 4600,* www. thepalm.com. From the perfect steaks to the Nova Scotia lobsters flown in daily, the traditional American food is impeccable at this acclaimed Northern Italian steakhouse with New York origins. Lunch Mon–Fri 11.30am–3pm, dinner Mon–Thu 3–10pm, Fri 3–11pm, Sat 5–11pm, Sun 5–9.30pm.

Sushi Gen $$–$$$ *422 East Second Street, tel: 213-617 0552,* www. sushigen-dtla.com. The melt-in-your-mouth toro and salmon understandably attract crowds of people to this gem of a sushi restaurant in Little Tokyo. Go at lunch to beat the crowds and take advantage of the reasonably priced lunch specials. Lunch Mon–Fri 11.15am–2pm, dinner Mon–Fri 5.30–9.30pm, Sat 5–9.30pm.

Water Grill $$$–$$$$ *544 South Grand Avenue, tel: 213-891 0900,* www.watergrill.com. A stunning international seafood restaurant with a lively, upscale atmosphere and some of the best seafood Downtown. Lobster, crab, and oyster bar. Mon–Thu 11.30am–10pm, Fri 11.30am–11pm, Sat 5–11pm, Sun 4–10pm.

PASADENA

Dog Haus $ *105 N. Hill Avenue, tel: 626-577 4287,* www.doghaus.com. Excellent good-sized and generously built hot dogs and burgers with delicious toppings that will surely put a big smile on your face. This place is consistently busy and it can get really crowded at lunch time. Other locations in Los Angeles County. Daily 11am–10pm.

Parkway Grill $$$ *510 South Arroyo Parkway, tel: 626-795 1001,* www.theparkwaygrill.com. One of Pasadena's top restaurants, serving such eclectic California fare as fresh fish, black bean soup, and pizza in a two-level indoor garden setting. Lunch Mon–Fri 11.30am–2.30pm, dinner Mon–Thu 5.30–9.30pm, Fri–Sat 5.30–10.30pm, Sun 5–9.30pm.

THE VALLEY

Mistral $$–$$$ *13422 Ventura Boulevard, Sherman Oaks, tel: 818-981 6650,* www.mistralrestaurant.net. Straightforward, quality, and affordable French bistro fare is served in a warm and convivial atmosphere. Mon–Fri 11.30am–2.30pm, 5.30–10pm, Sat 5.30–10.30pm, Sun 5–9.30pm.

Wolfgang Puck Bistro $$ *1000 Universal City Plaza, #152 Universal City, tel: 818-985 9653,* www.wolfgangpuck.com. California pizzas, fresh pastas, and tasty salads designed by the master chef. Large outdoor patio. Sun–Thu 11am–9pm, Fri–Sat 11am–11pm.

LONG BEACH

Belmont Brewing Company $–$$ *25 Thirty-Ninth Place, tel: 562-433 3891,* www.belmontbrewing.com. Authentic brewery on the beach with a commanding view of the Long Beach skyline, Palos Verdes, and Catalina Island. Salads, sandwiches, pasta, meat, and fish entrées, and, of course, beer. Mon–Fri 11.30am–9.30pm, Sat 10am–10pm, Sun 10am–9.30pm; bar until midnight.

The Sky Room $$$–$$$$ *40 S. Locust Avenue, Long Beach, tel: 562-983 2703,* www.theskyroom.com. First opened in 1926, this classy restaurant atop the Breakers Hotel transports diners to an earlier era of fine dining, dancing, and entertainment, with stunning Art-Deco décor, California-French cuisine, romantic music, and panoramic views over the ocean and city. Extensive wine list. Reservations suggested. Mon–Thu 5.30–10pm, Fri–Sat 5.30pm–11pm, Sun 4.30–9pm.

ORANGE COUNTY

Crab Cooker $–$$ *2200 Newport Boulevard, Newport Beach, tel:*

949-673 0100, www.crabcooker.com. In this funky and fun dining room you'll get inexpensive mesquite-grilled fresh seafood. Sun–Thu 11am–9pm, Fri–Sat 11am–10pm.

Las Brisas $$$ *361 Cliff Drive, Laguna Beach, tel: 949-497 5434*, www.lasbrisaslagunabeach.com. Great Mexican cuisine, including seafood dishes, served on an outdoor patio or indoor dining room with marvelous views of the ocean. Mon–Thu 8am–10pm, Fri–Sat 8am–11pm, Sun 9am–10pm.

Medieval Times Dinner and Tournament $$$ *7662 Beach Boulevard, Buena Park, tel: 866-543 9637*, www.medievaltimes.com/buenapark. A wacky but original dinner-theater concept: you enjoy a fixed-price four-course meal (adults: $61.95; 12 and under $36.95) while watching knights on horseback and dueling sword fighters. Reservations advised. Dinner shows nightly, call castle for specific times; castle opens 90 minutes before showtime.

Steve's No. 4 Charbroil $ *6033 Warner Avenue, Huntington Beach, tel: 714-848 1422*. Steve's has been on the corner of Warner and Springdale for over 25 years, serving cheap breakfasts, great burgers and lunches. The family-run service is friendly and prices are very reasonable. Try the breakfast burrito but don't order a large fries unless you're ready to eat a lot. Daily 7am–9pm.

White House $$$ *887 South Anaheim Boulevard, Anaheim, tel: 714-772 1381*, www.anaheimwhitehouse.com. Award-winning northern Italian cuisine in a romantic mansion setting with log fires and elegant Victorian décor. Try the lobster ravioli or signature rack of lamb. Reservations required. Lunch Mon–Fri 11.30am–2pm, dinner nightly 5–10pm, brunch Sun 11am–3pm.

CATALINA ISLAND

Steve's Steakhouse $$$ *417 Crescent Avenue, Avalon, tel: 310-510 0333*, http://stevessteakhouse.com. Beautiful views over Avalon harbour and varied menu ranging from teriyaki chicken to surf n' turf. Daily lunch 11.30am–2pm, dinner 5–11pm.

A–Z TRAVEL TIPS

A Summary of Practical Information

A

ACCUMMODATIONS (See also Camping, Youth Hostels, and the list of Recommended Hotels starting on page 135)

Many top hotels offer special **promotional rates,** and winter travelers are likely to get a lower rate than during the summer tourist season, especially along the coast. It is always wise to have advance reservations: where available, use the toll-free 800, 844, 855, 866, 877 or 888 telephone numbers for making your reservations from within the US.

Hotel rates in Los Angeles are subject to a 15.57 percent tax, which is added on top of the quoted rates. Parking and telephone charges can add considerably to the bill. In addition, the better hotels have valet parking, which can cost from $6 to $40 or more per night; you are also expected to tip the valet at least $2 each time he delivers your car.

Beyond the hotel and motel options, self-catering **apartments** for longer stays (usually one-month minimum) are available. Oakwood Apartments (tel: 1-877 902 0832; www.oakwood.com) has properties in several locations throughout the city.

The Los Angeles Convention and Visitors Bureau (see page 131) publishes a **lodging guide**, as do most other information offices, listing a wide selection of accommodation options in and around the city.

AIRPORTS

Los Angeles International Airport (LAX) is one of the busiest airports worldwide, serving nearly 90 major airlines. It is located 17 miles (27km) from downtown LA, near the coast, off the 405 freeway. Planes arrive and depart from eight terminals and from the Tom Bradley International Terminal. The information number for LAX is 855-463 5252; www.lawa.org. Volunteer Information Professionals, who assist passengers with finding appropriate transportation or provide directions, can be found at information booths on the arrivals level of each LAX terminal.Frequent shuttle-bus service between terminals is provided free of charge. LAX shuttle buses are white with blue and green stripes. Board the 'A' shuttle under the LAX Shuttle sign. Fly Away buses provide cheap, 24-hour transport between Downtown and LAX (www.lawa.org/flyaway/default.aspx). There is also shuttle service to and from the Metro Rail Green Line Aviation Station. Plentiful taxis are also available.

Bob Hope Airport (BUR), formerly Burbank-Glendale-Pasadena Airport (tel: 818-840 8840; www.bobhopeairport.com) provides domestic services. It serves the San Fernando Valley as well as Los Angeles residents who prefer to avoid the chaos of LAX. Thirteen miles (20km) from downtown LA and less crowded than LAX, this airport is actually the better option for travelers arriving from other US cities and planning to stay in the valleys, Pasadena, Hollywood, or Downtown. (However, fewer shuttles and taxis frequent this airport, making ground transportation more problematic).

John Wayne (Orange County) Airport (tel: 949-252 5200; www.ocair.com), 16 miles (25km) from Anaheim, serves the Orange County region. Eight major domestic airlines fly here from around the country. Several airlines also serve the **Long Beach Airport** (tel: 562-570 2600; www.lgb.org).

B

BEACHES

Access to public beaches is free, but fees (between $5 and $10) are charged in parking lots (car parks). Pets, alcoholic beverages, and bonfires are prohibited. Lifeguards are on duty year-round during daylight hours. Always swim in front of an open lifeguard tower where possible and keep an eye out for warning signs.

For maps, guides, and further information about beaches, call the Marina del Rey Visitors' Information Center/Los Angeles County Beaches and Harbors Information Center at 310-305 9545 (www.visitmarinadelrey.com; 9am–5pm, recorded information 24 hours).

BUDGETING FOR YOUR TRIP

The prices below are approximate and vary with the establishment

Airport transfer. To Downtown: taxi $45+, Super Shuttle $17.

Bicycle rental. $7–$9 per hour, $20–$32 per day.

Bus and Metro fares. $1.75 base fare, 50¢ transfers. Specials: $7 day-pass; $25 weekly pass.

Car rental. Depending on the company and the season, prices can vary greatly. Count on $35–$50 per day with unlimited mileage (taxes and collision damage waiver included), usually less expensive by the week and by waiving the collision damage waiver.

Entertainment. Movies $10–$14, concert/dance $20–$60, theater $20–$65, nightclubs $10–$20 cover charge.

Hotels (double occupancy, per night, 5.57 percent tax is not included). Expensive $210 and up; moderate $110–$210, budget under $110.

Meals and drinks. Breakfast $5–$15, lunch $7–$20, dinner $12–$20 and up, beer $3.50 and up, mixed drink $5–$12, wine $5–$15 per glass, soft drink $1–$2, coffee $2 and up.

Museums. Adults $5–$15, children, students, and seniors $4–$12.

Parking lots (car parks). $2–$6 per hour; many have a maximum $5–$6 charge; Downtown ramps and hotel parking $12–$30 per day.

Sales tax. A sales tax of 9 percent is added to most purchases and restaurant bills.

Theme parks. Adults $50–$80, children $20–$74 entrance per day.

Tours. Half-day city tours $30 and up.

C

CAMPING

In nearby state or national parks a daily fee is generally charged per campsite and per vehicle. Information on the Santa Monica Mountains and camping can be requested from the **National Park Service** (tel: 805-370 2300; www.nps.gov/samo) or the **State Park Service** (tel: 916-653 6995 or 800-777 0369; www.parks.ca.gov). State park camping information and reservations are available by calling 800-444 7275 or at www.reserveamerica.com. You can also contact the visitor information centers at Big Bear Lake and Lake Arrowhead and on Catalina Island (see page 131) for details of camping in these areas.

CAR RENTAL (See also Driving and Money)

Major car rental firms include Enterprise (tel: 800-261 7331; www. enterprise.com), Dollar (tel: 800-800 4000; www.dollar.com), Hertz (tel: 800-654 3131; www.hertz.com), and National (tel: 800-222 9058; www.nationalcar.com). Prices vary on an almost daily basis, and automobile-club and other discounts are often available. Look into special weekly/weekend rates.

Collision damage waiver adds considerably to the cost. It's best to learn whether your own automobile insurance or credit card offers full coverage for rental cars and, if so, waive the collision damage coverage. Also, rates that include unlimited mileage are advised.

To rent a car, you will need a valid driver's license plus an International Driving Permit if your own license is in a language other than English. Many agencies set a minimum age for car rental at 21, others at 25. A major credit card is required for car rental.

CLIMATE

Los Angeles enjoys a temperate climate with low humidity. Daytime temperatures average 80°F (26°C) June–October and 69°F (20°C) November–May. The rainy season is November–March, although rainfall is moderate and periodic, broken by sunny days. The heat of summer, usually tempered by sea breezes, is more intense in the valleys and further inland. Monthly average temperatures are as follows:

	J	F	M	A	M	J	J	A	S	O	N	D
°C	18	19	21	22	23	25	28	28	28	25	23	20
°F	65	66	69	71	74	77	83	83	82	77	73	68

CLOTHING

Bring comfortable, casual clothes and shoes. In January and February you might want to pack clothes suitable for rain. Formal restaurants may require a jacket and tie for men and dress clothes for women; otherwise, casual chic is fine. Bring a jacket or sweater.

CONSULATES

Many countries maintain consulates or have overseas representatives in Los Angeles. Official embassies are in Washington, D.C.

Australia: 2029 Century Park East; tel: 310-229 2300; http://los angeles.consulate.gov.au.

Canada: 550 South Hope Street, 9th Floor; tel: 213-346 2700; www.losangeles.gc.ca.

Japan: 350 South Grand Avenue, Suite 1700; tel: 213-617 6700; www.la.us.emb-japan.go.jp.

South Africa: 6300 Wilshire Boulevard, Suite 600; tel: 323-651 0902; www.dirco.gov.za/losangeles.

United Kingdom: 2029 Century Park East, Suite 1350; tel: 310-789 0031; www.gov.uk/government/world/usa.

CRIME AND SAFETY (See also Emergencies and Police)

Like all urban areas in the US, there is crime in LA, but as infamous as LA's criminal activity is, statistically it fares well when compared with other major cities. Visitors should take the usual precautions.

The all-purpose emergency telephone number is **911**. For non-emergencies, call the local police department. Find the number in the phone book or ask your concierge.

D

DRIVING (See also Car Rental)

To get around the city easily you will have to drive. Drive on the right; pass (overtake) on the left. Unless there's a sign to the contrary, you can turn right on a red signal, providing you make a complete stop and check for pedestrians and traffic. Drivers and all passengers must wear seat belts; children under 8 must be in a child's car seat secured in the back seat unless they are 4 feet 9 inches tall (148 cm). Rental car companies now offer child seats. Pedestrians have the right-of-way at crosswalks. It is an offense to pass a school bus in either direction on a two-lane road when it is taking on or discharging passengers. Strict drunk-driving laws are enforced, and anyone found driving under the influence of alcohol will be arrested.

Motorcycles. It is illegal anywhere in the state of California to ride a motorcycle without a helmet.

Pedestrians. Jaywalking (crossing in the middle of the street or against a traffic signal) is a serious offense and carries a heavy fine.

Highways. Divided highways are called freeways, and LA has the world's most extensive freeway system. They are generally the fastest way to cross town, but avoid them during rush hours (7–9.30am and 3.30–7pm), when they are clogged with traffic. For information on freeway or highway conditions, call 800-427 7623 or visit www. sigalert.com.

Freeways have multiple lanes, especially where one or more freeways intersect, but lanes are usually clearly marked with their destination. Some routes have car pool lanes, usually the far left lane. It will be marked with diamonds, and it means you must have two or more people in the car to use that lane. (Use it with only one person in the car and you'll be fined close to $400.) Before setting out, study your map and determine the exact route you intend to take. Freeways have both a number and a name, and sometimes there are two names depending on which part of the city you're in and which direction you're heading. The list below should help you.

Alternate routes. Like everywhere else in the world Los Angeles roads are subject to constant maintenance work. Call the **California Transportation Department** (CalTrans) at 916-445 7623 or 800-427 7623 for an up-to-date recording on the status of all California roads or check online at www.dot.ca.gov/roadsandtraffic.html. If you want to drive across town, the 10 freeway usually provides easy access from Santa Monica to Downtown.

Speed limits. If there are no posted speed limit signs, the maximum speed is 25mph (40km/h), and 55mph (90km/h) on the freeways. Outside city limits, the limit on Interstate highways is 65mph (100km/h) with several 70mph (112km/h) segments.

Parking. Los Angeles has an abundance of parking restrictions, which are posted along the street. Be sure you're parked legally and not in an area that requires a permit during specified times. Vehicles parked in violation of parking regulations are quickly ticketed

Freeway Number Freeway Name
1 Pacific Coast Highway (PCH)
2 Glendale
5 Golden State/Santa Ana
10 Santa Monica/San Bernardino
22 Garden Grove
57 Orange
60 Pomona
90 Marina
91 Artesia/Riverside
101 Ventura/Hollywood
105 Century Freeway
110 Pasadena/Harbor
118 Simi Valley-San Fernando Valley
134 Ventura
170 Hollywood
210 Foothill
405 San Diego
605 San Gabriel River
710 Long Beach

and/or towed. A red line on the curb means no parking, a green line indicates parking for 20 minutes only, and a white line means passenger loading and unloading only. Have a supply of coins for parking meters, although some of the newer ones do take credit cards. LA's parking lots (car parks) may be expensive for short-term stays but are cheaper than fines.

Gas (petrol) stations. Most service stations stay open in the evening and on Sunday. Most are self-service. If you have a credit card you can generally pay at the pump. Otherwise, you will have to go inside and pay in advance before the pump will be activated; you get a refund if you overpay. There are several grades of gasoline (petrol): regular unleaded (the cheapest) will suffice for most rental cars.

Breakdowns, accidents, and insurance. The **American Automobile Association (AAA)** offers its assistance to members of affiliated organizations from abroad. It also provides travel information within the US. Check the phone directory for the branch nearest you. **AAA**'s Emergency Road Services number is 800-AAA-HELP.

If you have car trouble on the freeway, try to pull off the road to the right shoulder where there are emergency call boxes; get out on the passenger side away from traffic. If your car stalls in a traffic lane, turn on your emergency flashers and stay inside with your seat belt fastened while you wait for a passing patrol car. Never cross the freeway to reach a call box. Most accidents must be reported to the police at once. If one occurs, make sure you get the driver's license number and car license plate of all parties involved for your insurance claim.

E

ELECTRICITY

Throughout the United States the standard is 110 volts, 60 cycle AC. Plugs usually have two flat prongs. Overseas visitors without dual-voltage travel appliances will need a transformer and adapter plug.

EMERGENCIES (See also Medical Care and Police)
All-purpose emergency number: **911**

G

GAY AND LESBIAN TRAVELLERS

West Hollywood is the center of gay and lesbian life in LA. The magazine *Frontiers* (www.frontiersmedia.com) offers information on local LGBT events, arts, and entertainment. The annual LGBT Film Festival Outfest (www.outfest.org) is a popular event. For more information, you can also contact the Los Angeles LGBT Center (www.lalgbtcenter.org), the world's largest provider of LGBT services. The center has six branches in the city. In a historic moment, same-sex marriage was legalised throughout the US in June 2015.

GETTING THERE

By air from North America. Direct flights connect many American and Canadian cities to Los Angeles. Special fares are available on these competitive routes. Certain US airlines offer bargains for foreign travelers who visit several American destinations. Fly-drive vacations, including flight, hotel, and rental car, are offered by many airlines.

International flights. All the major international carriers have either direct or one-stop flights to Los Angeles from Europe and the main Pacific airports. Fares vary widely according to the season, but discounted fares to Los Angeles are usually available. There are various APEX fares if you book two to three weeks in advance and stay between seven days and six months.

By rail. Amtrak is America's passenger railway company. LA's Amtrak terminal is located Downtown at Union Station, 800 North Alameda Avenue. You can travel nationwide from here; coastal routes go north to Santa Barbara, Oakland, and Seattle and south to San Diego. For information call 1-800-872 7245; www.amtrak.

com. The Amtrak stations in Orange County are at Anaheim, Santa Ana, Fullerton, San Juan Capistrano, San Clemente, and Irvine.

By bus. The Greyhound bus terminal for long-distance coach travel is located Downtown at 1716 East Seventh Street. For additional terminal locations in the area, or for fare and schedule information, call 213-629 8401 or 1-800-231 2222; www.greyhound.com.

By car. The excellent Interstate freeway system criss-crosses the United States and links LA with all regions of the country.

GUIDES AND TOURS

Many tour companies are listed on the website run by the Los Angeles Convention and Visitors Bureau (www.discoverlosangeles. com; see page 131). Long-established firms include Starline Tours (323-463 3333; www.starlinetours.com), which take passengers past movie stars' homes; Dearly Departed Tours (tel: 855-600 3323; www. dearlydepartedtours.com), a tour of Hollywood's most infamous murders, deaths, and scandals. The Los Angeles Conservancy (tel: 213-623 2489; www.laconservancy.org) offers excellent walking tours of downtown LA. Details of self-guided walking tours of other areas can be obtained from tourist information offices (see page 131).

M

MEDIA

Radio, television and DVDs. Most hotel rooms have television and many have radio. Stations generally broadcast around the clock, and there are several foreign-language stations. The nationwide commercial networks are CBS, 4 ABC, 7 ABC, and Fox. Channel 28 (KCET) is a non-commercial educational, independent television channel. Many hotels also offer a range of cable-TV programs. Note that DVDs bought in the US will only work outside the US and Canada on 'Multi-Region' DVD players, so check yours first.

Newspapers and magazines. *The Los Angeles Times* (www.latimes.

com) is LA's main daily newspaper. The 'Calendar' section carries arts and entertainment listings; the Friday and Sunday editions are extensive. *Los Angeles Magazine* (www.lamag.com), published monthly, has interesting features about LA life and excellent restaurant and entertainment listings. A number of weekly and monthly publications are also good sources of information. They include the *LA Weekly* (www.laweekly.com), the best of the free weeklies for listings of what's on around town and the *Downtown News* (www.ladowntownnews.com).

Foreign-language newspapers. Foreign newspapers and magazines are sold at large newsstands, and at Book Soup bookstore (8818 Sunset Boulevard; tel: 310-659 3110; www.booksoup.com).

MEDICAL CARE (see also Emergencies)

No vaccinations are required or recommended by health authorities, unless you are arriving from an area with cholera or yellow fever.

Health care, especially hospitalization, is extremely expensive in the United States. Some hospitals might even refuse treatment without proof of insurance. Overseas visitors should therefore make arrangements before leaving home (through a travel agent or an insurance company) for **health insurance** with a high level of coverage.

If you do need **medical assistance**, contact any of the major hospitals. Most have 24-hour emergency (trauma) rooms. These include: St. John's Hospital and Health Center (2121 Santa Monica Boulevard; Santa Monica; tel: 310-829 5511); Cedars-Sinai Medical Center (8700 Beverly Boulevard; tel: 800-233 2771; http://cedars-sinai.edu); and Hollywood Presbyterian Medical Center (1300 North Vermont Avenue; tel: 213-413 3000; http://hollywoodpresbyterian.com/. For emergencies, dial 911.

Drugstores (pharmacies). Several drugstores stay open late or even 24 hours a day. You may find that some medicines obtainable over the counter at home are available only by prescription in the US, and vice versa. The large pharmacy chain Rite Aid (www.riteaid.com) has numerous locations throughout the LA area.

MONEY

Currency. The dollar ($) is divided into 100 cents (¢). **Banknotes:** $1, $2 (uncommon), $5, $10, $20, $50, and $100. Larger denominations are not in general circulation. All notes are the same size and the same green color, so be sure to double-check before you pay for something. **Coins**: 1¢ (known as a penny), 5¢ (nickel), 10¢ (dime), 25¢ (quarter), 50¢ (half dollar, less common). Dollar coins are rarely encountered.

Banks and currency exchange. Banks are generally open 9am–5 or 6pm Monday–Friday or Saturday. Other foreign-exchange outlets include **World Banknotes Exchange,** downtown at 520 S. Grand Avenue, Suite L100 (tel: 213-627 5404; www.wbxchange.com) and **Travelex**, 8901 Santa Monica Boulevard inside US Bank (tel: 310-659 6093; www.travelex.com).

Credit cards. Major credit cards are accepted in most hotels, shops, and restaurants. You may be asked for supplementary identification.

Money transfers. To find the nearest money transfer location, call **Western Union** at 800-325 6000; for Spanish speakers, call 800-325 4045; for money orders call 1-800-999 9660 (http://westernunion.com).

O

OPENING HOURS

Shops. Department stores and shopping malls are generally open 10am–9pm on weekdays, 10am–6 or 7pm on Saturday, and 11am–5 or 6pm on Sunday. Individual shops are generally open Monday–Saturday from 9 or 10am to 5.30 or 6pm. In trendy shopping areas such as Melrose Avenue, shops often stay open until 11pm.

Museums. Normally 10am–5pm, but many open longer at least one night a week or on Sunday. Most museums are closed on Monday or one other day of the week.

Banks. Generally Monday–Friday or Saturday 9am–5 or 6pm.

Post offices. Most branches open at 8.30 or 9am and close at 5pm, though some close later. Some are open on Saturdays, as well.

P

POLICE

Police wear dark blue uniforms and usually travel by car, motorcycle, or bicycle. In an emergency, dial **911**. The Los Angeles Police Department (LAPD) can be reached at 1-877-275 5273 or at www.lapdonline.org.

POST OFFICES

The US Postal Service deals only with mail. Check with your hotel concierge for the branch office nearest you. Post offices are generally open 8.30 or 9am–5pm Monday to Friday, and some are open 9am–3.30pm on Saturday. You can usually purchase stamps at the front desk in your hotel and at drugstores and grocery stores. Letters can be mailed from the hotel, or dropped in one of the blue mailboxes located throughout the city. For more information, call the Postal Answer Line toll free at 1-800-275 8777 or visit www.usps.com.

PUBLIC HOLIDAYS

When certain holidays (such as Christmas) fall on a Sunday, banks, post offices, and most stores close on the following Monday. They close on Friday if those holidays fall on a Saturday.

New Year's Day January 1
Martin Luther King Jr. Day Third Monday in January
Presidents' Day Third Monday in February
Memorial Day Last Monday in May
Independence Day July 4
Labor Day First Monday in September
Columbus Day Second Monday in October
Veterans' Day November 11

Thanksgiving Fourth Thursday in November
Christmas December 25

S

SMOKING

Smoking is banned in city restaurants and bars, although trendy spots have a tendency to ignore the rules. Laws vary in surrounding communities, but all restaurants are required to have a nonsmoking section. Smoking is also prohibited in most public spaces.

T

TELEPHONES

The American telephone system is run by several private, regional companies. Coin- or credit card-operated phones are found in most public places, including hotel lobbies, drugstores, gas (petrol) stations, bars, restaurants, and along the streets. For directory assistance (information) dial **411**. When calling long-distance remember that evening (after 5pm) and weekend rates are often much cheaper.

The Greater Los Angeles area has four **area codes**: **310** (Westside, Beverly Hills, Santa Monica, and Los Angeles International Airport); **213** (Downtown LA); **323** (Hollywood); and **562** (Long Beach). Other area codes are **818** (San Fernando Valley), **626** (San Gabriel Valley and adjacent areas), **714** and **949** (Orange County), and **909** (Riverside and San Bernardino counties).

Callers dialing from one area code to another must always dial 1 plus the appropriate area code and seven-digit number. Local long-distance charges sometimes apply; these are based on a zone system and are difficult to work out in advance.

TELEVISION TICKETS

Tickets for most television show recordings on all networks are now handled by companies such as Audiences Unlimited (tel: 818-260-0041; www.tvtickets.com) or TVTix (tel: 818-985-8811; www.tvtix.com). Tickets can also be obtained in person on the day of the show. They are usually limited to two per person and are given on a first-come, first-served basis. All tickets are free and are offered online for most shows starting about 30 days prior to the show date. If you need to write in for tickets for specific shows, this information will come up on the website. TVTix also operates a second website, www.beinamovie.com, which can help you take part in a movie crowd scene. For *The Price is Right*, call 855 447 7423 or go to cbs.com for that and other CBS shows. Paramount Studios tickets are available through Audiences Unlimited, above.

TIME DIFFERENCES

Los Angeles is in the Pacific time zone, 8 hours behind GMT. From the second Sunday in March to the first Sunday in November, the clock is advanced 1 hour for Daylight Saving Time (GMT minus 7 hours). The chart below shows the time worldwide when it is noon in Los Angeles.

Los Angeles	Chicago	New York	London	Sydney	Cape Town
noon	2pm	3pm	8pm	6am	10pm

TIPPING

You should add 18 percent to restaurant and bar bills. If service has been very good, 20 percent or more is appropriate. Cinema/theater ushers are not tipped, but doormen who provide a service (calling a cab, etc) and cloakroom attendants should be given no less than one dollar. Tip the parking valet when he brings your car for you (not when he parks it). Some general guidelines:

Porter $1–$2 per bag

Hotel housekeeping $1–$2 per day except for one-night stays, or $7–$15 per week

Hotel concierge $5 for tickets or restaurant reservations ($10 or more if they're hard to get)
Taxi drivers about 15 percent
Tour guide 10–15 percent
Parking valet $2

TOURIST INFORMATION

The **Los Angeles Convention and Visitors Bureau** runs the site www.discoverlosangeles.com, which contains a visitors' guide to the city.
Visitor information centers. Most visitors' centers will gladly send you tourist information:

Hollywood Visitor Information Center, 6801 Hollywood Boulevard, at Hollywood and Highland, Hollywood, CA 90028; tel: 323-467 6412. Monday–Saturday 9am–10pm, Sunday 10am–7pm.

Union Station, 800 N. Alameda St. Port of Los Angeles, Berth 93, Pacific Cruise Ship Terminal, San Pedro, tel: 310-514 9484

Anaheim/Orange County Visitor and Convention Bureau, 800 West Katella Avenue, Anaheim, CA 92802; tel: 855-405 5020; http://visit anaheim.org.

Big Bear Lake Resort Association, 630 Bartlett Road, Big Bear Lake, CA 92315; tel: 800-424 4232; www.bigbearinfo.com.

Catalina Island Chamber of Commerce and Visitors Bureau, PO Box 217, Avalon, CA 90704; tel: 310-510 1520; www.catalinachamber.com.

Lake Arrowhead Communities Chamber of Commerce, 28200 California 189, Lake Arrowhead, CA 92352; tel: 909-336 1547; www.lake arrowhead.net.

Long Beach Area Convention and Visitors Bureau, 301 E. Ocean Boulevard, Suite 1900, Long Beach, CA 90802; tel: 562-436 3645 or 800-452 7829; www.visitlongbeach.com.

Palm Springs Desert Resorts Communities Convention and Visitors Authority, 70–100 Highway 111, Rancho Mirage, CA 92270; tel: 760-770 9000 or 1-800-967 3767; www.visitgreaterpalmsprings.com.

Pasadena Convention and Visitors Bureau, 300 E. Green Street,

Pasadena, CA 91101; tel: 626-795 9311 or 1-800-307 7977; www. visitpasadena.com.

TRANSPORTATION

Although Los Angeles has an extensive bus and now rail and subway network, use of a car is generally recommended because of the distance between sights and attractions and the travel time involved. But for short trips, or for carefree sightseeing at low cost, it's easy to ride the MTA, which is getting more comprehensive all the time.

Buses/rail transit. The Los Angeles County Metropolitan Transportation Authority (MTA) provides bus, light rail, and subway transportation in the metro area. Subway and light rail now connect Downtown with Hollywood, Universal City, Pasadena, and many tourist destinations. The Metro Orange Line serves the San Fernando Valley with new MetroLiner buses. The Expo Lines light rail system operates between Downtown Los Angeles and Culver City, with the lastest extension servicing Santa Monica. For information on MTA bus/rail/subway services and routes, call 323-GO METRO (226 6883), or consult the Trip Planner on its website, www.metro. net. Base fare is $1.75, plus 50¢ for transfers. You must have the exact fare or a token; drivers do not give change. A day pass, good on all Metro buses and rail lines, is $7; weekly passes are $25.

The Los Angeles Department of Transportation operates the DASH shuttle system (tel: 213-808 2273; www.ladottransit.com/ dash) Downtown during the daytime, linking the major business, civic, and entertainment centers (50¢ per ride; free transfer). It also runs the Commuter Express system. Separate DASH systems also operate around Hollywood and throughout the city. A similar shuttle system, the Passport, operates in Long Beach.

Taxis. There are taxi ranks at airports, train and bus terminals, and major hotels. Otherwise they are radio-dispatched and must be ordered by phone. Cabs will stop when hailed on the street, but they are infrequent.

Ferries. There are several services between the coast and Catalina Island. The Catalina Passenger Service operates the Catalina Flyer (tel: 949-673 5245; www.catalinainfo.com) once daily to and from Newport Beach: round-trip fares are $70 adults, $65 seniors (60+), $53 children 3–12, and $6 children under 2. Catalina Express (tel: 1-800-481 3470, 800-622 2354; www.catalinaexpress.com) offers several voyages a day from San Pedro, Long Beach, and Dana Point: round-trip fares are $74.50 adults, $68 seniors (55+), $59 children 2–11, $5 children under 2 (Dana Point departures slightly higher).

Bikes. A public bike-share system is scheduled to be launched in spring 2016 with 1,100 bikes at 65 stations in Downtown Los Angeles as a pilot project. Bikes will be available 24 hours a day and a smartphone app will provide information about their availability. Planned locations of dock stations include Union Station, the Convention Center, Staples Center, Grand Park, the Seventh Street Metro stop, Grand Central Market, Pershing Square, the Arts District and the future Figueroa Cycle Track (the city's first protected bike lane is located on Figueroa Street). In 2017, the bike-share scheme will be expanded to Pasadena. Eventually, 4,000 bicycles will be rolled out.

TRAVELERS WITH DISABILITIES

A number of properties have rooms for the disabled with handicapped-accessible features as well as wheelchair-accessible transportation and recreational facilities.

TDD telephone lines are available for the hearing impaired. Contact the California Relay Service for the Hearing Impaired: (Voice) 800-735 2922, (TDD/TTY) 800-735 2929.

Los Angeles County Metropolitan Transportation Authority's buses are equipped either with automatic wheelchair lifts, or, in the newer buses, low-floor access. The DASH system is similarly equipped. You can contact the Metro Wheelchair Lift Hotline (800-621 7828).

VISAS AND ENTRY REQUIREMENTS

Canadians need to present a valid passport, a NEXUS card, FAST-card or enhanced driver's license (EDL) as evidence of their nationality. See www.voyage.gc.ca for more information. Under the visa waiver program, UK, Irish, Australian, and New Zealand citizens do not need a visa for stays of less than 90 days in the US, only a valid 10-year passport and a return airline ticket. All passports must be machine readable, and visitors should check the current rules on biometric passports: www.travel.state.gov. The airline will issue a visa waiver form. Since September 11, 2001, new security arrangements have meant that non-American nationals are often called upon to produce photo ID. Plan to carry your passport with you at all times, or photocopy it and carry around the copies.

Duty-free allowances. You will be asked to complete a customs declaration form before you arrive in the US. When returning to your own country, restrictions will apply: depending on the country, usually around 200 cigarettes or 50 cigars or 250g tobacco, 2 liters wine or spirits.

YOUTH HOSTELS

Hostels offer modest, low-cost alternative lodging – for all ages. Call for prices, restrictions, and reservations. The following hostels are in the Los Angeles area: Banana Bungalow (603 N Fairfax Avenue, West Hollywood, CA 90036; tel: 323- 655 2002; www.bananabungalow.com) is centrally located and provides low-cost tours and shuttles to major attractions. There is another location on Hollywood Boulevard. Hosteling International Los Angeles (1436 Second Street, Santa Monica, CA 90401; tel: 310-393 9913; www.hilosangeles.org) is the largest on the coast, located in the center of Santa Monica's beach action.

RECOMMENDED HOTELS

To make direct reservations with a hotel, we have included addresses (all in California, abbreviated CA) and telephone numbers and websites. Check-out time is generally 11am–12pm, with check-in usually available from 3pm to 4pm. All hotels accept major credit cards.

Rates vary greatly according to season and availability; many hotels offer special weekend packages, business rates, and promotions. Ask about such discounts when booking. We have used the following symbols to indicate room prices (two persons in a double room, per night):

$$$	over $210
$$	$110-$210
$	under $110

HOLLYWOOD

Best Western Plus Hollywood Hills Hotel $$ *6141 Franklin Avenue, Hollywood 90028, tel: 323-464 5181, toll-free 800-287 1700,* www.best western.com. Family-friendly, with a Hollywood theme. The guest rooms are divided into a newer motel-style building with a courtyard pool and an older building with large hotel-style rooms, many of which have kitchens. 86 rooms.

Chateau Marmont $$$ *8221 Sunset Boulevard, Hollywood 90046, tel: 323-656-1010,* www.chateaumarmont.com. Perched above the Sunset Strip, this is the discreet hideaway beloved of film stars and rock gods. If you're sitting in the bar, keep your *eyes* peeled to spot the celebrities. Choose between a suite, penthouse, garden cottage, or hillside or poolside bungalow.

Hollywood Roosevelt Hotel $$$ *7000 Hollywood Boulevard, Hollywood 90028, tel: 323-856 1970,* www.hollywoodroosevelt.com. Site of the first public Academy Awards, an historic hotel with classic, Spanish-revival décor and movie-star memorabilia. Courtyard, hot tub, pool, restaurant, cocktail lounge, and jazz club. 302 rooms and 80 suites.

MID-WILSHIRE

Beverly Laurel Motor Hotel $$–$$$ *8018 Beverly Boulevard, Los Angeles 90048, tel: 323-210 3076,* http://beverlylaurelmotorhotel. com. The basic motel-style rooms jazzed up with Art-Deco furnishings and colorful touches, as well as the cute courtyard pool, make this a favorite spot with young travelers in particular. Make sure to try out the adjoining hip late-night diner that serves good American-style food. 52 rooms.

The Orlando $$$ *8384 W. Third Street, Los Angeles 90048, tel: 323-658 6600, toll free 800-624 6835,* www.theorlando.com. Hip European-style boutique hotel with large rooms, a short walk from good restaurants and shopping areas, such as the Beverly Center, Third Street, and Farmers Market. Amenities include free internet access in public areas, saltwater swimming pool, fitness center, restaurant, lounge. 98 rooms.

WEST HOLLYWOOD

Mondrian Hotel $$$ *8440 Sunset Boulevard, West Hollywood CA 90069, tel: 323-650 8999, toll-free 800-606 6090,* www.mondrian hotel.com. This trendy, celebrity-frequented hotel plays on scale and illusion and exudes Hollywood attitude. Minimalist chic rooms usually come with kitchens and provide VIP access to the outdoor lounge, the SkyBar. 237 rooms and suites.

The Standard $$–$$$ *8300 Sunset Boulevard, West Hollywood 90069, tel: 323-650 9090,* www.standardhotel.com. One of the hippest hotels on the strip, with cool rooms, pool, workout room, vista terrace, restaurant, bar, and live DJ at the front desk. The lobby regularly features art videos and live performances. 138 rooms, 2 suites.

Sunset Tower Hotel $$$ *8358 Sunset Boulevard, West Hollywood 90069, tel: 323-654 7100,* www.sunsettowerhotel.com. Historic luxury hotel with landmark Art-Deco façade. Pool and terrace with city views, health center, sauna, library, restaurant, bar, and lounge. 74 rooms and suites.

BEVERLY HILLS

Four Seasons at Beverly Hills $$$ *300 South Doheny Drive, Los Angeles 90048, tel: 310-273 2222, 310-786 222,* www.fourseasons.com. Refined luxury accommodations with excellent service and lots of celebrity-watching potential. Rooms are well appointed and have small balconies and beautiful bathrooms. Excellent fourth-floor pool and outdoor gym, a spa, concierge, restaurants, lively cocktail lounge. 285 rooms.

L'Ermitage Beverly Hills Hotel $$$ *9291 Burton Way, Beverly Hills 90210, tel: 310-278 3344, toll-free 877-235 7582,* www.lermitagebh.com. The highly-acclaimed ultra-luxury hotel is modern-minimalist and high-tech. The stylish lobby lounge and rooftop restaurant (with panoramic views), swimming pool, spa, gym, and sauna are second only to the accommodations, which start at 600 sq ft (56 sq m) and come with huge bathrooms, wet bars, four phone lines, personal fax machines, huge TVs, DVDs, and fancy stereo systems. 100 rooms, 19 suites.

The Regent Beverly Wilshire $$$ *9500 Wilshire Boulevard, Beverly Hills 90212, tel: 310-275 5200,* www.fourseasons.com. The elegant lobby of this historic hotel at the base of Rodeo Drive gives way to sumptuous rooms with plush furnishings and luxurious marble baths. Pool, fitness center, spa with steam room and sauna, restaurant, bar, shops. 395 rooms and suites.

CENTURY CITY

Hyatt Regency Century Plaza $$$ *2025 Avenue of the Stars, Los Angeles 90067, tel: 310-228 1234, toll-free 888-591 1234,* www.centuryplaza.hyatt.com. Business hotel with spacious accommodations featuring marble baths and attractive furnishings. Landscaped garden, restaurant, cocktail lounge, pool, fitness center, spa with café, business center, shops. 726 rooms and suites.

SANTA MONICA

Cal Mar Hotel Suites $$$ *220 California Avenue, Santa Monica 90403, tel: 310-395 5555, toll-free 800-776 6007,* www.calmarhotel.com.

Large apartment-style suites surrounding a courtyard pool – perfect for families. Coin laundry. A few blocks from Third Street Promenade and the beach. 36 suites.

Loews Santa Monica Beach Hotel $$$ *1700 Ocean Avenue, Santa Monica 90401, tel: 310-458 6700, toll-free 888-332 0160,* www.loews hotels.com. Casually luxurious beachfront hotel with a five-story glass atrium and outdoor swimming pool. Perched above the beach, two blocks from Santa Monica Pier. Some rooms have ocean views. Two restaurants, bar, pool, Jacuzzi, sundeck, fitness facility with steam and dry saunas; business center, bike and skate rental. 325 rooms, 17 suites.

Shangri-La Hotel $$$ *1301 Ocean Avenue, Santa Monica 90401, tel: 310-394 2791, toll-free 877-999 1301,* www.shangrila-hotel.com. Stylish Art-Deco design makes this 1939 beachside hotel near the Santa Monica Pier an architectural gem. In 2008 the hotel was completely refurbished with a contemporary twist, including such amenities as high-speed internet and sound systems, lavish suites, elevated pool and cabanas, chic rooftop bar and gourmet restaurant. 71 rooms and suites.

Shutters on the Beach $$$ *One Pico Boulevard, Santa Monica 90405, tel: 310-458 0030,* www.shuttersonthebeach.com. The only hotel in Santa Monica right on the beach. Exquisitely appointed rooms in luxury cottage-style setting. Public areas with fireplaces and original artwork. Two restaurants and bars, pool, Jacuzzi, sauna, health club, spa, and bicycle and skate rental. 186 rooms, 12 suites.

DOWNTOWN

Figueroa Hotel $ *939 S. Figueroa Street, Los Angeles 90015, tel: 213-627-8971,* www.figueroahotel.com. A onetime YWCA has been transformed, Hollywood-style, into an exotic, Moroccan-inspired reverie. Happily, it's also a bargain by LA standards. Rooms have wrought-iron beds and there's a pool out back for enjoying the California sun.

Hilton Checkers Hotel $$$ *535 South Grand Avenue, Los Angeles 90071, tel: 213-624 0000, toll-free 800-445 8667,* www.hilton.com. Historic and intimate deluxe boutique hotel. Rooms elegantly appointed with antiques and fine artwork. Gourmet restaurant and lobby bar, rooftop pool, and Jacuzzi. 188 rooms and suites.

Omni Los Angeles Hotel $$$ *251 South Olive Street, Los Angeles 90012, tel: 213-617 3300, toll-free 888-444 6664, www.omnilosangeles. com.* Downtown's cheeriest business hotel, next to MOCA, is brightened with artworks, while the spacious rooms are of contemporary design. Lounge, restaurant, executive floor, health club, pool, and saunas. 453 rooms and suites.

Westin Bonaventure Hotel $$$ *404 South Figueroa Street, Los Angeles 90071, tel: 213-624 1000, toll-free 800-353 1254, www.westin. com/bonaventure.* The busy atrium lobby gives way to shops, 17 restaurants, lounges, and numerous services. Glass elevators with spectacular city views transport guests to the revolving rooftop restaurant as well as the small but comfortable guest rooms. Outdoor pool, with floor-to-ceiling views, executive floor, spa, and health club. 1,354 rooms, 135 suites.

SAN FERNANDO VALLEY

Holiday Inn Burbank $$–$$$ *150 East Angeleno Avenue, Burbank 91502, tel: 818-841 4770, toll-free 800-311 1216, www.holiday-inn.com.* Towers with restaurant, pool, sauna, business facilities. 383 rooms, 102 suites.

Sheraton Universal $$–$$$ *333 Universal Hollywood Drive, Universal City 91608, tel: 818-980 1212, toll-free 800-325 3535, www.sheraton. com/universal.* Large, upscale rooms, some with sweeping views of the Hollywood Hills; five minutes from Universal Studios, Amphitheater, CityWalk. Pool, whirlpool, gym, restaurant, lobby bar, gift shop. 436 rooms and suites.

PASADENA

The Langham Huntington Hotel and Spa $$$ *1401 South Oak Knoll Avenue, Pasadena 91106, tel: 626-568 3900, www.pasadena.langham*

hotels.com. A stunning, historic pastoral resort that opened in 1907. Picture Bridge and Japanese gardens. Three restaurants, three lounges, pool, Jacuzzi, executive floors, fitness center, and tennis courts. Afternoon tea available daily. 380 rooms, suites, and cottages.

LONG BEACH

Hotel Queen Mary $–$$ *1126 Queens Highway, Long Beach 90802, toll-free 877-342 0742, 877-342 0738, www.queenmary.com.* Formerly the world's largest passenger ship, this historic liner is now docked in the harbor and converted into a hotel. Several restaurants, bar, spa, and on-board shopping. Tours are available. 307 unique staterooms and suites.

Westin Long Beach $$–$$$ *333 East Ocean Boulevard, Long Beach 90802, tel: 562-436 3000, toll-free 800-937 8461, www.westin.com/long beach.* Offering spacious rooms with full bay-window and ocean views. Situated across from the Convention Center. Restaurant, lobby bar, pool, fitness center, saunas, business center. 469 rooms and suites.

ORANGE COUNTY

Anaheim Majestic Garden Hotel $$ *900 S. Disneyland Drive, Anaheim 92802, tel: 714-778 1700, toll-free 844-227 8535, www.majesticgarden hotel.com.* This hotel is fashioned after a medieval castle, with period décor, courtyards, and waterfalls. There's a Disneyland shuttle, and facilities include a restaurant, lounge, arcade, fitness center, and pool. 489 spacious rooms and suites.

Candy Cane Inn $$ *1747 South Harbor Boulevard, Anaheim 92802, tel: 714-774 5284, toll-free 800-345 7057, www.candycaneinn.net.* Budget-priced considering the amenities. Lovely, family-friendly motel with attractive landscaping, pool with children's wading area, Jacuzzi, free continental breakfast, and complimentary Disneyland shuttle. 171 rooms.

Disneyland Hotel $$$ *1150 Magic Way, Anaheim 92802, tel: 714-778 6600, www.disneyland.com.* Connected to the theme park by the monorail, this hotel extends the Disney formula with classic-Disney decorations, landscaped gardens, a marina with pedal boats, fantasy water show, and a variety of family activities. Numerous restaurants and lounges, three swimming pools, and entertainment. 990 rooms.

The Disney's Paradise Pier Hotel $$$ *1717 S. Disneyland Drive, Anaheim 92802, tel: 714-999 0990, www.disneyland.com.* Disney's more upscale hotel is adjacent to its sister property and honors the contemporary Disney characters. Restaurant and two bars, conference facilities, rooftop pools with a waterslide, and a fitness club. 489 rooms.

Newport Beach Marriott Hotel and Spa $$–$$$ *900 Newport Center Drive, Newport Beach 92660, tel: 949-640 4000, toll-free 866-440 3375, www.marriott.com.* Overlooks Newport Harbor yacht basin and the beach and ocean. Restaurant, lounge, lighted tennis courts, two pools, fitness center, and whirlpool. 512 rooms, 20 suites.

The Westin South Coast Plaza $$–$$$ *686 Anton Boulevard, Costa Mesa 92626, tel: 714-540 2500, toll-free 888-627 7213,* www.westin southcoastplaza.com. Comfortable, spacious rooms with luxury appointments. Central location for coastal and inland Orange County attractions. Adjacent to the Performing Arts Center and South Coast Plaza shopping center. The excellent restaurant offers indoor/outdoor seating. Cocktail lounge, pool, tennis courts, fitness center. 393 guest rooms.

CATALINA ISLAND

Hotel Metropole $$$ *205 Crescent Avenue, Avalon 90704, tel: 310-510 1884, toll-free 800-541 8528, www.hotel-metropole.com.* Situated on the beachfront in the Metropole Market Place. Some of the rooms with ocean views, fireplaces, spas, and private balconies. Restaurant, rooftop sundeck, and Jacuzzi. 48 spacious rooms and suites.

INDEX

INSIGHT ⊙ GUIDES POCKET GUIDE

LOS ANGELES

First Edition 2016

Editor: Kate Drynan
Author: Donna Dailey
Updated by: Katarzyna Marcinkowska
Head of Production: Rebeka Davies
Picture Editor: Tom Smyth
Cartography Update: Carte
Update Production: AM Services
Photography Credits: Corbis 7T; CTTC 4TC,
5MC, 6ML, 46, 50, 54, 73, 89, 91; David Dunai/
Apa Publications 4MC, 4ML, 4TL, 5TC, 5M,
5MC, 5M, 6TL, 7M, 7TC, 8L, 8FR, 9, 9R, 11, 12,
14, 20, 22, 24, 26, 28, 33, 41, 45, 49, 52, 56, 58,
60, 63, 64, 66, 77, 80, 82, 84, 93, 95, 96, 100,
101, 104; Disney Enterprises 75; Getty Images
7M, 16, 30; iStock 6ML, 35, 37, 38, 68, 71, 79,
86, 102; Joe Mabel 6MC; Public domain 18;
Shutterstock 5T, 6TL, 43
Cover Picture: Shutterstock

Distribution

UK: Dorling Kindersley Ltd,
A Penguin Group company, 80 Strand, London,
WC2R 0RL; sales@uk.dk.com
United States: Ingram Publisher Services,
1 Ingram Boulevard, PO Box 3006, La Vergne,
TN 37086-1986; ips@ingramcontent.com
Australia and New Zealand: Woodslane,

10 Apollo St, Warriewood, NSW 2102,
Australia; info@woodslane.com.au
Worldwide: Apa Publications (Singapore) Pte,
7030 Ang Mo Kio Avenue 5,
08-65 Northstar @ AMK, Singapore 569880
apasin@singnet.com.sg

Contact us

Every effort has been made to provide accurate
information in this publication, but changes are
inevitable. The publisher cannot be responsible
for any resulting loss, inconvenience or injury.
We would appreciate it if readers would call our
attention to any errors or outdated information.
We also welcome your suggestions; please
contact us at: hello@insightguides.com
www.insightguides.com

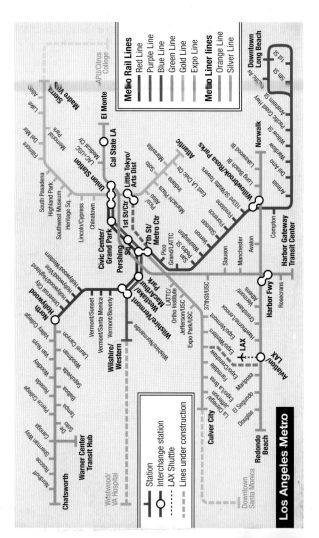

The Betrayal of Dissent

THE BETRAYAL OF DISSENT

Beyond Orwell, Hitchens and the New American Century

Scott Lucas

Pluto Press

LONDON • STERLING, VIRGINIA

First published 2004 by
Pluto Press
345 Archway Road, London N6 5AA
and 22883 Quicksilver Drive, Sterling, VA 20166–2012, USA

www.plutobooks.com

Copyright © Scott Lucas 2004

The right of Scott Lucas to be identified as the author of this
work has been asserted by him in accordance with the Copyright,
Designs and Patents Act 1988.

British Library Cataloguing in Publication Data
A catalogue record for this book is available from the British Library

ISBN   0 7453 2198 4 hardback
ISBN   0 7453 2197 6 paperback

Library of Congress Cataloging in Publication Data applied for

10   9   8   7   6   5   4   3   2   1

Designed and produced for Pluto Press by
Chase Publishing Services, Fortescue, Sidmouth, EX10 9QG, England
Typeset from disk by Stanford DTP Services, Northampton, England
Printed and bound in the European Union by
MPG Books, Bodmin, Cornwall, England

Contents

To my constant dissenters, Ryan and Lauryn

Acknowledgements

This book was meant to be no more than a short polemic, spurred by the interaction of George Orwell with the 'Left' and Big Brother and by the castigation of those who questioned the rush to a War on Terror after 11 September 2001. For me, it has turned out to be much more.

I am grateful to Anne Beech, who rescued and guided this project at a late stage, and to the staff of Pluto. I am indebted to Frances Stonor Saunders, who encouraged me to test initial ideas in the *New Statesman* and who set an example with her own work. Over the past 18 months, many friends and colleagues, willingly or unwillingly, shared my anxieties and hopes. I thank in particular Liam Kennedy, for his unfailing calm input and reassurance; David Ryan, for the enthusiasm he sparked with his approach to US foreign policy; and Seyed Mohammad Marandi and Saied Reza Ameli, for a valuable perspective outside 'America'. Maria Ryan is officially the Research Assistant for this book; unofficially, she has been essential in developing and refining its arguments.

To Helen Laville, I offer this book as thanks for the past and hope for the future.

Mark Twain

The loud little handful – as usual – will shout for the war. The pulpit will – warily and cautiously – object ... at first. The great, big, dull bulk of the nation will rub its sleepy eyes and try to make out why there should be a war, and will say, earnestly and indignantly, 'It is unjust and dishonorable, and there is no necessity for it.' Then the handful will shout louder. A few fair men on the other side will argue and reason against the war with speech and pen, and at first will have a hearing and be applauded, but it will not last long; those others will outshout them, and presently the antiwar audiences will thin out and lose popularity. Before long, you will see this curious thing: the speakers stoned from the platform, and free speech strangled by hordes of furious men... . Next the statesmen will invent cheap lies, putting the blame upon the nation that is attacked, and every man will be glad of those conscience-soothing falsities, and will diligently study them, and refuse to examine any refutations of them; and thus he will by and by convince himself that the war is just, and will thank God for the better sleep he enjoys after this process of grotesque self-deception.

Introduction

> The intellectual's role generally is to uncover and elucidate the contest, to challenge and defeat both an imposed silence and the normalized quiet of unseen power, wherever and whenever possible.
>
> Edward Said[1]

This is a story of two lists compiled and disseminated by 'decent' men.

The first list is in a modest, somewhat battered, 'quarto notebook with a pale-bluish cardboard cover'.[2] Inside, on 65 pages in red and blue ballpoint and pencil, there are approximately 135 names. Many have annotations beside them. Stephen Spender, whom George Orwell had labelled a 'pansy poet' in the 1930s before the two began corresponding, was again a 'Sentimental sympathiser, & very unreliable. Easily influenced. Tendency towards homosexuality'. Charlie Chaplin, admired by Orwell in 1941 for 'his power to stand for a sort of concentrated essence of the common man, for the ineradicable belief in decency that exists in the hearts of ordinary people', was now identified with the cryptic '??'.[3] J.B. Priestley was not only a 'Strong sympathiser, [with] possibly ... some kind of organisational tie-up' and 'Very anti-USA', he had also made 'huge sums of money in USSR'. Cecil Day-Lewis, the Poet Laureate, was evaluated as 'Previously C.P. [Communist Party]. Probably not now completely reliable.' There was apparently some hope for Isaac Deutscher, the historian who would later write an incisive critique of *Nineteen Eighty-Four*, as he 'Could change??'

These names, and others such as Paul Robeson, Richard Crossman, Harold Laski and Henry Wallace, could be found in the twentieth and final volume of Peter Davison's comprehensive catalogue of Orwell's life and works. There were 38 suspects, however, who were still beyond us until June 2003. Davison, the Orwell Archive, which kept the blue notebook

1

safe from readers' eyes, and the British Government would not reveal them. For these unknown individuals were those whom George Orwell, defender of free thought and clear prose, foe of Big Brother, offered up to British Intelligence.

On 29 March 1949, Orwell, gaunt and tubercular, was lying in a Gloucestershire sanatorium. Three months earlier, he had completed a frantic retyping of the final draft of *Nineteen Eighty-Four*, but the effort had exhausted him. In April, he would pursue his last hope for recovery, the experimental antibiotic streptomycin. By the start of the following year, he would be dead.

This late winter day, however, the author was in good spirits, for he was receiving a special guest. Celia Kirwan was well connected to the literary world: the sister-in-law of Arthur Koestler, she had worked as an editorial assistant on the journals *Horizon* and *Polemic*, both outlets for Orwell's essays. In 1946, soon after the death of his wife, Orwell had become infatuated with Kirwan and quickly proposed marriage. She 'gently refused him', but they remained close friends.[4]

By 1949 Kirwan had a professional as well as personal interest in seeing Orwell, as she was working for the top-secret Information Research Department (IRD). Created in January 1948 by a Labour Government trying to manoeuvre between Stalin's Soviet Union and the capitalism of the United States, the IRD was working with the Foreign Office and MI6 to generate and distribute pro-British and anti-Communist propaganda at home and overseas.[5] The IRD's standard operating procedure was to pass useful 'information' to journalists, authors, trade unions and voluntary associations, who would then disseminate the material under their own names.

During her visit, Kirwan just happened to 'discuss some aspects of [IRD's] work' with Orwell. She reported, 'He was delighted to learn of them, and expressed his wholehearted and enthusiastic approval of our aims.' Unable to write for IRD because of his health, the author eagerly suggested the names of others who could be helpful. As she departed, Kirwan 'left some material with [Orwell]' and promised to send 'photostats of some of his articles on the theme of Soviet repression of the arts, in the hope that he may become inspired when he is better to take them up again'.[6]

It is unclear whether Orwell mentioned the blue notebook to Kirwan. If he had, it would not have been much of a revelation to her, as the roll-call of the suspects was probably annotated by Arthur Koestler. In any event, within a week Orwell was asking Richard Rees, the millionaire who had published the author's first essays, to retrieve the list from the bedroom of his London flat. With the names before him, he pondered his selection carefully, writing to Rees, 'The whole difficulty is to decide where each person stands, & one has to treat each case individually.' A day later, he sent Kirwan the 38 who merited the IRD's further attention.[7]

Beyond the celebrity of Charlie Chaplin, J.B. Priestley or Michael Redgrave being proffered to British Intelligence, the suspects are bland fare. There were two Soviet agents, the jailed physicist Alan Nunn May and Peter Smollett of the wartime Ministry of Information, who had intervened to stop Jonathan Cape publishing *Animal Farm* as an anti-Soviet fable. There was Tom Driberg, the flamboyant Labour MP who was in contact with MI5 as well as officials from the Soviet Embassy. Then, however, it was a case of the *Daily Express*'s correspondent, Alaric Jacob, who dared to think during the Second World War that the Soviet society was 'basically a just one', of *Guardian* reporters and editors who did not sufficiently criticise Moscow, of a prominent historian like E.H. Carr whose interpretation was the 'wrong' one, of a novelist like Naomi Mitchison who apparently was a 'silly sympathiser', or of a Nobel Prize-winning physicist like Patrick Blackett whose transgression is still unclear.[8]

No, the significance of 'The List' is not what it says about the 38, but what it offers us about Orwell.

The second list was compiled more than 50 years later in another time of crisis. Unlike Orwell's, this rogues' gallery was offered not to the British Intelligence Services or even to a love interest, but to all of us. It has emerged over a period of months. Indeed, additions are still being made today.

From 19 September 2001, eight days after the attacks on the World Trade Center and the Pentagon, Christopher Hitchens profiled the mad, bad and dangerous for his readers. There were Noam Chomsky and his nefarious allies, Howard Zinn and Norman Finkelstein. John Pilger was coupled with Harold Pinter. Tariq Ali was 'ridiculous' and Robert Fisk 'a reactionary simpleton'.[9] Sam Husseini, the director of Washington's Institute for Public Accuracy, was beyond acceptability, as were all Hitchens' former colleagues at *The Nation*. Even Nelson Mandela was 'stupid' and 'crass', speaking 'garbage'.[10]

This time, the naming of names was above board. There was no need to debate the merits or ethics of cooperating secretly with the Intelligence Services. Hitchens' 'freedom' and 'clarity of thought' openly acknowledged that the need was not to engage with dissent, but to close it off. The contrarian, running with the mainstream, allowed no other contrarians.

A half-century, including the end of one long Cold War and the start of a new one, separates them, but Orwell and Hitchens are now joined. Both purportedly are iconic representatives of the 'Left' who distinguished themselves by attacking faulty comrades who strayed, cynically or naively, towards the enemy. Both are purveyors of a distinct and exalted Englishness, elevated above the defects of the Europeans and guaranteed to refine the crude sensibilities of Americans. Both are the exponents and supposed embodiment of a clarity of language which will transport the clarity of a decent moral, political and social vision.

Such tributes are self-perpetuating, for from his first sketches, Orwell was conscious that he was establishing a reputation. He would manufacture an unsuccessful battle with the 'literary cliques' who supposedly kept his novels in check and then convert it into the successful, selfless defence of virtue against alleged political cliques. With his 'good prose ... like a windowpane', he would 'make political writing into an art' from the 'starting point [of] ... a feeling of partisanship, a sense of injustice'.[11] He would be the 'man who is always fighting against something, but who fights in the open and is not frightened, the face of a man who is generously angry – a free intelligence, a type hated with equal hatred by all the smelly little orthodoxies which are now contending for our souls'.

And, as Orwell constructed himself for the reader through his study of the 'nineteenth-century liberal' Charles Dickens, so Hitchens, in the guise of a biography of Orwell as well as his political essays and extended 'letter' to an acolyte, has rendered himself the decent contrarian. He is the virtuous intellectual, guarding moral and political purities even if (and indeed because) this sets him apart from supposed comrades.

There is nothing inherently wrong in this process, either about the authors or the positions they are establishing. Rare is the writer who, interpreting the world for his audience, does not use sleight-of-pen to promote himself. What is unsettling is that Orwell and Hitchens are also joined in an effort to diminish, ridicule or even shut out completely the views of others. The literary and political battlefield they set out is never a level one; they occupy the higher ground because of the alleged shortcomings of foes and colleagues. They stand on the shoulders of straw men.

Thus the 'early' Orwell crafts the extraordinary Part II of *The Road to Wigan Pier* as an extended polemic against any and all who would claim the mantle of Socialism, the Orwell of the Second World War carps at pacifists as accomplices of Fascism, and the 'late' Orwell spends his final years assailing the Left as apologists and even adjuncts of Soviet Communism. Hitchens picks out Chomsky for totemic distortion and ridicule and, ignoring others who raise equally troublesome questions and objections, draws his caricature of a deviant Left which deserves obsolescence.

In his *Letters to a Young Contrarian*, Hitchens resurrected an Orwell column from November 1945 to exalt his subject and himself as society's honourable dissenters, highlighting truths no matter how unpleasant they might be:

Whenever A and B are in opposition to one another, anyone who attacks or criticises A is accused of aiding and abetting B. And it is often, objectively and on a short-term analysis, that he is making things easier for B. Therefore say the supporters of A, shut up and don't criticise: or at least criticise 'constructively', which in practice always means favourably. And from this it is only a short step to arguing the suppression and distortion of known facts is the highest duty of a journalist.[12]

Hitchens' intent is clear: because he and George dared criticise the 'Left', they are accused by that same 'Left' of abetting Conservative Governments, imperialist exploiters, capitalist schemers, sinister US foreign policies. They will prevail, however, their freedom of thought and expression vanquishing any who would oppose them.

Yet, what if the As and Bs of Orwell's world were filled in as 'anyone who attacks or criticises anti-Communist policy is accused of aiding and abetting the Soviet Union ... Therefore say the supporters of anti-Communist policy, shut up and don't criticise'? Or 'anyone who attacks or criticises the War on Terror is accused of aiding and abetting Al-Qa'eda'? Or 'anyone who attacks or criticises the occupation of Iraq is accused of aiding and abetting Saddam Hussein'? Suddenly the 'anyones' whom Orwell always fought and often accused from the 1930s to his death, the 'anyones' whom Hitchens today labels as appeasers of Serbo-Fascism/Islamo-Fascism/Iraqi Fascism do not appear so villainous, and the decency of the supposed contrarian is no longer so absolute.

This book is a polemic, but it does not seek to invert the process of naming, to cast Orwell and Hitchens as 'wrong', while those comrades who have been besmirched and belittled by them, and the many more who are ignored because they are setting out challenges which cannot be easily dismissed, suddenly emerge as 'right'.

No, this is simply a request to call the spade of 'contrarian' political writing a shovel; a shovel that is not brought down on the heads of those with power, but on the heads of those exposing and confronting that power, a shovel that is not wielded against the state but for it. Orwell and Hitchens, for all the proclamations of their individualism, never operated as maverick intellectuals when they defined the limits of acceptable opinion. Instead, they manoeuvred within a wider social and political environment in which, far from challenging the agencies of the Government, they could be complicit with them, identifying and tagging that dissent which could not be permitted.

The significance of Orwell's notebook, absolved by Hitchens as a 'party game', did not lie in the identification and black-listing of Communists. Orwell's designated enemies were those on the 'Left', irrespective of Communist affiliation, who had caused offence by pursuing differing Socialisms, differing theories (or even the very notion of economic or social 'theory'), differing perspectives on British foreign policy. In the Manichaean world of the Cold War, Orwell finally left no ground between support of the freedom-loving West and the tyrants of Moscow. For those who tried to occupy such ground, the outcome was a naming and shaming not only in Orwell's essays, but also in the selection and handover to those whom Orwell could have parodied elsewhere as 'Big Brother'. It was an outcome in harmony with the ideology and strategy of a US Government which declared, long before Joseph McCarthy, that Communist subversives lurked everywhere, 'each carrying with [them] the germs of death for society'.[13]

Christopher Hitchens' public roll-call of offenders is unlikely to expose any concealed Islamic fascists or servants of Saddam. That, however, was never the objective. Just as Ari Fleischer, the White House press secretary, had warned, 'Watch what you say, watch what you do',[14] Hitchens would silence those who asked for a consideration of US foreign policy as well as of 'Islamic fundamentalism' in the setting for 9–11, those who posted any alternative to a US-led military campaign in Afghanistan, those who examined the probable cause, plan of action and possible consequences of US unilateralism in the toppling of Saddam Hussein and occupation of Iraq. And all this, of course, was just fine for a Bush Administration which had made clear, 'Either you are with us or you are with the terrorists.'[15]

This is not a conspiracy, a deception by which 'free' intellectuals carry out the will of political masters. Indeed, the promotion of the individual thinker proceeding objectively, against tyrannical foes from Stalin to bin Laden to Saddam, is even more effective in silencing those who are supposedly too naive or too deceitful to oppose these menaces. It is this silencing that is vital to a 'manufacture of consent' for the wars which are supposedly being fought in our name and for our good. And it is this silencing that must always be challenged. As George Monbiot, who has always escaped Hitchens' notice, wrote in October 2001: 'Democracy is sustained not by public trust but by public scepticism. Unless we are prepared to question, to expose, to challenge and to dissent, we conspire in the demise of the system for which our governments are supposed to be fighting. The true defenders of America are those who are now being told that they are anti-American.'[16]

1

Orwell, Policeman of the 'Left'

In 1942 the American journal *Partisan Review* set up a debate between three pacifists, D.S. Savage, Alex Comfort and George Woodcock, and the pacifist-turned-patriotic warrior George Orwell on 'Pacifism and the War'.

Savage was a poet who held to pacifism as a 'moral phenomenon' and who claimed (as had Orwell up to 1940) that Britain's prosecution of the war was leading to Fascism at home rather than vanquishing it abroad. Comfort, destined for fame as the author of *The Joy of Sex*, was a physician, novelist, poet and 'aggressive anti-militarist', who added that in this environment, 'It looks as if Mr Orwell and his warlike friends were being not objectively but constructively supporters of the entire philosophical apparatus which they quite genuinely detest.' It was the anarchist Woodcock, however, who laid the most damaging charge:

> If we are to expose antecedents, Orwell does not come off very well. Comrade Orwell, the former police officer of British imperialism (from which the Fascists learnt all they know) in those regions of the Far East where the sun at last sets for ever on the bedraggled Union Jack! Comrade Orwell, former fellow-traveller of the pacifists and regular contributor to the pacifist *Adelphi* – which he now attacks! Comrade Orwell, former extreme left-winger, ILP partisan and defender of Anarchists (see *Homage to Catalonia*)! And now Comrade Orwell who returns to his old imperialist allegiances and works at the BBC conducting British propaganda to fox [mislead] the Indian masses![1]

Orwell was in no mood to compromise. He established, 'Pacifism is objectively pro-Fascist. This is clear common sense … I am not interested in pacifism as a moral phenomenon.'

Although he offered to differentiate between individuals in his judgement of 'true intellectuals', no examples were given, as he continued to target 'the Catholic gang, the Stalinist gang, and the present pacifist or, as they are sometimes nicknamed, the Fascifist gang'. As for his past, Orwell offered a response to the charge that he served imperialism in Burma and at the BBC. However, he renounced the 'independent' Marxist organisation POUM, which he had hailed in *Homage to Catalonia*, and somehow failed to mention his pacifist proclamations of 1937–39.

The most impressive feature of Orwell's reply was a passage in which he combined his portrayal of pacifists as accomplices of National Socialism with the denunciation of others who might have joined him in the fight against imperialism:

> As an ex-Indian civil servant, it always makes me shout with laughter to hear, for instance, Gandhi named as an example of the success of non-violence. As long as 20 years ago it was cynically admitted in Anglo-Indian circles that Gandhi was very useful to the British Government. So he will be to the Japanese if they get there. Despotic governments can stand 'moral force' till the cows come home; what they fear is physical force. But though not much interested in the theory of pacifism, I am interested in the psychological process by which pacifists who have started out with an alleged horror of violence end up with a marked tendency to be fascinated by the success and power of Nazism.[2]

More than 60 years later, after all the celebration of the decency of Orwell, the sharpness of his pen is disorienting. How can his legendary defence of freedom of thought and expression be reconciled with his sweeping dismissal of erstwhile allies, his jibes at those fighting for independence, his ridicule of others pursuing a role for the intellectual and writer in critical times?[3] The abrupt, if equally unsettling, answer is that it cannot, at least not through the iconic St George.

Orwell wrote of John Galsworthy, '[He] was a bad writer, and some inner trouble, sharpening his sensitiveness, nearly made him into a good one; his discontent healed itself, and he reverted to type. It is worth pausing to wonder in just what form the thing is happening to oneself.'[4] If Orwell followed this advice, his self-analysis would have revealed an aspiring novelist who, facing not only the outer troubles of imperialism, economic deprivation and the threat of war, but also inner concerns over women, finance and reputation, 'sharpened his sensitiveness' in political essays, literary criticism and newspaper columns. His discontent never healed itself, however. It may have yielded two memorable novels, but it cast doubts on Orwell's 'Socialism', his treatment of women and even the position of the common person whose cause he supposedly championed.

Orwell was neither consistent nor complete. Indeed, what emerges on closer examination is not the depth but the superficial immediacy of his assurance, to 'which we have got to cling, as a life-belt, ... that it is possible to be a normal decent person and yet to be fully alive'.[5] The author wrote in *The Road to Wigan Pier*:

> I had at that time no interest in Socialism or any other economic theory. It seemed to me then – it sometimes seems to me now, for that matter – that economic injustice will stop the moment we want it to stop, and no sooner, and if we genuinely want it to stop the method adopted hardly matters.[6]

His approach would change little in the following years, as he espoused an 'English Socialism' which was 'not ... doctrinaire nor even logical'.[7] As he summarised in 1947, 'I became pro-Socialist more out of disgust with the way the poorer section of the industrial workers were oppressed and neglected than out of any theoretical admiration for a planned society.'[8]

The simplicity of a political and social philosophy based on this supposed instinctive sense of decency lent Orwell the advantage of flexibility. He could contemplate as late as May 1937 joining a Communist brigade in Spain but, within weeks, castigate the Spanish Republican Government and its Red supporters as the primary threat to democracy and the working class. He could sneer on the eve of the Second World War at 'Quakers shouting for a bigger army, Communists waving union jacks, Winston Churchill posing as a democrat',[9] yet on the strength of a dream in August 1939, decide 'that I was patriotic at heart, would not sabotage or act against my own side, would support the war, would fight in it'.[10] He could work as the literary editor for the Labour Party's newspaper *Tribune*, yet shrug with resignation after Labour's historic access to power in the 1945 General Election, 'One cannot take this slide to the Left as meaning that Britain is on the verge of revolution .... The mood of the country seems to me less revolutionary, less Utopian, even less helpful than it was in 1940 or 1942 .... Heaven knows whether this Government has any serious intention of introducing Socialism, but if it has, I don't see what there is to stop it.'[11]

Unfortunately, the reluctance to delve beyond a basic response of decency also made Orwell a far from straightforward defender of the oppressed and powerless. With few exceptions, his portrayal of women was at best patronising and at worst fearful and vindictive. Working-class women could be pitied as the young woman 'kneeling ... in the bitter cold, on the slimy stones of slum backyard, poking a stick up a foul drain-pipe' or derided, such as the 'half-witted servant girl with huge body, tiny head and rolls of fat at back of neck curiously recalling ham-fat', the landlady who, 'as usual, does not understand much about politics but has adopted her husband's views as a wife ought to' and the abominable Mrs Brooker, 'a soft mound of fat and self-pity'.[12] A fictional creation might be a female version of the struggling Orwell (Dorothy in *A Clergyman's Daughter*), a paragon of patient virtue (Rosemary in *Keep the Aspidistra Flying*) or a flawless saint (Winston's mother in *Nineteen Eighty-Four*), but she might also be an anchor pulling a worthy husband into mediocrity (Hilda in *Coming Up for Air*). The heroine collapses under her burdens or our scrutiny to re-emerge in simpler, 'essential' form. Julia in *Nineteen Eighty-Four*, unwilling or unable to pursue the Revolution with her intellect, is only 'a rebel from the waist down',[13] but the washerwoman is transformed from a 'monstrous woman' into the maternal ideal of 'strong arms, a warm heart, and a fertile belly'.[14]

Similarly Orwell, the anti-imperialist, was never really at ease with the 'natives'. The corrupt local magistrates, exotic women and ignorant mobs in *Burmese Days* had factual counterparts in African soldiers portrayed as 'a flock of cattle', leaders such as Gandhi who were 'deliberately making trouble' and intellectuals going 'out of their way to antagonise those likeliest to help them'.[15] Orwell's reaction to Nehru's famous question, 'Who dies if India lives?' was the sneer, 'How impressed the pinks will be.'[16] In contrast, the scourge of British rule was writing in 1936 that 'it was still possible to be an imperialist and a gentleman'.[17] He later assured, 'It may be that all that [Anglo-Indians] did was evil, but they changed the face of the earth.'[18]

And Orwell was a far from secure bulwark for the working class. *The Road to Wigan Pier*, for all the power of its observation, ended with a chocolate-box portrait of 'Father, in shirt-sleeves, sits in the rocking chair at one side of the fire reading the racing finals, and Mother sits on the other with her sewing, and the children are happy with a penn'orth of mint humbugs, and the dog lolls roasting himself on the rag mat.'[19] Other portrayals were less flattering, such as the reduction of the real-life National Unemployed Workers' Movement to 'the same sheeplike crowd – gaping girls and shapeless middle-aged women dozing over their knitting – that you see everywhere else',[20] or *Nineteen Eighty-Four*'s fictional proles as degraded, Lottery-chasing drunkards and crazed old men. Orwell risked hoisting himself with his own damning petard: 'The trouble is that the socialist bourgeoisie, most of whom give me the creeps, will not be realistic and admit that there are a lot of working-class habits which they don't like and don't want to adopt.'[21]

Fortunately for Orwell, there were easy exits from his suspect depictions. One was the sudden proclamation of the maxim at the start of the Second World War, 'We are in a strange period of history in which a revolutionary has to be a patriot and a patriot has to be a revolutionary.'[22] This contrived equation elevated Orwell above all others, since the nationalism of his opponents was 'the habit of identifying oneself with a single nation or other unit, placing it beyond good and evil and recognising no other duty than that of advancing its interests',[23] while he was simply an Englishman speaking for an ideal English revolution of decency happening 'in a sleepy, unwilling way'.[24]

Confronted at first-hand with the intricacies of a Spanish Civil War where military strategy clashed with social and economic revolution, where the threat to the Republican Government were the factions within its ranks as much as the 'fascists' without, Orwell had taken refuge in the 'crystal split' of the individual. The difficulty of explaining the sudden move from pacifist to warrior was justified by a home country of 'solid breakfasts and gloomy Sundays, smoky towns and winding roads, green fields and red pillar-boxes ... a land where the bus conductors are good-tempered and the policemen carry no revolvers'.[25] And the complications of an emerging Cold War in which the path of social progress had to be negotiated between Washington and Moscow were met with repeated declarations of clear language equalling clear thought and an honest politics, a defence of 'certain moral and intellectual values whose survival is dangerous from the totalitarian point of view'.[26]

Orwell never set aside the label of 'Socialist'. In 1941, for the first and arguably the last time, he set out a programme. Its six points included nationalisation of key industries, land and banks, limitations on top incomes, reform of the educational system and independence for India.[27] Eight years later, months before his death, he would rebut American critics seizing *Nineteen Eighty-Four* as a condemnation of postwar Britain as well as Communism:

> My recent novel is NOT intended as an attack on Socialism or on the British Labour Party (of which I am a supporter) but as a show-up of the perversions to which a centralised economy is liable and which have already been partly realised in Communism and Fascism.[28]

The difficulty was that Orwell rarely saw how his socialist dream could be achieved. Wartime hopes for the English Revolution gave way by 1943 to the glum assessment that 'the forces of reaction have won hands down' and anticipation of 'the dreary world which the American millionaires and their British hangers-on intend to impose upon us'.[29] Orwell's future was one in which his son would have to be a farmer as 'that may be the only job left after the atom bombs'[30] when, foreshadowing *Nineteen Eighty-Four*, there were 'three great empires, each self-contained and cut off from contact with the outer world ... [in] an epoch as horribly stable as the slave empires of antiquity'.[31]

The working class for whom the battle was supposedly being waged were not smart enough to claim this future; trying to uplift them, Orwell had 'all the time the sensation of kicking against an impenetrable wall of stupidity'.[32] So he could only offer a benediction in a final review, using Oscar Wilde's *The Soul of Man under Socialism* to sigh:

> Socialism, in the sense of economic collectivism, is conquering the earth at a speed that would hardly have seemed possible 60 years ago, and yet Utopia, at any rate Wilde's Utopia, is no nearer .... The trouble with the transitional periods is that the harsh outlook which they generate tends to become permanent.[33]

Had Orwell, like Winston Smith, fought the honourable crusade of the lone liberal? Perhaps, but for more than 20 years, there was always a negative dimension. From his days in Burma, when Eric Blair of the Imperial Police took potshots at the 'Left' journal *Adelphi*, to the moment when he strode into the same *Adelphi*'s office and described 'himself as a Tory anarchist but admitt[ing] the *Adelphi*'s socialist case on moral grounds',[34] to the caricature of the *Adelphi* editor and Orwell's patron Richard Rees in *Keep the Aspidistra Flying* as Ravelston, the naive millionaire, 'apologizing, tacitly, for the largeness of his income',[35] the creation of 'Orwell' always rested on the denigration of threats, real or imagined, from the 'Left'.

Up to 1936 Orwell put on no false left-wing airs, preferring to be called 'a kind of intellectual anarchist'.[36] There were omens, however, of battles to come. Orwell wrote to a friend of the evening when, having ventured to Rees's flat to borrow money, he learned that his benefactor was at a socialist meeting. Orwell followed and recalled, 'I spent three hours with seven or eight Socialists harrying me, including a South Wales miner who told me – quite good-naturedly, however – that if he were a dictator he would have me shot immediately.'[37]

When Orwell chose confrontation with the 'Left' in *The Road to Wigan Pier*, it was far more than a skirmish. It had to be. For all the power of his observations of economic deprivation in northern England, Orwell had reached a troublesome impasse at the end of Part I. To his noble miners, his working class family sitting in the parlour, his woman poking a blocked drainpipe with a stick, his unemployed and bedridden, he could offer nothing beyond the visceral insistence that willpower alone could stop economic injustice. He had no knowledge of Adam Smith, no Karl Marx, no John Maynard Keynes, whose *General Theory of Unemployment* had been published four years earlier. He did not provide the context of history from the cataclysm of the First World War through the General Strike to the fall of the Labour Government in 1931. Orwell's social and economic vision did not notice the Jarrow March, in which hundreds of the unemployed marched 300 miles from north-east England to London, and he glimpsed only briefly groups like the National Unemployed Workers' Movement.

Orwell's solution to his quandary was a sustained attack, not on the leaders and systems that had brought the crisis of Part I, but on the organised activism of Socialists. He would give no quarter for 'everyone who uses his brain knows that Socialism, as a world-system and wholeheartedly applied, is a way out'. The movement consisted of either the 'warm-hearted, unthinking' Socialists from the working class or the 'intellectual, book-trained' Socialist from the middle class, 'out of touch with common humanity' with his 'soggy half-baked insincerity' and 'his pullover, his fuzzy hair, and his Marxian quotation'. These woeful figures were joined by a 'prevalence of cranks', including 'every fruit-juice drinker, nudist, sandal-wearer, sex-maniac, Quaker, "Nature Cure" quack, pacifist, and feminist in England'.[38]

Yet Orwell had no alternative beyond his diatribe. He contended that Socialists must capture the 'exploited middle class',[39] but he had no Socialism to put forward. He had already ruled out a mobilisation of the working class: too passive, misguided or ignorant, they could be no more than pawns in political games. Observing a meeting led by Oswald Mosley, Orwell concluded, 'It struck me how easy it is to bamboozle an uneducated audience.'[40]

Forget the revolution, Orwell's immediate fight was with his own publisher, Victor Gollancz, who had commissioned *The Road to Wigan Pier* and ensured a mass readership by featuring it as a selection for the Left Book Club. Gollancz's transgression was to write a Foreword for the LBC edition: 'It is indeed significant that so far as I can remember (he must forgive me if I am mistaken), Mr Orwell does not once define what he means by Socialism; nor does he explain how the oppressors oppress, nor even what he understands by "liberty" and "justice".'[41]

If Gollancz had wanted to silence Orwell, he could have withheld the Left Book Club offer or even suspended publication of the manuscript. Instead, he had offered a difficult challenge to his author. Orwell, who was not going to give up access to a large audience by renouncing the edition, thanked Gollancz for the Foreword as a discussion 'that one always wants'.[42] He was left, however, with no answer to the allegation of vagueness.

So Orwell moved practically. Gollancz could still publish his novels, but the author would find another distributor for his non-fiction. As he told a fellow writer, 'It is rather a good idea to have a foot in both the Gollancz and Secker [rival publisher] camps.'[43] Meanwhile, he began denouncing Gollancz in his correspondence, informing friends that 'Gollancz is of course part of the Communism-racket'.[44]

Orwell had not yet embraced Socialism, but he had already measured the distance between himself and the Socialist movement he was defining. Front-line service in the Spanish Civil War only confirmed the split. He vented his spleen against 'hack-journalists and the pansy Left', 'parlour Bolsheviks' and 'sleek little professors'.[45] He exposed the Spanish Communists and their Soviet supporters as the forces that could be blamed for a Republican Government targeting erstwhile allies amongst the Anarchists, Trotskyists and other Marxist groups, rather than the nationalist insurgency. And he waged his campaign from the moral high ground, his first-hand experience of both battle and Barcelona's turmoil giving him the edge over *New Statesman* editors supporting the Republicans from a distance.

Yet Orwell simplified events and causes, and not just for the sake of literary clarity. Any complexities, such as the role of religion and regional divisions, the relationship between the Republican Government and the Soviet Union (and the effect on that relationship of the refusal of the British and French Governments to intervene against the Nationalists), or tensions between urban and rural areas, were absent from *Homage to Catalonia*. Even the title of the book was misleading, with Orwell offering little about the special position of Catalonia within Spanish politics.

Orwell recognised that, with only a partial view of these complexities, he was far from secure in his moral elevation. Indeed, his service with the militia of POUM, the 'independent' Marxist party, had come from circumstance rather than choice: he initially tried to join the International Brigades but was turned down. Furthermore, until spring 1937 he had accepted the Republican Government's case that groups such as POUM were undermining the war effort with their insistence on more radical economic and social changes. Only atop POUM's headquarters in Barcelona in May 1937 would Orwell set his political stance.

Despite this genesis and its selective approach, *Homage to Catalonia* stands as the brave work of a brave man, inspiring later dissidents such as Noam Chomsky.[46] Immediate virtue, however, carried the seeds of long-term vice. Orwell, setting himself up as the contrarian who was exposing the corruptions and hypocrisies of British counterparts, was building a stage where he was always right and the 'Left' was always wrong. If *The Road to Wigan Pier* had demeaned the Socialists who might offer a rebuttal, *Homage to Catalonia* established that Orwell's 'crystal spirit' alone was decent and just. The critic Q.D. Leavis anointed him 'the only man of letters we have whom we can imagine surviving the flood [of real Socialism] undisturbed'.[47]

Orwell was far from a constant saint. Over the next five years, he would join the Independent Labour Party only to put it behind him, embrace pacifism only to condemn pacifists as accomplices of Fascism, place hope in enlightened intellectuals only to dismiss them as quislings, raise up the common people only to condemn them as stupid and indolent, and turn former allies into nemeses not only of Orwell but of England. And, far from pursuing any sustained consideration of his opponents' views, Orwell preferred *ad hominem* condemnation of defective characters. He targeted the poet W.H. Auden, explaining, 'Mr Auden's brand of amoralism is only possible if you are the kind of person who is always somewhere else when the trigger is pulled.'[48] He vilified Stephen Spender, pausing for a moment after he began corresponding with the poet: 'Funny, I had always used him and the rest of that gang as symbols of the pansy Left, and in fact I don't care for his poems to speak of, but when I met him in person I liked him so much and was sorry for the things I had said about him.'[49] Yet a year later, Auden and Spender were once more among those writers 'attracted by a form of Socialism that makes mental honesty impossible'.[50]

The technique was quite simple and quite effective. Once Orwell had established his own position, he associated any possible challengers with the broadest of injustices. It was not enough to claim a position against imperialism; Orwell had to ensure that the 'Left', whom one might have assumed to be his allies, were turned into supporters of British rule: 'The majority of left-wing politicians and publicists are people who earn their living by demanding [a decolonisation] that they don't generally want.'[51] When Orwell became a pacifist, 'the greater part of the Left' had to be associated with a 'war against Germany' and with 'the fascising process, which will ultimately mean associating themselves with wage-reductions, suppression of free speech, brutalities in the colonies etc.'[52]

One of the political themes of Orwell's underrated novel, *Coming Up for Air*, published in 1939, was a devious Leftist plot to embroil Britain in a conflict with Germany. In a memorable scene, the naive or deluded audience at a Left Book Club meeting were harangued by 'a mean-looking chap ... with a bald head which he'd tried rather unsuccessfully to cover up with wisps of hair', who rails against the Nazis and 'Bestial atrocities .... Hideous outbursts of sadism .... Rubber truncheons .... Concentration camps .... Iniquitous persecution of the Jews'. Orwell's protagonist concluded, 'What's he doing?

Quite deliberately, and quite openly, he's stirring up hatred. Doing the damnedest to make you hate certain foreigners called Fascists.'[53]

When Orwell the pacifist embraced the passivity of the writer Henry Miller and told readers, 'Give yourself over to the world-process, stop fighting against it or pretending that you control it; simply accept it, endure it, record it', he still stood guard against the '9 out of 10 British Socialists [who] turned into Jingoes' at 'the first real threat to British interests'.[54] Yet months later, when Orwell the patriot wholeheartedly embraced war, the 'Left' was suddenly populated with dangerous pacifists and those mired in shame 'of their own nationality ... whose hearts have never leapt at the sight of a Union Jack [and who] will flinch from revolution when the time comes'.[55] Even if the Soviet Union was now fighting with 'England', Orwell could still link all his evils, identifying the 'quisling intellectual'[56] who gave shelter to a Fascist–Communist axis in which 'Germany [was] going Bolshevik because of Hitler and not in spite of him'.[57]

Orwell had stood on so many different soapboxes and denounced so many enemies by the height of the Second World War that he risked becoming a band of one. Indeed, he had prepared for this situation with his extraordinary attempt to become Charles Dickens in 1940. In an extended essay ostensibly critiquing the Victorian author's work, Orwell lauded Dickens as 'a subversive writer, a radical, one might truthfully say a rebel'. In the final paragraph, Orwell revealed his broader motive. Dickens, 'express[ing] in a comic, simplified and ... memorable form the native decency of the common man', looked into a mirror and saw not only himself but his twentieth-century successor:

> It is the face of a man who is always fighting against something, but who fights in the open and is not frightened, the face of a man who is generously angry – in other words, of a 19th-century liberal, a free intelligence, a type hated with equal hatred by all the smelly little orthodoxies which are now contending for our souls.[58]

The problem was that, without followers from somewhere, Orwell's crusade of decency would be a lonely, and ultimately unsuccessful, one. He tried to meet the challenge with the manifesto of 1941, *The Lion and the Unicorn: Socialism and the English Genius*. Ostensibly the cause was a proper Socialism, in contrast to the nasty variant Orwell had identified throughout the 1930s. Yet, as with *The Road to Wigan Pier*'s Part I, any Orwellian conception of this Socialist future was ultimately a diversion. The manifesto devoted several pages on a basic exposition of a six-point programme including nationalisation of key industries, land and banks, limitations on top incomes, reform of the educational system and independence for India and other British colonies. Orwell could go no further, however, his lack of economic and political theory leaving him with his Socialism which was 'not ... doctrinaire, nor even logical'.[59]

No matter, for Socialism was peripheral to Orwell's far easier mission, the proclamation of 'Englishness'. *The Lion and the Unicorn* was a vehicle for a cultural nationalism that knew no complexity. The reader was assured,

> Above all, [England] is your civilization, it is you. However much you hate it or laugh at it, you will never be happy away from it for any length of time. The suet puddings and the red pillar-boxes have entered into your soul. Good or evil, it is yours, you belong to it, and this side of the grave you will never get away from the marks that it has given you.[60]

Orwell was so wedded to the wonders of Englishness that the 'Socialist' was willing to make allowances for those at the more privileged end of the political and economic spectrum. While he noted a 'decay of ability in the ruling class', he added that they were 'morally fairly sound'. Their faults lay in aptitude rather than malice: 'What is to be expected of them is not treachery, or physical cowardice, but stupidity, unconscious sabotage, an infallible instinct for doing the wrong thing.' Thus the author of *The Road to Wigan Pier* could blithely assure the reader that 'patriotism is usually stronger than class-hatred'.[61]

If only Englishness could have guaranteed the revolution. At first, Orwell assured himself, as well as his readers, that there was no need for European-style bloodshed: 'Like all else in England, [the revolution] happens in a sleepy, unwilling way, but it is happening …. The right men will be there when the people really want them, for it is movements that make leaders and not leaders movements.'[62] It was clear, however, that the common men and women would be following, rather than alongside, Leader Orwell. Insecure and inconsistent in his description of the masses, Orwell worried that the working class were 'more frightened than the middle class'[63] and compounded this with back-handed praise of their lack of intelligence: 'But of course at times their stupidity has stood them in good stead. Any European nation situated as we are would have been squealing for peace long ago.'[64]

Failing to get an armed Home Guard for his movement, Orwell settled for a temporary contract with the BBC, producing programmes for India and Southeast Asia. While he was behind the desk and in the studio, 'an orange that's been trodden upon by a very dirty boot',[65] his leaderless troops drifted. By the end of 1944, he had given up, 'There has been no real shift of power and no increase in genuine democracy. The same people still own the property and usurp all the best jobs.'[66] If Orwell's personal fortunes improved when he left the BBC and became literary editor of *Tribune*, the newspaper backed by the Labour Party, his glimmer of a better future had come and gone. Even Labour's unexpected victory over Winston Churchill in the 1945 General Election would not restore faith since, 'on the Left, political thought is a sort of masturbation fantasy in which the world of facts hardly matters'.[67] Britain was 'less revolutionary, less Utopian, even less helpful than it was in 1940 or 1942'. [68]

Of course, the ultimate cause of Orwell's failure had to be the Socialists. Sometimes the 'Left' were mistreating his fellow intellectuals: 'There is no knowing just how much the Socialist movement has lost by alienating the literary intelligentsia, but it has alienated them, partly by confusing tracts with literature, and partly by having no room in it for a humanistic culture.'[69] Sometimes the intellectuals became the problem: 'In the last 20 years Western civilisation has given the intellectual security without responsibility .... He has been in the position of a young man living on an allowance from a father whom he hates. The result is a deep feeling of guilt and resentment, not combined with any genuine desire to escape.'[70]

So it was that Orwell would spend the final years of his life securing a posthumous reputation, not through revolution fulfilled, but through revolution betrayed. *Animal Farm* was a powerful fairy tale, the clarity of its language offering a devastating allegory of the Soviet Union from 1917 to 1941; however, it ended tragically because its heroes, too stupid, naive or stoic, must fail. Just before the publication of *Animal Farm*, Orwell had written of the 'semi-anaesthesia in which the British people contrive to live';[71] his animals, having tasted freedom only to lose it to the new tyrants, return to that state. Richard Rees, Orwell's friend and lifelong defender, confessed, 'What is pathetic ... in both *Animal Farm* and *1984* is the helpless, inert, and almost imbecile role which [Orwell] attributes to the common man.'[72]

Hope can be recovered only if one argues that *Animal Farm* was not a projection of what must happen but of what must be prevented or altered. The American backers, including the CIA, of the film version of *Animal Farm* left no doubt by changing the ending, the animals finding their strength to chase both the pigs and the capitalist men from the farm. And Orwell did write a special preface to an edition for Ukrainian displaced persons, envisaging liberation from the Soviet Union for a model such as England, 'a country in which people have lived together for several hundred years without knowing civil war, in which the laws are relatively just and official news and statistics can almost invariably be believed, and, last but not least, in which to hold and to voice minority views does not involve any mortal danger'.[73]

Such hope was exceptional for Orwell, however, with his focus on ever-present enemies. He awkwardly tried to separate his Englishness from the threatening nationalisms of 'neo-Toryism', 'Zionism', 'political Catholicism', 'Celtic nationalism', 'colour feeling', 'class feeling' and even 'pacifism'.[74] He claimed supremacy over the 'Left' by holding up his honest and clear expression over the writing of those allied with or corrupted by influences such as 'the totalitarian outlook': 'The direct, conscious attack on intellectual decency comes from the intellectuals themselves.'[75] He used the honourable objective of guarding against slovenly language to attack old enemies such as the political and economic theorist Harold Laski.[76] He put forth 'liberal values' to deride the physicist J.D. Bernal, whose advocacy of cooperation with the Soviet Union became 'subservience to the Soviet Union'.[77]

Orwell declared in 'Why I Write', his autobiographical manifesto, 'Every line of serious work that I have written since 1936 has been written, directly or indirectly, against totalitarianism and for democratic socialism.'[78] It was a false balance. In the series of important essays published between 1945 and 1948, as well as in his columns in *Tribune*, there was little on socialism. References to the Labour Government of Clement Attlee, who reminded Orwell of 'a recently dead fish, before it has time to stiffen',[79] were limited and churlish, and, as George Woodcock, who had mended relations with Orwell, noted, 'Any enthusiasm [for Labour] cooled perceptibly and rapidly.'[80] Only in 1948, in the American journal *Commentary*, would Orwell offer a fuller evaluation, expressing disappointment that the Attlee Government had not brought fundamental changes in British society, although he did not identify what those fundamental changes should be, and resigning himself to the notion that any socialist principles would give way to the fight for economic survival. The criticism was a bit of the pot calling the kettle black; Orwell had already written off Socialism with the reduction of left-wing thought to a 'perfectionist ideology' with 'a whole series of unadmitted contradictions'.[81]

Instead, Orwell was defining and refining his anti-Communism. The author was far from an absolute Red-baiter. He worried that the ten-year sentence on the scientist Alan Nunn May, convicted of passing secret information to the Soviet Union, was too harsh, and he was involved with his good friend Arthur Koestler in the Freedom Defence Committee, formed in 1945 after the prosecution of an anarchist newspaper for anti-militarist propaganda.

Orwell's 'freedom' still turned on the identification and monitoring of a supposed Fifth Column, however, with the call in his *Tribune* column 'to discover which individuals are honest and which are not'.[82] In the summer of 1946 he warned in his 'London Letter' written for America's 'Left' but staunchly anti-Communist *Partisan Review* that, while the number of open Communists and their supporters might be limited, they had assumed importance because of their placement in key positions in trade unions, Parliament and the press: 'It is a fact that the Communists are at present the main danger to the Government and might become a real political force if some calamity abroad – for example, large-scale fighting in India – made the Government's foreign policy acutely unpopular.'[83] Even literary criticism could be used for Orwell's fight, with the redemption of a 'Tory radical' with 'reactionary' politics, Jonathan Swift, because of 'his attack ... on what would now be called totalitarianism'.[84]

Orwell the lone liberal was no longer alone. In the US a coalition of Democrats and former radicals were forming round the notion of a 'vital center', which would not only defend the economic and social programmes of the New Deal, but also pursue an 'anti-Communist liberalism'. Years before Joseph McCarthy made his allegations of widespread Communist penetration of the US Government, a 'mainstream' of intellectuals was pursuing a virtuous campaign against any enemy within. Arthur Schlesinger, Jr, the historian who defined the movement, declared in *Life* magazine in July 1946, 'With history breathing down their necks, Communists are working overtime to expand party influence, open and covert, in the labor movement, among Negroes, among veterans, among unorganized liberals.'[85]

Orwell, perhaps unwittingly, was playing his part in the formation of an anti-Communist network linking 'private' activists with the efforts of the state. He and Koestler had already proposed 'psychological disarmament', with free distribution of British newspapers, books and other materials within the Soviet Union when a US union official, Francis Henson, approached Orwell in March 1946 about the work of the International Rescue and Relief Committee. Orwell advised Koestler to make contact, and the IRRC was soon asking the émigré to carry out a speaking tour of the United States.

During the extended visit, Koestler outlined his ideas for psychological warfare against the Soviet Bloc to William Donovan, the head of America's wartime intelligence service, the Office of Strategic Services. He met the political theorist James Burnham, Arthur Schlesinger, Sidney Hook, Daniel Bell, Lionel Trilling, Dwight Macdonald and James Farrell. All would eventually be involved in the much-heralded formation of the anti-Communist Congress for Cultural Freedom in 1950, with its not so open relationship with the US Government.[86] The IRRC, from its inception, had close links with officials in Washington; later, the CIA would provide funding. The Congress for Cultural Freedom was not only financed but created by US Intelligence Services, working closely with the 'private' intellectuals.[87]

Orwell, unlike Koestler, was never a central figure in the network. Indeed, he had a deep scepticism of American power and American culture. During the Second World War, his *Tribune* column had satirised drunken, aggressive GIs, and his essays went even further in the denunciation of a violent society:

> Who, without misgivings, would bring up a child on the coloured 'comics' in which sinister professors manufacture atomic bombs in underground laboratories while Superman whizzes through the clouds, the machine-gun bullets bouncing off his chest like peas, and platinum blondes are raped, or very nearly, by steel robots and 50-foot dinosaurs?[88]

However, in the emerging Cold War, Orwell made the fundamental decision, 'If one were compelled to choose between Russia and America .... I would always choose America.'[89] When he did, he may have sacrificed any hope for his 'Socialism'. In 1947, for the first and perhaps only time after the war, he dwelt on the possibility of a 'democratic Socialism [which] must be made to work throughout some large area'. With North America caught up in capitalism and the Soviet Union in the grip of the Communist Party, this Socialism had to emerge from a *'federation of the western European states'* shed of their colonial dependencies.[90]

For a moment, Orwell might have joined a British strategy which amounted to more than trailing in America's Cold War wake. In January 1948 the Attlee Government embarked on a global gamble to establish a 'Third Force' between Washington and Moscow. The Prime Minister told the nation in a radio broadcast, 'Our task is to work out a system of a new and challenging kind, which combines individual freedom with a planned economy, democracy with social justice.' The Cabinet confirmed the intention 'to develop our power and influence to equal that of the United States of America and the USSR .... We should be able to carry out our task in such a way which will show clearly that we are not subservient to the United States or to the Soviet Union.'[91]

Could Britain have led a Third Force? The question, possibly the most significant of the early Cold War, was moot, for economic weakness as well as fear of a Soviet incursion into Western Europe led to British deference to the dollar and NATO. And Orwell had left behind any Western European bloc for 'Ingsoc' and the world of *Nineteen Eighty-Four*.

The universal fame of Winston Smith's Oceania did not obscure the contentious portrayals in the book. There was the issue of its misogyny, be it the frigidity of Winston's wife Katherine or the sexuality of his mistress Julia, which prompts thoughts of rape and conquest: 'He would flog her to death with a rubber truncheon. He would tie her naked to a stake and shoot her full of arrows like Saint Sebastian. He would ravish her and cut her throat at the moment of climax.'[92] There was the treatment of the 'proles', which far from empowering them, 'excludes the working class from history and fails to give any place in the revolutionary cast, other than the supporting role, the proverbial extras'.[93]

Most importantly, *Nineteen Eighty-Four* was the culmination of an Orwellian career which, for the 'Left', now offered little except recrimination. As Orwell put it, his aim was to present 'totalitarian ideas [that] have taken root in the minds of intellectuals everywhere ... to draw these ideas out to their logical consequences'.[94] When one of Big Brother's functionaries proclaims, 'It's a beautiful thing, the destruction of words',[95] the spectre of Leftist foes such as Harold Laski was raised once more.

It could be argued that Orwell's depiction of totalitarianism was not limited to the Soviet menace, that he was writing of his feared 'three great empires' carving up the world, that he was illustrating the hazards of technology which could be used, by 'democratic' as well as tyrannical systems, to enslave rather than liberate. Those fighting the Cold War in 1949 were not bothered by such nuances, however. As Orwell's publisher Fredric Warburg had privately warned, 'Here is the Soviet Union to the nth degree, a Stalin who never dies, a secret police with every device of modern technology.'[96] In the promotion of *Nineteen Eighty Four* by the Cold Warriors, the Party of Oceania was the Communist Party of 1948, and that was that. Harcourt Brace, the novel's American publishers, did not correct such impressions, but used them to market the book. They approached J. Edgar Hoover, the head of the Federal Bureau of Interrogation, for an endorsement: 'We hope you might be interested in helping to call this book to the attention of the American public – and thus, perhaps, helping to halt totalitarianism.'[97]

So, in a United States where President Harry Truman had declared, 'There isn't any difference in totalitarian states. I don't care what you call them, Nazi, Communist or Fascist',[98] exalted voices could designate *1984* (the title was re-presented for the American market) as the bible for a new crusade. The reviewer for the *New York Times* proclaimed the book 'a great work of kinetic art', for 'no other work of this generation has made us desire freedom more earnestly or loathe tyranny with such fulness'.[99] Philip Rahv of *Partisan Review* proclaimed:

> This novel is the best antidote to the totalitarian disease that any writer has so far produced …. I recommend it particularly to those liberals who still cannot get over the political superstition that while absolute power is bad when exercised by the Right, it is in its very nature good and a boon to humanity once the Left, that is to say 'our own people', takes hold of it.[100]

Orwell had lost control. For almost 15 years, he had put forth a 'Socialism' which targeted his comrades; now he watched from his sickbed as others used his masterwork to bury Socialism once and for all. Orwell tried to hold back the US magazines cheering his portrayal of a 'Left' dystopia: 'I do not believe that the kind of society I describe necessarily will arrive, but I believe ... that something resembling it could arrive.'[101] The burial could not have begun, however, had Orwell not handed the shovel to would-be adversaries. Warburg commented when he first read his author's manuscript:

> This I take to be a deliberate and sadistic attack on socialism and socialist parties generally .... It seems to indicate a final breach between Orwell and Socialism, not the Socialism of equality and human brotherhood which clearly Orwell no longer expects from Socialist parties, but the Socialism of Marxism and the managerial revolution.[102]

In the end, Orwell's 'negative' attacks on the Left and Socialism had no 'positive' alternative, for Orwell had left a seminal book which 'offered no way out of our century's ordeals'.[103] For whom was the Revolution being fought? The 'common man' of *The Road to Wigan Pier* and *The Lion and The Unicorn* had ended up as a travesty in *Nineteen Eighty-Four*, making a mockery of Winston's declaration, 'If there is hope, it lies in the proles.'[104] Far from being empowered or even ennobled, the working class were either good-hearted but passive or threatening and irrational, such as the old prole in the pub who can offer 'nothing but a rubbish-heap of details'.[105] The paradox of *Nineteen Eighty-Four* – 'until they become conscious they will never rebel, and until after they have rebelled they cannot become conscious'[106] – once more renders the common people dependent on a far-seeing leader such as Orwell. The only problem was that he had no place to lead them.

So Orwell's final months were spent not in the pursuit of a socialist future, but in the dogged oversight of his 'suspects'. Even the non-violence of the assassinated Gandhi was criticised:

> There is reason to think that Gandhi ... did not understand the nature of totalitarianism .... It is difficult to see how Gandhi's methods could be applied in a country where opponents of the regime disappear in the middle of the night

and are never heard of again .... Is there a Gandhi in Russia at this moment? And if there is, what is he accomplishing?[107]

Then there were the fellow travellers. When an Ukrainian refugee asked for some of Laski's publications, Orwell warned, 'Have nothing to do with Laski and by no means let a person of that type know that illicit printing in Soviet languages is going on in the allied zones.'[108] After Dwight Macdonald sent him a book on Henry Wallace, the Progressive Party candidate challenging President Truman in 1948, Orwell responded, 'Very good, and I am urging Gollancz to publish it over here. I am afraid Wallace may well cause "our" man [Truman] to lose the election, and then Lord knows what may happen.'[109]

In a letter to George Woodcock, Orwell tried to establish a guideline for anti-Communist activity: 'It is a matter of distinguishing between a real and merely theoretical threat to democracy, and no one should be persecuted for expressing his opinions, however antisocial, and no political organisation suppressed, unless it can be shown that there is a substantial threat to the stability of the state.'[110] He was less discriminate in public exchanges, however. In January 1947 Konni Zilliacus, a Labour MP who advocated cooperation with the Soviet Union, challenged Orwell by demanding to know if the author was calling him a secret member of the Communist Party. Orwell offered no substantive case on Zilliacus's denial that he was a 'crypto-Communist'. Instead, he made his case by noting, 'What else could he say?' and 'If what I have suggested is obviously untrue, why does he get so hot and bothered about it?' The legal and political defence of freedom had given way to guilt by association:

What I believe, and will go on believing until I see evidence to the contrary, is that [Zilliacus] and others like him are pursuing a policy barely distinguished from that of the CP [Communist Party], and that they are in effect the publicity agents of the USSR in this country .... I could not prove that in a court of law any more than I could have proved before the war that the Catholic Church was sympathetic to Fascism.[111]

Orwell's list, those 135 names that he collected, showed to Arthur Koestler for comment and annotation, the 38 that he offered up to the British Intelligence Services, was not a sudden aberration or a 'party game'. Its handover to an official of the British Intelligence Services was not a special show of affection for an old flame or a response to an imminent Soviet threat to life and liberty. And its power did not reside in the 'black-listing' of any particular individual, but in a wider symbolism. For most of his writing, Orwell had patrolled the borders of Socialism as a lone ranger of decency. He had established himself as the authoritative voice of dissent, in part to limit the dissent of others. He had used decency and morality to discredit others as indecent and immoral. Having warned of the power of the state, he had discreetly shared his campaign with the state.

And, now that he was dead, others would use 'Orwell' to carry on that campaign.

2

The Canonisation of St George

In a 1947 essay Orwell commented on the true measurement of 'quality' in a writer:

> In reality there is no kind of evidence or argument by which one can show that Shakespeare, or any other writer, is 'good'. Nor is there any way of definitely proving that – for instance – Warwick Beeping is 'bad'. Ultimately there is no test of literary merit except survival, which is itself an index to majority opinion.[1]

Orwell could just as easily have been predicting the conditions of his future success. Beyond the merits of his language, beyond the power of his observation, beyond his proclaimed virtue, there was an immediacy about his writing. Four months before his death, the Soviets exploded an atomic bomb and Mao Zedong's Communist Party took control of China. Two weeks after he passed away, Senator Joseph McCarthy told a women's club in Wheeling, West Virginia, that there were 205 Communists inside the US State Department. Five months after he was buried, Britain would follow the United States into the Korean War.

And only ten days after Orwell's friends said their last goodbyes at University College Hospital, President Harry Truman authorised the development of a document numbered NSC 68, the global blueprint for the defeat of Soviet Communism. Before the authorisation of the hydrogen bomb, before the expansion of economic and military aid to anti-Communist allies around the world, before a four-fold increase in the staff and a ten-fold increase in the budget for covert operations, before the support of anti-colonial regimes such as the French in Vietnam, there was the declaration of freedom's war:

The idea of freedom is the most contagious idea in history, more contagious than the idea of submission to authority. For the breadth of freedom cannot be tolerated in a society which has come under the domination of an individual or group of individuals with a will to absolute power .... Our free society, confronted by a threat to its basic values, naturally will take such action, including the use of military force, as may be required to protect those values.[2]

For Cold Warriors on both sides of the Atlantic, 'Orwell' was a powerful weapon, ready to be used. US covert operators, based in a specialist unit called the Psychological Warfare Workshop, allegedly approached Orwell's widow Sonia about the film rights to *Animal Farm*. Sonia, who had married the dying author in October 1949, set an unusual price: an introduction to Clark Gable. The Americans eagerly delivered. *Animal Farm*, produced by CIA contact Louis de Rochemont and with script advice from the CIA-supported American Committee for Cultural Freedom, was released as an animated feature in 1954.[3] Even the CIA's rival, the FBI, declared that the film 'hit the jackpot'.[4] (The film *1984*, with live actors rather than cartoon animals, was distributed two years later.[5] The rights were acquired by Peter Rathven, the former President of RKO, who financed films on behalf of the US Information Agency in the 1950s. Sol Stein, the executive director of the CIA-supported American Committee for Cultural Freedom, provided advice on the screenplay.)[6]

Orwell's admirers in the British services also played their part. The IRD developed an *Animal Farm* comic strip, which was distributed by British Embassies and published in India, Burma, Eritrea, Thailand, Mexico, Venezuela and Brazil. When *Animal Farm* was reissued in an illustrated edition in 1954, Christopher Woodhouse helpfully reviewed it for the *Times Literary Supplement*:

There is a long way to go yet; but there is a long time ahead too. *Animal Farm* will not, like Uncle Tom's Cabin, contribute to changing history within a decade or so, but it probably has as good a chance as any contemporary work of winning its author a place – unacknowledged, of course, among

Shelley's legislators of the world .... If the worst comes to the worst and [Orwell] fails as a legislator, he is then virtually certain of immortality as a prophet.[7]

Woodhouse did not declare, and the *Times Literary Supplement* did not mention, that he was an officer in MI6, the British overseas Intelligence Service.[8]

These episodes, though colourful, were not the making of 'Orwell'. For the author to endure, there had to be a long term veneration beyond the patronage of shadowy Government agencies. Indeed, the eulogies sought to place Orwell beyond the Cold War. Julian Symons stretched the author across time and class, citing his faith in 'the revolutionary power of the proletariat' as 'an Edwardian, even a Victorian' figure 'whose unorthodoxy was valuable in an age of power worship'.[9] Stephen Spender, either forgiving of or oblivious to Orwell's protracted assault on his reputation, lauded the author as 'an Innocent, a kind of English Candide of the twentieth century. The Innocent is ordinary because he accepts the value of ordinary human decency.'[10] For the BBC, Orwell was 'a lonely, courageous figure passing with detached honesty and without rancour across the mudbanks of corruption',[11] while George Woodcock elevated his former adversary with the words of *Homage to Catalonia*, enshrining Orwell as 'The Crystal Spirit'.[12]

Yet, however exalted the tributes, they could not escape the context of the US confrontation with Soviet Communism. Tom Hopkinson's clever obituary linked literature and politics: 'I know only two present-day works of fiction before which the critic abdicates; one is Arthur Koestler's *Darkness at Noon*, the other Orwell's *Animal Farm*.'[13] Koestler in turn separated Orwell from dubious comrades by lauding his friend and political ally as 'the only writer of genius among the *littérateurs* of social revolt between the two wars', but it was V.S. Pritchett who offered the enduring image that placed the author as first among Socialist equals: 'George Orwell was the wintry conscience of a generation which in the thirties had heard the call to the rasher assumptions of political faith.'[14]

The most important sculpting of 'Orwell' came from the United States, where *Homage to Catalonia*, the ideal text given its portrayal of Leftist betrayal, was finally being published. Lionel Trilling, selected to write the introduction, defined Orwell as the moral middle way needed to endure and win the Cold War. Orwell had told the truth 'in an exemplary way, quietly, simply, with due warning to the reader that it was only one man's truth'. Doing so, he had set the standard for an author exalting his country and his countrymen while retaining his individuality:

> It is hard to find personalities in the contemporary world who are analogous to Orwell. We have to look for men who have considerable intellectual power but who are not happy in the institutionalized life of intellectuality; who have a feeling for an older and simpler time, and a guiding awareness of the ordinary life of the people, yet without any touch of the sentimental malice of populism; and a strong feeling for the commonplace; and a direct, unabashed sense of the nation, even a conscious love of it.[15]

British versions of the tribute were even less subtle. T.R. Fyvel, who had collaborated with Orwell since the outset of the Second World War, set up the icon, 'The word saintly was used by one of his friends and critics after his death, and – well – perhaps he had a touch of this quality.'[16] Christopher Hollis placed the author above all other Cold Warriors:

> In an age when all good things were desperately assailed by tyrants, [when] so many at one time or another belittled the dangers on the one flank in order to concentrate on the dangers of the other, he almost alone from first to last dealt out his blows impartially and defended without fear and without compromise the cause of liberty and the decencies from whatever quarter they might be assailed.[17]

A variant on the theme enshrined Orwell's Englishness. John Atkins, in the first 'unauthorised' biography, began, 'The common element in all George Orwell's writing was a sense of decency .... The special connotation of this English word is a complex of English living and English attitudes.'[18] Stephen Spender argued, 'He had a kind of quality about him that reminded one of plain living, bread and cheese, English beer, and so on.'[19]

At a glance, there is nothing untoward about the canonisation of St George. It was convenient, if not necessarily deliberate, that Orwell's work was crafted in such a way that it could easily be mobilised to hold up the values of a 'free world' purportedly facing the threat of Communism. Yet, just as Orwell could not take his eyes off the supposed foes whose 'menace' helped him make his reputation, so his hagiographers could define him as virtue only through comparison with the vices of others. He was the buttress against an English intelligentsia that wanted 'a breakdown of law and order which would produce a situation in Britain comparable to that in St. Petersburg [Russia] in 1917'.[20] He was the 'noble and colourful figure, large in act and vision, the almost complete opposite of the narrow-visioned academics who have closed in during the present generation on the literary worlds of both Britain and North America'.[21]

To challenge this vision of Orwell directly was foolhardy, for it merely set up the critic as one of the Leftists who were narrow of mind and short of sight. A statement such as that of the British historian A.L. Morton that 'Nineteen Eighty-Four is, for this country at least, the last word to date in counter-revolutionary apologetics' already verged on self-parody,[22] but even sharper assessments, such as the caveat of the New Republic's George Mayberry that 'Orwell's enthusiastic vision of an equalitarian socialism might have been paired with a recognition of the fact that the "road to socialism is paved with bedbugs"', were quickly dismissed.

No, if 'Orwell' was to be confronted, not only the writer but the times which made him had to be challenged. If the author had risen with the Cold War, he could also fall with it.

Isaac Deutscher, the historian named in Orwell's list of suspects passed to British Intelligence in 1949, was the first critic to make a serious mark. In 1954 he wrote an essay on Nineteen Eighty-Four which noted that, once the author was gone, he and his novel were being re-created 'as a sort of ideological super-weapon …. A book like 1984 may be used without much regard for the author's intention. Some of its features may be torn out of their context, while others, which do not suit the political purpose which the book is made to serve, are ignored or virtually suppressed.'[23] Thirteen years later, Conor Cruise O'Brien used revelations of CIA funding of intellectuals and authors (though not Orwell, whose own relationship with the Intelligence Services was still almost 30 years from discovery) to assert that St George, 'a Tory eccentric with a taste for self-immolation', had been a convenient model for imitators who were secretly sponsored by the US Government.[24]

These very occasional cavils were little more than a distraction. Deutscher's critique was tucked away in a collection of essays on 'Russia', and O'Brien's challenge was for the elite audience of the journal *The Listener*. Then, in the 1970s, 'Orwell' was confronted by Raymond Williams.

Williams had the scholarly weight to throw a good punch. Indeed, if Orwell had helped make popular culture a 'respectable' subject for analysis in the 1940s, Williams had put cultural studies at the centre of academic debate. More importantly, just as Orwell ostensibly challenged the 'Left' from within rather than without, Williams was claiming the same political territory as his subject. And he did so, not with an instinctive Orwellian 'Socialism', but with the ability to call forth and develop social, economic, political, and cultural theory.

There was one other matter. Williams, like Orwell, could also write clearly. His 1971 paperback was only 94 pages long but the argument was as substantial as that of biographies five times the length. Not only Orwell's writings but 'Orwell' himself were creations which served the interests of the author and, after his death, those with political and social agendas. Any activist could hold up Orwell as a beacon of their viewpoint, 'Right' or 'Left', for 'the contradictions, the paradox of Orwell, [were] paramount'.

This inevitable and incessant claiming of 'Orwell' could occur not because the author was being betrayed, but because he had left a space for others to fill: 'Orwell recognises and emphasises the complexity [of England], but he does not develop any kind of thinking which can sustain and extend a critical analysis of structures .... Orwell hated what he saw of the consequences of capitalism, but he was never able to see

it, fully, as an economic and political *system*.' Nor was Orwell
unaware of this. Instead, he had tried to establish the safeguard
of a decent superiority, the 'successful impersonation of the
plain man who bumps into experience in an unmediated way
and is simply telling the truth about it'.[25]

Orwell's defenders had to rebuild the edifice, and they did
so with a moral fervour that would do credit to their hero. If
Williams had the sharpness of analysis, they had the solidity
of the thousands of personal documents catalogued, released
and published in part by the Orwell Archive in the late 1960s.
The standard-bearer of biographers, Bernard Crick, confronted
Williams by avoiding any confrontation with the argument
that Orwell was a creation. Instead, he erased the contradictions to resurrect the 'real' author, returning him to the exalted
simplicity of 'decency'. Orwell was a Socialist but he was an
English Socialist, a man concerned with morality rather than
high intellect and theory: 'What was remarkable in Orwell
was not his political position, which was common enough, but
that he demanded publicly that his own side should live up
to their principles, both in their lives and in their policies,
should respect the liberty of others and tell the truth.'[26]

Others would follow at decent intervals to rally the troops.
Michael Shelden offered *Orwell: The Authorised Biography* in
1991. Promoted as a corrective to Crick's 'reporting Orwell's
actions without commenting much on the motives and
feelings behind them',[27] the book gilded the icon with
assertions such as 'one of his remarkable qualities was his
ability to face grim possibilities without losing all hope' and
'he was always analysing, always standing to one side and
observing, trying to make sense of this life'.[28] Jeffrey Meyers
produced another narrative in 2001; the title, *Orwell: Wintry
Conscience of a Generation*, linked 50 years of veneration.

Orwell also received a boost from the combination of
coincidence and cataclysm. For obvious reasons, the advent of
1984 raised the author's profile, becoming a convenient peg
for the reassertion of political significance cloaked in a superior
morality. As Robert Mulvihill asserted in a collection of essays
based on one of the numerous Orwell conferences: 'Because
of its underlying moral commitments and its identity of
problems central to the democratic political experience, *1984*

is a story for all seasons. The novel continues to provoke us to consider the substance of political decency and the threats to its survival.'[29]

Five years later, the collapse of the Soviet Bloc, which had been Orwell's ultimate foe, prompted another celebration. However, whereas *1984*'s most prominent cheerleaders had been politicians and the tabloid press, Communism's fall inspired the elegies of political philosophers who, like Orwell, had also sought a telling victory within the Left. Richard Rorty exulted, 'In the forty years since Orwell wrote, ... nobody has come up with a better way of setting out the political alternatives which confront us.'[30] Michael Walzer was even more dramatic, 'The story of the last man was not intended to be his last word on politics. Nor need it be ours, so long as we speak with the terrifying awareness that was his gift.'[31]

With the apparent demise of both Napoleon and Big Brother, at least in their Soviet guises, it appeared that Orwell could be retired in eternal glory. In 1998, Peter Davison completed a 20-year project to publish almost all of Orwell's writing. If the 20 volumes added little that was not already known, Davison could confirm his longtime subject as the embodiment of the values of the 'liberal' society of the twentieth century: 'Orwell's virtues are at their most attractive in his incredible determination to be a writer, whatever the difficulties and disappointments; in his passion for what he saw as social justice ... to strive against the "beastly" for "decency" and, in writing to achieve that, to fight against the insistence of censors and publishers to "garble" what he said.'[32]

However, Davison's reference to the 'garbling' of Orwell betrayed an annoying gap in his quest for completion. As Williams had noted, the decent Left did not have an exclusive hold on their champion. When the John Birch Society could use '1984' as the last four digits of its phone number even as the Black Panthers were putting Orwell on the syllabus of the Oakland Community School,[33] the faultlines were far from clear, and Orwell's adoption by the 'Right' had even more resonance in the Reagan–Thatcher 1980s. The title of Norman Podhoretz's otherwise inconsequential article jumped the Left's claim: 'If Orwell were Alive Today, He'd be a Neo-

Conservative.'[34] No less an authority than the *Sun*, Rupert Murdoch's best-selling tabloid, amplified:

> As 1984 opens, we have been spared the Orwell nightmare. We have liberty under Margaret Thatcher. We have hope of a better tomorrow.
>   Yet all these things are not automatic.
>   *We have to deserve them. We have to earn them.*
>   *We must be vigilant every day in 1984 and beyond to preserve them from any assault.*[35]

Bernard Crick, who had defined Orwell against the predations of Raymond Williams, scrambled to cover his other flank with ever-loftier language: '[Orwell had] on the one hand a sensibility and perception that is close to observable experience and intensely practical, but [he was] on the other hand Pilgrim with his eyes raised toward Zion, head-in-the-air while feet necessarily tramp through the Slough of Despond and Vanity Fair.'[36] Crispin Aubrey tried to bridge any gap between the 'freedom' of Right and Left: '[Orwell's] unorthodox, libertarian position should appeal in fact to many on the current British left concerned for a broader, more humanitarian socialism.'[37]

The complications of 'liberalism', however, were an opportunity not only for Podhoretz's NeoCons but also for those on the 'Left' who were unwilling to accept their icon. For some, it might be a settling of scores with an Orwell 'kidnapped by the forces of reaction' to become 'the patron saint of current Cold-War doublethink',[38] but more important critiques were emerging. An examination of Orwell's factual and fictional treatment of women was finally emerging in the analyses of Deidre Beddoe ('some of the most obnoxious portrayals of women in English fiction') and Daphne Patai ('manhood is the basic issue'). Beatrix Campbell linked gender and class when she not only raised Orwell's treatment of the 'common man', but then observed that the author ignored 'the culture of women, their concerns, their history, their movements' to make 'women the bearers of his own class hatred'.[39]

Of course, 'Orwell' survived, if only through the repetition of the old mantras of a decent Englishman standing against scurrilous subversives.[40] Feminist quibbles were met with the casual dismissal that they were 'fundamentally wrong-headed',[41] while John Rossi boasted of true heroes, 'Orwell never lost his faith in the rugged sense of the English people and their simple patriotism. They, and not the upper classes or the hopelessly degenerated intelligentsia, would save England.'[42] John Rodden used a book on the battle for Orwell's reputation to make his own sweeping claim that Orwell was 'a "true" intellectual .... He flayed the Left intelligentsia in order to fortify it, not to weaken it.'[43]

But did Orwell's defenders see the far greater threat of 'victory'? For more than 40 years Orwell and his work inevitably settled within a Cold War environment. If that Cold War was disappearing, it might be taking 'Orwell' with it. Peter Davison seemed to recognise the danger, for he tried to invoke the author in an ongoing fight against evil regimes and evil men who could suddenly appear, even at home:

> Were we able to hope that such regimes had no place in the modern world and that they would never arise in Britain, the 'necessity' for *Nineteen Eighty-Four* would disappear and the novel itself could become a footnote, a mere 'problem in intellectual history'. Until that happy and unlikely state occurs, it will remain an essential warning.[44]

The revelations about Orwell's cooperation with British intelligence services were damaging not because they turned him into a threatening agent of the Right, but because they cast him as a Cold War anachronism.

In May 2001, Timothy Garton Ash tried to establish 'Orwell in Our Time' with the contention, 'The three dragons against which Orwell fought his good fight – European and especially British imperialism; fascism, whether Italian, German or Spanish; and communism, not to be confused with the democratic socialism in which Orwell himself believed – were all either dead or mortally weakened. Forty years after his own painful and early death, Orwell had won.' But, with all three dragons slain, where was St George's next test of virtue? Garton Ash could only provide a far less spectacular role, 'If I had to name a single quality that makes Orwell still essential reading in the 21st century, it would be his insight into the use and abuse of language.'[45]

Britain's Home Secretary Jack Straw tried a different tactic, wielding Orwell to 'Blame the Left, not the British': 'Given the Left's tendency to wash their hands of the notion of nationhood, it's unsurprising our perception of Britishness became a conservative one',[46] but the ploy only highlighted that Orwell was becoming an omnipresent cultural cliché, used for every phenomenon from closed-circuit television to the surfeit of 'reality' programmes. He had been defeated, not by the devious 'Left' but by the mundane triumphs of a post-1984 Oceania in which, as one analyst summarised, 'some people have given up on politics and gone shopping'.[47] A comment in 2000 on the latest wonder of British television (appropriately, by Jonathan Freedland, one of Britain's leading political columnists) was illustrative: 'Just this once, believe the hype. *Big Brother* was billed as the summer's monster hit, and it is. Part gameshow, part docusoap, the Channel 4 programme has not just edged in front of BBC1 in the ratings. It has pulled off a trick thought possible only in television's golden past – creating a shared, collective experience. Sixteen years after 1984, Britain can declare: "Big Brother, we're watching you."'[48]

And then Christopher Hitchens wrote *Orwell's Victory*. And then came 9–11.

3

Christopher Hitchens: Becoming George

My worry has more to do with another thing Orwell warned about – the willingness of people to police themselves, and to believe anything that they're told. Especially the willingness of intellectuals and academics to become worshippers of whomever is in power, or passers-on of whatever the reigning idea is. Conformity, in other words. That will always carry on being a threat.

Christopher Hitchens, October 2002[1]

The front cover of *Orwell's Victory* displays the author in extreme close-up. He is photographed in near-profile, head bowed in concentration, a cigarette dangling from his mouth. It is a portrait of earnest endeavour, and it is reassuringly familiar.

For the reader of Orwell's fiction, it is the same snapshot (albeit not as tightly cropped) used for the cover of Penguin's latest edition, published in 2000, of *The Complete Novels*. For the consumer of Orwell's personal life, it is one of a series of photos taken in the domestic workplace of Orwell's Canonbury flat in 1945. The full frame reveals that Orwell, in tweed jacket and open-necked shirt, is intent on the typewriter on his desk.

A curious item catches the eye. The at-ease attire and the rumpled but striking face establish the eternal image of the writer, but it is the cigarette that is distinctive. Commonplace in the 1940s, it is a rarity on the book jackets of the new millennium.

So it is striking to see the cigarette on the front cover of *Letters to a Contrarian*. Casually seated, Christopher Hitchens holds it as a natural extension of his literary detective's attire, the collar on the trenchcoat turned up. A couple of days' stubble are apparent, as is the intent but slightly fatigued gaze. Unlike Orwell, Hitchens is facing the camera, but in his look of defiance, the equation is made. He, the self-described contrarian, is the keeper of dissent, ready to confront opponents in his own camp as well as those on the other side.

The reader is to conclude: just as George Orwell defined himself as Charles Dickens, so Christopher Hitchens has become George Orwell.

The interpretation is not left to a chance connection of two photographs. Nor is the union limited to Hitchens' judicious choice of phrases, such as his aspiration 'to graduate, from being a "bad boy" ... to becoming a cummudgeon"',[?] invoking an Orwell who was 'by no means' a saint, sometimes brusque, but always virtuous.[3] It is not confined to the Orwellian dicta of *Contrarian*: 'Always look to the language'; 'One should strive to combine the maximum of impatience with the maximum of scepticism, the maximum of hatred of injustice and irrationality with the maximum of ironic self-criticism.'[4]

In the introduction to *Orwell's Victory*, written as Hitchens was polishing *Contrarian*, Hitchens proclaims, 'George Orwell requires extricating from a pile of saccharine tablets and moist hankies; an object of sickly veneration and sentimental over-praise, employed to stultify schoolchildren with his insufferable rightness and purity.'[5] This rescue is a magician's act. The author eulogised by writers from Symons to Woodcock to Crick to Davison is a far from 'moist' combatant of indecent language and behaviour, but the audience is to be led astray by the false image so the 'real' Orwell can be revealed as tough, sometimes cantankerous and, eventually, on the honourable side of the argument. Possibly just like Hitchens.

Orwell concluded his metamorphosis into Dickens by looking at both himself and his predecessor in a mirror; Marcel Proust lends Hitchens a mirror for a less modest introduction to both George and Christopher:

> The men who produce works of genius are not those who live in the most delicate atmosphere, whose conversation is the most brilliant or their culture the most extensive, but those who have had the power, ceasing suddenly to live only for themselves, to transform their personality into a sort of mirror, in such a way that their life, however mediocre it may be socially and even, in a sense, intellectually, is

reflected by it, genius consisting in reflecting power and not in the intrinsic quality of the scene reflected.[6]

It is far from surprising that Hitchens' Orwell is not only a steadfast foe of imperialism but also the father of post-colonial studies, whose portrayal of the 'natives' becomes a 'keen and sad interest in the passivity and docility of the victims'.[7] He is not only an Englishman standing for an 'English tradition that has had to be asserted against British authorities time and again', but also an Englishman whose ideas are 'for universal consumption'.[8] Rough edges are filed away, with Hitchens mentioning Orwell's 'ill-natured remarks on homosexuals ... [and] his occasional lapses about Jews', but moving on swiftly, never to return to the topic.[9] Any concerns over Orwell's portrayal of his 'distraught ... relationship with the female sex' are refined by Hitchens' analysis 'that Orwell liked and desired the *feminine* but was somewhat put on his guard by the *female*' and assuaged with the note:

> We are still witnesses to, and participants in, the battle over what is and what is not, in human and sexual relations, 'natural'. At least it can be said for Orwell that he registered his participation in this unending conflict with a decent minimum of hypocrisy.[10]

Hitchens, as the rescuer of the 'contrarian', can spin gold from flaws: 'He had to suppress his distrust and dislike of the poor, his revulsion from the "coloured" masses who teemed throughout the empire, his suspicion of Jews, his awkwardness with women and his anti-intellectualism ... [to become] a great humanist.'[11] He can wave away Orwell's inconsistencies by refashioning the author. The 'real' Orwell of 1939 had rejected war with Germany, in part because it could be used to justify British imperialism. But through the magic of Hitchens' words, Orwell makes a brave stand against imperialism by insisting on a showdown with Hitler:

> There were a lot of people, a very large number in fact, in 1940, for example, not just in England but in Europe and America, who would say, 'Well, this Nazi business in Poland

is pretty rough, obviously, but look at how the British behave in India. Why should we pick a side?' [Orwell] sort of knew by the same instinct that I hope your readers have why that stinks as a means of arguing.[12]

Hitchens can even rewrite history by presenting the literary Messiah, unloved even in his own country:

He was very much reviled. He never had a steady publisher. He never had a steady outlet for his magazine writing. He was always broke. He was always ill. And he was kept to a very minority limited audience and not recognized for his contribution until after he was dead.[13]

A doubting Thomas might note that, apart from Kingsley Martin of the *New Statesman*, there were few who disliked Orwell as a person, and apart from the *Daily Worker* and the *New Masses*, few who reviled him for his writing. He never lacked for outlets for his essays from the *Adelphi* in 1930 through *Tribune* and *Partisan Review* during the war to *Horizon* and *Polemic* after 1945. He had a steady publisher for his fiction in Victor Gollancz, even after the two parted ways over *Homage to Catalonia*, and he then had a secure arrangement with Fredric Warburg for his nonfiction and for *Animal Farm* and *Nineteen Eighty-Four*. *The Road to Wigan Pier* reached a 'mass' audience through the Left Book Club, *The Lion and the Unicorn* was distributed widely to bolster the war effort, and *Animal Farm* and *Nineteen Eighty-Four* were international best-sellers.

Beyond the required depiction of decency, far more of interest links Orwell and his re-maker. Behind the celebratory statement, 'The reason to revere him is that he was correct on the three great issues of the century that's just ended (the end of European imperialism, fascism and Stalinism)',[14] there is the shadow of the issues of social and economic deprivation, which have been erased from the book. In 150 pages the only mention of Orwell as a Socialist is immediately qualified, not by reference to the conditions that he was supposedly challenging, but by Hitchens' unsupported caveat: 'The egalitarian and socialist sees simultaneously the fallacy of state-ownership and centralization.'[15]

For Hitchens (as well as Lionel Trilling, from whom he took the observation), it is 'sportsmanship and gentlemanliness and dutifulness and physical courage' that have become the 'revolutionary virtues'.[16] There is no mention of theory, and 'historical context' is discredited as a 'shady alibi'.[17] Indeed, there is no need at all for a defined social, economic or political position because 'what [Orwell] illustrates ... is that "views" do not really count; that it matters not what you think, but *how* you think; and that politics are relatively unimportant'. Yet, far from setting Orwell and Hitchens aside, this elevates them, for 'principles have a way of enduring, as do the few irreducible individuals who maintain allegiance to them'.[18]

Instead, not as much in unwitting emulation of Orwell's own priorities as in his conscious cleaving to the 'contrarian', Hitchens batters at the old enemy of the 'Left'. Far more substantial than any exposition on Orwell's own writing are Hitchens' critiques of those who dare question. *Orwell's Victory*, with only two references to Socialism, devotes more than 30 pages to a Left which, 'too stupid','too compromised' or 'twisted' to recognise the truth, responds 'to the very name of Orwell ... [with] a shiver or revulsion'. Not only Raymond Williams, Hitchens' arch-villain, but those alongside him, such as Isaac Deutscher and E.P. Thompson, and those who followed, including Edward Said and even Hitchens' good friend Salman Rushdie, are to be exposed for their distortions with an 'animus' against Orwell which 'has been allowed to depose the ordinary intellectual standard'.[19]

Hitchens' attack is one that does not split hairs so much as take an axe to heads, with little regard for the collateral damage. Setting out after E.P. Thompson, Hitchens sabotages his own critique by beginning with Thompson's assessment, '*Inside the Whale* must itself be read as an apology for quietism.' Unable or unwilling to challenge this substantial claim, Hitchens searches for a detail and then mangles it. In this case, Thompson's supposed lapse is to claim, 'Orwell found confirmation of his "world-process" in the *Managerial Revolution* of the ex-Trotskyist, James Burnham'; Hitchens retorts that 'Orwell was one of the very few commentators to see the sinister influence of [Burnham's] preachings'.[20] Of course, the riposte is an illusion: Orwell's pessimistic vision after the Second World War, bereft of 'Socialism' and 'freedom', both endorsed Burnham's projection of the 'three great empires' and bemoaned this 'sinister' outcome.

At least the reply to Thompson has some connection with the original source. Hitchens' correction of Rushdie, who also focuses on Orwell's 'passivity', is the wild insistence that Rushdie is 'taking phrases that Orwell puts in the mouths of others, and attributing them to their author'. A ten-second glance at the essay 'Inside the Whale' would confirm that Orwell's conclusion is his own, and no one else's:

> At this date it hardly even needs a war to bring home to us the disintegration of our society and the increasing helplessness of all decent people. It is for this reason that I think that the passive, non-co-operative attitude implied in Henry Miller's work is justified. Whether or not it is an expression of what people *ought* to feel, it probably comes somewhere near to expressing what they *do* feel.[21]

The fundamental problem for Hitchens, which he evades by assaulting the 'Left', is that Orwell's pacifism between 1937 and 1939 culminated as war approached with withdrawal into the self. Hitchens' explanation, unsupported and unfounded, is that Orwell was 'so horrified by the cynicism and stupidity of the Conservatives in the face of fascism that he fell for some time into the belief that "Britain", as such or as so defined, wasn't worth fighting for'. This alchemy of Orwell's far from consistent approach into the exalted claim that he 'was forever taking his own temperature' rests uneasily with Hitchens' later promotion of Orwell's 'steady attitude to the obvious'.[22]

Hitchens is on more secure ground when he selects two sentences from Edward Said which are far from convincing in their challenge to Orwell's 'bourgeois' character. Yet it is not necessary to note that Hitchens has chosen a Said review of an Orwell biography rather than consider (or even mention) Said's extended essays in which his assessment of Orwell is developed with more precision. For Hitchens inadvertently saves his intended victim, attacking Said's observation that Orwell the reporter has shown 'Asiatic and African mobs rampaging' by insisting that Orwell is criticising British imperialism. As with the attempted demolition of Thompson, the tactic does not refute but complements Hitchens' opponent: Orwell could both snap at the Empire, even if that criticism wavered at times, and in reportage ('Shooting the Elephant') and fiction (*Burmese Days*) display hordes of irrational, threatening natives.[23]

Reducing Deutscher's critique to the 'solecism' of one sentence, Hitchens hurriedly concludes, 'He judges Orwell's *Nineteen Eighty-Four* not as a novel or even as a polemic, but by the possibility that it may depress people,' and places Deutscher alongside 'priests and censors [who] have adjudged books to be lacking in that essential "uplift" which makes them wholesome enough for mass consumption'. Set aside supposed solecism: this is misreading on the grandest scale. In the 15 pages beyond Hitchens' selected sentence, Deutscher carefully placed *Nineteen Eighty-Four* in a Cold War context. He described the novel's 'borrowing' from Evgeny Zamyatin's *We* to assert that Orwell's question about Zamyatin – did he 'intend the Soviet target to be the special target of his satire'? – could also be asked about Orwell's objectives and conclusions. It is this judgement of both novel and polemic that leads Deutscher to assert, 'Orwell intended *1984* as a warning. But the warning defeats itself because of its underlying boundless despair.' The real problem is not that Deutscher is measuring 'uplift', but that he is denying the possibility of it to Hitchens: without a way out, the novel contributes to the 'despair' of the Cold War rather than Orwell's victory beyond it.[24]

By this point it seems that Hitchens may be exhausted. Then we discover that these skirmishes are just the preliminary to the main event: the public execution of the 'prime offender', Raymond Williams.

This strategem was established long before *Victory* and *Contrarian*, for Williams is the critic who must die so that 'Orwell' and Hitchens can flourish. With his interdisciplinary approach to literature, culture, economics and politics, Williams had exposed a process in which the political and social façade of 'objectivity' could be used by Orwell, and by those who upheld his legacy, to occupy a privileged position. Doing so, he anticipated the strategy with which Hitchens would attempt to take over that position in a new century.

Hitchens launched his attack in a 1999 essay on 'George Orwell and Raymond Williams', devoting all but a few hundred of more than 7,000 words to the critic rather than the author. Hitchens' misrepresentation of Williams' supposed 'misrepresenting' of Orwell is a triumph of bravado. Unable to grapple with Williams' thesis of 'Orwell' as a construction, but needing to do so to defend Orwell as an icon of morality, Hitchens opined that the process 'came to strike Williams as something almost sinister'. Repelled by but unable to deal with Williams' allegation that *Nineteen Eighty-Four* risked an equation of 'Ingsoc' with English Socialism, Hitchens made up a new interpretation: '[The book] should in Williams's view have been a dystopian satire on the form of dictatorship – National Socialism – that had just been defeated and destroyed, rather than on the form – "People's Democracy" Stalinism – that had just annexed Eastern Europe.' Faced with Williams' reading that the Orwellian vision ended in pessimism rather than the triumph of the individual, Hitchens had to convert that critique into 'Williams's call for a novel about totalitarianism that has a happy ending'. (Of course, it was not Williams but the filmmakers behind *1984*, backed by the US Government, who provided that happy ending.)

With enough style, however, the specifics do not matter. In Orwellian fashion, Hitchens accused Williams of bad language: 'almost bureaucratic' prose with 'a surreptitious element of pseudo-objectivity', 'lethal lapses into tautology'. He lashed Williams to villains on the Right, notably Norman Podhoretz. With a stroke of the pen, he turned Williams' closing homage to Orwell – 'We are never likely to reach a time when we can do without his frankness, his energy, his willingness to join in' – into 'a weak way of saying that this example was something to note, perhaps, but also to try and forget'.[25]

It is difficult to summarise the 20 pages devoted to Williams in *Orwell's Victory* because much of the text rambles far beyond the tangential. Hitchens starts his argument with several paragraphs in what seems no more than a coy attempt to charge Williams with borrowing, 'losing', and plagiarising from an Orwell manuscript on the novelist George Gissing. There is an attempt to prove Williams' 'hidden bias' because he claimed that Orwell used the word 'little' to diminish his targets. Hitchens' case for Williams' supposed acceptance of totalitarianism is his description of Orwell as a vagrant; unfortunately, the passage chosen by Hitchens has no such reference.

What remains in Hitchens' constructions, after one takes out the diversions and distractions, are the snide jabs: 'What Williams means to imply, but is not brave enough to say, is that Orwell "invented" the picture of totalitarian collectivism.' (Cowardice is a mean-spirited red herring. Only the most predetermined of assaults could turn Williams' compliment – 'He was a humane man who communicated an extreme of inhuman terror' – into a supposed insult to Orwell.)[26] Just as Orwell freely labelled his foes as accomplices and collaborators with fascism, National Socialism and Communism, so Hitchens will not rest until Williams is seen not only as an appeaser but as a devoted follower of the Red Menace: 'Of Stalin's "community", at that epoch [the late 1930s], Williams formed an organic part. Nor, by the time he wrote *Culture and Society* [1958], had he entirely separated from it.'[27]

Any purported evaluation of Williams is merely loading the gun for character assassination. One allegation of 'his ... inability to do so much as master the plot' not only verges on but dives into the obtuse. Presenting Williams' charge that Orwell's working class in *Animal Farm* and *Nineteen Eighty-Four* are too stupid to have any agency, thus leaving the revolution to a lone 'rebel', Hitchens trills, 'Williams even quoted the paragraph on the proles [from *Nineteen Eighty-Four*] that controverted what he had just said.' Indeed, Williams dwells on Winston Smith's declaration, 'If there was hope, it must lie in the proles', but the possibility that the critic may have been highlighting Winston's sentimental illusions, illusions shattered by Orwell's rendering of the decadent, ignorant denizens of the 'prole' section, is either too challenging or too inconvenient for Hitchens' one-man tribunal.[28]

Williams was not acting as a Stalinist operative when he penned the books that would be instrumental in launching cultural studies, nor was he a Communist stooge when he offered his evaluation, in his writing and interviews, of Orwell in the 1970s. He was opening up a space for the debate that 'Orwell' was as much a construction serving the interests of himself and others as he was an eternal truth-teller. But Hitchens does not want debate; he wants to be the last man standing. And, for that last man to be George/Christopher, the 'Left' must be chopped down once and for all.

Of course, this destruction must be seen as an act of virtue. Hitchens devotes an entire chapter of *Orwell's Victory* to 'The List' and 'the recent absurd fuss ... manured in the soil by those who had never forgiven [Orwell] for the stubborn rectitude he evinced between 1936 and the time of his death'. Any consideration that Orwell cooperated with the British Intelligence Services must be an 'utter distortion of Orwell's motives and methods', so Hitchens insists on a 'matter of record' that Orwell's list is of 'Stalinized intellectuals' and that the Information Research Department 'was unconnected to any "Thought Police"'.

This summary dismissal 'objectively' establishes that everyone in Orwell's notebook, from Richard Crossman to the former US Ambassador to Moscow Joseph Davies to *Picture Post*'s Tom Hopkinson (who later wrote a glowing eulogy to Orwell) to former Mayor of New York Fiorello La Guardia to the theologian Reinhold Niebuhr (who was subsequently an influence on the Cold War warriors of the Eisenhower Administration), is 'Stalinized'. At the same time it 'objectively' fails to mention that the IRD worked closely with MI6 as well as the Foreign Office. But, perhaps in recognition that any prolonged stand on his objectivity might unsettle it, Hitchens has already skipped away to another explanation of 'simple facts': Orwell's list is no more than a 'game [which] consisted of guessing which public figures would, or would not, sell out in the event of an invasion or a dictatorship'.

Hitchens dances back and forth throughout the chapter. On the one hand, Orwell's list was part of an honourable 'confrontation with the poisonous illusion that the Soviet system had a claim on the democratic Left'. On the other, in case anyone still lingers on the notion that passing the list to British Intelligence compromised this honour, it was a 'relatively trivial episode' in which 'nobody suffered or could have suffered from Orwell's private opinion'.[29] (Andy Croft has identified the possible effect on one of Orwell's suspects, the poet Randall Swingler. Shortly after the meeting between

Orwell and British Intelligence, Swingler was blacklisted by the BBC and effectively fired from teaching when his extramural classes were closed down.)[30]

Orwell must be exonerated and uplifted for Hitchens to become the beacon for another generation. *Letters to a Contrarian* is not just Hitchens' benevolent response to his students in the New School in New York, sitting at his feet for 'any advice to the young and the restless; any counsel that would help them avoid disillusionment'.[31] It is not just the fulfilment of Basic Books' marketing idea of a *Letters ...* series as a 'how-to' guide for becoming a contrarian, a therapist, a lawyer or even a golfer. This is Hitchens' would-be masterstroke: if he can claim the role of the honourable loner, if he can talk with crowds and maintain his virtue, then he can move against any perceived threat, not just including but especially those from the 'Left'. He can claim 'free' thought while querying the use of freedom by dangerous intellectuals. He can claim the position of 'dissent' while shutting down any dissenters. He can state any position without the burden of complex political, economic or social consideration. He can walk away from any contradictions or burdensome queries, for his stance *a priori* is the correct one.

The question remains, however: what brought the contrarian to this point? Why, in 2001, would it be necessary to look to Orwell and the past to preserve Christopher Hitchens for the future? The answer lies in an incident two years earlier: soon after he wrote articles in *Vanity Fair* and *The Nation* absolving Orwell of his contact with the IRD, Hitchens would fight for his career and reputation against the allegation of 'snitching'.

The personal had always been part of the political for Hitchens. The aura of the 'bad boy' was never just the badness of a radical socialist who might reignite 1968 in editorial offices in London, Washington and New York. It was also the personal badness: his well-known proclivities, the blunt and quite earthy remarks to friend and foe alike, the behaviour fostering the urban legend that Hitchens was the model for Tom Wolfe's decadent English journalist Peter Fallow in *Bonfire of the Vanities*.[32] By the mid-1990s, after 25 years from Oxford

University to London's *New Statesman* to *The Nation*, *Vanity Fair* and the New York–Washington loop, it was the in-your-face badness of knocking down those supposedly beyond scrutiny, the Royal Families and Mother Theresas of the world.

None of this, however, put distance between Hitchens and others on the 'Left'. Stands against the monarchy and future Catholic saints could be taken without division, and even more important positions, such as Hitchens' condemnation of the 1989 Iranian *fatwa* against Salman Rushdie, were also shared.[33] Then, in the spring of 1999, the intersection of the personal and the political reached a critical juncture for Hitchens.

The story is now part of the salacious scandal of the Clinton years. The furore over the President's relationship with his intern, Monica Lewinsky, had contributed to his impeachment, and the Senate was conducting the trial that would determine whether Clinton would be thrown out of office. Hitchens' dramatic cameo in the affair came when he and his wife, Carol Blue, offered affidavits to the Congressmen prosecuting the case. Hitchens affirmed that Sidney Blumenthal, his close friend since the 1980s and an aide to Clinton, had told him that the President had described Lewinsky as a stalker. The allegation ultimately meant little to the trial – Clinton would escape conviction by a clear margin in February – but it could have meant a jail sentence for Blumenthal, who had denied to Congressional investigators that he had made any such remark.

Hitchens was suddenly engulfed by a firestorm of debate among the elite of the press and East Coast society. At the end of 1998, Alexander Cockburn, a fellow columnist at *The Nation*, had vigorously debated with Hitchens whether Orwell 'snitched' with his passing of names to the IRD.[34] The historical was now the contemporary, as Cockburn declared, 'As a Judas and a snitch, Hitchens has made the big time.'[35]

Maureen Dowd began tracking 'Christopher Snitchens' in her *New York Times* column.[36] Others were even more damning, deflating Hitchens' politics to the pettiness of the personal: in Britain, Mark Steyn wrote of 'Chris the contrarian who gets in to [*Washington Post* editor] Kay Graham's dinner party only to pass out in the soup and throw up on the rug', while in the

US, Dowd's colleague Frank Rich turned post-Cold War crisis into the 1950s US situation comedy *Leave it to Beaver*:

> The fate of anti-Communism isn't at stake – nor even the fate of the Clinton Presidency. What is on the line are the guest lists of certain Washington dinner parties, a lot of lawyers' fees and Mr. Hitchens's continued ability to command a spotlight on All-Monica talk shows. This catfight isn't Chambers-vs.-Hiss but Beaver-vs.-Eddie Haskell, less suitable for CNN than for [the American cable channel] Nick at Nite.[37]

Eventually, the Blumenthal showdown would prove to be the making of Hitchens the contrarian. At the time, however, it put him on an unsettling defensive. Even before Cockburn's missive appeared, Hitchens was sacrificing himself on *Meet the Press*, the Sunday morning mediator of American politics, by passing the blame to Lindsey Graham, the Congressman who questioned him. Hitchens assured the audience that he would endure contempt of Congress charges before seeing Blumenthal serve five years in jail for perjury.[38] In *The Nation*, he tried to ally himself and Blumenthal as victims of the real villain: 'It is just thinkable that this could end with Clinton walking free, with his subordinates made to suffer for him yet again and with C. Hitchens cited for contempt.'[39]

Over the following months, Hitchens retreated into a self-reflection that never remained private. In April the 'Boy Who Can't Help It', as the profile labelled him, greeted a reporter for *New York* magazine with a glass of Scotch in his hand, a grin and a quip, 'I've started without you.' Over the Johnnie Walker Black, Hitchens moved into a lifelong tale of sadness. From the regret, 'I've been thinking of just turning up at Sidney's and walking in when they open the door for Elijah [Hitchens' son] … I've decided it would be too theatrical,' he worked backwards to the tragedy of a life marked by a tense home, rigid boarding schools and, ultimately, his mother's suicide.

Hitchens was careful to leave a path out of depression and regret, however. As the *New York* reporter concluded her profile, 'Hitchens isn't likely to lie low. Inevitably, he will find a new way to make mischief. After all, he's an agitator, a bad boy. "I am frightened, really frightened, of being bored," he tells me late one evening, in the tone of a small child fearful of the dark. "Boredom creates a physical sensation of terror in me." Lives like his are not for the faint of heart; sometimes boring is better.'[40]

Two years later, Hitchens would reassure himself and his readers, 'The life of an oppositionist is supposed to be difficult.' But, in 1999, being a contrarian had become far more than an intellectual pose and 'a badge of honour'; it was a necessity for personal salvation. And, conveniently, Hitchens had a cause which could rescue him: Kosovo.

In early April, after NATO forces began bombing to force the withdrawal of Serb forces from Kosovo, Hitchens launched a series of four articles on the conflict in *The Nation*. As the 'contrarian' now tells the story, these articles were a valiant defence against 'Serbo-fascism' and the Western leftists who appeased Serb leader Slobodan Milosevic. Reading them offers a very different, far more confused picture.

Hitchens' first 'Minority Reports' did not support the NATO air attacks. Instead, he defined them as the 'bloody blundering' of his nemesis Clinton, their objective to force Milosevic to the negotiating table where 'the likeliest outcome [was] obviously a de facto partition of an "ethnically cleansed" Kosovo'. Hitchens claimed 'the "line of the day" among administration spokesmen, confronted by masses of destitute and terrified refugees and solid reports of the mass execution of civilians, [was] to say that "we expected this to happen"', and warned, 'If they want to avoid being indicted for war crimes themselves, these "spokesmen" had better promise us that they were lying when they said that.'[41]

Throughout May, Hitchens continued to portray a conspiracy between the Clinton Administration and the Serb leadership that they were supposedly attacking: 'Pentagon and NATO officials have even mused that the complete expulsion of Albanians from Kosovo would give the alliance a big military advantage' in 'this objective collusion, between the aims of Milosevic and the aims of NATO'. Yet, whatever his outrage at this 'collusion', Hitchens never proposed that the West ally with or even offer support to the Kosovars who were the victims of Milosevic's actions. His most substantive proposal was that 'a principled peace movement in this country should at least attempt to contact the few genuine Serbian internationalists, ask them what they think and inquire how they can be helped'.[42]

Contrary to the later presentation of his valiant position, Hitchens did not argue that the 'ethnic cleansing' of Kosovo preceded the NATO bombing. Instead, in harmony with critics of the war such as John Pilger, he made clear that he believed 'the cleansing interval ... was both provoked and provided by the threat of air attacks on other parts of Yugoslavia'. NATO's action was not the salvation of the Kosovars but the sacrifice of those people, as well as 'good' for the sake of a Clinton-backed 'carve-up [of Kosovo that] might have been in the works from the start'.[43]

Hitchens had put himself in a Janus-like position. His flailing against 'those who say that NATO is doing the right thing by taking an antifascist position at last' could have been adopted by those protesting against the West's intervention, yet he was also slinging criticism at those 'who speak smugly about how all this bombing has upset the Serbian democrats'. Orwell had positioned himself as a valiant opponent of both would-be warriors and pacifists, but he had done so at different points in his career. Hitchens had achieved the impossible by assaulting everyone at once.

The problem for the contrarian was that, until the 'Serb internationalists' whom he promoted rose up and took Belgrade, he had no way to resolve his different battles. He could only jeer from the sidelines, be it at the 'drunken, robotic militias' of Serbia or 'the obligatory "double standards" passage' of those who wondered why others besides the Kosovars, such as the Kurds in Turkey or the East Timorese, were not being defended by NATO and US planes.[44] Edward Herman, the lesser-known but equally incisive colleague of Noam Chomsky, exposed Hitchens' dilemma: 'He is captured by the demonization of Milosevic and clearly accepts the western establishment's elevation of the removal of the demon to top priority, although he finds it painful that the instrument of removal of this beast must be his old enemy Bill Clinton.'[45]

Herman threw down a challenge which Hitchens would eventually have to confront: 'Perhaps "moral right" is irrelevant to explaining NATO policy in Yugoslavia.' Hitchens had made an awkward start in the fourth of the Minority Reports, printed in mid-June, by revising his account of ethnic cleansing: NATO had finally chosen the war option 'when the sheer exorbitance of the crimes in Kosovo became impossible to ignore'.[46] The conversion would take the best part of two years, however, in a series of returns to Kosovo.

Hitchens acknowledged one abrupt change of position – 'much of the left – including myself for a time – consoled and continues to console itself with the half-truth that intervention only made matters worse' – only to make an even more important, unacknowledged U-turn. In 1999, he had slammed NATO for claiming 'antifascist' intervention, but a year later he was the leading advocate of such action: 'The Kosovo war marked the first and only time in the twentieth century that ethno-fascism was stopped, and reversed, while it was still in progress.' At last, he could seize the moral high ground, 'The NATO intervention repatriated all or most of the refugees and killed at least some of the cleansers. I find I have absolutely no problem with that.'[47]

Yet Hitchens never could sweep away his initial castigation of NATO for prompting the Kosovar catastrophe. At best he could try the 'retrospective justification',[48] put out by NATO officials, that there was a Serbian 'Operation Horseshoe' which would have expelled the Kosovars if the West had not begun military operations. Nor could he ever explain what he was 'for', beyond the notion of a Serbian Internationalist Brigade and the claim of a number of Serbs who were quite happy to be part of NATO-occupied Kosovo. And there were the challenges that he had not met, from Herman's assertion that Hitchens had ignored the plight of Kosovo's Serbs to the broader contention that the war against Milosevic was for the interests of Western power rather than any righting of moral wrongs.

Unable or unwilling to deal with complexities, Hitchens had fallen back on simplicity. Far from coincidentally, his warm embrace of the defeat of 'ethno-fascism' occurred in an article which began with a vivid description of the shortcomings of international reconstruction efforts in Kosovo. Hitchens pondered, 'The absence of principle and direction is palpable and visible' and was confronted by a question which shook his newfound faith in NATO's military campaign: 'You live in Washington. Why not ask what half a day of bombing cost, compared to what we need here?' Unable to tell his inquisitor 'that this irony – if it is an irony – is subject to diminishing returns', Hitchens offered the consolation of Serbo-fascism's demise.[49]

Still, even if Hitchens never replied to Herman, even if his essays safeguarded their contradictions, he could slip the punches. As Herman's rebuttals were published in the 'alternative' electronic journal *Z-Net*, only the most devoted Web surfers and readers of *The Nation*, which published an extended Letter to the Editor from Herman in June 2001, would have known of the challenge to Hitchens' supposedly consistent position.

Herman's critique was also overshadowed by a general cessation of hostilities between Hitchens and his supposed Leftist enemies. Some personal animosity sparked by the Blumenthal affair would remain, as in the case of Hitchens' break with Alexander Cockburn. If this could be overcome, however, the contrarian's attention to the evils of the Clinton Administration could be tolerated, given that many on the 'Left' had their difficulties with the behaviour and policies of the President. Indeed, a claim which pre-dated Kosovo, such as the 'wag the dog' criticism of Clinton for the 1998 bombing of a Sudanese pharmaceutical factory, could reunite Hitchens and prominent anti-war essayists such as Noam Chomsky.

There was also common ground because Hitchens, in stark contrast to his later incarnation, was hostile to a Bush Presidency. Hitchens not only endorsed the independent candidacy of Ralph Nader, but also blasted comrades such as *The Nation*'s Eric Alterman for using the 1968 Presidential election (won by Richard Nixon, with the third-party candidate George Wallace receiving almost 10 million votes) to suggest support for Nader 'would allow a dangerous Republican into the White House'.[50] Appearing on the national talk show *Hardball* a week before the election, he decried Bush's use of English and his lack of culture and sophistication.[51]

And then there was *The Trial of Henry Kissinger*. Hitchens, in a case first made in *Harper's* in a two-part essay and then published as a paperback, did not simply point to Kissinger's complicity in the shadier operations of US foreign policy from 1968 through 1977 and call for the prosecution of the Nobel Peace Prize winner for capital crimes. He also indicted the political culture that had embraced the great statesman: 'We charge Henry Kissinger with murder for [intervention in Chile between 1970 and 1973], and we say that the society that tolerates it is tolerating murder, too. And that's, therefore, a big reproach to a society that claims to be bound by law and responsive to justice.'[52] Some might complain that Hitchens did not recognise, let alone cite, activists and authors who had laid the evidence against Kissinger in the 1970s, but he had succeeded in reaching a large audience with the prosecution of one of the standard-bearers of US foreign policy in the Cold War and beyond.

For Hitchens, however, any truce with the 'Left' was an uneasy one. He later asserted:

> I tried to say to the left you're mad if you think this guy [Clinton] is one of us. I guess now if I was to produce a video of him dismembering a child, it wouldn't make any difference because they think he's their guy. So I became unmoored from the liberal left because I thought, I'm wasting my time trying to pitch the argument to them that way.[53]

No doubt part of this was an *ex post facto* jockeying for moral position, but both *Contrarian* and *Orwell's Victory*, essentially completed before 9–11, had demonstrated that Hitchens was not only willing but aspiring to set himself apart from any comrades. He would stand guard against 'identity politics'.[54] He would side with 'a poor white ... good ol' boy family rather than [a] bookish or pointy-headed bleeding heart',[55] for after all, 'most of the intellectual class were fatally compromised by accommodation with one or other of these man-made structures of inhumanity [imperialism, fascism, and Stalinism]'.[56]

The 'unaffiliated radical', the title that Hitchens eventually adopted, was not born on 11 September 2001; rather, the tragedy of that day served as a rite of passage.[57] In this self-anointed role as protector of the good and right, Hitchens used Orwell as the sanctioning deity. Asked in an interview for *Salon*, 'If one were to look at your writing, say, since Sept. 11, there are threads of Orwell in it, aren't there? Whether or not they're cited', Hitchens replied modestly, 'Well if someone wanted to say that, I wouldn't feel I had to repudiate it.'[58]

Of course, there would be the application of *Nineteen Eighty-Four*'s nightmare fantasy to the enemies of the moment:

> The unspeakable degradation that was inflicted last week by the Big Brother on the people of Iraq, forced once again to gather adoringly, unanimously and terrified, and not only to turn out to vote 100 percent, but to turn out to vote 100 percent the same way [for Saddam Hussein] …. The discovery that the Democratic People's Republic of Korea, while its people have been starving and screaming with hunger and pain and the absence of all culture, has been choosing to spend all its resources on the enrichment of uranium. Who will say, in the face of this, that the relevance of George Orwell belongs in the past?[59]

But, even more importantly, Orwell could be used as a cudgel against the enemy at home. In a footnote added at the last moment to *Orwell's Victory*, Hitchens assailed 'a number of intellectuals and pseudo-intellectuals [who] affected a sort of neutrality between the victims of New York and Pennsylvania and Washington and the theocratic fascists of Al Quaeda and the Taliban' by quoting from Orwell's essay 'Notes on Nationalism':

> There is a minority of intellectual pacifists, whose real though unacknowledged motive appears to be hatred of western democracy and admiration of totalitarianism. Pacifist propaganda usually boils down to saying that one side is as bad as the other, but if one looks closely at the writings of the younger intellectual pacifists, one finds that they do not by any means express impartial disapproval but are directed almost entirely against Britain and the United States.[60]

(By mid-2002, Hitchens could not only cite Orwell, but act as a medium for the dead author: 'I know what he would say about the grand question of the moment which is, there's no comparison, can or should be made, no moral equivalence, between the United States, whatever its shortcomings and the war of theocratic absolutism, which rejoices in the destruction of non-believers. I mean that's the totalitarianism of our day and the same sorts of people he would have loathed are making their crummy little excuses, their little point scoring abasements of themselves.')[61]

When there was a danger of Hitchens finding himself on the same ground as his foes, as in the common criticism of US internal security measures, 'Orwell' could elevate Hitchens above the deluded opposition: 'I think those who think that "1984" is here are silly, because what would they have left to say if it really arrived? (And those who claim this while carrying water for Milosevic and Saddam and Kim Jong Il are, I begin to think, beyond the reach of contempt.)'[62] And when Hitchens couldn't fit hand-in-glove with Orwell, he remedied this by remaking his icon. Signing off the Preface to *Contrarian* 'Stanford, California, Independence Day 2001', the 'contrarian' rescued Orwell for the American Millennium:

> The only thing he didn't get right was the United States .... But I think that would have changed had he lived another ten years. I think that his friends in New York would have persuaded him to come over.[63]

4
9–11

The narrative is now well established. The attacks on the World Trade Center and the Pentagon not only destroyed buildings and claimed thousands of victims, they shattered the 'Left'. The call for peaceful resolution of conflict, let alone the critique of US foreign policy as the source of that conflict, could no longer be accepted.

Some recalcitrants held out against this logic. They did not necessarily line up with the enemy, but they failed to decide, and to proclaim that decision loudly, when it was time to choose sides. Fortunately, there were others who not only recognised the need to support 'America', but to embrace that choice by striking down any who questioned a War on Terror that soon became a War on the Taliban. Christopher Hitchens was one such 'liberal'.

So it comes as a surprise, re-reading the initial reactions to 9–11, to find that this narrative has an element of artifice, one reinforced by Hitchens' later claim that he felt 'exhilaration' at the prospect of a 'clash of civilisations' with 'theocratic fascism'.[1] Instead, for several days after the shock, there was a different contrarian, one suspending the choice for the question 'Why?', one willing to look beyond the 19 hijackers and their network to interrogate others beyond Ground Zero.

Hitchens began writing within hours of the attack, starting with the personal: Barbara Olson, a Washington lawyer and wife of the Bush Administration's Solicitor General, was aboard American Airlines Flight 77 when it was flown into the Pentagon. Through the pain of that loss, Hitchens identified an innocent 'America' cruelly assaulted. He expanded the attack on the US and its citizens into a challenge to 'civilization'. He did not, however, designate America's enemy in religious, ethnic or national terms.[2]

Nor did he concentrate on that enemy in columns over the following two days. While Hitchens joined the general suspicion of Osama bin Laden and linked the attacks to the turmoil of the Middle East, he saw the complication: 15 of the 19 hijackers had come from Saudi Arabia, a long-time ally of the US. More importantly, Hitchens did not leap into the future but took a step back, insisting that Americans must ponder how events had led to the tragedy of the previous Tuesday morning: 'One day into the post-World Trade Center era, and the question "how" is still taking precedence over the question "why".' If he had a target for his queries, it was not a 'terrorist' – they had perished with Barbara Olson and their captured passengers – but George Walker Bush:

> More than ever this week, we were reminded that this President is essentially a frontman: A slight and malleable figure who was invented by a committee of stronger men as an 'electable' symbol.
>   He is a shadow framed by powerful advisers and handlers, a glove puppet with little volition of his own and a celebrated indifference to foreign affairs.[3]

In the 72 hours after the first strike, Hitchens had shared in the cries of grief, but he had not joined the quest for retribution. His thoughts were closer to the questions of Susan Sontag, who would soon be high on the list of intellectuals pilloried for suggesting that the actions of the US Government might have been part of a political environment fostering 9–11. Indeed, Hitchens would be challenged by Leon Weiseltier, who also savaged Sontag, in *The New Republic* (fortunately for his later reputation as the honourable inter-ventionist of the 'Left', he was not named, only quoted as a 'contrarianism-artist').[4]

But then something happened. Five days passed before the *Evening Standard* published Hitchens' next commentary on 19 September. 'Reflect[ing] that at my age I might never again feel carefree', he was ready for vengeance. The enemies had emerged: the Serbo-Fascists of 1999 had been replaced by the Islamic Fascists:

> The people who destroyed the World Trade Center, and used civilians as accessories ... are fighting for the right to

throw acid in the faces of unveiled women in Kabul and Karachi. They didn't just destroy the temple of modernity, they used heavy artillery to shatter ancient Buddha statues in Bamiyan earlier this year, and in Egypt have plotted to demolish the Pyramids and the Sphinx because they are un-Islamic and profane.

Look at what they do to their own societies, from Algeria to Afghanistan, and then wonder what they might have in mind for ours.

And these extremists might have allies, if only by default, amongst those on the 'Left' who were not ready for the fight: 'Liberal masochism is of no use to us at a time like this, and Muslim self-pity even less so. Self-preservation and self-respect make it necessary to recognise and name a lethal enemy when one sees one.'[5]

For Hitchens, Osama bin Laden was secondary to the threat within, his search for enemies sparked by the replies of Noam Chomsky to enquiries from a number of journalists in the days after 11 September. Chomsky began, 'The terrorist attacks were major atrocities', and later reiterated, 'That this was a horrendous crime is not in doubt.' In between the two statements, however, he had made a comparison:

In scale [the attacks of 9–11] may not reach the level of many others, for example, Clinton's bombing of the Sudan with no credible pretext, destroying half its pharmaceutical supplies and killing unknown numbers of people (no one knows, because the US blocked an inquiry at the UN and no one cares to pursue it).[6]

If Chomsky witnessed a 9–11 in which 'the primary victims, as usual, were working people: janitors, secretaries, fireman, etc.', he also envisaged a future in which those primary victims would be 'Palestinians and other poor and oppressed people' abroad and those enduring 'harsh security controls' at home, a future in which 'the crime [became] a gift to the hard jingoist right' of a US Government whose 'likely … actions' would 'trigger possibly more attacks like this one, or worse'. He concluded by citing Robert Fisk of the *Independent*: 'This is not the war of democracy versus terror that the world will be asked to believe in the coming days. It is also about American missiles smashing into Palestinian homes and US helicopters firing missiles into a Lebanese ambulance in 1996 and American shells crashing into a village called Qana and about a Lebanese militia – paid and uniformed by America's Israeli ally – hacking and raping and murdering their way through refugee camps.'[7]

There was a time when Hitchens had vigorously defended Chomsky against distortion and character assassination. In a 1985 essay, he recalled seeing Chomsky lecture at Oxford 16 years earlier: 'Chomsky seemed to suggest that you need not politicize the academy in order to take a stand, but that if you did not take a stand, then you were being silent about a surreptitious politicization of it.'[8] He then took on those who were accusing Chomsky of 'minimising the Khmer Rouge atrocities in Cambodia' and endorsing the denial of 'the historical reality of the Jewish Holocaust'. And, for good measure, he castigated the media and academia alike for ignoring Chomsky's 1983 work *The Fateful Triangle* on US policy towards Israel and neighbouring states. Hitchens concluded, 'Whether he is ignored, whether he is libeled, or whether he is subjected to an active campaign of abuse, Chomsky is attacked for things that he is thought to believe, or believed to have said.'[9] (Hitchens would later declare, reviewing *The Culture of Terrorism*, that Chomsky 'is nearly the only person now writing who assumes a single standard of international morality not for rhetorical effect, but as a matter of habitual, practically instinctual conviction'.)[10]

Hitchens had differed from Chomsky, at least in degree, when both contributed articles on Bosnia for the *Boston Review* in 1993;[11] however, the two would not clash directly until December 1999, after the Kosovo conflict and the start of Hitchens' skirmishes with Chomsky's friend and co-writer, Edward Herman. Hitchens charged that Chomsky, in *The New Military Humanism*, was guilty of 'double standards' in criticising NATO's bombing of Yugoslavia while supporting intervention in the case of East Timor.[12] Chomsky replied, 'There is a double standard only if the intentions are humanitarian .... My book found no evidence of benign intent [over

Kosovo] ... hence no double standard but rather the familiar single standard of pursuit of power interests with little concern for human consequences.'[13] Hitchens, after the cheap jibe, 'It is no disgrace to be condescended to by Noam Chomsky nor to be instructed in matters of formal logic and argumentative procedure', wrestled with double standards before settling on a simpler call, 'We appear to be in a new era, where old reflexes serve us less well. However, this does not relieve us of our responsibility to take the side of the victims, as Chomsky once taught me and many others to do.'[14]

The exchange foreshadowed more bitter confrontations over 'liberal intervention'. Hitchens would criticise the 'Left' for its failure to support military action but, after Chomsky based a rebuttal on logical exposition, would set aside the detailed confrontation for a general call to moral authority. With the apparent clarity of 9–11 and with Chomsky already set up as America's 'perpetual dissenter', Hitchens finally seemed to have a bead on his target.

Hitchens took aim through his 'Minority Report' on the website and pages of *The Nation*. He began with an article claiming knowledge of a 'masochistic e-mail traffic ... from the Chomsky–[Howard] Zinn–[Norman] Finkelstein quarter'. For Hitchens, there was no need to establish that such traffic even existed in order to expose its fallacies:

> I know already that the people of Palestine and Iraq are victims of a depraved and callous Western statecraft. And I think I can claim to have been among the first to point out that Clinton's rocketing of Khartoum – supported by most liberals – was a gross war crime, which would certainly have entitled the Sudanese government to mount reprisals under international law .... But there is no sense in which the events of September 11 can be held to constitute such a reprisal, either legally or morally.[15]

Discovering 'not all readers liked [his] attack', Hitchens went even further four days later on the *Nation*'s website. After skewering another dissenter, Sam Husseini of the Institute for Public Accuracy, Hitchens praised the heroes who wrestled with the hijackers of United Airlines Flight 93, which crashed in Pennsylvania: 'One iota of such innate fortitude is worth all the writings of Noam Chomsky, who coldly compared the plan of September 11 to a stupid and cruel and cynical raid by Bill Clinton on Khartoum in August 1998.' He sneered that any such equation was 'to abandon every standard that makes intellectual and moral discrimination possible. To put it at its very lowest, and most elementary, at least the missiles launched by Clinton were not full of passengers. (How are you doing, Sam? Noam, waaaup?)' After a closing volley that Chomsky 'described the whole business [of NATO intervention] as a bullying persecution of – the Serbs!', Hitchens assured the reader, in tones reminiscent of Orwell's denunciation of pacifists in 1942:

> I have no hesitation in describing this mentality, carefully and without heat, as soft on crime and soft on fascism. No political coalition is possible with such people and, I'm thankful to say, no political coalition with them is now necessary. It no longer matters what they think.[16]

Hitchens could not confront his adversary directly, for Chomsky did not allege that the Sudanese deaths were the intended outcome of a short-term American action. Instead, investigations had established that 'tens of thousands of people – many of them children – … suffered and died from malaria, tuberculosis, and other treatable diseases' after the destruction of the pharmaceutical plant.[17] So, rather than debate Chomsky's specific point, Hitchens ruled that only the immediate and intentional effects of 'terrorism' were appropriate:

> The malicious premeditation is very evident and manifest …. The cruise missiles fired at Sudan were not crammed with terrified civilian kidnap victims. I do not therefore think it can be argued that the hasty, politicised and wicked decision to hit the Al-Shifa plant [in Sudan] can be characterized as directly homicidal in quite the same way.

Having set this criterion, Hitchens could then render his verdict, 'There is no facile "moral equivalence" between the two crimes.'[18]

The different approaches of the two combatants, played out through a series of replies and rejoinders, meant that no resolution was possible. As Chomsky noted in his final statement:

> [Hitchens] begins by placing his question 'before the house': 'Can the attacks of September 11 be compared to an earlier outrage committed by Americans? And should they be so compared?' *His* question. If he wants to consider that question, fine, but I didn't raise it or discuss it, nor will I now.[19]

But, of course, no resolution was intended. The specific debate was simply a sideshow in the wider spectacle of Hitchens' devious and decadent Left.

Even before the dénouement of the debate with Chomsky, who would stand forever condemned of 'intellectual and … moral disgrace',[20] Hitchens had marched on in a long comment for the *Spectator*, introduced on the cover as 'Damn the Doves'. Sam Husseini was again put on trial to establish that any dissent was 'denial' through 'the simple refusal to admit that a painful event has occurred', 'a cheery rationalisation of something ghastly' or 'a crude shifting of blame'.[21]

Hitchens also used his collection of brief thoughts for the *Guardian* to scatter charges. A poem of Edna St Vincent Millay's was a reminder that 'the American pacifist and anti-militarist tradition hasn't always been so morally dull'.[22] A note on the 1973 coup in Chile which slew Salvador Allende and brought Augusto Pinochet to power observed, 'I haven't yet heard anyone insult our comrades by saying that Chilean democrats took out their righteous rage about this by committing mass murder in Manhattan, but these days one has to be ready for infinite stupidity.'[23] And there were not one but two references to the double menace of the playwright Harold Pinter and the journalist John Pilger, who had adopted 'that renowned Muslim-baiter Slobodan Milosevic' as 'their last brave cause'. Hitchens pictured himself 'looking out at a gutted Capitol or charred White House and reading Pinter or Pilger on how my neighbourhood had been asking for it'.[24]

Hitchens had finally overstepped the mark. Pinter, with six other artists, may have written to the *Independent* to warn, 'Out of the carnage and rubble of a new crusade [against Afghanistan, Iraq, and other countries] will come new terrorists even more desperate and ruthless than before',[25] but that was far from applause for the attacks on New York and Washington. Pinter and Pilger each wrote to the *Guardian*, and Hitchens was forced into a retraction for the first and only time. Only Pinter was acknowledged, and then only for the 9–11 reference, and even then Hitchens blamed the incident on the failure of an editor to remove his misstatement, but still, 'At a time like this, it is very important that there be no jeering or witch-hunting.'[26]

For Hitchens, this was no more than a minor annoyance. Pinter may have received an apology, but Chomsky and the other masochists of the Left had no access to the 'mainstream' media in the US and Britain. So Hitchens advanced as a 'lone' intellectual, albeit one secured by numerous supporters as a 'singularly insightful ... critic of American policy and culture', the 'honourable man of the left', and the 'authentic voice of dissent'.[27]

The march was carried out in double-quick time. With the image of the Islamic fascists well established, Hitchens could erect the alternative of American greatness, from the 'exemplary' response of its citizens towards Muslims in the United States to 'the huge reserve strength' which could withstand future atrocities.[28] And he could cast his eyes beyond the upcoming war against Afghanistan to the next venue for battle, say, an assault on Iraq or a strike against Hezbollah:

I had to confess my worries to another administration person the other night. 'So what you are telling me,' I said, 'is that the only ones apart from me who worry about under-reaction are wholly owned subsidiaries of the Ariel Sharon lobby?'

'That's about it,' he replied, a touch too contentedly for my taste.[29]

There were awkward moments. The English columnist Julie Burchill cheerfully became a born-again supporter of the US,

'11 September turned me triumphantly and shamelessly around. Christopher Hitchens is my hero.' But she added an uncomfortable twist, 'Still, I knew I was right about the Soviets in Afghanistan; like the democracies in Spain, we could have stopped them there.'[30] Other new confederates, such as Ramesh Ponnuru in the *National Review*, were ruthless in the reduction of Hitchens' 'liberalism':

Liberals should not support the war because the Taliban is hostile to feminism. They should support it because they are patriots. That is why most of them actually do support it. They are better than their ideology.[31]

But the 'contrarian' had succeeded, an invaluable icon for an America which could be reassured that this was one foreigner who was a steadfast ally against the delusions of others on the 'Left', 'a Brit with a green card [who felt] more passionately about 11 September than most native-born Americans'.[32] He was vital at an uncomfortable moment in late October when American bombing and covert operations appeared to be making little impact on the Taliban, when there was uncertainty about supporting the Northern Alliance as the replacement for the Afghan regime, when there was pressure to suspend military operations both to allow humanitarian supplies into Afghan regions before winter snows arrived and to respect the period of Ramadan. As Michael Kelly put it bluntly in *The Washington Post*, 'Liberals and leftists who work in politics or who are serious about politics (such as the writer Christopher Hitchens and the political philosopher Michael Walzer) have pretty much lined up on the side of the government and the public, which is the side of giving war a chance.'[33]

When uncertainty suddenly turned into triumph in November with the fall of Mazar-e-Sharif and Kabul, Hitchens could celebrate not only the fall of the Taliban, but also the demise of the bad Left with a 'Ha Ha Ha to the Pacifists':

Looking at some of the mind-rotting tripe that comes my way from much of today's left, I get the impression that they go to bed saying: what have I done for Saddam Hussein or good old Slobodan or the Taliban today?

Well, ha ha ha, and yah, boo. It was obvious from the very start that the United States had no alternative but to do what it has done. It was also obvious that defeat was impossible.[34]

Not only Oliver Stone but bell hooks, who sinned by referring to a 1963 race-related bombing in Alabama as 'state terrorism', and Susan Sontag with her 'disdainful geopolitical analysis', were held up for further ridicule.[35]

It remained only to sweep aside any remaining qualms about civilian casualties or the state of opinion in the Islamic world to establish the general rule for future action:

War is hell .... But religious fascism is hell as well. Not only is it hell, but it also demands and guarantees war. Thus a victory over it is something that peace-lovers should actively welcome.

How strange and how sad that so few of them do.[36]

There was now the certainty of superiority: 'If, as the peaceniks like to moan, more bin Ladens spring up to take [Osama's] place, I can offer this assurance: Should that be the case, there are many, many more who will also spring up to kill him all over again .... We are both smarter and nicer, as well as sur-prisingly insistent that our culture demands respect, too.'[37]

At the same time that he was doing his victory dance, newspapers on both sides of the Atlantic were reviewing (and, in the case of the *Guardian*, extracting) *Letters from a Contrarian*. Although many of the compliments were at best back-handed ('the blend of the debonair and the moralizing ... can be well nigh insufferable, but give him his due – it probably wows undergraduates'), he had apparently 'written a sales brochure for radical sensibility as an attractively stylish posture' with a 'combination of dogged truth-telling and tactical snideness'. And although one shrewd reviewer noted, 'when, in a text littered with mentions of "my dear friend Salman Rushdie", "my dear friend Martin Amis" and so on, Hitchens counsels his readers not to mind the loneliness of dissent, even his dear friend Gore Vidal might want to tell him to come off it', others were captivated by the contrarian's image:

> How refreshing, in these times when what passes for public debate sounds more like a chorus humming one note than the cacophony of conflicting opinions it should be. How refreshing to come upon the Hitch so unapologetically truculent, so eager to scandalize and offend, if that's what it takes to draw attention to scandalous and offensive circumstances.[38]

Hitchens had reached the public intellectual's summit, exalted as an 'honourable man of the left', but already he faced the principle of entropy. The exultant 'Ha Ha Ha', far from killing off opposition, had given the enemy an opening. A *Guardian* reader noted crisply that the 'criticisms of leftist and ethnic minority anti-war movements bears no resemblance to the actual debates in these communities'.[39] George Monbiot captured the essence of Hitchens' 'smarter and nicer' slogan, 'This new triumphalism is sliding effortlessly into a new imperialism. It conflates armed and ethical success, munitions and morality', and then offered the prescient warning that the 'repetition of Mrs Thatcher's injunction – "just rejoice, rejoice" – may prove to be a little premature'.[40] Joan Smith in the *Independent* marvelled:

> It has been fascinating to watch [Hitchens] shift politically in recent weeks, heaping ad hominem abuse on 'peaceniks' and making the demonstrably absurd claim that the US had no alternative to the bombing …. His transformation is so complete that a friend of mine watched an entire edition of the BBC's Question Time 10 days ago under the impression that one of the panellists, clearly present to air his reactionary views, was Christopher. It was in fact his thoroughly delightful but ferociously right-wing brother, Peter.[41]

For victory was never complete. The stoic fortitude of Americans had suddenly disappeared in scares over anthrax, air crashes and passengers with box-cutters, and Hitchens' swagger was not so bold: 'Has there ever been such a contrast between supreme confidence overseas and round-the-clock jitters at home? ... The whole cult of "national security" depends upon the cultivation of national insecurity.'[42] He found that his new comrades in the War on Terror could be too enthusiastic, proposing the torture of suspects: 'There will have to be vigilance to ensure that such moronic and inhuman views (and people) are handled with tongs from now on.'[43]

And what was to come after Kabul and the imminent conquest of other towns such as Kandahar and Kunduz? Hitchens reached the end of the year with the recitation, 'We are rid of one of the foulest regimes on earth, while one of the most vicious crime families in history has been crippled and scattered', and a parting shot at Chomsky. But the jibe at his old nemesis was a strained distortion, giving the false impression that Chomsky had predicted millions of deaths in Afghanistan from American military operations,[44] and Hitchens left hostages to fortune, 'It remains to help the Afghan exiles to return, to save the starving and to consolidate the tentative emancipation of Afghan women.'[45]

It was not just that Osama bin Laden had not been captured or killed. US authorities were already announcing their lack of interest in long-term 'nation-building' in Afghanistan. Not only the War on Terror but life after the war was moving through an inconclusive transition. Hitchens was adrift – how many times could he repeat the proclamation of victory?

In early January the columnist-turned-warrior paused, as 'the continued bombing of remote caves and hillsides [began] to look like a piece of grand-opera petulance, a sort of pique at the failure of Osama bin Laden or [Taliban leader Mullah] Omar to do us the favour of a "dead or alive" appearance'. Worse, his presumption that a ground assault was being delayed by 'the fear of taking casualties' would soon be tested with unfortunate results.[46] US forces moved into eastern Afghanistan, only to be embarrassed in Operation ANACONDA when they were pinned down for up to 48 hours by enemy ambushes. Eight soldiers died, and American commanders aborted the effort.

Hitchens fretted. He worried about the US relationship with Israel, the corporate crisis fostered by the collapse of Enron, the problems of Americanism, the lack of serious news coverage on television and the cold of Washington DC.[47] He gave Henry Kissinger, America's 'own war criminal', a kick for old time's sake.[48] Gaps were appearing in his support for the Bush Administration: not only was he voicing concern about 'the question of proportionality' in the protracted bombing of Afghanistan, he was joining the criticisms of indefinite detention, both of prisoners from the Afghan conflict and of other 'terrorists', at Camp X-Ray on the US base at Guantanamo Bay, Cuba: 'There is no Devil's Island solution to this crisis.'[49] There was even a hint of the 'what did George know before 9–11?' controversy, which would flare up the following summer: 'We're left now with the appalling situation of a national security regime, which has for years been given millions of dollars to talk loud about national security and terrorism. It seems it knew, or could have known about and had identified, many of the perpetrators of the September 11 aggression, but did not do so.'[50]

On the first anniversary of the Bush inauguration, Hitchens reviewed his description of the President as 'uncultured … uneducated … incurious … a glove puppet and proud of it'. His updated compliments were far from straightforward – 'the measure of Bush's success' was that he had 'not sought to outgrow his limited stature' – and he dared to speculate that Bush's recent choking on a pretzel may have had something to do with a fall from the wagon.[51] As for Bush's advisers, with his heavy-handed approach to internal security, Attorney General John Ashcroft 'now appear[ed] to believe that he has been reborn as the tsar of Russia'.[52] There was more than a touch of irony, given Hitchens' patrolling of dissent, in the complaint, 'On the home front, I am told by Ari Fleischer, the semi-articulate White House spokesman to "watch what you say".'[53] And there was a reversal of fortune when, appearing on MSNBC's national talk show *Hardball*, which had feted him weeks earlier, Hitchens called the death penalty 'barbaric'. The host, Chris Mathews, reminded him:

> That's your opinion. Living over here, you must live with our social mores. We believe it's an appropriate response if someone kills somebody to get knocked off themselves.

When Hitchens persisted in his protest, he was chided to 'stick with [the discussion of] John Walker [Lindh]', the US citizen being tried for fighting with the Taliban.[54]

There was more disenchantment to come. The Bush Administration, opening up the post Afghan battlefront, declared the 'Axis of Evil' of Iraq, Iran and North Korea. Hitchens was unimpressed with both the rhetoric and the possibilities: '[Axis and evil] fail, both as terms and as description, to live up to the high moral tone that was properly set by those events [of September 11] .... I am asked to endorse in advance any move that might be made by an overconfident superpower whose leaders appear to be making up foreign policy as they go along. For some reason, this doesn't make me feel any safer.'[55]

The contrarian needed to renew himself with another cause, one which offered a fresh triumph over the real enemy of the 'Left'. So, having just derided the notion of an Axis of Evil, Hitchens prodded the Bush Administration for being too cautious in its campaign against Saddam Hussein, 'One has to inquire how it is that an American government, so apparently decided on a new Iraqi regime, can afford to be so indifferent to the actual Iraqi opposition.'[56] Bolstered by the prospect of a new war, Hitchens could turn the troubled aftermath of Afghanistan into hope:

> It's just as well for our troops to have experience in this kind of warfare, because we'll be fighting these people for a long time. Not necessarily in Afghanistan, but people like that .... It's useful practice, because they will have to keep on killing them.[57]

And he could renew his personal campaign: 'I'm not surprised at criticism from the "Ramadanistas" – the ones who said we should wait around until they decide to regroup. I don't care what they think .... It's one long bleat from these guys and gals.'[58]

Unfortunately, no sooner had the call to war been sounded than another complication intervened. In March, the escalating conflict between Israel and Palestine became a front-page crisis with suicide bombings in Israel and Israeli military operations in the West Bank, culminating in the 'massacre' at Jenin, the siege of Yasser Arafat's headquarters and the stand-off at the Church of the Nativity in Bethlehem. Hitchens, a long-time supporter of a Palestinian state, had to join George Bush in setting aside Iraq and addressing the issue. As he had asked only days earlier, 'Can any attack on Iraq be justified without a parallel settlement for the Palestinians?'[59]

For the first time since 9–11, Hitchens fell into disillusion-ment and despair. In an extraordinary commentary for the *Mirror*, the latest version of the contrarian vied with his earlier incarnation. Hitchens began with a jab at the Left in defence of the President: 'Bush "gets" [the War on Terror], in a way that many liberal intellectuals have failed to', but he then proposed his transformation into an honourable opponent of the Administration. He wrote that the notion of 'America's war' had eclipsed earlier hope of 'the chance to bond with other civilised societies' and betrayed 'the essential smallness of George Bush'. Because this was a criticism which fit all too well with those put by observers such as Susan Sontag and even Noam Chomsky, who had urged international cooperation to address the threat raised by Al-Qa'eda, Hitchens hastened to maintain his distance from the dovish tendency:

> Unlike the cults who now wish us harm, we are not conditioned to worship leaders or to blindly follow demagogues. Any criticism of the commanders in chief must be a criticism we are willing to share among ourselves, because this right and this duty is, among many other such rights and duties, what we are fighting about in an argument which we did not start but must be willing to finish.[60]

Through this negotiation of his position, Hitchens would criticise Bush and his advisers, but he would do so as the proper defender of the War on Terror-*cum*-War on Iraq. He maintained the vigilance over the 'thousands of immigrants … rounded up in the US after September 11', juxtaposing

Ashcroft's negation of 'the rights of the accused' with Bush's argument 'that US soldiers should be exempt from international law', while explaining to his readers, 'The US Administration refuses to say whether it wants a military junta in Baghdad, a monarchy, a vassal – or even an Iraqi state at all.' Specifically, 'the Bush Administration ... has been keeping the Iraqi opposition at arm's length.'[61]

And this was not all. Hitchens was noticing other faultlines in the War on Terror. Like bombs of the martial military junta he had vilified, Hitchens recalled that the original network of the 9–11 attackers relied not only on camps in Afghanistan, but also on the funding and logistics of America's supposed friends: 'The bin Laden/Mullah Omar crime family was trained in Afghanistan by the Pakistani secret police and paid for by Saudi Arabian money. The American "national security" class looked (and looks) upon the Pakistani secret police and the Saudi Arabian royal family as friends and allies.'[62]

Yet, a year after 11 September, Hitchens' opposition was not one of restraint on the Administration; to the contrary, he was more hawkish than the hawks. The Bush Administration had committed itself only to the liberation of Iraq; Hitchens wanted much more. He not only sought a specific, if ill-defined, place for an 'Iraqi opposition' (presumably, this was the Iraqi National Congress which, contrary to the impression given by Hitchens, had been fostered and nurtured by agencies of the US Government) to take power after Saddam; he also sought campaigns against the Saudi and Pakistani regimes who had been essential to the American prosecution of the War on Terror or, at least, the War on Afghanistan. He railed in frustration, 'The obscurantists and fanatics [of Riyadh and Islamabad] were nurtured in the bosom of the same "national security" apparatus that so grotesquely, if not criminally, failed to protect our civil society a year ago', even as he clung to the conclusion, 'The very complexity and subtlety of the task is one of the things that makes this war worth fighting.'[63]

Caught up in complexities that defied the simplicity of his good versus others' evil, Hitchens took refuge in the War on the Left. He lashed out at Tariq Ali, in his 'ridiculous' book *The Clash of Fundamentalisms*, as 'Wrong. Wrong twice. As wrong as could be.'[64] He assured, 'Only a complete moral idiot can believe for an instant that we are fighting against the wretched of the earth. We are fighting, as I said before, against the scum of the earth.'[65] He proudly gloated that a long-time enemy had joined the 'dovecote' over Iraq: 'I must say, however, that Henry Kissinger has never let me down, as a person to consult before making up my own mind.'[66]

And he escaped by sheltering within the inevitability of war. On 18 September, Hitchens noted that the attack on Iraq was 'going to happen' and worried:

> No assurance has been required, at least in public, that the Israeli government will stay out of it. No programme either for democracy or for Kurdish self-government has been produced.
>
> It seems Washington is willing to let all this wait until after the crux moment, which is approaching a great deal faster than most people appreciate.[67]

Seven days later, none of this mattered, for 'the long period of unwise vacillation and moral neutrality seems to be drawing to a close, and this is a good thing in itself'.[68]

Finding resolution through simplicity, Hitchens left himself only one path for his writing. There would be no return to the questioning of the contradictions in a foreign policy which targeted Afghanistan and Iraq but absolved Saudi Arabia and Pakistan, to the criticism of 'homeland security', to anything less than a portrayal of George Bush as the capable President. Hitchens' contributions in autumn 2002 to *Vanity Fair* would be anodyne paeans to 'America' through a journey along the old Route 66 and a promotion of the US abroad in his depiction of Qatar, which had virtuously agreed to site a US base for future military operations: 'To the extent that Qatar has an "Arab street", it half wishes it were a street somewhere in America.'[69]

The only way forward was to complete the demolition of the 'Left'. In October 2002, Hitchens petitioned for divorce from *The Nation* (which, despite being part of the delusional fringe, published its essayist's rude goodbye in a final 'Minority Report' and noted 'with keen regret' the loss of 'his eloquent and passionate voice and his elegantly crafted prose'). According to Hitchens, the final break was prompted by the request of the magazine's editors, marking the first anniversary of 11 September, for readers' letters. He was simply appalled at the responses:

Most of those letters in an ordinary week would not have been chosen for publication because they just weren't up to the standard. They were very weak and badly written. Instead of which there were three pages of them, all of which said: 'Here's what Sept. 11 means to me – I've discovered I live in a fascist state.' I said, 'Well, that's goodbye.' I don't want to have anything to do with reinforcing that kind of public opinion.[70]

Hitchens' farewell began with a lecture on Iraq which established beyond doubt that a 'crazy' and thieving 'sadistic megalomaniac', Saddam Hussein, had: 1) 'acquired some of the means of genocide and hopes to collect some more'; 2) supported international nihilism by allowing the Palestinian Abu Nidal to shelter in Baghdad in his final years; and 3) 'rejoice[d] in the attacks on New York and Washington and Pennsylvania'. It was '70 percent likely' that an Iraqi official had met Mohammad Atta, one of the hijackers of 9–11, and there were 'suggestive links' between Baghdad and a 'gang' who also had 'suggestive links' with Osama bin Laden.[71]

Having confirmed himself in his wisdom, Hitchens could offer doubts about the Bush Administration for not being forceful enough on Iraq and Iran, as well as allowing 'the Palestinian plight ... to worsen', establishing his credentials for an objective observation of the real enemy:

It's obvious to me that that 'antiwar' side would not be convinced even if all the allegations made against Saddam Hussein were proven, and even if the true views of the Iraqi people could be expressed .... I have come to realize that [*The Nation*] takes a side in this argument, and is becoming the voice and the echo chamber of those who truly believe that John Ashcroft is a greater menace than Osama bin Laden.[72]

A few days later, Hitchens redoubled his charges and his invective. The 'peace-mongers', with their 'moral relativism', 'not only ... ignore the anti-Saddam civilian opposition, [they sent] missions to console the Ba'athists in their isolation, and speak of the invader of Kuwait and Iran and the butcher of Kurdistan as if he were the victim and George W. Bush the aggressor'. The anti-war movement was reduced to one organisation, the International Action Center, chaired by former Attorney General Ramsay Clark, which was 'a sinister sect' and 'quasi-Stalinist group'. These Leftists were appeasers of 'the Socialist Party of Serbia, the Ba'ath Party of Iraq and the Workers' Party of North Korea', employing 'arguments as contemptible as those on whose behalf they have been trotted out'.[73]

Covering his Left flank with the credentials that he had 'done a good deal of marching and public speaking about Vietnam, Chile, South Africa, Palestine and East Timor in his time (and would do it all again)', Hitchens returned to the breaking point of Kosovo. His position of 1999 had been concerned more with Serb internationalists than the Kosovars, but it was now recast as preventing 'the extermination of [Europe's] oldest Muslim minority'. Chomsky, even though he had praised the removal of the 'brutal and corrupt' Milosevic regime as 'an important step forward for the region',[74] was vilified as having 'thought and [written] of national-socialist and Orthodox Serbia as if it were mounting a gallant resistance to globalization'.

Hitchens had nothing left but insults and the dream of another 'Ha Ha Ha'. Reduced to charging the 'affectless, neutralist, smirking' Left with preferring Jimmy Carter to George Bush, he warned, 'I am booked to have a reunion in Baghdad with several old comrades who have been through hell. We shall not be inviting anyone who spent this precious time urging democratic countries to give Saddam another chance.'[75]

This time he would not get away unchallenged. Katha Pollitt, a former colleague at *The Nation*, revealed Hitchens' new clothes – 'What kind of contrarian leaves a column – called "Minority Report," no less – because too many of the readers disagree with him?' – and his straw men. She noted the false equation, 'The antiwar movement equals the left and the left equals the followers of Ramsey Clark, defender of Slobodan Milosevic and assorted Hutu *genocidaires* and other thugs, who is the founder of the International Action Center, which is closely linked to ANSWER, a front for the Workers World Party', and then brought out all those whom Hitchens had tried to place in the shadows:

> You know that Edward Said, Ann Snitow, Doug Henwood, Laura Flanders and Adolph Reed care as much about human rights as you do, don't regard Saddam Hussein as a people's hero, don't secretly gloat over 9/11 .... Why do you write as if these antiwar voices – or Vietnam Veterans Against the War, or the National Organization for Women, or your presidential candidate of choice, Ralph Nader – did not exist? ... Why aren't Mark Danner, Aryeh Neier and Ronald Dworkin on your radar screen? Who died and made Ramsey Clark commissar?[76]

Pollitt had struck home. Hitchens blatantly misrepresented her description of the anti-war rally in Washington,[77] converted the marchers into 'those who ... have attended demonstrations the message of which they don't really understand', and then allied them with 'right-wing' foes such as 'the Scowcroft–Eagleburger reactionaries, the majority of the CIA and the Pat Buchananite isolationists'. Pollitt responded, 'You set the equation up so that there is no way to oppose invading Iraq except to be a coward or a covert admirer of dictatorship and theocracy.'[78]

Of course, there would be more tributes to Hitchens, the 'independent radical', after *The Nation* bust-up. *Salon*, the electronic magazine, profiled him as the 'in-house contrarian', confirming, 'The term "the American left" is as near to being meaningless or nonsensical as any term could really be in politics'. Two weeks later, Hitchens would appear as *Slate*'s new columnist, offering covering fire for the Administration's 'armchair generals' ('Shall we inquire into the "armchair" or otherwise sedentary lives of those who sympathized with Milosevic, or who published euphemisms about al-Qaida, or who went on fatuous hospitality trips to Baghdad and ended up echoing Baathist propaganda?'), defining 'anti-Americanism' and foreseeing a benevolent American imperialism. He appeared in forums on the East and West Coasts, in New York humiliating the writer Vivian Gornick (guilty of heaping too much praise on Orwell's Englishness, she was rewarded with a Hitchens remark about 'languorous fellatio'), at Berkeley expounding on the relevance of Orwell and his Englishness. The Toronto *Globe and Mail* reported, 'He's absolutely certain he's right'; the *Star* faithfully recorded his summary of the Left's 'head-in-the-sand' failings.[79]

But, without 'Minority Report' to keep controversy stoked, without the regular appearances in the *Guardian*, with only the 'attack Iraq now' refrain, Hitchens was appearing far from timeless. A diatribe on National Public Radio in October 2002, opening and closing the argument in less than two paragraphs, exhausted all possibilities:

One is not confronting an insurgency by people deprived or oppressed in the Third World or anything of the kind; instead, one is confronting an aggressive totalitarian dictatorship that's proved its credentials both as aggressive and as totalitarian many, many times and whose megalomaniacal leader quite obviously does not understand ... the rationality of things like deterrence and containment, who's repeatedly proved he's not a rational actor in his own country or outside.

And so the question will be, for anyone willing to confront it seriously: Would you rather confront such a person now or later at a time of his choosing and under circumstances where he might, as [North Korean leader] Kim Jong Il now can, himself practice deterrence, or would you just rather fold the whole tent and say, 'Well, let him get on with it'? And, after all, as people who, like your last caller and as many of the peace movement, as they like to call themselves, say, not have a war with Iraq at all, except the war is not going to be with Iraq or on Iraq, and the propaganda betrays itself in the slogan just as the Iraqi people were humiliated last week – publicly, massively degraded by being forced, I mean to say, to affirm that Iraq is Saddam and Saddam is Iraq. All those who say we don't want a war with Iraq are making the same mistake. This is a confrontation with someone who doesn't represent the Iraqis, but who does represent a totalitarian, aggressive principle.

When a questioner challenged, '[You're] spending a lot more time attacking the Left than [you are] actually attacking the very, very weak case that the administration has made for the war against Iraq', Hitchens spent several minutes of free association avoiding that case before proving his enquirer's point: 'It's just that you really do seem to find Mr. Bush more irritating than Mr. Hussein. In that respect at least, you disagree with the majority of the people of Iraq and Kurdistan.' Inconveniently, the questioner pressed on, 'By your logic, then, I should also support the bombing of North Korea tomorrow because we have actual evidence that North Korea … has weapons of mass destruction,' forcing Hitchens' last-stand refrain, 'So, again, you see, you're trying an idiotic – oh, I don't mean to insult you, but I do mean to make you try and think again. You're trying a foolish double-standards comparison where one doesn't apply.'[80]

Occasionally, Hitchens realised the problems with his simple dedication to the new war. He told *Salon*, 'The problem of post-Saddam Iraq is a grave one, no matter how the post-Saddam stage is reached.'[81] He was in the depths of pessimism when *Newsweek* gave him the opportunity to pass comment on 2002: 'Possibly in no year have relations between America and the rest of the world been more fraught. Certainly in no year have they declined so precipitously from the height of the preceding one.'[82]

'Orwell' could save Hitchens from such troublesome doubts. The promotion of *Orwell's Victory*, retitled *Why Orwell Matters* for the US market, kept the contrarian in the public eye. George gave him the pretext to insist, '[Orwell] would have seen straight though the characters who chant "No War On Iraq"',[83] and to recycle anti-Left arguments in the guise of clear 'language'.

Hitchens again commanded, 'Don't say "war on Iraq" or "with Iraq," there is no sense in which it can be said that Saddam Hussein represents the Iraqi people.' (At no point did Hitchens acknowledge that, in his clearly defined 'war against

Saddam', the Iraqi people rather than the leader were likely to be the first casualties and those dealing with the long-term consequences.)[84] He again ruled out any consideration of 'cause' for enemy action, leaping to the Saddam–Osama secret marriage: 'Enfolded in any definition of "terrorism", it seems to me, there should be a clear finding of fundamental irrationality. Al-Qaida meets and exceeds all of these criteria, to a degree that leaves previous nihilist groups way behind.'[85] A discourse on 'evil' became the pretext for an attack on the 'reactionary simpleton', Robert Fisk.[86] Only in a consideration of the term 'weapons of mass destruction' did Hitchens offer a fresh analysis, exposing the motive of the US Government in its use of the phrase:

You could not properly 'inspect' or diagnose Iraq, after all that's been endured and discovered, without being in control of it. Thus, those who emphasize 'WMDs' might as well be honest and admit that they are talking partly about latency. And those who sincerely want to see a genuine invigilation ought to confess that 'inspection' is only another demand for (and condition of) 'regime change'.[87]

Unfortunately for Hitchens, the Orwellian posturing soon wore thin. Lacking fresh ideas or perspectives, he was too wedded to attack to keep his cloak of 'decency'. In a February 2003 interview, after one more recitation of Saddam's bond with 9–11's terrorists ('there may be a sort of understanding between his people and al-Qaeda, a sort of non-aggression pact') and another invocation of 'democracy' based on little more than the assertion of 'an open society' in Kurdistan, he enlivened the discussion by wishing that Al Gore and Hillary Clinton 'get some sort of wasting disease'. He capped the interview with the end of his political journey. Not only did he defend the President he had long derided as ill-educated, ill-mannered and unfit for office ('Gore and wife say that Bush is picking a fight with Iraq? Fuck them'), he swore allegiance: 'I'd vote for Bush. The important thing is this: Is a candidate completely serious about prosecuting the war on theocratic terrorism to the fullest extent? Only Bush is.'[88]

So the 'contrarian' could support his President while criticising 'a certain kind of arrogance and hubris about this administration that fills me with horror [with] the reappointment of people ... who've shown their contempt for Congress and for the democratic process, and shown their contempt for other people's constitutions, and democratic processes as well, and have ... visited aggression and atrocity on other people'. And, even as he proclaimed, 'Bush Marching to War? Nonsense,' he could walk hand-in-hand with that Administration towards a long-ordained display of American shock and awe.[89]

5

Beyond the Spirit of '68

Eight months into the War on Terror, there was a staged battle at the Institute of Education in London. With the failure to round up Osama in Afghanistan or to round up allies for a showdown with Baghdad, there was a lull in the page 1 headlines. Despite this respite, or perhaps because of it, there was expectation among those in the intellectual know. Christopher Hitchens was going to slug it out with Tariq Ali.[1]

There were others on the podium. Onora O'Neill, who had just delivered the Reith Lectures on human rights, was being practical: 'What is the evidence of an orthodox Islamic Empire? ... What can be done to build trust amongst peoples seeking a way forward?' Anatole Lieven, the Carnegie Endowment fellow and *Times* columnist, thoughtfully negotiated a position where he had supported retaliation against Al-Qa'eda but now feared that the American-led war on terrorism, absent 'a new commitment to humanitarian principles and a new sense of international law and international institutions', would never succeed. Jacqueline Rose, with her Freudian approach to language, would link the rhetoric of Hitchens to that of Osama bin Laden, Tony Blair, and Ariel Sharon: 'At best, two boys in a playground fighting, at worst two dead men talking ... very exciting, very ineffectual, and very dangerous.'

But, unfairly perhaps, it was the two men at opposite ends of the table who brought out most of the audience. The rivalry had been on tour: Hitchens and Ali debated in Washington the previous month in an exchange so heated that Michael Berube asked 'whether Christopher might not consider hiring media consultants from Al-Jazeera to help him with his self-presentation',[2] and that morning they had traded charges of 'untruth', 'pacifis[m], neutralis[m]' and 'warmonger[ing]' on the *Today* BBC radio programme until the presenter, John

Humphrys, separated them, 'We'll have to leave them there and let them decide on it all.'[3]

On this occasion, Hitchens would come off far worse. He started with quick jabs at Ali, 'I'll try to avoid casuistry as well as prolixity' and 'I hope we have heard the last of [easy sneering at George Bush]; we have certainly heard the first of it.' He stood for the 'defence of civil and secular society' against 'theocratic fascism' in a fight which was 'global, to the knife, to the finish.' He was soon knocked off his polemical stride, however.

It was not Ali who landed the telling punches in response. He provided barbed comments on the 'thinker President' and the 'old [US] agent' Hamid Karzai and noted the complications of the Pakistani situation and Saudi support for Al-Qa'eda, but he stumbled when challenged if he would support any Western intervention in 'developing' countries, such as the British operation in Sierra Leone. Instead, Rose rattled the contrarian. Hitchens had embarked on another global charge against Islamic movements that had pressed for *sharia* law in Nigeria, burned synagogues in Tunisia and London, and persecuted Jews when Rose levelly noted her concern at Hitchens' evocation of the Dreyfus affair: 'It was the French, not Islamic theocracy, that put Dreyfus on trial.' When she received applause, Hitchens snapped his disdain, 'You'll clap anything.'

Inadvertently, Hitchens had donned the mantle of the 'lone' intellectual, no longer taking on Ali but the entire 'Left' audience. He lashed, 'I won't bore you with all that moral mushy stuff [about airliners, stuffed with terrified passengers, used as cruise missiles], even if many of you have already forgotten it.' Booed for evading a question with derision, he upped the ante, 'If you knew how you sound when you hissed, you wouldn't do it. You sound like such berks.' Finally, he resigned with a sneer, 'Anyone can get more applause than me .... If you haven't understood anything I've said up to now, you won't understand what I would say now.'

The clash fizzled out, although Hitchens still provoked, mock-applauding the audience and telling an elderly questioner, 'I assume you are from the subcontinent .... You will never have a problem with [religious extremism]. Your ideology will not allow that.' The gentleman replied in agitation, 'I am not from the subcontinent', drawing Hitchens' non-apology, 'We can all make mistakes', and, off-mike, 'Well, he certainly looks like he's from the subcontinent.'

There was something unsettling about the evening. (Not for Hitchens – any bruising of his ego would be salved by the post-debate festivities with the coterie of London columnists who awaited him.)[4] The unexpected emergence of Rose and, to a lesser extent, Lieven as the challenging contributors rather than Hitchens and Ali only highlighted the event behind the event: this wasn't meant to be as much a resolution of the future of the War on Terror as a contest for the Spirit of '68.

In *Letters to a Contrarian*, Hitchens referred to himself as 'a grizzled soixante-huitard, or survivor of the last intelligible era of revolutionary upheaval'.[5] More than 30 years later, the protesters from the streets and the universities were 50-somethings, and there was a legacy to be settled. As Frank Rich of the *New York Times* noted, the three protagonists of the Blumenthal affair of 1999 – Alexander Cockburn, Blumenthal and Hitchens – all 'had loose ties to the organized radical movement'.[6]

If Rich took his observation from the exalted to the mundane, noting, 'Without a vibrant mass movement, [independent radical journalists] tend to become disoriented. Their careers loom more importantly as approaching middle or old age remind them about the need to feather their own nest,' 9–11 renewed the political struggle. *The Economist* may have insisted, 'The true comparison is not with 1969, but with 1939', and Michael Kazin in the *Washington Post* may have offered, 'Most liberals and a few chastened radicals view the Sept. 11 attacks through the prism of World War II', but the CVs of these combatants were firmly anchored in the 1960s. Joy Press, in the *Village Voice*, anointed Martin Amis and Christopher Hitchens as the 'belligerati', and Tariq Ali was soon promoting the term for the 'fond purring and trite eulogies' of 'new empire loyalists' such as Hitchens and Salman Rushdie.[7] This internecine scrapping was eye-catching, but unhelpful. Complex debates on the morality and efficacy of the 'War on Terror' were reduced to a settling of scores between veterans of the movement – the *Observer*'s summary of the London debate patronised Lieven as 'Hitchens with more nuances' and failed to notice the presence of Rose.[8] With this storyline, Hitchens could represent his barracking of former comrades as a broader quest for the decent survival of 'revolution'. The *Guardian*'s introduction to the extracts from *Contrarian* proclaimed:

> The spirit of 1968 may be a distant memory, but a new generation of radicals live in hope of making the world a better place. Christopher Hitchens offers them the wisdom of a seasoned campaigner.[9]

In this post-1960s procession, Hitchens' train would be carried by John Lloyd. A former editor of the *New Statesman*, Lloyd had already embarked on a crusade against the 'bad' Left. He had been upset by the May Day 2001 demonstration, 'a mockery of democratic dissent, at times violent (though in minor ways) and wholly uninterested in reason or explanation', and noted that George Monbiot had also disapproved of the violence on the day.[10] Yet, whereas Monbiot redoubled his efforts for demonstration and protest, Lloyd found coherence after 11 September in a simple test. Tony Blair's 'Third Way', framed by Anthony Giddens and Robert Cooper, was the only way forward, and those who did not follow it, especially the 'anti-globalisation groups', were tagged: 'The left must revive the drive for "cosmopolitan democracy," giving voice to the excluded billions. It will fail if it persists in anti-Americanism.'[11] If the Far Right were in the ascendent in Europe, this irrational Left, with its criticism of a 'good' America, was to blame. If a figure such as the Italian political philosopher Toni Negri wrote a best-selling book on 'Empire', it must be the legacy of an intellectual violence of the 1970s: 'with others in the global movements, [Negri has] taken a position that describes a moral equivalence between the US and its allies, on the one hand, and terrorism of all sorts on the other.'[12] In a conflation worthy of Orwell and Hitchens, Lloyd mixed all the elements of protest, treated them with the 'with us or against us' formula, and produced a frightening concoction. By early 2002, he was proclaiming that the 'traditions of pacifism, individualism and anti-fascism now meet another: anti-Americanism, not confined to the left in developed states, but most virulent on [sic] it, inspired by powerful (among the young) prophets as Professor Noam Chomsky, sharpened by the anti-globalisation movement which tends to equate America with capitalism'. According to Lloyd, for these bad Leftists, 'imperialism and crimes of America are the only matter which may enter the discussion', marking 'an abdication of the left's own attachment to enlightenment rationalism'.[13]

There was a self-defeating quality to Lloyd's work. With its appearance in the same publications that had featured Hitchens, it smacked of 'me, too'. And there was a limit to how many times he could beat the drum. Unable to vent all his fury through his essays, Lloyd wrote a Letter to the Editor accusing the *New Statesman* of 'abdicat[ing] criticism and analysis for denunciation and cynicism'. The editor, Peter Wilby, responded, 'There is no reason why John, who is a regular contributor, should have a privileged position to attack the editorial line of the *New Statesman*'; Lloyd screamed censorship to any newspaper or journal that would listen.[14]

Perhaps in recognition that if you can't surpass your hero, promote him, Lloyd offered the iconic portrait of the 'America-loving' belligerati on the six-month anniversary of 9–11. The same *New Statesman* that was supposedly censoring him offered space for 'In Bed with Bush: Rushdie, Hitchens and Amis cosy up to America'. (What is more, there was a classic front cover. The Hitch is sitting up in bed, cigarette once more in hand, eyes piercing the camera, tucked with computer imagery under an American flag duvet and a teddy bear with George Bush's superimposed face. Snuggling against each of Hitchens' shoulders, pulling Old Glory tightly around them, are Salman Rushdie and Martin Amis.)

Lloyd's paean struggled for clarity, even as it fused his trio (and himself) in 'the war ... between the decent left, which is on the side of those willing to fight Islamic fascism, and the rigidly anti-American left'. The blanket call for a 'Left' intervention did not regard any specific case such as Afghanistan or Iraq. Instead, Lloyd used the general definition of a national interest of halting 'mass murder' to smuggle in a vaguer call to arms against all 'regimes that use the paraphernalia and practices of fascism'.

Where the essay was telling, in implications both deliberate and unwitting, was the re-marking of 1968: 'Hitchens sees, among the generation whose most active spirit were far leftists, "a new politics" of engagement emerging, pointed up by such figures as Joschka Fischer and Daniel Cohn-Bendit.' Lloyd's leap was to equate this engagement, first and foremost, with 'anti Americanism'. He cited Rushdie's warning that the 'ideological enemy that may turn out to be harder to defeat than militant Islam' was 'anti-Americanism, which is presently taking the world by storm', and quoted with glee Amis' rejection of Chomsky: 'Anti-Americanism doesn't impress me as a very rational position.'

The irony, of course, was that the Spirit of '68 was never a clarion call to ensure a proper 'America' by joining it in intervention, but a stand against that intervention in Vietnam, given Washington's far from clear defence of human rights. To reclaim the spirit, Lloyd had to make it over as the embrace of American power. He quoted Hitchens:

> I do think America is a great idea. I think the American revolution is the only one which has lasted, the only one left. It still has a dynamic. It is the only one capable of a universal application.

Even this was not enough for Lloyd, who extended the point with the plaudit 'that this brought [Hitchens] close to the position of Francis Fukuyama ... that the values derived from the American revolution represent the highest achievement of political economy and that there can now be no credible challenge to them'. (Lloyd might have been blissfully unaware that Fukuyama, along with Donald Rumsfeld, Dick Cheney and Paul Wolfowitz, was a member in the mid-1990s of the Project for a New American Century, which called for an American superiority of power – economic and military as well as cultural and ideological – over any other country or group of countries.)[15]

Lloyd's selling of the new Spirit of '68 soon ran into difficulties, not because of snide Leftist critiques without, but from implosions within. Rushdie may have draped himself in the real Stars and Stripes for the cover of a French magazine,[16] but he was always a more cautious and nuanced supporter of 'America' than the bedtime variety observed by the *New Statesman*. True, he had written with scorn that 'America-hating has become a badge of identity, making possible a chest-beating, flag-burning rhetoric of word and deed that makes men feel good', and a fortnight after Lloyd's reverie, he added, 'The cleaning of those stables [in Afghanistan] by the US deserves a far better press than it is getting', praising the 'sheer gravity [with which] Americans, young and old, liberal and conservative, have been thinking and feeling their way through personal tragedy and global crisis'.[17]

Yet Rushdie was asking 'the world' to take note of these American people, not because they were supporting their government, but because they might be challenging it. Like the deviant Left, he reeled off a list of catastrophes brought on by the arrogance of the real 'belligerati', 'the hawks among America's makers of foreign policy'. He made an assertion that could have come from the 'anti-America' textbook: 'If America gets into bed with scumbags, it loses the moral high ground, and once that ground is lost, the argument is lost with it.' He even noted with foresight, 'If Saddam and his cronies are to be unseated, it's important to find a successor regime that doesn't require decades of propping up.'[18]

Like Hitchens, Rushdie warned about 'Islamists'.[19] Like Hitchens (and Lloyd), he moved from the religious to the secular variant of Islamic evil, considering action against Baghdad as 'a case that ought to appeal not just to militaristic Bushie-Blairite hawks but also to lily-livered bleeding-heart liberals'.[20] However, he never dropped his reservations about the US Government and 'its string of foreign policy mistakes .... A sober look at the case against America may serve US interests better than the patriotic "let's roll" arguments that are being trumpeted on every side.' Challenging Iraq, the Bush Administration risked unleashing 'a generation-long plague of anti-Americanism that may make the present epidemic look like a time of rude good health .... A war of liberation might just be one worth fighting. The war that America is currently trying to justify is not.'[21]

Amis was also proving a tenuous member of the belligerati, never fully engaging with the new Islamic enemy. When his initial response to 9–11 finally escaped existential reflection about 'the worldflash of a coming future', it failed to offer a ringing endorsement of the new US mission: 'Unless Pakistan can actually deliver Bin Laden, the American retaliation is almost sure to become elephantine. Then terror from above will replenish the source of all terror from below: unhealed wounds.'[22] Several months later, Amis wandered around religion and literature, took a passing shot at all creeds, singling out militant Islamists as 'misologists – haters of reason', and beat a final retreat from his own considerations: 'Even the plodding logic of the traffic lights looked obsolete. Why drive on the left? Why drive on the right?'[23] John Pilger flayed the departing writer:

> [Amis] had nothing to say about 'the conflicts we now face or fear', as he put it. Why not? Where was the spirit of Orwell and Greene? Where was a modest acknowledgement of history: a passing reflection on the impact of rapacious great power on vulnerable societies, which are the roots of the current 'terrorism'?[24]

If Amis was still willing to offer a quote on the shallowness of others such as Chomsky, his main concern in his writer's hideaway in Ecuador was defining himself through the past rather than the present. In summer 2002 he made his historical point with the publication of *Koba the Dread: Laughter and the 20 Million* and a series of newspaper and journal pieces both publicising and extending the book. The problem was not the shocked reiteration of the evidence – Stalin was indeed a very bad man, responsible for millions of deaths – but that those deaths became the platform for Amis's personal journey: he wrote a letter to his late father, a sympathiser with Communism, he heard his daughter's wailing as the cries of the gulag, he was disturbed when tyranny was converted into laughter by acquaintances who are 'old comrades'.

One of the 'old comrades' (indeed, the person raising a laugh with that greeting at a gathering in London) was Christopher Hitchens, who received an open letter from Amis:

It is still obscure to me why you wouldn't want to put more distance between yourself and these events than you do, with your reverence for Lenin and your unregretted discipleship of Trotsky .... Do you admire terror? I know you admire freedom.[25]

Amis set a high bar for Hitchens, reconstructing their friendship at the *New Statesman* in the mid-1970s by describing a Trotskyist who sold the *Socialist Worker* on the street corners at the weekend and delivered prose with 'the sense that the truth could be postponed'. The 'old comrades' line from 1999 became 'the laughter of forgetting .... It forgets the Twenty Million [victims of Stalin]'.

A welcome for Amis' exposure of fellow-travelling would have required, if not a recantation of Hitchens' personal views, then a renunciation of most of his past. So, having reconstructed himself to take on the deviant Left, Hitchens adjusted once more to fend off the anti-Communist wing of the political spectrum. Once more, the best defence was a good offence: in a review in *The Atlantic*, Hitchens took Amis to the woodshed of history and political philosophy, but first he set on the personal, the 'self-righteousness and superficiality that let [Amis] down' and the 'want of wit ... even about a feeble joke, [that] compromises his seriousness'. The Parthian shot returned to the personal, complementing John Pilger's challenge about Amis's contemporary retreat: 'Be very choosy about what kind of anti-communist you are, and be careful not to confuse the state of the world with that of your family, or your own "internal organs".'[26]

In his own 'open letter' in the *Guardian*, Hitchens revelled in retaliation. Double-edged sympathy ('Hardened as I am to hostile or philistine reviews, I can still imagine that you must be at least disappointed by the treatment you have been getting') gave way to a redress of history, with Hitchens playing his part in 1968 in Grosvenor Square, in Cuba, with 'old friends from Spain and Portugal and Greece', 'in close touch with student and worker groups in Poland and Czechoslovakia', all the while standing against the Soviet descendants of Stalin. It was Hitchens who fought the good fight then, with Amis keeping his distance at Oxford, and it was Hitchens who fought it now, while Amis sat in 'a pretty cushy spot in Uruguay'. So it was Hitchens who could admonish his 'dearest friend … giving pleasure to those who don't love you, as I do': 'Don't. Be. Silly.'[27]

Any reconstructed Spirit of '68 had been shattered. John Lloyd tried to recover the situation by using Amis' *Koba* for some contemporary Red-hunting: 'The British government has nobody in it of the prominence in the far left of D'Alema, Jospin, Scully or Fischer but it has its own figures with a reckoning still to make …. They were in great error, or worked with those who were, and they have let fall a great silence.'[28] Unsurprisingly, it was a call echoed by sections of a US press still fighting the Cold War: 'The question Amis asks [Hitchens] – "Do you admire terror?" – is not easily ducked. And it's the question that Amis is asking of all the apologists, all the infatuated.'[29]

Hitchens had won the battle but lost his belligerati; indeed, the skirmish with Amis threatened to expose the Contrarian's New Clothes. With his defence of the 'New Left' of the 1960s, his break with that 'Left' in the new millennium stood out in even greater relief. Almost all his named targets were veterans of the period: on the American side, Cockburn, Chomsky, Zinn and Sontag; for Britain and the Commonwealth, Pinter, Pilger and Tariq Ali.

Hitchens had demonstrated how Amis had set up a cartoonish New Left for Koba, but once he asked the question, 'How [had] the Left … degraded itself into little more than the appeasers of Islamic fascism?', it became clear that Hitchens' own struggle in the Age of Terror was never with an actual 'Left' but with a caricature of it. He never engaged, or intended to engage, with the diversity of expression in the aftermath of the attack. Pilger, Hitchens' token Left appeaser, had characterised Islamic peoples as victims of the 'West', and Tariq Ali, Hitchens' future sparring partner, had thrown the first punch: 'To say that the Manhattan and Pentagon bombers are "fascists with an Islamic face" can help whip up a war-frenzy, but it solves nothing, apart from being a wrong-headed analogy.'[30] However, there were other, equally pointed criticisms of US power, from Robert Fisk's warning that 'there will be inevitably, and quite immorally, an attempt to obscure the historical wrongs and the injustices that lie behind yesterday's firestorms', to Seumas Milne's 'They can't see why they are hated', to Rana Kabbani's assertion that 'terror has come home'.[31] There was the damning assessment of the *New Statesman* that 'American values too easily come over as shallow and hypocritical', even as one of its editors wrote in the same issue of 'the American Dream'. Charlotte Raven reminded readers, 'A bully with a bloody nose is still a bully.'[32]

Specific challenges extended Raven's query about a wronged and innocent nation. Jonathan Freedland criticised President Bush and questioned US foreign policy, 'A Washington or a Lincoln would have struggled to deal with this crisis. But today's Americans don't have a Washington; they have a W.'[33] Frances Stonor Saunders tellingly forecast 'the end of the open society' in the US; the *Guardian* chronicled the American possession of biological weapons and its refusal to support any international treaty challenging them.[34] As for the new enemy, Dilip Hiro noted that US insistence on maintaining troops in Saudi Arabia had fuelled the antagonism of Al-Qa'eda, and that mainstay of Leftism, *The Economist*, noted that the American government had reaped 'a bitter harvest' with its earlier support of Osama bin Laden.[35]

Most writers recognised that action must be taken against those responsible for the attacks on the World Trade Center and Pentagon, but the call for a 'civilised way' did not translate into unconditional support for a unilateral American response. Ahdaf Soueif warned against that, with the purported 'clash of civilisations', 'You could almost say that US officialdom, the media, and Hollywood dreamed this nightmare into reality.'[36] Fred Halliday emphasized a reliance on international law, Martin Woollacott advised caution and Jonathan Steele insisted that US use of force would 'only exacerbate the wider problem of international terror. The world must say so directly.'[37] Polly Toynbee warned against 'this swashbuckling nonsense about absolute good and evil', as Jon Snow suggested a 'war against hatred'.[38]

In this panoply of considerations, all of which appeared in the week following 9–11, Edward Said offered a touchstone commentary. Far from condoning or turning a blind eye to the attacks, Said set out a scathing criticism of any movement using 'Islam' to justify such violence:

> What is bad about all terror is when it is attached to religious and political abstractions and reductive myths that keep veering away from history and sense. This is where the secular consciousness has to try to make itself felt, whether in the US or in the Middle East. No cause, no God, no abstract idea can justify the mass slaughter of innocents, most particularly when only a small group of people are in charge of such actions and feel themselves to represent the cause without having a real mandate to do so.

Said had not abandoned his critique of US foreign policy and its 'mostly hidden sordid interests', but, searching for 'a still more critical sense of the actuality', he sought an alternative to the clash of civilisations between Washington and its new enemy: 'Demonisation of the Other is not a sufficient basis for any kind of decent politics, certainly not now when the roots of terror in injustice can be addressed, and the terrorists isolated, deterred, or put out of business.'[39]

Said's quest for some understanding was followed days later by the challenge of Arundhati Roy's essay, 'The Algebra of Infinite Justice'. She set the uncomfortable requirement of moving beyond an immediate reaction to events, and risking opprobrium for doing so, in a single paragraph:

> America's grief at what happened has been immense and immensely public. It would be grotesque to expect it to calibrate or modulate its anguish. However, it will be a pity if, instead of using this as an opportunity to try to understand why September 11 happened, Americans use it as an opportunity to usurp the whole world's sorrow to mourn and avenge only their own. Because then it falls to the rest of us to ask the hard questions and say the harsh things. And for our pains, for our bad timing, we will be disliked, ignored and perhaps eventually silenced.

The history of American involvement in Afghanistan since 1979, including its collaboration with Pakistan to support the

Taliban's rise to power, the willingness of US politicians to accept the deaths of 500,000 Iraqi children over the past decade and the forthcoming cost of 'a climate of war', was invoked to raise 'the equivocating distinction between civilisation and savagery, between the "massacre of innocent people" or, if you like, "a clash of civilisations" and "collateral damage"'.[40]

The depth of these critiques pointed not to a failure of thought on the 'Left', but to a consideration which went beyond the casual response of retaliation. The crisis was not for those who set out the complexity of past and future courses of action, but for counterparts who desired an easy acceptance of the War Against Terror. As Madeleine Bunting noted, 'There is a danger that, as Yeats put it, the centre cannot hold; that the ground on which stand efforts for tolerance, mutual understanding and respect, is eroded by the Us and Them mentality.'[41] George Monbiot stated cogently:

> The left is able to state categorically that Tuesday's terrorism was a dreadful act, irrespective of provenance. But the right can't bring itself to make the same statement about Israel's new invasions of Palestine, or the sanctions in Iraq, or the US-backed terror in East Timor, or the carpet bombing of Cambodia. Its critical faculties have long been suspended and now, it demands, we must suspend ours too.[42]

Hitchens' diatribes offered a way out. They not only dovetailed with other denunciations such as Michael Gove's attack upon 'Guardianistas' but, as the wisdom of a former torch-bearer of the 'Left', provided legitimacy for them. Never mind that doubts were not the exclusive property of Hitchens' erstwhile comrades, that the *Independent* was calling for diplomacy rather than war, that Brenda Maddox in *The Times* was querying the link between the Taliban and Osama bin Laden, that John Humphrys was noting, 'It's not anti-American to see both sides of the argument', and that the *Daily Mail* was questioning the evidence of Al-Qa'eda's responsibility for 9–11.[43] Leave aside the concern of the chronicler of American power, Arthur Schlesinger Jr, 'I don't see any form of drastic military action that will not rebound against us.'[44] The reduction of dissent to a simple-minded, knee-jerk betrayal of the Spirit of '68 could dismiss any troublesome questions.

Such a conflation drew on high-profile incidents. On BBC's *Question Time*, US Ambassador Philip Lader was confronted with hostile comments from members of the audience. As with Hitchens' own initial questions, the points were far from irrelevant; however, they did not fit a mood of unreserved mourning for American loss. More than 600 viewers complained to the BBC, and the Director-General, Greg Dyke, apologised for 'an inappropriate programme to broadcast live just two days after the attacks in the US'.[45]

The *London Review of Books* served as another villain after it asked a range of contributors for their immediate reactions. Tariq Ali pointed to causes, such as past American activity in the Middle East and the Israel–Palestine dispute as well as Egyptian and Saudi sources of 'fanaticism', to warn that the challenge came from the educated middle class. Amit Chaudhari charged, 'America has been a great, self-appointed proponent of democracy in the modern world, while, in actuality, it has treated it as a nuisance and an obstruction when it gets in the way of its self-interest', and Paul Foot looked beyond the US, 'The attention of the world's leaders is focused on a single, dreadful act that gives them the excuse they need to gun the engines of oppression.' Even the American contributor Eric Foner worried, 'I'm not sure which is more frightening: the horror that engulfed New York City or the apocalyptic rhetoric emanating daily from the White House.'

While some statements were too close to 'the United States had it coming' for comfort – Mary Beard used that very phrase – the *LRB* collection was far from a festival of anti-Americanism. There was none of the applause for the attack that Hitchens anticipated; Neal Ascherson reflected, 'Once there was a time when the most evil people on earth were ashamed to write their crime across the heavens.' James Buchan found hope that tragedy provided an opportunity for Iran to reconcile with the West, while Lorraine Daston called for a war on terrorism in which 'the new challenge [was] addressed to anthropologists and historians, sociologists and theologians, students of the symbolic rather than the technical'.[46]

If the majority of submissions had a common theme, it was a concern directed at Washington that, as Ascherson phrased it, 'Leaders are writing "Retribution" on the clouds. Nothing good will come of that.' This, however, was more than enough for the journal's detractors to point to delusional intellectuals. Ian Buruma in the *Guardian* reduced the contributors to

professors of this or that, raving on about 'cowboy' President Bush, about the crassness of Hollywood movies, about the Vietnam War, about US-sponsored globalisation, about capitalism, and, of course, about US and Israeli atrocities against Iraqis and Palestinians .... What is so nauseating is the smug way with which most of them squander their freedom by missing the point and yet write as though they are being tremendously brave in doing so, as though damning US foreign policy or ridiculing George Bush's English is a sign of bold dissidence.[47]

The conflation of the anti-war argument did not constitute a rebuttal of it, however. Given Hitchens' animosity towards 'anti-Americanism', one might have expected some reference to the forthright views of Fisk, Milne, Raven and Kabbani. There would be none, however, let alone any engagement with the more specific analyses of American politics, power and ideology as well as the complexities of the situation in Africa and Central Asia. Hitchens' 'clash of civilisations' could not withstand such a protracted examination.

If there was any consideration of the position of the 'Left', it came not from the contrarian but from the deviants within. Milne continued to warn that US intervention in Afghanistan was 'lurching toward catastrophe', Gary Younge labelled it a 'war against the weak' and Monbiot highlighted America's 'backyard terrorism', but Freedland and Toynbee were beginning to define a support of 'Operation Enduring Freedom', searching for a 'hard liberalism' in defence of military action.[48]

The quest was marked out in leader columns. The *Observer* had quickly moved from a call for justice through law, not military action, to acceptance of a 'just war'. As the first American bombs fell, both the *Guardian* and the *Independent* were equivocal, with the former assuring, 'It needs to be said as clearly and as unemotively as possible at the outset that the US was entitled to launch a military response', before pondering, 'Whether this particular military action is wise is another matter. We hope, of course, that it is. That will depend above all upon whether the armed action strikes effectively at its targets.'[49]

These continuing debates cast Hitchens' 'Ha Ha Ha' as a crude parody, its target not the Taliban who were fleeing Kabul but those who dared look beyond the immediate question of military victory. The article was far from the only one. Charles Moore in the *Daily Telegraph* wrote, 'The same siren voices who, almost as soon as the bombing campaign had commenced, wrote it off as a failure, or who called for a ceasefire during Ramadan, are now wringing their hands over the "power vacuum" that the sheer speed of the Taliban collapse has supposedly created. They are wrong again.' Anne McElvoy and David Aaronovitch lobbed jibes in the *Independent*: McElvoy's 'Terrible news from the front: we're winning the war .... If the Taliban are depressed, think how much worse it is for the anti-war lobby in the west. How can something that was supposed to go so wrong go so right?' and Aaronovitch's helpful guidance:

> This Sunday, a lot of people are planning to come to London as part of what organisers promise will be a 'massive turnout' for their demonstration. The slogan for that march is a simple one: Stop the War. Here's a bit of well-intentioned advice for the most open-minded of those with tickets for the coach, and it, too, is very simple. Don't go. Have the flu. Stay at home. Do something constructive instead. You are wasting your time.[50]

There was more than a hint of relief in these sentiments: weeks earlier, when the war had apparently stalled, doubters had been characterised as 'Nazi appeasers' by the Armed Forces Minister Adam Ingram, Minister for International Development Clare Short had alleged that humanitarian agencies operating in Afghanistan 'want[ed] to raise money in their own countries and therefore want to be in the news',[51] and no less a figure than Chelsea Clinton had explained, 'It's hard to be abroad right now. Every day I encounter some sort of anti-American feeling. Sometimes it's from students, sometimes it's from a newspaper columnist, sometimes it's from "peace" demonstrators.'[52]

Yet the shallowness of these crushing rebuttals would be exposed in the following weeks and months. Hitchens and his fellow celebrants continued their victory jig, but dissent did not evaporate with the declaration of triumph in Kabul. Robert Fisk and Brenda Maddox raised doubts over the Northern Alliance, and the *Observer* noted the return of 'warlords' to authority.[53] Both the *Observer* and the *Guardian* reported, within two weeks of Kabul's fall, that opium production was rising sharply with the ousting of the Taliban. Nick Cohen identified the uncertain future of aid to rehabilitate Afghanistan, a warning that would be borne out in following months as refugees remained in the camps (and, in many cases, returned to them after trying to resettle) and Afghans awaited restoration of water and electricity supplies and the rebuilding of houses. Even the liberation of women from the Taliban, highlighted in the Western media, came under scrutiny. As women were effectively excluded from the *loya jirga* reconstructing Afghanistan's government and the Ministry for Women tried to operate with no funds, Peter Beaumont reported in the *Observer*, the 'tyranny of veil is slow to lift'. Polly Toynbee was still asking a year after the liberation of Kabul, 'Was it worth it? ... 9 out of 10 women still wear the burqa .... This is [still] an apartheid society ... [Women say] "We wear the burqa because we are still afraid."'[54]

Investigative reporters were also uncovering some uncomfortable realities of the war. The 'just war' apparently had resulted in the execution of thousands of prisoners, prompting questions from the United Nations Human Rights Commissioner, Mary Robinson. Seymour Hersh in the *New Yorker* described how Pakistanis who fought with the Taliban and Al-Qa'eda in Kunduz were airlifted, with US connivance, from the city before it fell to the Northern Alliance.

And, far from resolving the War on Terror, the vanquishing of the Taliban raised new questions far beyond Afghanistan. Rupert Cornwell asked about a future where the 'self-centred'

US tried to lead the world. Michael Boyce, Britain's Chief of Defence Staff, warned, 'We have to consider whether we wish to follow the US's single-minded aim to finish Osama bin Laden and al-Qa'ida or to involve ourselves in creating the conditions for nation-building or reconstruction as well.'[55] David Clark, the former Labour Minister, declared that 'Blair must stand up to Bush'.[56] As for the war at home, columnists such as Ronan Bennett and Nick Cohen assailed the Government's anti-terrorism plans as the sanctioning of 'internment'.[57]

The US detention of several hundred captured fighters on the Guantanamo Base in Cuba brought these fears over the wielding of US power and the dismissal of basic civil rights to the fore. When John Sutherland of the *Guardian* related Camp X-Ray to a manual for torture, it was far from an isolated complaint from the 'Left'. Stephen Glover, an ardent supporter of the 'special relationship', expressed regretful outrage, and the *Daily Telegraph* lambasted Washington for threatening the distinction 'between civilised society and the apocalyptic savagery of those who would destroy it'.[58] Meanwhile, Richard Norton-Taylor linked Camp X-Ray to domestic 'justice', highlighting Britain's unlimited detention of up to a dozen Muslims without charge at Belmarsh Prison in Kent, and Faisal Bodi declared that, with such internment, 'We have no loyalty to this state.'[59]

With Hitchens now joining in the doubts over Camp X-Ray and certain members of the Bush Administration, it appeared that he had been reunited with his Leftist masochists. Fortunately for the contrarian, such a reunion could still be avoided.

If 'dissent' had escaped immediate execution, the intellectual proponents of a US-led War on Terror could always rely on the media, even the supposed outlets of the 'Left', to give them an identity and public forum while placing the burden of proof on the sceptics of military action. Andy Beckett's post-Kabul post-mortem for the *Guardian* examined Tariq Ali's comment that 70 per cent of those in anti-war marches in London, in a British movement 'larger than anywhere except Italy', were between 18 and 25; however, it hid this behind the interrogations, 'Did the left lose the war?' and 'So did the left get it all wrong – and does it matter?', claims such as 'The anti-globalisation movement has drawn up a sophisticated economic policy, but not a foreign policy', and descriptions of activists as weary, unconvincing, naive and a bit paranoid.[60]

In contrast, days after John Lloyd presented his pro-American trio, the *Guardian* offered an open platform for pro-intervention columnists to review their victory proclamations after the fall of Kabul. Despite the subsequent tensions in Afghanistan and beyond, none recanted and only Henry Porter wavered, wondering why British troops were taking over the fight in Afghanistan from the Americans. Michael Gove of *The Times* safeguarded his earlier exultation, 'It's incumbent on the political leaders to explain that it's not a quick process', and David Aaronovitch reassured, 'I'm not prepared to flounce out of the room now that things have become difficult.' Robert Harris chided those who doubted, '[Al-Qa'eda and the Taliban] will be beaten. They will run out of weapons. It's not like before, when the superpowers were arming them. It's not going to be a picnic, but it's not like Vietnam or anything like that.'[61]

And, if the first unifying crisis in the War on Terror was becoming far too complicated, another one could be found to revive the denunciation of the 'Left'. The Bush Administration's decision in February 2002 to relaunch the War on Iraq once more reduced troublesome complexity to 'with us or against us', or, in the words of Margaret Thatcher, a contest where 'Islamism is the new bolshevism'.[62]

As in the weeks after 9–11, the American move for a crusade to liberate Baghdad brought a wide range of opposition. Seumas Milne did not mince his words, 'Can the US be defeated?' Will Hutton announced, 'Time to stop being America's lap-dog' and Nick Cohen intoned, 'Blair's just a Bush baby.'[63] Jonathan Freedland ridiculed Washington's announcement of a 'potential marriage' between Saddam Hussein and Al-Qa'eda, John O'Farrell snapped, 'I had PE teachers more intelligent than George Bush' and Rod Liddle suggested nuking the Belgians with 'a dossier of fabricated evidence, supposition and pure guesswork – which will show that Belgium is presently developing weapons of mass destruction, sponsoring terrorism abroad, and producing cheap, subsidised steel for export'.[64] Mary Riddell expanded on all these sentiments with a sharp analysis of a US campaign designed for the sake of revenge, oil and 'a Pax Americana from Georgia to the Philippines', contrasting this with her plea for a humanitarian alternative:

If Afghanistan looks a flawed success, then the idea that Mr Bush can bomb Baghdad into something along the lines of the Prince of Wales's Poundbury seems truly fantastic. Should an elusive salvation still exist for Iraq, it lies in targeted sanctions, more food aid, plus global co-operation on weapons treaties and regional action on oil smuggling. Mr Blair should press for those and unhitch himself fast from the Bush game of swagger and double jeopardy.[65]

This time, there was no immediate round-up of these sentiments as the knee-jerking of a deluded 'Left', even when the *London Review of Books* put itself in the dock with the ill-advised refusal to print a David Marquand review offering support for Tony Blair.[66] There were too many troublemakers for the *Daily Telegraph*'s 'Useful Idiots' watchdog to cope, and Hitchens appeared to be preoccupied with his running feuds with fellow alumni of '68. The Bush Administration, inconvenienced by the Israeli–Palestinian dispute and the sudden threat of a nuclear exchange between India and Pakistan over Kashmir as well as the failure of Tony Blair to wave the dossier damning Saddam Hussein, stood down the immediate alert for war.

Yet any thought that 'dissent' had not only survived but triumphed ran the risk of hopeful illusion. The invocation of the 'Axis of Evil', followed by the restoration of Saddam as Public Enemy Number One, served long-term purposes. First, it skipped away from other challenges, notably questions over the progress of the War on Terror. The Bush Administration could trumpet the second campaign of the war for freedom with the assurance that, in the words of *The Times*, 'the first phase, not yet over, is politically the easiest'.[67] It did so even as Operation ANACONDA was grinding to failure in eastern Afghanistan, amidst American deaths and elusive Taliban and al-Qa'eda leaders, as Fred Halliday was summarising the failure of international cooperation after 9–11, and as a series of commentators, such as Abdel Bari Atwan in the *Observer*, were warning that US strategy was turning most of the Islamic world, and not just the 'fundamentalists', against it.[68]

By intention or convenient coincidence, the War on Iraq could divert attention from the 'quagmire' on the West Bank and US reluctance or inability to offer any move towards resolution. It could relegate to the back pages the US-supported (and possibly US-sponsored) coup against President Hugo Chavez of Venezuela and the confirmation that the US had adopted the policy of 'pre-emptive' strikes, including the use of nuclear weapons, against non-nuclear powers. It could turn its back on the continued failure to deliver aid to the 'liberated' Afghan people as the country, beset by assassinations (some attempted by the CIA) and rivalry between 'warlords', emerged as an uneasy collection of regions. The Axis of Evil could expand to include an enemy such as Cuba and contract once more as soon as US hostility towards Havana came under scrutiny.

Second, the Bush Administration had set the parameters for any future debate. The call for war might not have been taken up by American allies in the spring but, at the least, it had bumped alternatives off the agenda. The formula would no longer be Iraqi acceptance of inspections in exchange for removal of sanctions but, at most, Iraqi acceptance to forestall US-led military operations. Even if certain voices had raised objections to war the first time around, they might not do so on the next occasion.

So in August, having prepared the media with a series of far from subtle leaks, the Administration's 'hawks' renewed their charge, with Vice President Dick Cheney declaring that Iraq was on the verge of acquiring nuclear weapons. In previous weeks, even John Simpson in the *Daily Telegraph* had been warning, 'I had never seen Britain and the United States more separated from each other', quoting senior British officials on the arrogance of an Administration led by 'a bear of very little brain'. Now this was set aside for the fundamental query – yes or no – of whether Britain would support US use of force.

The BBC, rediscovering a bravery for confrontation lost with the *Question Time* incident after 9–11, featured Michael Moore grappling with former New York City mayor Ed Koch and a former US Attorney General, while Sheik Hamza Yusuf Hanson offered an Islamic perspective; Koch screeched that the audience was biased, but this programme would not be disowned by the BBC's leadership.[69] When hundreds of thousands marched through London in mid-September, Yasmin Alibhai-Brown celebrated 'a spectacular coming together of various tribes and individuals' to put a series of difficult questions to Tony Blair, and Euan Ferguson and the *Observer* threw back the rhetoric hurled by the march's detractors: 'A big day out in Leftistan ... old and new radicals joined forces to make the Stop the War coalition feel more like the start of something.'[70] If one listened closely, some new voices could be heard: the Archbishop of Canterbury joining other religious leaders when he saw 'no grounds whatsoever for taking any military action', the Government's chief legal adviser insisting that 'regime change' violated international law, John Nichol, the British pilot held by the Iraqis as a POW in the first Gulf War, commenting, 'Do I think that bombing Iraq would make the world a safer place? No', and Bill Morris, the head of the Transport and General Workers' Union, lashing out, 'When we said on September 11 that we support our prime minister, we didn't say we would support the government undermining our liberty, our freedom, and our democracy. And we didn't say that we should declare war on Islam as we have seen.'[71] Even the actor Woody Harrelson took time out from his West End performances to write as 'an American tired of American lies'.[72]

However, this coming-out of dissent as 'mainstream', rather than the preserve of a few Guardianistas and professional malcontents, only highlighted the greater challenge. The marchers gathered, but only a few days later, the agenda returned to 'US hard line on Iraq leaves full-scale invasion a "hair-trigger" away'.[73] Tony Blair's long-anticipated dossier of Saddam's evils might turn out to be 'weasel words', 'a deliberate misreading of the facts' and 'a desperate quest' for the logic of war, but his performance at the Labour Party conference a week later could make the case for 'engagement abroad ...

soberly and convincingly'.[74] If the Bali bomb in October prompted the reminder, 'The war on terror is not working', that War on Terror was duly replaced by the United Nations 'ultimatum' to Iraq.[75]

The perpetual repetition of the 'proper' course of action always supported, and even fostered, the containment of protest on the 'Left'. The comments of Andrew Sullivan on an 'anti-Americanism ... designed to demonize the United States as a whole' or Michael Gove about 'Saddam's useful idiots' had long ago become the bellowing of pantomime cattle, and one could predict Bill Emmott's homage to US power or the *Sunday Telegraph*'s loving portraits of Condoleezza Rice, 'Bush's secret weapon', and the 391st Fighter Squadron of the US Air Force.[76] More effective in containing opposition were the revelations in the *Sunday Times* by Bob Woodward, once an investigative reporter who challenged power, of the wisdom and leadership of the President.[77] Similarly the journalist Polly Toynbee, for all her doubts about a strike on Baghdad, proclaimed after Blair's conference speech, 'This great government .... Now is the time to celebrate New Labour's success – before war and recession come along to spoil it all.'[78] Timothy Garton Ash preferred an air of resignation, 'Washington is at war. Washington is going to war.'[79] The *Guardian*'s leader column whimpered, 'More than ever, Europe needs to pull together, to stand up for the values and ideas it holds in common. As ever, there is little sign that it can or will.'[80] Journalist Jackie Ashley noted, 'Instead of a debate over war, there's been a national shrug,' and foretold the future:

> We are going to war, but Tony hasn't quite got round to telling us. By the time we wake up from our Christmas hangovers, the momentum will be unstoppable; just as in 1914, once the armies were moving, it was too late to alter the railway timetables.[81]

Sure enough, a supposed bastion of the 'Left', the *Observer*, slipped in December towards an acceptance of what was now presented as the inevitable: 'If it's war, it has to be legitimate.' Provided the US passed 'all information [it] holds ... quickly

... to the inspectors', provided that 'the 27 January report [of the inspectors] is as thorough as possible' and provided the 'inspectors ... had every opportunity to establish whether any reported discrepancies in Iraq's account of its military capability are substantive', the United Nations could trigger the conflict.[82] On 19 January, even though the US had not passed its information to the inspectors (and, indeed, had 'belittled and obstructed' them; as one inspector noted, 'The US will start a war whenever they want anyway, regardless of what we find'),[83] even though the report was eight days distant, and even though the inspections process was estimated to require up to a year to complete, the *Observer* concluded, 'We find ourselves supporting the current commitment to a possible use of force .... If Saddam does not yield, military action may eventually be the least awful necessity for Iraq, for the Middle East and for the world.'[84]

Other columnists circled round the central issue. Nick Cohen continued to press his argument against measures for internal security, advanced by 'our modern mob ... in Downing Street and Fleet Street, New Scotland Yard and the BBC', while wrestling with his dilemma over Iraq. Like some American advocates of war, Cohen pointed to the hope of introducing democracy (endorsing, in particular, the exiles of the Iraqi National Congress), but he also acknowledged the likelihood that American and British intervention would have baser motives and outcomes: 'By pinning his hopes on a new dictator, Tony Blair has placed himself on the wrong side of the debate in the Bush Administration.'[85] At least Cohen was working through his position while swiping at the 'master evaders' of the anti-war movement; less honourable were David Aaronovitch's lashings of hyperbole against the bogeymen. He turned debate about the historical and contemporary influence of the pro-Israeli lobby on American foreign policy into 'the ultimate Jewish conspiracy theory' and sniped at the *New Statesman* and its 'cannibalistic tendencies'.[86]

For all these efforts, dissent could not be banished with a 'Ha ha ha'. Indeed, unlike in autumn 2001, it was becoming part of the everyday discourse and debate, far beyond a usual suspect such as Chomsky advising, 'Drain the swamp and there will be

no more mosquitoes' or Pinter describing 'the American administration [as] a bloodthirsty wild animal'.[87] Former Conservative
ministers Douglas Hurd and Douglas Hogg and the former
Permanent Undersecretary of the Ministry of Defence, Michael
Quinlan, made their concerns public.[88] The newly appointed
Archbishop of Canterbury, Rowan Williams, brought the
objections of clergy across all denominations into a pointed
Christmas message: 'It is as if the wise, the devious and the
resourced can't help but make the most immense mistakes of
all. The strategists who know the possible ramifications of
politics miss the huge and obvious things and wreak yet more
havoc and suffering.'[89] Ghada Karmi wrote of 'a deep and
unconscious racism [which] imbues every aspect of western
conduct towards Iraq – and by extension the Arabs in general'.
Her claim of the tragedy 'that the Arabs themselves – those
who are providing facilities for this war – should have colluded
with an enterprise so irrational, destructive and demeaning' was
echoed in Said's plea: 'Will no one come out into the light of
day to express a vision for our future that isn't based on a script
written by Donald Rumsfeld and Paul Wolfowitz, those two
symbols of vacant power and overweening arrogance? I hope
someone is listening.'[90] Toynbee, shifting once more between
euphoria and unease, charged, 'By becoming Bush's chief
vassal, Blair has humiliated Britain on the world stage as well
as making us a prime al-Qaida target …. As the prime advocate
of a joint European defence policy, he threw away the chance
to bring Europe together and reconnect its citizens with a sense
of purpose in the union.'[91] Martin Kettle simply demanded,
'Who will speak for England?'[92]

There was now a general unease with the march to conflict
and a 'grass roots' display of opposition. As Milne declared,
'Direct action will not simply be justified, it will be a
democratic necessity.'[93] For the first time, the press sustained
attention to dissent. The *Observer*, in coverage which fitted
uneasily with its conversion to a just conflict, noted, 'Anti-war
protests span the globe', and spent four pages on 'the great war
debate'.[94] The *Independent on Sunday* went even further with
a page 1 trumpeting of 'A world against the war', declaring
'Global protest delivers a resounding "No"' with the 'Voices
against war: actors, writers, warriors, citizens'.[95] *The Times*

featured, without any denigration beyond the headline 'Peaceniks', the development of the 'unlikely alliance' against war.[96] The *Independent* and *Guardian* chronicled the objections of residents of Peoria, Illinois, and Bagdad, California, to an attack upon Iraq.[97]

The commitment in September 2002, no matter how token on the part of the United States, to go through the inspection process before smiting Saddam had opened up a space which could not be closed down. Even the *Sunday Times* had to accept that the United Nations must be 'methodical': 'Take Time, then Act'. Objections by Security Council members and European allies, notably France and Germany, to any shortcuts to military action could not be set aside, even if Paris and Berlin were labelled the 'Axis of Weasels' by *The Times* columnist Ferdinand Mount. The interlude was filled not only with stories of Baghdad's evils, but also of support by US officials such as Rumsfeld of Saddam Hussein in the 1980s, of schemes by those same officials since 1998 to overthrow their ally-turned-enemy in Baghdad, of US readiness to use nuclear weapons against new foes, and of its resort to torture against old ones.[98]

But if the *Observer* was leaving the peace camp, the *Independent on Sunday* was making a dramatic entrance. A week after its presentation of the anti-war march in London, the newspaper issued a front-page declaration, 'Stop. Think. Listen: Stop the rush to war. Think of the consequences. Listen to reason', and pointedly noted 'the growing number of voices expressing concern' despite the support of all other Sunday broadsheets for an attack. The editorial was accompanied by the sharp commentary of Robert Fisk, 'Does Tony have any idea what the flies are like that feed off the dead?' and a series of readers' protests against military intervention.[99] The *Guardian* was maintaining its position that there was no evidence to justify war; the *Independent* was more cautious in calling for more time for inspections but was jabbing at Blairite support for Bush, including a heralded whip-round of seven other European leaders backing US action, as a 'show of weakness'.

Only six days after 9–11, the sociologist Richard Sennett offered a prescription/proscription for the 'Left' in the *Guardian*. While he worried, 'I have no idea how to fight terrorists effectively.

I suspect our rulers do not, either', and accepted, 'We Americans need to change our behaviour towards others in order to make ourselves ultimately more secure', he set limits on protest and criticism:

> That sign 'An Eye for an Eye = Blindness' seems to me only to waken memories of Vietnam, when such simplistic recipes split the US apart. What holds civil society together is neither ideology nor shared sorrow, and not even religion; it is the capacity to act effectively together day by day, toward some common purpose.[100]

The tactic would become a familiar one. Just as Orwell had defined discussion of 'Socialism', of Englishness and of the Cold War by marking out the unacceptable, so the guardians of the proper response, however well-meaning their advice, would try to foreclose any wayward interventions.

Vigilance against the weak-kneed and the weak-willed was maintained, of course, by more traditional foes. Between 9–11 and the fall of the first bombs on Afghanistan, Andrew Neil railed at the 'apologists for terror who dominate the opinion pages of the hard-left *Guardian*, henceforth better known as the *Daily Terrorist*', Richard Littlejohn exposed 'the silly anti-American propagandists of the fascist Left press', Janet Daley found the 'hatred and foaming malevolence' of an 'intellectual decadence' which was 'repulsive', and Michael Gove converted that decadence into the 'Guardianistas' of the 'Prada-Meinhof gang'. Stephen Glover put forth the equation, 'To demonise the Americans is to follow the example of Osama bin Laden', and Bryan Appleyard identified 'Yankophobes' as 'morons ... too villainously stupid to get the message', making him 'sick of [his] generation's whining attitude, its wilful, infantile loathing of the great, tumultuous, witty and infinitely clever nation that has so often saved us from ourselves'. Mark Steyn made the greatest leap of polemical imagination, picturing himself 'in some weepy CNN montage of dead commuters' because of pro-Palestinian apologists amongst 'third-rate *Guardian* columnists'.[101]

But, precisely because they were expected, such comments did not constitute effective policing of the 'Left'. That duty was taken up by those who could claim credentials, past or present, within the movement. Aaronovitch set up the watch on 21 September when he railed at a letter signed by Pinter and others, 'Pinterism is all around, wearing its badges stating, "Don't blame me, I'm against it, whatever it is," and is as wrong as ever.'[102] Commentators, wittingly or otherwise, began using the slang of derision such as 'peaceniks'.[103] Some resisted the easy labelling of 'good' and 'bad', such as Will Hutton's reclamation of 'hard liberalism' to challenge, rather than embrace, proposed American and British military action, but they were often lost in the tide of disdain.

Every so often columnists would check to ensure the 'Left' knew its place. Ian Buruma chided, 'Two things, in my experience as a *Guardian* columnist, are guaranteed to cause maximum annoyance; or perhaps just one thing: any argument in defence of Israel or the United States.'[104] Henry Porter wrote in the *Observer* that he could absolve the 'doves' of 'a morally reprehensible error because the majority of people who were opposed to the war were so for highly civilised reasons'. However, since they had sinned by portraying as 'self-evidently barbarous' those who supported the war in Afghanistan, the 'peace party' had to accept

> its failure to stand up for the democratic achievements of the last 100 years and for the reign of liberal values in which we thrive and indeed possess the freedom to debate the enormous issues that now face the world .... The hawks may forgive but they won't forget that was ... a matter of personal judgement and moral choice.[105]

With decency barred to those who might question the 'War on Terror', those prosecuting the campaign could move in. Charles Clarke, the Chairman of the Labour Party, explained how the Left loved America. Labour Minister Peter Hain, best known for his long-time opposition to apartheid in South Africa, lashed out at 'the anti-interventionist left [as] politically bankrupt' and set it up as the unwitting accomplice of an 'agenda driven by hawks on Capitol Hill, let off the hook by rejectionists worldwide'.[106]

Whatever Hitchens' personal motivation for his vilification of the '68 'peaceniks', he served a vital role in this stage-managing of decent comment. He was the ultimate sheriff, keeping a wary eye out for any who dared take a pot-shot at the war that he helped define and defend. If Nelson Mandela dared label Blair 'George Bush's Foreign Minister', then he must be lacking in 'political courage' and spouting 'garbage'.[107]

However, by the end of 2002, the sheriff seemed to be leaving little more than a shadow. In Britain the articles had ceased, the commentaries (except for very occasional contributions to the *Mirror* and *Evening Standard*) had abated and references to the honourable contrarian were scattered. Even the *Vanity Fair* showcase had become little more than martial whooping:

> This will be no war – there will be a fairly brief and ruthless military intervention. The president will give an order. [The attack] will be rapid, accurate and dazzling .... It will be greeted by the majority of the Iraqi people as an emancipation. And I say, bring it on.[108]

It would be Peter, not Christopher, Hitchens who would be featured on *Any Questions*; however, far from preserving the family reputation, Peter the ferocious right-winger would risk appeasement of Saddam Hussein:

> To start a war is incredibly dangerous. You do not know what you are going to unravel. You sow the wind, and you may very easily reap the whirlwind. I don't think however bad Saddam Hussein's regime is, and it is, however many weapons that he has, and I'm sure that he does have weapons of mass destruction ... these are not arguments for starting a war. They are arguments for other responsible actions ....
>
> The baby talk which is constantly thrown at us suggests that the people who are putting forward this case for war don't even take their own argument seriously. I think they should start treating us as adults.[109]

Dissent seemed to have spread beyond Christopher's grasp. Still, he could rest assured that, if he was no longer the exalted prophet in his native land, he might hold attention in the US where he now lived.

6

Our Friends in America

Americans ought to know [why the attacks of 11 September occurred] .... The fact is, if I wrote this story now, thousands of people would write into the *Washington Post* and say, 'Fire the guy.' My editors are right: we're not ready for this.

T.R. Reid, the London bureau chief of the *Washington Post*, 22 September 2001[1]

It would be crude hindsight to assert that dissent in the United States was shut down on 9–11. There was no need to quash a dissent of 'celebration', for there was no such cheering of downed planes and collapsing buildings. The nearest any commentators ventured to the 'America had it coming' heresy was the double-act of evangelists Jerry Falwell and Pat Robertson. Falwell explained:

The abortionists have got to bear some burden for this because God will not be mocked. And when we destroy 40 million little innocent babies, we make God mad. I really believe that the pagans, and the abortionists, and the feminists, and the gays and the lesbians who are actively trying to make that an alternative lifestyle, the ACLU [American Civil Liberties Union], People for the American Way, all of them who have tried to secularise America, I point the finger in their face and say, 'You helped this happen.'

Robertson endorsed the thesis, 'I totally concur, and the problem is we have adopted that agenda at the highest levels of our government.'[2]

Beyond the grief and horror, there was chaos. In the near-panic after the first strikes, with President Bush being shuttled through the hinterland, with the Vice President ordering the shooting-down of any other hijacked aircraft,[3] with the FBI mobilising to round up the vaguest of 'suspects' (more than 1,100 people would be detained without charge in the days after 9–11), careful deliberation over the causes of the terrorist assaults was not high on the Government's agenda.

Yet, even as the full impact of the attacks was being felt, the media were calling not only for America to regroup, but to find the unity of purpose to strike back. Television networks were broadcasting under the banners of 'America at War', 'America United', 'America Strikes Back'. Even before Bush's 'Wanted: Dead or Alive' declaration, Fox News featured a visual of Osama in a sniper's scope; its chairman, Roger Ailes, a former adviser to Richard Nixon and Ronald Reagan, warned the Administration, 'The American public would tolerate waiting and would be patient, but only as long as they were convinced that Bush was using the harshest measures possible.'[4]

Newspaper columns reinforced the message, with the *Washington Post* calling for a unifying purpose and the *New York Times* heralding 'the first American war of the 21st century'. Others invoked the precedent of Pearl Harbor and the Second World War, with the *Dallas Morning News* quoting Winston Churchill in a 'bombed-out' London 'when Britain stood virtually alone against Adolf Hitler's war machine' and the *Atlanta Journal-Constitution* taking aim at the 'cowardly enemy'.[5]

The US Government did not need to direct the prevailing national mood. After George Bush belatedly returned to Washington to display authority, more than 90 per cent of the public supported the President as he changed the target from the Afghan caves to Kabul itself. When Bush ad-libbed to rescue workers at Ground Zero, 'I hear you, the rest of the world hears you, and the people who knocked these buildings down will hear all of us soon', the guttural response of 'USA! USA! USA!' heralded the resurgence of an Americanism that would have its revenge.

Yet there were more cautious, if not dissonant, voices. Pat Buchanan, never before accused of a 'dovish tendency', argued against US intervention for 'empire'. And, establishing a penchant for cutting against the grain of media comment, Maureen Dowd and Paul Krugman of the *New York Times* each chided the Administration. Dowd ridiculed the President for pressing ahead with Missile Defence in the days after 9–11, 'What's the sense of rushing to create a $60bn defense shield to protect against a Trojan horse [of terrorism]?', and Krugman warned Bush against the 'opportunism' of pursuing the 'disastrous idea' of a tax cut.[6]

These sentiments, if they were acknowledged, were met with resistance and antipathy. Mary McGrory wrote that journalists asking questions with any hint of scepticism were inundated with furious calls calling them a disgrace to their profession and even traitors'.[7] Politically, however, not even this was enough. Bush had declared in his speech of 20 September to the Congress that everyone was either 'with us or … with the terrorists'.[8] Dissent, at least at the level of the 'mainstream', was to be placed beyond acceptability.

On 17 September, the *New Yorker* devoted its 'Talk of the Town' section to the immediate reactions of writers to 9–11. Contributors included John Updike, Jonathan Franzen, Amitav Ghosh and Roger Angell, but all would be overshadowed by the furore over the thoughts of Susan Sontag. These were the impressions and expressions destined to be the centrepiece of unacceptable dissent:

> The disconnect between last Tuesday's monstrous dose of reality and the self-righteous drivel and outright deceptions being peddled by public figures and TV commentators is startling, depressing. The voices licensed to follow the event seem to have joined together in a campaign to infantilize the public. Where is the acknowledgement that this was not a 'cowardly' attack on 'civilization' or 'liberty' or 'humanity' or 'the free world' but an attack on the world's self-proclaimed super-power, undertaken as a consequence of specific American alliances and actions? How many citizens are aware of the ongoing American bombing of Iraq? And if the word 'cowardly' is to be used, it might be more aptly applied to those who kill from beyond the range of retaliation, high in the sky, than to those willing to die themselves in order to kill others. In the matter of courage (a morally neutral virtue): whatever may be said of the perpetrators of Tuesday's slaughter, they were not cowards.

Our leaders are bent on convincing us that everything is O.K. America is not afraid. Our spirit is unbroken, although this was a day that will live in infamy and America is now at war. But everything is not O.K. And this was not Pearl Harbor. We have a robotic president who assures us that America stands tall. A wide spectrum of public figures, in and out of office, who are strongly opposed to the policies being pursued abroad by this Administration apparently feel free to say nothing more than that they stand united behind President Bush. A lot of thinking needs to be done, and perhaps is being done in Washington and elsewhere, about the ineptitude of American intelligence and counter-intelligence, about options available to American foreign policy, particularly in the Middle East, and about what constitutes a smart program of military defense. But the public is not being asked to bear much of the burden of reality. The unanimously applauded, self-congratulatory bromides of a Soviet Party Congress seemed contemptible. The unanimity of the sanctimonious, reality-concealing rhetoric spouted by American officials and media commentators in recent days seems, well, unworthy of a mature democracy.

Those in public office have let us know that they consider their task to be a manipulative one: confidence-building and grief management. Politics, the politics of a democracy – which entails disagreement, which promotes candor – has been replaced by psychotherapy. Let's by all means grieve together. But let's not be stupid together. A few shreds of historical awareness might help us to understand what has just happened, and what may continue to happen. 'Our country is strong', we are told again and again. I for one don't find this entirely consoling. Who doubts that America is strong? But that's not all America has to be.[9]

Sontag's was far from the only observation that 9–11 was not a manifestation of evil isolated from the realities of US foreign policy. Joel Rogers had written in *The Nation*, 'Our own government, through much of the past fifty years, has been the world's leading "rogue state".'[10] Katha Pollitt dared to question Old Glory, 'My daughter, who goes to Stuyvesant High School only blocks from the World Trade Center, thinks we should fly an American flag out our window. Definitely not, I say: The flag stands for jingoism and vengeance and war.'[11] The forcefulness of Sontag's language and her reputation pushed her to the front, however, and by calling to account America's media as well as America's politicians, she had become more than a nuisance.

The tarring party was led by Charles Krauthammer, a syndicated columnist featured in *Time* and the *Washington Post* and on national talk shows. On 21 September, he parroted Orwell's 'clarity' to define good and bad opinion:

> In the wake of a massacre that killed more than 5,000 innocent Americans in a day, one might expect moral clarity. After all, four days after Pearl Harbor, the isolationist America First Committee ... formally disbanded. There had been argument and confusion about America's role in the world and the intentions of its enemies. No more ....
>
> And yet, within days of the World Trade Center massacre, an event of blinding clarity, we are already beginning to hear the voices, prominent voices, of moral obtuseness.

Not content to douse Sontag's questions with overblown assertions about 'good' and 'evil', Krauthammer inserted into her essay points that Sontag never raised – 'perhaps she means that America should have abandoned Israel' – to offer the ultimate caricature of moral cowardice and treachery: 'What Sontag is implying, but does not quite have the courage to say, is that because of these "alliances and actions," such as the bombing of Iraq, we had it coming.'[12]

It requires only a glance at Sontag's *New Yorker* comment to recognise Krauthammer's distortion of what Gary Younge called her 'subtle, if strident tone that preferred complexity to simplicity and met intellectual challenges head on'. Far from being 'anti-American', she was calling for a display of what was best with 'America'. Like Chomsky, like Zinn, her dissent rested on a faith in an American 'public' who, asked to think and learn beyond the straitjacketed pronouncements of its leaders and broadcasters, would contemplate what should be done in light of what had gone before. As Sontag later commented, 'I thought I was writing centrist, obviously mainstream common sense. I was just saying, let's grieve together, let's not be stupid together.'[13]

The time needed for contemplation, however, did not fit the agenda of a War on Terror which was to be immediate and without reservation. For the sake of 'clarity', Sontag could not be allowed to separate 11 September 2001 from 7 December 1941; the example of the Second World War, rather than Korea or Vietnam, had to be paraded to put a just war beyond doubt. The questioning of American motivation as anything other than the purest pursuit of reparation for victims, and of security for all others, had to be depicted as sinister.

From there, it was a short step from supposed moral obtuseness to alliance with 'evil'. The *Weekly Standard* awarded the Susan Sontag Certificate, 'recognizing inanity by intellectuals and artists in the wake of terrorist attacks'. One article in *The New Republic*, a journal for which Sontag had written, began, 'What do Osama bin Laden, Saddam Hussein and Susan Sontag have in common?' Another declaimed, 'Only in a free, open society such as ours could people actually be arguing that it is courageous to murder thousands of civilians but cowardice to climb into a fighter plane to defend those same civilians.'[14] (The magazine also assisted readers by establishing an 'Idiocy Watch'.)

Sontag was effectively silenced and removed from public view. Then the hunt was on for others. Andrew Sullivan sounded the warning, 'The decadent left in its enclaves on the coasts is not dead – and may well mount what amounts to a fifth column.'[15] Within days of 9–11, the American Council of Trustees and Alumni issued an all-points bulletin on the Internet and in print for 'subversive' university lecturers and students. Led by activists such as Senator Joe Lieberman, former Vice Presidential and current Presidential candidate, and Lynne Cheney, former chairman of the National Endowment for Humanities and current wife of the Vice President, ACTA pursued its mission for 'academic freedom, excellence and accountability' by publishing the report *Defending Civilization: How Our Universities are Failing America and What Can Be Done About It*. It explained:

Rarely did professors publicly mention heroism, rarely did they mention the difference between good and evil, the nature of Western political order or the virtue of a free society. Indeed, the message of many in academe was clear: BLAME AMERICA FIRST.

The 115 transgressions listed included the campus poster 'Our grief is not a cry for war' and the statement of a Harvard lecturer criticising those 'who are deploying rhetoric and deploying troops without thinking before they speak'.[16]

Another website, Campus Watch, was launched to 'monitor and gather information on professors', particularly American scholars of the Middle East, 'who fan the flames of disinformation, incitement and ignorance'. Immediate targets included Stanford's Joel Beinin, the head of the Middle East Studies Association, Georgetown's John Esposito and 'Edward Said, [who] can be held responsible for a large portion of the morass of today's Middle East Studies departments'. When more than 100 academics protested by asking to be added to the list, the website's creator, Daniel Pipes responded with an expanded dossier of 154 'apologists for suicide bombings and militant Islam'. Such apologists were soon 'inundated with hostile spam, rendering their e-mail accounts almost useless', 'spoofed' with 'their identities ... stolen and thousands of offensive e-mail messages sent out in their names', and more than one received death threats by telephone.[17]

The charge in the *New York Post* against staff and students at City University of New York, holding a teach-in on 'Threats of War, Challenges of Peace', was that they had held 'a hard core America-bashing festival': a CUNY trustee made clear, 'I would consider that behavior seditious at this time.'[18] The University of South Florida fired Sami al-Arian, a Professor of Computer Science, in December 2001 for unspecified 'terrorist connections' after he appeared on the Fox News Channel and host Bill O'Reilly repeatedly told him, 'If I were with the CIA, I'd follow you wherever you went.'[19] (The firing was still being disputed in the courts in February 2003 when al-Arian was arrested on federal charges of affiliation with Islamic Jihad.)[20]

No sector of public life was beyond policing. At a high school in Alexandria, Virginia, students from the Amnesty

International Club put up posters with the slogan 'War Will Only Kill More'. These were torn down by staff, re-posted and torn down again. A student who wrote an essay criticising US foreign policy was asked for another paper on a less 'offensive' subject.[21] In West Virginia, a student was suspended for applying to start an anarchy club and wearing a T-shirt 'Against Bush, Against Bin Laden'. Security agents questioned a North Carolina student for 'anti-American activity' when someone reported that she had a wall poster criticising George Bush's support of the death penalty. Anti-war activists were barred from flights as security risks, and one passenger was turned away for carrying a novel by the anarchist Edward Abbey.[22] Two activists from Voices in the Wilderness, a group dedicated to non-violence, asked for 4,000 stamps, ones not with the American flag on them; they were questioned at length by police and a Federal postal inspector.[23]

Even those in the media who generally supported the Administration's get-tough approach might find their career threatened for a suspect statement. Bill Maher, the host of the national late-night talk show *Politically Incorrect*, sinned when he observed:

We have been the cowards, lobbing cruise missiles from 2,000 miles away. That's cowardly. Staying in the airplane when it hits the building, say what you want about it, it's not cowardly.[24]

Though Maher was a vigorous opponent of Arab and Islamic 'fundamentalism', he had to be punished. There was an immediate call for a boycott of any company that advertised on *Politically Incorrect* until the broadcaster ABC dropped the programme. The President's press secretary, Ari Fleischer, chipped in with, 'There are reminders to all Americans that they need to watch what they say, watch what they do. This is not a time for remarks like that; there never is.' *Politically Incorrect* was reprieved from the initial onslaught after Maher apologised, 'In no way was I intending to say, nor have I ever thought, that the men and women who defend our nation in uniform are anything but courageous and valiant, and I offer my apologies to anyone who took it wrong', but it was dropped in spring 2002.[25]

Even in this environment, there was a significant movement for peace, but it was contained in the media through limited attention or a broader 'perspective'. As a CNN senior executive admitted in August 2002, 'Anyone who claims the US media didn't censor itself is kidding you. It wasn't a matter of government pressure but a reluctance to criticise anything in a war that was obviously supported by the vast majority of the people.'[26] Vigils held across the US, the most prominent in New York's Washington Square, were reported with some sympathy in sections of the overseas press but treated as a footnote to events by American media. Andrew Jacobs reported in the *New York Times*, 'The drumbeat for war, so loud in the rest of the country, is barely audible on the streets of New York'; however, his article did not appear until 20 September, after dozens of other reports had emphasised public unity and 'the case for war'. An article the next day on 'A Nation Challenged: Campuses' further defined the issue:

> In some places, there were echoes, however faint, of the Vietnam era. Yesterday, for instance, demonstrations for peace were held on 146 campuses in 36 states, some of them drawing hundreds of chanting students. But on many of those same campuses and elsewhere, students spoke in almost romantic terms about giving their generation its chance to be the greatest [for military action].[27]

Vanity Fair, which had commissioned an article from Gore Vidal before the terrorist attacks, returned the essay after 11 September for 'market reasons'.[28] The views of Noam Chomsky, despite articles and interviews with overseas journalists which would become the collection *9–11*, were mentioned just twice in the *New York Times* between September and December 2001. (In an article summarising anti-war sentiment in the US, he was identified in the opening paragraph as 'the perennial dissenter'; the other reference quoted Hitchens' dismissal of Chomsky in *Letters to a Young Contrarian*.)[29] The views of Edward Said, despite his position at Columbia University, were ignored by the newspaper except for two articles from the Cultural Desk, one on 'Arab intellectuals', the other on the state of post-modernism after 9–11.[30] In contrast, the 'pundit' Ann Coulter, who called for the assassination of Arab/Muslim leaders and the conversion of their populations to Christianity and regretted that the *New York Times* had not been blown up, appeared on NBC's *Today*, MSNBC's *Hardball* and CNN's *Crossfire*. She was profiled in *Newsday*, the *New York Observer* and the *New York Times* and defended in the *Wall Street Journal* and *National Review Online*.[31]

Dissent was being drowned out by the seismic roar of an American 'culture of retribution' – Walter Isaacson, the president of CNN, warned, 'If you get on the wrong side of public opinion, you are going to get into trouble' – and those who spoke against this retribution did so only as fodder for hostile interviewers and more appropriate 'experts'. When Ibrahim Ramey of the Fellowship of Reconciliation spoke for an international legal process rather than bombing, Fox News' Bill O'Reilly snapped, 'Mr Ramey, with all due respect, that's a pie-in-the-sky Goldilocks answer that's going to allow terrorism to continue', and called for backup from his other guest, an academic at the conservative Heritage Foundation: 'Am I wrong, doctor?' O'Reilly and the audience were assured, 'Well, non-violence is a long tradition in the United States, but in this instance, it's one that will get you killed.' Before Arundhati Roy was interviewed on ABC's *Nightline*, host Ted Koppel offered a viewers' advisory:

Some of you, many of you, are not going to like what you hear tonight. You don't have to listen. But if you do, you should know that dissent sometimes comes in strange packages.[32]

Some who might be concerned about such treatment of dissent had already found hope in the saluting of the Flag. Indeed, protesters who had rejected or even burnt the Stars and Stripes during the war in Vietnam could now embrace the national symbol. As Todd Gitlin explained, 'It's an affirmation of solidarity. It's not an affirmation that America deserves to rule the world, just that America is a community entitled to public affection.'[33] Thomas Friedman wrote of playing 'The

Battle Hymn of the Republic' 'over and over, often singing along as I drove ... [This was] a moment of American solidarity, with people rallying to people and everyone rallying to the president.'[34]

With these images, as well as the more strident rejection of any nay-saying, the call to battle was sounded. A survey by Fairness and Accuracy in Reporting of the *New York Times* and *Washington Post* opinion pages for the three weeks from 9–11 found that 'columns calling for or assuming a military response to the attacks were given a great deal of space, while opinions urging diplomatic and international law approaches as an alternative to military action were nearly non-existent'.[35] Another content analysis of *Newsweek* and *Time* 'found that the news magazines minimized voices of opposition and instead focused on American unity, highlighted the importance of core American values, shifted blame away from the U.S., emphasized the U.S. role as the only superpower on the international stage, and demonized the enemy'.[36] In June 2002, 64 per cent of editors questioned by the Pew International Journalism Program assessed the media's coverage of foreign news as 'fair' or 'poor'.[37]

The admission came months after the event, however. In the meantime, the shutdown or setting aside of dissent reserved the airwaves for 'acceptable' opinion. When CNN told its American viewers of 'alleged' civilian casualties of US bombing in Afghanistan, anchormen were instructed to add the tagline, 'We must keep in mind, after seeing reports like this, that the Taliban regime in Afghanistan continues to harbour terrorists who have praised the September 11 attacks that killed close to 5,000 innocent people in the US.'[38] John Burns assured the readers of the *New York Times* that foreign peoples really did like the United States, leading the way for Thomas Friedman to claim repeatedly that all would be well if Arab countries followed a US model of 'democracy'. William Safire was blunter, heralding the resurgence of the American Empire.

By early October, the *New York Times* framed an acceptable Left as 'dissent [that] seemed more to anticipate events rather than react to them' even as 'the White House [was] talking of a carefully calibrated response'. (The next day, the bombing of Afghanistan began.) Jonathan Alter of *Newsweek* warned any dissenters, 'Blame America at your peril.' Michael Kelly in the *Washington Post* separated good from evil as a direct descendant of Orwell. Drawing from the author's listing of enemies in the Second World War, Kelly wrote, 'The American pacifists ... are on the side of future mass murders of Americans. They are objectively pro-terrorist .... That is the pacifists' position, and it is evil.'[39]

So when Ralph Nader addressed a 'Democracy Rising Rally' in San Francisco on 11 October, the only mention of the event in the *San Francisco Chronicle* was a comment about Nader's 'address [to] a large group of his fellow malcontents'.[40] When Mary Robinson, the UN High Commissioner for Human Rights, called for a bombing pause to allow more aid into Afghanistan, there was no need for any coverage in the US media, apart from a passing comment from *Washington Post* columnist Mary McGrory two weeks later. As CBS anchorman Dan Rather noted much later (but only on the BBC and not in the United States, where he continued to present the news):

> It is an obscene comparison – you know I am not sure I like it – but you know there was a time in South Africa that people would put flaming tyres around people's necks if they dissented. And in some ways the fear is that you will be necklaced here, you will have a flaming tyre of lack of patriotism put around your neck. Now it is that fear that keeps journalists from asking the toughest of the tough questions, and to continue to bore in on the tough questions so often. And again, I am humbled to say, I do not except myself from this criticism.[41]

Hitchens and his American peers assumed an important role in the War on Dissent by providing an alternative 'Left' which could be embraced. Michael Walzer was asking in *Dissent*, 'Can there be a Decent Left?' given a 'guilt, produced by living in [the US] and enjoying its privileges', accompanied by 'festering resentment, ingrown anger, and self-hate'. The Orwellian answer was 'to put decency first' by not blaming one's own country so often and blaming others a lot more.[42] Joe Klein waved credentials as a 1960s activist to quell British objections over Camp X-Ray:

While all the carping pains an Anglophile like me, most Americans don't give a fig about what you think .... And there is an old American saying which I think I've just invented: Before you get up on your high horse, be sure you are not riding an ass.[43]

(Later, in a series of Euro-trotting essays for the *Guardian*, he would uphold Italian Prime Minister Silvio Berlusconi at the expense of troublemaking trade unionists, a France which was a decaying throwback to the 1970s and a Germany rendered inert by a 'frantic ... thoughtfulness'.)[44] Thomas Friedman joined Klein in waving away weak-willed Europeans as he praised the President for updating the 'madman' approach to foreign policy:

[The Bush team's] willingness to restore our deterrence, and to be as crazy as some of our enemies, is one thing they have right. It's the only way we're going to get our turkey back.[45]

Yet Matthew Engel's comment in the *Guardian* at the end of January 2002, 'To complain is to be unAmerican', was only a partial perspective. Space for criticism might not come in discussion led by acceptable monitors such as Hitchens, but it could arise from complications in the political and military prosecution of the War on Terror. Throughout November and December and even into the New Year, the sudden capitulation of the Taliban overshadowed the failure to kill or capture Osama bin Laden and the instability of the 'new' Afghanistan. However, after trumpeted successes of US Special Forces turned out to be false, Howard Kurtz of the *Washington Post* reported, 'War Coverage Takes a Negative Turn', with 'a few reporters in Afghanistan ... challenging the official accounts' and 'some journalists [saying] the news business has been too passive'. Borrowing language from the Enron corporate crisis occurring at the same time, Mark Thompson of *Time* remarked, 'We are the auditors of this operation. Sometimes you get the feeling there's a little too much Arthur Andersen going on.'[46]

For the first time, the mainstream press began delving into less salubrious motives for intervention in Afghanistan, such as a column in the *Chicago Tribune*, 'Pipeline Politics Taint US

War'.[47] The *New York Times* finally called for 'the White House [to] seek the informed partnership of Congress and the American people', and Paul Kennedy, the British-born historian based at Yale, countered the unilateral sneering of Klein and Friedman:

> There is a deep yearning abroad these days for America to show real leadership .... It would be a leadership marked by a breadth of vision, an appreciation of our common humanity, a knowledge that we have as much to learn from others as we have to impart to them ....
>
> Were that to happen, we would fulfill America's promise – and probably get a surprise at just how popular we really are.[48]

Stories of opposition were being told and retold, spurred by the 'alternative' medium of the Internet. Michael Moore's *Stupid White Men*, a broad indictment of American politics and society, had initially fallen victim to 9–11, with Rupert Murdoch's HarperCollins ordering the pulping of the 50,000 copies ready for distribution. The book was saved by a 'librarians' revolt', started by an audience member who heard Moore's tale and spread it across discussion boards. HarperCollins relented, and by March the book was top of the *New York Times*' best-seller list for non-fiction. (In February 2003, it was still in the Top 10 and going into its 45th printing.)

Far from checking the emerging protest, the Bush Administration's shift of focus to Iraq provided further opportunity for criticism; as Friedman complained, 'President Bush thinks the axis of evil is Iran, Iraq, and North Korea, and the Europeans think it's Donald Rumsfeld, Dick Cheney, and Condoleezza Rice.'[49] The former arms inspector Scott Ritter, now a vocal critic of US policy towards the 'phantom threat' of Saddam Hussein, began to receive attention.[50] There was even a return to the pre-9–11 belittling of the President. Aaron Sorkin, the creator of the fictional White House in the *West Wing*, claimed, 'We're simply pretending to believe that Bush exhibited unspeakable courage at [baseball's] World Series by throwing out the first pitch at Yankee Stadium or that he, by

God, showed those terrorists by going to Salt Lake City and jumbling the first line of the Olympic opening ceremony. The media is waving pom-poms and the entire public is being polite.' On the six-month anniversary of 9–11, the *Observer* did a cultural tour of Sorkin, Michael Moore, the comedienne Sandra Bernhard, *New York Times* writer Frank Bruni's tale of 'the unlikely odyssey of George W. Bush' and Alexandra Pelosi's documentary *Journeys with George* to proclaim, 'Suddenly it's cool to be rude about Dubya again.'

'Dissent' was not just cultural jibes, however, and it was no longer the muttering of a lone Congresswoman or a soon-to-be-silenced intellectual. Robert Byrd, an elder statesmen in the Senate, criticised the President's 'sabre-rattling' and compared it to the Gulf of Tonkin resolution, which authorised large-scale US intervention in Vietnam, 'Shrouded in ambiguity and cloaked in deep secrecy, this administration continues to suddenly, and sometimes unexpectedly, drop its decisions upon the public and Congress, and expect obedient approval, without question, without debate, and without opposition.'[51] Representative Dennis Kucinich was charging that the Bush Administration was funding an undeclared war by taking money from 'education, housing for the elderly, health care, and transportation' and offering a 'Prayer for America':

> Let us pray that we have the courage to replace the images of death which haunt us, the layers of images of September 11th, faded into images of patriotism, spliced into images of military mobilization, jump-cut into images of our secular celebrations of the World Series, New Year's Eve, the Super Bowl, the Olympics, the strobic flashes which touch our deepest fears, let us replace those images with the work of human relations, reaching out to people, helping our own citizens here at home, lifting the plight of the poor everywhere.
>
> That is the America which has the ability to rally the support of the world.[52]

Meanwhile, Representative Cynthia McKinney was raising even more uncomfortable questions, 'What did this Administration know, and when did it know it, about the events of September 11?', alleging that 'persons close to his administration are poised to make huge profits off America's new war'.[53] In the *New York Times*, Frank Rich declared, 'The Bush Doctrine RIP', given American alliances with states, such as Saudi Arabia and Pakistan, which could be accused of supporting terrorism.[54] 'The widest ranging group of opponents of government policy since September 11' issued the Not in Our Name statement – 'Let it not be said that people in the United States did nothing when their government declared a war without limit and instituted stark new measures of repression' – and a group of 128 US intellectuals sent a public letter to European counterparts requesting 'a sane and frank European criticism of the Bush administration's war policy'.[55] Even Thomas Friedman, who had carried the flag for an American democracy around the world, now cast 'blame' on President Bush 'for squandering all the positive feeling in America after 9/11'.[56]

There was worse to come with the Administration's muddling in the worsening Israeli–Palestinian conflict and the fallout from the Enron débâcle. Vice President Dick Cheney came under scrutiny for secret meetings with energy companies and for his tenure as Chief Executive Officer of the Halliburton Corporation, amidst charges that he moved to the vice-presidency from the company with a $36 million payout while leaving behind an unstable pension fund and a merger that left Halliburton liable for billions in asbestos-related lawsuits. White House records showed that Cheney's aide Lewis 'Scooter' Libby sold up to $225,000 in energy company shares just as the Administration was drafting plans for an expansion in energy production. Even President Bush was caught up in the sudden media scrutiny, with re-examination of alleged insider trading when he was Chief Executive Officer of the Harken Corporation.[57] The *National Enquirer*, better known for fanciful tales of sex and celebrity scandal, revealed, 'The Enron Corporation gave the Taliban millions of dollars in a no-holds-barred bid to strike a deal for an energy pipeline in Afghanistan – while the Taliban were already sheltering terror kingpin Osama Bin Laden!'[58] In this case, the hyperbole rested on an element of truth.

Belatedly, the press began asking Cynthia McKinney's question – Had the Administration had advance warning about the possibility of a 9–11-type attack? With further revelations of advance intelligence that was not heeded, 'in a single day, the capital's media climate [was] transformed'.[59] Condoleezza Rice had asserted in May, 'I don't think anybody could have predicted that these people would take an airplane and slam it into the World Trade Center'; three months later the admission of an FBI whistleblower established that agents had notes that a suspect might be planning exactly that type of operation. (A Congressional committee subsequently established that, between 1994 and 2001, US intelligence had warnings of a dozen plots of a similar nature.)[60] The White House was finally forced to admit that President Bush was shown briefings that Osama bin Laden might be planning hijackings.

Helen Thomas of Hearst Newspapers began criticising an 'imperial Presidency ... with Americans turning into a new silent majority and Congress into a bunch of obeisant lawmakers'.[61] Maureen Dowd, who had never shown proper respect for Bush, laughed at a European tour in May where the President showed off his Texas charm, noting that France's President Jacques Chirac was 'always saying that the food here is fantastic, and I'm going to give him a chance to show me tonight' and chiding a US reporter who asked a question to President Chirac in French: 'Whoa! The guy memorises four words and he plays like he's inter-continental. I'm impressed! Que bueno! Now I'm literate in two languages.'[62] Reuters and other services gleefully reported that Bush nicknamed Russian President Vladimir Putin 'Poot-Poot' and accepted his new friend's explanation of caviar production, 'Experts take the eggs from the fish, then they sew it up and let it go back into the [river] Volga.'[63] Dana Milbank of the *Washington Post* presented Bush's novel use of language, such as his offer 'to help Russia securitize the dismantled nuclear warheads' and his reference to the 'unalienable rights in the Declaration of Independence'.[64]

Public support for President Bush's handling of the War on Terror remained above 70 per cent. However, there was now a political and cultural space to express 'dissent' in the mass media. Chomsky made his one and only appearance on a far-from-welcoming CNN.[65] The Not in Our Name petition was acknowledged by the very newspapers that were being criticised for failing to challenge the Bush Administration's actions and rhetoric. The White House's unveiling of a 'pre-emptive strike' strategy was immediately challenged by commentators in the *Washington Post* and other newspapers. As Mark Morford of the *San Francisco Gate* framed the doctrine, 'Be pre-emptive and destructive and bomb-happy, or be a tree-hugging traitorous liberal commie sympathizer. There is no in-between.'[66] CBS News laughed at an Attorney General who was constantly finding 'dirty bombers': 'Who needs terrorists when we have John Ashcroft to scare us out of our pants?'[67]

Of course, the keepers of the proper American faith were still on the lookout for troublemakers. Jonah Goldberg maintained a steady rant in the *National Review*: '[Representative Cynthia McKinney is] dumber than rock salt and more repugnant than Yasser Arafat's three-week-old underwear.' 'The main reason Europeans hate Israel is that they hate America; and the main reason they hate America is that they really hate themselves.' 'Why does it seem like so many Islamic scholars, particularly the nasty ones, are blind? Does the Koran say that you can't ingest vitamin A?'[68] Andrew Sullivan, also known as 'Hitchens Lite', berated the 'confused left' through a diatribe against the 'purist class-war leftist' Michael Moore: 'There is ... barely a mention in Moore's book about the current war on terrorism .... It raises questions the left simply doesn't want to answer.' (Unfortunately for his analysis, Sullivan did not realise that *Stupid White Men* was printed before 9–11.)[69] Neil Cavuto of the Fox News Channel offered the sage advice to any foreigners who raised questions, 'I don't require a "thank you" when we give you a hand, but I don't expect the finger either.'[70]

The playground rhetoric betrayed the weakness that, with their caricatures of the 'enemy', these guardians were missing or avoiding the diversity of criticism. In August 2002, when the Bush Administration renewed the campaign for military action against Iraq, opponents included Brent Scowcroft and James Baker, both leading advisers to the first President Bush, Dick Armey, the Republican leader in the House of Representatives, and the veteran neo-conservative commentator William

Buckley.[71] The *New York Times* was being pilloried as the paper where 'super-liberals have to rise to the defense of suicide bombers', and a federal appeal was inconveniently ruling that the Administration's conduct of hundreds of deportation hearings in secret was illegal.[72] Even Thomas Friedman now had doubts about the wisdom of 'craziness':

> [Bush] shows real contempt for the world, and a real lack of seriousness, when he says from the golf tee ... 'I call upon all nations to do everything they can to stop these terrorist killers. Thank you. Now watch this drive.'[73]

Appropriately, Sontag reappeared with a comment for the first anniversary of 9–11, 'Real wars are not metaphors – they have a beginning and an end. But the war that has been declared by the Bush administration will never end. That is one sign that it is not a war but, rather, a mandate for expanding the use of power.'[74] Maureen Dowd, as acerbic as ever, mocked the crusade for 'Texas on the Tigris', and the *Washington Post*'s William Raspberry declared that Bush's case 'fails morally. War ... needs a firmer basis than that the slimeball [Hussein] was happy about 9/11 and I'm still sore about Poppy [the first President Bush].'[75] Simon Schama published his 'Whiff of Dread for the Land of Hope', with its scathing denunciation of the President.[76] The *Los Angeles Times* summarised, 'Mr. Bush had plenty of capital to spend after Sept. 11. Sadly, on issue after issue, most of that capital is still in the bank, depreciating by the day', a comment echoed and extended in papers from Madison, Wisconsin to Missoula, Montana to Honolulu, Hawaii.[77]

Amidst large demonstrations in New York, Washington DC and other cities, disquiet had spread far beyond the usual suspects and those who could be easily mocked (such as Barbra Streisand with her fax for Democrats to 'get off the fence and go on the offensive').[78] James Fallows of the *Atlantic* noted the 'blowback' that had not been envisaged before intervention in Afghanistan, 'If we can judge from past wars, the effects we can't imagine when the fighting begins will prove to be the ones that matter most.'[79] The editorial writers at *American*

Prospect also warned, 'If the fighting turns ugly and there are large numbers of civilian casualties – if we have to level the very cities we say we are liberating – American legitimacy in the eyes of the world and of the Iraqis will be shot', and put forth an argument paralleling the 'nutcase' allegations of Cynthia McKinney about Bush's use of 9–11: 'The suspicion will not die that the administration turned to Iraq for relief from a sharp decline in its domestic political prospects, corporate scandals, and the fall of the stock market.'[80]

Perhaps most significant were the doubts being put by defenders of the American way. Fareed Zakaria, who had written in *Newsweek* immediately after 9–11 that 'for the rest of the world it is the end of the free ride', cautioned that the US should 'gain the legitimacy that comes through an international consensus. Without this cloak of respectability America will face a growing hostility around the world.' Friedman set aside his campaign for American-led democracy to warn, 'Iraq cannot prevent an American victory. But it might be able to extend a war over weeks and months, imposing significant costs and putting on a bloody show for the rest of the world.'[81] The *Atlanta Journal-Constitution*, far from a bleeding-heart publication, commented, 'Invasion would mark the next step towards an American empire ... [Key Bush Administration officials] envision the creation and enforcement of a Pax Americana.'[82] Even Joe Klein began to fret, 'The rush to war, the tendency of conservatives (and their propagandists) to go berserk whenever legitimate questions are raised, the giddy moral certainty in the air, the fact that we are not talking about one quick war against a psychopath but about a fundamental shift in American policy that may shape the world for the next 50 years – all this should cause us to pause, slow down, and talk this over.'[83]

When Congressmen such as Jim McDermott alleged, 'This president is trying to bring to himself all the power to become an emperor – to create Empire America', and national churches such as the United Methodists (President Bush's denomination) declared, 'It is inconceivable that Jesus Christ would support this proposed attack', the assessment of Anthony Lewis in the *New York Review of Books* that 'the fear of looking unpatriotic inhibits dissent' risked the appearance of obsolescence.[84] Yet precisely because, in the words of the *Guardian*'s Ed Vulliamy, 'the uprising of the intelligentsia has burst its banks', the need to contain any potential flood was reinforced.[85]

Once more, the best method was to turn the 'Left' against itself, to invoke the 'proper' Spirit of '68. Another veteran, Greil Marcus, swung wildly as 'the bile rose in [his] throat' at Chomsky, Fisk, Zinn and Sontag, their arguments supposedly 'told [him] that everyone and anything the United States was or might be attacked by is in fact the direct creation of the United States'. In Marcus' world, those who examined the causes of 9–11 were the real controllers of debate and opinion, seeking 'to close questions, not to open them – as if [theirs were] the only voices brave enough to say what had to be said'.[86]

Todd Gitlin, member and then chronicler of Students for a Democratic Society, prominent scholar of the media and US politics, followed up his post-9–11 adoption of the US flag with an assault on the 'left-wing fundamentalist' in January 2002. No specific fundamentalist was named, but the reader was assured that 'on the left, both abroad and at home, [there was] smugness, acrimony, even schadenfreude, accompanied by the notion that the attacks were, well, not a just dessert, exactly, but … [a] damnable yet understandable payback … rooted in America's own crimes of commission and omission … reaping what [the] empire had sown'. So the 'patriotic fervor' which Gitlin had embraced turned into the allegation that, for the deviant 'Left', 'America is seen as all of a piece, and it is hated because it is hateful – period. One may quarrel with the means used to bring it low, but low is only what it deserves.' The substantive evidence, when it was finally presented, was the standard litany that 'Noam Chomsky [had] bent facts' in his comparison of the 1998 Sudan attack with 11 September, that Edward Said exulted in writing of 'a superpower almost constantly at war, or in some sort of conflict, all over the Islamic domains'. Arundhati Roy's essay of September 2001 became a 'queenly declaration' in which 'she was in the grip of a prejudice invulnerable to moral distinctions'.[87]

Gitlin's major contribution would come in October 2002, at the same time that Hitchens was spitting his resignation at the

Nation. Gitlin, unlike Hitchens, had not only expressed disquiet about the Bush Administration, but had come out in opposition to the 'puny' commitment to rebuilding Afghanistan, the gluing of 'Team Bush' to Israel's Ariel Sharon, and the 'hapless' and 'thuggish' policy against Iraq. But only a few weeks later Gitlin, after speaking at an anti-war rally, denounced in full Hitchensian voice the protestors who supposedly had 'a refusal to face a grotesque world ... a near-total unwillingness to rebuke Saddam Hussein, and a rejection of any conceivable rationales for using force'. Inevitably the opposition was converted into the naive followers of the 'morally tainted' and 'doomed' Ramsay Clark, the former US Attorney General who now 'belong[ed] to the International Committee to Defend Slobodan Milosevic'.

Gitlin's concluding flourish was the quotation of Marc Cooper of the *Los Angeles Times*:

If the left is not for Hussein and is also opposed to economic sanctions, what is it for? If the left is for containment instead of invasion, then isn't it the U.S. armed forces that must do the containing? ... If at the end of the day, Hussein does foil weapons inspections, what is to be done then?[88]

Once more dissent was turned into a caricature, once more any thoughtful criticism was dismissed for the delusions of the 'old Left at its worst'. The suggestion that removal of sanctions might be linked to confirmation of the disposal of Iraq's weapons of mass destruction (a proposal being discussed by the United Nations as late as May 2002, before the latest American drive for war), the possibility of a policy based not on US armed forces but on international enforcement, the concept that Saddam Hussein might not foil weapons inspections, provided the US did not sabotage this course of action: all this was removed from discussion.

George Packer, in the guise of a studied examination of liberals and their approach to intervention, began by tilting the arena: 'This is not a constructive liberal antiwar movement.' With this introduction, he could pretend a nuanced study of 'liberal hawks' as 'people, who generally have little trouble making up their minds and debating forcefully, talked themselves through every side of the question'. Michael Walzer 'the theorist', Christopher Hitchens 'the romantic', David Rieff 'the skeptic', Leon Wieseltier 'the secularist' and Paul Berman 'the idealist', almost all of whom had written off others in the 'Left' as unacceptable for questioning the War on Terror, were given fawning treatment. 'Doves' never reappeared; instead, Packer closed with the 'liberal intellectuals' being re-fastened to intervention by the Iraqi exile Kanan Makiya, who 'met their hope of avoiding a war with an even greater hope, [giving] the people·in the room an image of their own ideals'.[89]

On occasion, those claiming to police the Left from within would give away the tactic by citing neo-conservatives. Michael J. Totten relied on the assertion of Robert Kagan, the academic closely linked to Bush's hawks, 'Yesterday's liberal intervention- ists, in Bosnia, Kosovo and Haiti, are today's liberal abstentionists. What changed? Just the man in the White House,' before throwing in an Orwell quote and launching into sub-Hitchens diatribe:

> If you don't join us now, when Saddam's regime falls and Iraqis cheer the US Marines, you are really going to feel like a jackass. And your jackassery will be exposed beneath klieg lights for all to see. Remember the Chomskyites who got everything wrong in Afghanistan? Remember the Europeans who wanted to give the Butcher in Belgrade one more chance? That is not where you want to be right now.[90]

With opposition reduced to the issue of 'good' vs. 'bad' activists, Republican gains in the mid-term Congressional elections were presented as a 'mandate for war'.[91] Between mid-September and early February, 380 of 414 stories on Iraq on NBC, ABC and CBS television came from the White House, Pentagon and State Department.[92] Inevitably, the United Nations resolution insisting on renewed inspections was converted into a last-chance saloon for Baghdad: 'Hussein will be disarmed. Just how that happens is up to him.'[93] The *New York Times*, which had stood aside from war in October – 'Bush said, "Approving this resolution does not mean that military action is imminent or unavoidable." The country should hold him to that' – was back on board by December:

> Had Baghdad kept its word [in 1991], its non-conventional weapons would long ago have been destroyed and the sites where they were developed permanently monitored. If careful scrutiny of Iraq's new report shows it to be still defaulting on its promises, it will have forfeited the chance for a peaceful solution.[94]

John Hughes offered assurance in the *Christian Science Monitor* that the war would be just and laudable: 'Exposing a large chunk of the Islamic world to democracy is a noble goal .... It might set an example for other Arab lands wallowing in backwardness and despair.'[95]

Hostages were being left to fortune, however. Complications in the fight for freedom were exposed when the Administration backed away from a showdown with North Korea, which not only claimed to have nuclear weapons but brazenly evicted UN monitors and withdrew from the Non-Proliferation Treaty. The American claim that it could bring 'democracy' to Muslims through war in Iraq was so tenuous – in the words of one *Washington Post* columnist, 'Is it hopelessly cynical to imagine that democratization is a much lower priority than controlling Iraqi oil reserves, asserting our authority in that part of the world and (perhaps) avenging our president's father?'[96] – that supporters of the cause had to look beyond Washington for salvation. Thomas Friedman's pronouncement, 'Blair for US president', might have been a quip aimed at Democrats rather than Bush, but the sentiment was repeated solemnly by the *New York Times* in January 2003: 'Blair seems to understand well as he carefully balances the role of public opinion in a democracy and the responsibilities of international leadership. Washington would do well to study his example.'[97]

As in Britain with its 'unlikely couplings' of protesters beyond the stereotyped Left,[98] dissent's 'useful idiots' were now in US streets. After the demonstrations in autumn 2002, the *Washington Post*'s ombudsman admitted 'the failure to report the news of the rallies when they occurred';[99] four months later, there were too many American participants in global protests to be ignored. Only days before, *Newsweek* had declared, 'Anti-war protests are happening all over the country and the world, but the mainstream media are hardly paying attention.'[100] Afterwards, even Fox News, the declared enemy of weak-kneed liberals, had to acknowledge, 'Crowds Cry for Peace in Washington, Across U.S., Around the World', and the *New York Daily News* admitted, 'W Pushes War, but People Push Back'.[101] CNN now presented anti-war activists, including 'human shields', in debates on the Showdown with Iraq and gave airtime to Yasmin Alibhai-Brown to critique the media's previous ignorance of dissenting opinion.

It was all too much for Hitchens. As hundreds of thousands joined protests in a number of US cities in mid-January, he gave up all semblance of argument. Invited by a Seattle 'alternative' newspaper to comment, he began gently, 'The editor of this rag told me of your upcoming "Potlucks for Peace" event and invited my comments, and at first I couldn't think of a thing to say.' He gathered himself enough to yell, 'Ever since that morning [of 11 September] the United States has been at war with the forces of reaction', but any addition of substance was a struggle. Even the charge sheet against Saddam and his support of 'terrorism' was stretched beyond breaking point: 'Saddam Hussein denounced the removal of the Sunni Muslim-murdering Slobodan Milosevic, and also denounced the removal of the Shiite-murdering Taliban.'[102]

Hitchens railed at 'Christians', including Jimmy Carter, 'peanut czar, home-builder, Nobel laureate, and Baptist big mouth', who dared question war in Iraq.[103] He warned that Saddam could 'put the world economy into a slump and kill millions of people' and named UN inspectors as accomplices of the crime: 'More time means [Saddam Hussein] could join the club that Kim Jong-Il of North Korea now belongs to .... And Mr. Kim Jong-Il got there with the help of Mr. Hans Blix.' He forged the links that could not be proved: '[It would be] rather unsurprising to find that so many of the al Qaeda refugees in Afghanistan have shown up in Baghdad.'[104] He even rewrote his personal history of 9–11: now he was no longer in Washington State but in Washington, DC, on that catastrophic day: 'I've seen the Pentagon burning from the top of my house. I've seen .... And where .... My daughter's school was just up across the river from that .... Very difficult to go ... tough time getting her back from school that day. The streets were jammed, panic, fire.'[105]

But after 16 months, after the high of the 'Ha ha ha' had been undone by the complications of a victory that never would be straightforward, all that was left was the sneer: 'Nothing seems to disturb the contented air of moral superiority that surrounds those who intone the "peace movement".'[106]

7

How we Dissent: On Bushmen and the 'Preponderance of Power'

The containment of dissent has often relied on 9–11 as a starting point, the response of the intellectual validated only if he or she began with the attacks to reach conclusions about the menace of 'Islamic fascism'. Any consideration that began with a cause preceding the event, such as Susan Sontag's reference to an 'attack ... undertaken as a consequence of specific American alliances and actions' or Mary Beard's 'feeling that all the "civilised world" ... is paying the price for its glib definitions of "terrorism" and its refusal to listen to what the "terrorists" have to say',[1] could be ruled out of order.

But of course the challenge of a Susan Sontag, a Mary Beard, a George Monbiot, an Edward Said and many others was that they dared to examine the world before 11 September 2001, to posit that the terrorist strike was not the only source of American policies and actions which had a vision far beyond Ground Zero. The Bush Administration had entered office dedicated to a strategy of 'preponderance of power', a 'blueprint for maintaining global US pre-eminence, precluding the rise of a great power rival, and shaping the international security order in line with American principles and interests'. The US military, 'the cavalry on the new American frontier', would be ready to 'fight and decisively win multiple, simultaneous major theatre wars'. If necessary, this superiority would be maintained through first strikes: 'To forestall or prevent ... hostile acts by our adversaries, the United States will, if necessary, act preemptively.'[2]

This strategy, with its 'nearly messianic vision'[3] of an American global role, was not tabled in January 2001 but more than a decade earlier, after the fall of the Berlin Wall. Held up by the first War on Iraq in 1991, it was re-presented at the end of the first Bush Administration in 1992 by Secretary of

Defense Dick Cheney and his assistants Paul Wolfowitz and Lewis Libby.[4] Wolfowitz and Libby, with Donald Rumsfeld, Richard Perle, Richard Armitage and George Bush's brother Jeb developed the concept through a private 'think tank', Project for a New American Century, launched in 1997.

The origins of PNAC lay in a 1996 article, 'Toward a Neo-Reaganite Foreign Policy', by William Kristol, a lynchpin of the neo-conservative challenge to Bill Clinton, and the Yale academic Robert Kagan. Complaining that 'in foreign policy, conservatives are adrift', they proposed a role of 'benevolent global hegemony' for an America that was supposedly drifting towards a 'reduced role in a post-Cold War world'. Kristol's key position within Washington's networks and Kagan's emerging academic profile forged a PNAC of aspiring politicians, former Government officials, businessmen and intellectuals which, by the eve of the 2000 Presidential election, would confirm, 'At present the United States faces no global rival. America's grand strategy should aim to preserve and extend this advantageous position as far into the future as possible.' Its 90-page guide to political, economic and military strategy would be the bedrock of the new Administration's approach, its only misstep coming in the failure to identify the 'terrorist' as the primary threat, 'While reconfiguring its nuclear force, the United States also must counteract the effects of the proliferation of ballistic missiles and weapons of mass destruction that may soon allow lesser states to deter U.S. military action by threatening U.S. allies and the American homeland itself.'[5]

PNAC was complemented by 'academic' centres such as the American Enterprise Institute and activist groups such as the Jewish Institute for National Security Affairs, with members such as Cheney, Perle, John Bolton, the future Undersecretary of State, and Douglas Feith, future Undersecretary of Defense, and the Center for Security Policy, which would provide 22 members of the second Bush Administration.[6] Their output included a 1996 paper, 'A Clean Break: A New Strategy for Securing the Realm', prepared for Israeli Prime Minister Binyamin Netanyahu by Perle and Feith. The Americans advised Israel to scrap the Oslo Accords with Palestinian leaders, to 'shape its strategic environment by weakening, containing and even rolling back Syria' and to 'focus on removing Saddam Hussein from power in Iraq – an important Israeli strategic objective in its own right' as first steps towards removing anti-Israeli governments in Syria, Lebanon, Saudi Arabia and Iran.[7]

All these activists would become members of, or consultants to, the second Bush Presidency. Supporting Rumsfeld at the Pentagon, Perle chaired the advisory Defense Policy Board with members such as Henry Kissinger and Newt Gingrich. Building on the work of PNAC, JINSA and CSP, Perle's influential group would build a strategy based on regime changes, an approach summarised by a Perle adviser in August 2002 (including the recommendation of 'an ultimatum to the House of Saud') as 'Iraq as the tactical pivot, Saudi Arabia as the strategic pivot [and] Egypt as the prize'.[8]

The strategy provided a general framework which extended the Clinton Administration's identification of 'rogue states', namely Cuba, Iran, Iraq, Libya and North Korea. Now the threat was no longer from specific enemies; it was general and global, and the US must be prepared for unilateral 'pre-emption' of this danger. Some officials even hailed the 'clash of civilisations' thesis set out by academics and consultants such as Samuel Huntington in the 1990s. Donald Rumsfeld told the *Daily Telegraph*: 'If one looks down from outer space on earth, you find a couple of handfuls of countries that are generally like thinking, and they tend to be in Western Europe and North America. They have freer political systems, and freer economic systems, and tend not to covet the land or property or lives of other nations.'[9]

A starting point for the strategy was to assert US power while removing the nuisance of the Iraqi leadership. Many of the veterans of the first Bush Administration had rued the failure to depose the Iraqi leadership in the first Gulf War, blaming Colin Powell among others for ceasing fire and abandoning the Shi'a and Kurd rebellions;[10] even in their 1990s exile from Government, they sought redress. The Project for a New Century began lobbying President Clinton in January 1998 for 'a full complement of diplomatic, political and military efforts' to remove Saddam Hussein from power,[11] and the group declared in a September 2000 document, 'The

United States has for decades sought to play a more permanent role in Gulf regional security. While the unresolved conflict with Iraq provides the immediate justification, the need for a substantial American force presence in the Gulf transcends the issue of the regime of Saddam Hussein.'[12] During the Presidential campaign, 'various great and worthy men trooped down to Austin to teach George Bush about the world. And by and large, they told him that Iraq was unfinished business.'[13] From Inauguration Day, Perle's Defense Policy Board was considered by some 'in the State Department, on Capitol Hill ... as "the cabal", ... a group in the Pentagon, aligned with some people outside of government, that is absolutely determined to lay the groundwork for a strategy to get Saddam out with the use of American military troops'. Inside the Administration, Undersecretary of Defense Wolfowitz provided the strategic framework while Cheney emphasised that access to Persian Gulf oil was a necessity and priority for US foreign policy: 'Iraq remains a destabilising influence to the flow of oil to international markets from the Middle East.'[14]

The first casualty of the strategy was not Saddam Hussein, however, but an international approach to these priorities. Once again, the strategy of the second Bush Administration harked back to the Defense Policy Guidance set out by Cheney, Rumsfeld and Wolfowitz as they left office in 1993:

> While we favor collective action to respond to threats and challenges in this new era, a collective response will not always be timely and in the absence of US leadership may not gel .... Neither can we allow our critical interests to depend solely on international mechanisms that can be blocked by countries whose interests may be very different to our own.[15]

Inevitably, the strategy fostered concern and possible division, particularly with America's supposed partners in Western Europe. Within weeks of the Bush Administration's taking office, Rumsfeld had greeted allies by warning of 'actions that could reduce NATO's effectiveness by confusing duplication or by perturbing the transatlantic link' and by pointedly refusing to use the term 'European Union'.[16] During the President's first visit to Europe in June 2001, insults were traded by newspapers and even officials across the Atlantic. As one analysis in *USA Today* offered:

> While in Europe this week, President Bush faced recalcitrant European leaders who, among other issues, disagree with the United States' use of the death penalty. This is interesting in as much as:
>
> Spain is a country that gave us the Inquisition. England had a king who continued his tennis match while his wife was being beheaded at his command. France is the country that came up with the 'humane' way to carry out a death sentence, the guillotine. And Germany gave the world an innovative use of gas ovens.[17]

The tragedy of 9–11 did not sweep aside existing US strategies and approaches. Away from the War on Terror, American unilateralism would continue to provoke, with withdrawal from or limitation of the Anti-Ballistic Missile Treaty, International Criminal Court ('to protect the country's top leaders from being indicted, arrested or hauled before the court on war crimes charges'), the Kyoto protocol on the environment, international conventions on biological and chemical warfare, the accord on land mines, the international conference on racism and the International Agreement on Children's Rights. The Administration would even try, unsuccessfully, to block a UN vote on an anti-terror resolution.[18]

Meanwhile, the complications and hypocrisies of the War on Terror were being exposed. Stories began to emerge of US entanglements that contradicted official policy and might even have contributed to 9–11, such as the $23 million of equipment sold to Saddam Hussein by Cheney's Halliburton before January 2001;[19] the international investment empire of the Carlyle Group, with board members including the elder George Bush and John Major meeting clients such as the bin Laden family;[20] negotiations with the Taliban for an oil and gas pipeline across northern Afghanistan (manoeuvres including, among others, future Afghan President Hamid Karzai, future Bush special envoy Zalmay Khalilzad, Halliburton and the Carlyle Group);[21] an American approach in July 2001 to high-level Pakistani officials (who proceeded to tell the Taliban) proposing an attack upon Afghanistan in October;[22] or the Clinton Administration's 'game plan to remove al-Qaida from the face of the earth', which only reached Bush's desk on 9 September 2001.[23] A few 'alternative' correspondents noticed the place of oil after 9–11 in the War on Terror – three days after the first American bombs fell, the US Ambassador to Pakistan told the Pakistani Oil Minister that the pipeline was back on the table 'in view of recent geopolitical developments'.[24]

Nor did the future hold out brighter prospects for the American pursuit of its war. Afghanistan's Cabinet ministers were assassinated and, after an attempt on President Hamid Karzai's life, bodyguards were brought in from a Virginia 'private military corporation'.[25] US bombers continued to hit civilians, such as an attack on several villages in July 2002 in which up to 80 people died,[26] the CIA took up an alternative policy of assassinating leaders of Afghan factions, including some with no connection to Al-Qa'eda,[27] and details emerged of American involvement in the torture, murder and 'disappearance' of Taliban prisoners.[28] With the lifting of the Taliban's ban on opium production, there was a 1,400 per cent increase in the harvest of poppies.[29] Women who attended the *loya jirga* confirming the new political system 'faced the threat of violent backlash': the Minister for Women's Affairs was accused of blasphemy and forced from office (no replacement was appointed) and 'in much of the country outside of Kabul, the crossfire of rival factions … left women immensely vulnerable and victimized anew by a wave of rapes and other forms of sexual violence'.[30] Madeleine Bunting in the *Guardian* reflected:

> By the time of the first anniversary of the fall of Kabul it will no longer be possible to ignore the accumulation of these awkward details, and we will be embarrassed to be reminded of our naive triumphalism. The war was a crude and clumsy intervention which did little for the wretched Afghans, and even less for the struggle against terrorism.[31]

The chilling appearance was that key members of the Bush Administration could care less about such questions and other inconveniences such as the Israeli–Palestinian dispute; the priority was the display of American might. Rumsfeld had signalled in May 2001, as the US failed for the first time to be voted onto the UN Human Rights Commission:

People who never believed the United States had a monopoly on all political wisdom or all economic wisdom or all cultural wisdom now don't feel grateful for the role the United States was playing to the same extent, and so they're perfectly willing to express their views. That's fine. We don't have a monopoly on all wisdom in the world, and we can live in that world very successfully.[32]

An American diplomat explained the unilateralist mission in more prosaic terms: 'These guys at the Pentagon – Wolfowitz, Perle, Doug Feith – when they lie in bed at night, they imagine a new book written by one of them or about them called, "Present at the Recreation". They want to banish the wimpy Europeanist traditional balance of power, and use the Iraq seedbed of democracy to impose America's will on the world.'[33]

Rumsfeld had laid out the Administration's policy of a 'pre-emptive strike' in March 2001 with the principle that the US should 'act forcefully, early, during [a] pre-crisis period' with the might 'necessary to prevail, plus some', a principle confirmed publicly 15 months later by President Bush in a speech at West Point: 'A military that must be ready to strike at a moment's notice in any dark corner of the world. And our security will require all Americans to be forward looking and resolute, to be ready for preemptive action when necessary to defend our liberty and to defend our lives.'[34] The US not only pulled out of the ABM Treaty, but was dismantling oversight of the missile defence programme as work began on a site in northern Alaska.[35] Even the revelation at the end of 2002 that the US was staging 'successful' tests with 'easy-to-spot decoys' as targets did not prove an obstacle.[36] As the defence budget was scheduled to rise by 35 per cent by 2007, bringing it to $451 billion per year, military bases were rapidly expanded and placed, for the first time, in countries such as

Uzbekistan and Kyrgyzstan. Special forces were deployed in the Philippines, Djibouti, Indonesia and former Soviet republics such as Georgia, and supplementary military assistance was earmarked for interests such as oil pipelines in Colombia.[37] The Administration abandoned a pledge, made in 1978, not to use nuclear weapons against non-nuclear states;[38] and for good measure the Pentagon drew up a contingency list of seven targets (China, Russia, Iran, Iraq, North Korea, Syria and Libya).[39] The Department of Defense was also 'building up an elite secret army with resources stretching across the full spectrum of covert capabilities'.[40]

In this context, 9–11 was not the foundation for US foreign policy, but a 'transformative moment' enabling the Bush Administration's strategy. Condoleezza Rice asked, 'How do you capitalize on these opportunities?' Another official admitted, 'Without Sept. 11, we never would have been able to put Iraq at the top of our agenda.'[41] (The most sinister report of 2002 was that Rumsfeld sought to create more 'opportunities' on which the US could capitalize: his Defense Science Board proposed a 'Proactive, Preemptive Operations Group (P2OG) ... [to] carry out secret missions designed to "stimulate reactions" among terrorist groups, provoking them into committing violent acts which would then expose them to "counterattack" by U.S. forces'.)[42]

The excuse of a post-9–11 threat for the pursuit of a strategy developed months, even years earlier, was sharply confirmed in September 2002 when the new National Security Strategy used 'terrorism' to target 'aggressive regimes seeking weapons of mass destruction'. Six days later, Rice 'accused Iraqi President Saddam Hussein's regime of helping Osama bin Laden's followers develop chemical weapons', Rumsfeld claimed 'bulletproof' evidence of a link, and President Bush predicted 'that Al Qaeda [would] become an extension of Saddam's madness and his hatred and his capacity to extend weapons of mass destruction around the world'.[43]

Even as Manhattan was being enveloped in dust on 11 September, Rumsfeld had tried to turn disaster into immediate potential. Although all intelligence pointed to Al-Qa'eda's hand in the attacks, the Secretary of Defense ordered, 'Judge whether [information] good enough hit S.H. [Saddam Hussein].

Not only UBL [Osama bin Laden].' He added, 'Go massive. Sweep it all up. Things related and not.'[44] The following day Wolfowitz and Rumsfeld lobbied the Administration for a strike on Iraq; Colin Powell held out against the idea, and Bush decided that the battle would have to await victory over Osama bin Laden.[45]

Wolfowitz, Rumseld and their allies bided their time, even as Powell asked military commanders 'to keep these guys in a box'.[46] As Perle reasoned, 'I would have gone after Iraq immediately. I would not have relegated it to some subsequent phase. But it's all right, as long as we get to Phase 2.'[47] The Project for a New Century provided the rationale in a letter to Bush nine days after 9–11:

> It may be that the Iraqi government provided assistance in some form to the recent attack on the United States. But even if evidence does not link Iraq directly to the attack, any strategy aiming at the eradication of terrorism and its sponsors must include a determined effort to remove Saddam Hussein from power in Iraq. Failure to undertake such an effort will constitute an early and perhaps decisive surrender in the war on international terrorism.[48]

James Woolsey, the former director of the CIA, was despatched to Europe to find evidence linking the Iraqi Government to 9–11 (months later, he was still searching). The US Government also tried to tie Saddam Hussein to the 'anthrax letters' of October 2001 before moving to the 'weapons of mass destruction' pretext.[49] Fortunately, planning did not depend on any proof of these assertions: Woolsey's trip to Europe included consultation with Iraqi National Congress officials and other exiles based in London, and President Bush accepted the Defense Policy Board's recommendation 'to depose Saddam Hussein by giving armed support to Iraqi opposition forces across the country' with orders to 'the CIA and ... senior military commanders to draw up detailed plans for a military operation that could begin within months'.[50]

But Baghdad, like Kabul, was never the final destination of the American campaign. Privately, President Bush told Condoleezza Rice, 'Fuck Saddam. We're taking him out;'[51]

publicly, he broadened US targets with his labelling of the 'Axis of Evil'. The 'conservative' commentator Robert Novak stripped away the covering rhetoric: '[The Administration] want a war as a manifestation of U.S. power in the world and as a sign that the United States is capable of changing the balance of power and the political map of the Middle East.'[52]

As early as May 2001, Cheney offered a cue for the mission beyond Iraq, identifying North Korea and Iran as parallel threats.[53] After 9–11, the Project for a New American Century constructed the rationale that the Hezbollah organisation in Lebanon was a primary threat to the 'free' world: 'We believe the administration should demand that Iran and Syria immediately cease all military, financial, and political support for Hezbollah and its operations. Should Iran and Syria refuse to comply, the administration should consider appropriate measures of retaliation against these known state sponsors of terrorism.'[54] Just before Bush's State of the Union address, Condoleezza Rice and her deputy, Stephen Hadley, asked for Iran to be added to the Axis of Evil, 'because denouncing the ruling theocracy might accelerate the incipient revolt they [saw] emerging in the street protests'.[55] While Saddam was to be confronted directly, the US would use 'soft power' to undermine a country allegedly under the control of the 'ayatollahs'.

So Bush used the 'with us or with the terrorists' rhetoric to 'warn Iran … that it must not try to undermine the new interim government of Afghanistan, or it will face consequences'.[56] Newspaper stories followed of Iranian intrigue, advisers and arms propping up the local Governor, Ismail Khan, in Herat in western Afghanistan and threatening the leadership of President Karzai.[57] Colin Powell emerged from his dovecote: 'We … see [Iran] doing some unhelpful things with respect to Afghanistan …. This is the time to stop terrorist organizations such as Hezbollah. This is the time to stop developing weapons of mass destruction. This is the time to stop trying to develop nuclear weapons.'[58]

Despite signs that the strategy was having the opposite effect, with many domestic critics of the Tehran government joining in protests against US intervention,[59] the

Administration and supportive media featured academic commentators who insisted:

> The best way that we can fight terrorism is to promote democracy and our American values. And that's what President Bush has started. And I think we will see change, within this year, probably – if the United States sticks to its guns, does not back-pedal from what the president has said.[60]

Iran, despite its historic opposition to Osama bin Laden and Al-Qa'eda, was converted into a 'safe haven' for the organisation, and the State Department's Richard Armitage went even further:

> Hezbollah may be the 'A-Team of Terrorists' and maybe al-Qaeda is actually the 'B' team. And they're on the list and their time will come .... We're going to go after these problems just like a high school wrestler goes after a match. We're going to take them down one at a time.[61]

The Axis label, far more dramatic, media-friendly and deceptive than 'preponderance of power', would be used to challenge North Korea, a tactic that had backfired dramatically by the end of 2002, and could be slapped at will on other countries. Assistant Secretary of State John Bolton added Cuba, Libya and Syria in May 2002, just as George Bush was setting tough conditions on easing the US embargo against Havana.[62] Even those who did not make it onto the list could be assured of US attention. In April a short-lived coup ousted Venezuelan President Hugo Chavez, as Condoleezza Rice explained, 'Just because Chavez was elected doesn't mean he exhibited democratic values.'[63] There had been significant local protest against Chavez, but the US Government had been glad to lend more than a helping hand, given Venezuela's status as a leading oil producer, the inconvenience of Chavez policies such as warm relations with Cuba and Chavez's statement that war on Afghanistan was 'fighting terrorism with terrorism'. The Venezuelan opposition was supported with almost $900,000, through 'independent' foundations, by the National Endowment for Democracy.[64] (Chavez returned to power after 72 hours, but pressure continued with national strikes, encouraged by US statements, beginning in November 2002 and lasting well into the New Year. When the strikes were called off, the *Washington Post* maintained the call for US intervention: 'Without more meddling, and soon, Venezuela will likely see the collapse of what was once one of Latin America's richest economies and strongest democracies.')[65]

Efforts abroad were complemented at home by 'a stunning disregard for the democratic principles of public transparency and accountability'.[66] While detainees languished indefinitely in Camp X-Ray without access to family or lawyers,[67] Attorney General John Ashcroft 'granted sweeping powers to the Federal Bureau of Investigation to spy on political organizations, religious groups and private citizens' with the suspension of 'ordinary Fourth Amendment requirements to listen in on phone calls, read e-mail and conduct secret searches' and 'the CIA ... expand[ed] its domestic presence'.[68] From September 2001 to March 2003, Ashcroft personally authorised more than 170 surveillances free from court oversight, compared to 47 such surveillances between 1981 and 2001,[69] as the FBI put into the skies a fleet of more than 80 'Nightstalker' aircraft 'to track and collect intelligence from suspected terrorists'.[70]

The FBI trawled libraries to check readers' records,[71] an Information Awareness Office for coordination of global surveillance, headed by Admiral John Poindexter of Iran–Contra fame, was established,[72] the 'top-secret Foreign Intelligence Surveillance Court of Review handed the government broad new authority ... to wiretap phone calls, intercept mail and spy on Internet use of ordinary Americans',[73] and Operation TIPS (Terrorist Information Prevention System) was proposed to give 'millions of American truckers, letter carriers, train conductors, ship captains, utility employees, and others a formal way to report suspicious terrorist activity'.[74] (TIPS was withdrawn after expressions of concern from Congress and the public, but the Justice Department persisted, handing over information to the top-rated television series *America's Most Wanted* so it could appeal for citizens' assistance.)[75] The mandatory Special Registration of immigrants from Muslim countries led to detentions and deportations; in California, 'hundreds of men, from teens on up, were handcuffed, shackled and, according to their lawyers, even hosed down in jail'.[76]

In this environment, where was 'dissent'? Christopher Hitchens noted and expressed concern over the domestic measures (as did 'hawks' such as William Safire) but, apart from Iraq, said nothing about US strategy and its expansion of operations abroad. Nor did most of his compatriots. While some like Thomas Friedman and Safire hailed the next campaign for democracy in Iran, none associated this with the objective of 'preponderance of power'. It took the *Sunday Herald*, 4,000 miles away in Glasgow, to reveal 'the blueprint for the creation of a "global Pax Americana"'.[77]

Resistance would have to come from sources outside the US. From the weeks after 9–11, the American media struggled with opinion polls which repeatedly displayed overseas hostility to US policies and operations. Unease with the War on Terror (on one memorable occasion CNN anchorman Wolf Blitzer was left gaping as a correspondent observed, after the bombing of Afghanistan began, that Pakistani public opinion concerning the Taliban and the US was 81–3 in favour of the bad guys)[78] fed into wider long-term concerns about Washington's regional and global strategies. A February 2002 poll of almost 10,000 people in nine Muslim countries found the common opinion that the United States was 'ruthless and arrogant', with residents by a 2-to-1 margin expressing an unfavourable opinion of the US and President Bush. Seventy-seven per cent thought the US bombing of Afghanistan 'morally unjustified' (vs. 67 per cent with the same opinion about the attacks of 11 September).[79]

The US Government tried a number of tactics to win over, or at least neutralise, this scepticism. The State Department's campaign was supervised by Charlotte Beers, the former head of the J. Walter Thompson and Ogilvy and Mather advertising agencies. Beers even brought with her the language of her profession, 'The important thing about our products is that they have to be marketed.'[80] Initiatives included the travelling exhibition of 'Ground Zero' photography by Joel Meyerowitz, illustrating US sacrifice and recovery and linked to 'local' displays such as the bombing of Britain in the Blitz and the strike against the US Embassy in Nairobi in 1998, the website display 'Muslim Life in America' and an attempt (coordinated with the White House and film and television executives) to put Muhammad Ali on Al-Jazeera.[81]

The Pentagon, not satisfied with these 'positive' efforts, went further. After 9–11, it had already paid more than $7.5 million for the services of the Rendon Group, the private consultancy famed for putting American flags in the hands of the liberated Kuwaiti populace in 1991 and for fostering the development of the 'opposition' Iraqi National Congress, including its failed attempt to take power in 1995.[82] Now the Department of Defense decided to create an Office of Strategic Influence 'to provide news items, possibly even false ones, to foreign media organizations as part of a new effort to influence public sentiment and policy makers in both friendly and unfriendly countries'. Proposals included 'sending journalists, civic leaders and foreign leaders e-mail messages that promote American views or attack unfriendly governments'; a senior Pentagon official confirmed, '[The initiative] goes from the blackest of black programs to the whitest of white.'[83]

The OSI was formally suspended after its plans were leaked to the media; however, according to *Der Spiegel*, 'the U.S. Defense Department ... developed a top-secret plan for bribing European journalists to produce more favorable articles on U.S. policy concerning Iraq.'[84] Rumsfeld indicated in November that the original programme for 'information' was being implemented:

I went down that next day [after the press revelations on OSI] and said fine, if you want to savage this thing, fine, I'll give you the corpse. There's the name. You can have the name, but I'm gonna keep doing every single thing that needs to be done and I have.[85]

At every step, however, the Government seemed to be frustrated by the unwillingness of foreigners to accept the universal truth of the American vision. Even in Europe, 55 per cent of those polled believed 'U.S. foreign policy contributed to the tragic event' of 9–11.[86] Henry Hyde, the arch-conservative Republican Senator, opined, 'How is it that a country that invented Hollywood and Madison Avenue has allowed such a destructive and parodied image of itself to become the intellectual coin of the realm?'[87] In July 2002 the Council on Foreign Relations produced a scathing analysis which highlighted 'America's shaky image abroad'; the President's advisers responded by blaming the State Department, notably Beers, and promising 'a White House role in global communications'.[88]

New and improved programmes were trumpeted, such as the Middle East Partnership Initiative (devised by Cheney's daughter Liz, a State Department official), with $25 million to bring Arab students to the United States, and Radio Sawa, given a $35 million budget to win over Middle Eastern populations with American music and 'information'.[89] Radio Farda, an updated version of the Cold War veteran Radio Freedom, began broadcasting to Iran in December 2002, and the US expanded support for satellite stations such as National Iranian Television. President Bush proclaimed, 'If Iran respects its international obligations and embraces freedom and tolerance, it will have no better friend than the United States of America.'[90]

All these efforts made little headway, however, as 'true dislike, if not hatred, of America [was] concentrated in the Muslim nations of the Middle East and in Central Asia'.[91] Even Coca-Cola cut its losses and moved operations from its Middle Eastern base in March.[92] In January 2003 the latest high-profile State Department campaign, a series of television advertisements for Muslim countries on the 'Shared Values' of Muslims in the United States, was abandoned after resistance from the Egyptian, Lebanese and Jordanian Governments. The problems were not only political: a specialist at the Council on Foreign Relations thought the ads 'extremely poor', 'It was like this was the 1930s and the government was running commercials showing happy blacks in America.'[93] In March 2003, Charlotte Beers resigned from the State Department for 'health reasons'.[94]

'Public diplomacy' might have satisfied the vision of a Thomas Friedman for the bequest of democracy to unenlightened territories but the message, for some reason, was still not getting through. Anne Kingston of Canada's *National Post* was blunt to the point of cruelty, proclaiming, 'Uncle Sam can't be sold like Uncle Ben's [wild rice]':

In the annals of great American marketing disasters, the attempt to sell 'brand America' will rank right up there with the introduction of the Edsel and the New Coke. No, let me rephrase that: The attempt to sell 'brand America' will likely rank as the worst American marketing disaster ever, bar none.[95]

The image of US intervention spreading democracy could always be undermined by revelations such as the inconvenience that, in Afghanistan, the CIA was carrying out torture of suspects at the Bagram air base.[96] It might be undone by truth-telling such as the comment of Yale professor Donald Kagan, a member of the Project for a New American Century and an adviser to the Bush Administration, 'People worry a lot about how the Arab street is going to react. Well, I see that the Arab street has gotten very, very quiet since we started blowing things up.'[97] It was not just a question of stubborn Arab and Central Asian populations; some of America's closest allies were still blocking progress through the War on Iraq. In Canada, 51 per cent agreed 'that Americans were behaving like bastards'.[98] More than 70 per cent of the French population expressed opposition and the vast majority of Germans backed the refusal of the Schroeder Government to join military operations.

Some American observers expressed a genuine bewilderment about European opinion. Melvyn Leffler, the historian who examined the US quest for 'preponderance of power' in the Cold War, said of his year at Oxford, 'I was stunned to realize that people here seem more fearful of American power than they are of the oppressiveness and hideousness of Saddam Hussein's regime.'[99] However, the response of US gatekeepers of opinion was not to investigate the reasons for this apparent short-sightedness, but to reduce it to stereotypes of weakness, self-hatred and delusion. Victor Davis Hanson in *Commentary* wrote 'of frustrated Europeans [who] have put their faith, mistakenly or not, in international bodies ... while pretending not to notice that American power alone is what has permitted them to dream that they inhabit a global fairyland of reasonable people'.[100] The American Enterprise Institute sponsored a roundtable Euro-thrashing with Jeffrey Gedmin of the Aspen Institute in Berlin ('How long can an alliance really function when key allies believe that building themselves up means cutting America down?'), Andrew Sullivan ('Grow up and join in – or pipe down and let us do it'), Mark Steyn ('A collapsed birthrate, accelerating immigration, lavish welfare, an evasive political culture, phony transnational structures: For Europe, this is the Perfect Storm'), Michael Kelly ('A century of American resolve, often in the face of European disdain, created a continent where not one of these [imperialism, fascism, Communism] lives as a serious force') and Jonah Goldberg ('We shouldn't allow the histrionics of "the Europeans" to distract us from taking the right route').[101] David Brooks in *The Weekly Standard* was rolling up his sleeves for a scrap with 'the bourgeoisophobes' of 'the entire Arab world and much of the rest of the world':

> Maybe in their hatred we can better discern our strengths. Because if the tide of conflict is rising, then we had better be able to articulate, not least to ourselves, who we are, why we arouse such passions, and why we are absolutely right to defend ourselves.[102]

Anatole Lieven had warned just after 9–11 that political differences would be exacerbated by different outlooks across the Atlantic, 'The cultural gap between Europeans and Republican America (which does not mean a majority of Americans, but the dominant strain of policy) will continue to widen. "Who says we share common values with the Europeans?" a senior US politician remarked recently. "They don't even go to church!"[103] However, these sentiments followed, rather than created, the strategy of the US Government; the influential PNAC report of September 2000 had pointed to Europe as the emerging threat to US pre-eminence.[104]

The catalyst for division would be the renewal of the campaign against Iraq. 'A senior administration official' noted, 'At some point the Europeans with butterflies in their stomachs – many of whom didn't want us to go into Afghanistan – will see that they have a bipolar choice: they can get with the plan or get off.' German Foreign Minister Joschka Fischer rebutted, 'Alliance partners are not satellites', and his French counterpart,

Herbert Vedrine, criticised 'simplistic' US policy with its 'growing unilateral temptation'.[105] When German Chancellor Gerhard Schroeder dared to question the American 'adventure', he was rebuked by the US Ambassador; after Schroeder's re-election, which owed much to his opposition to war against Iraq, Richard Perle advised, 'It would be the best thing if he retires.'[106]

By early 2003, 'alliance' was being maintained despite the fundamental wishes of the Bush Administration and, as Rumsfeld pejoratively labelled it, the 'old Europe' of France and Germany. The Secretary of Defense tipped off a US strategy to bypass the troublemakers by going directly to countries formerly in the Soviet bloc as well as seeking alternative partners such as Spain and Italy: 'Germany has been a problem, and France has been a problem. But you look at vast numbers of other countries in Europe. They're not with France and Germany on this, they're with the United States.'[107] Rumsfeld then linked Germany, for its anti-war position, to Cuba and Libya,[108] and Richard Perle opened hostilities with the French, '[We] must develop a strategy to contain our erstwhile ally or we will not be talking about a NATO alliance.'[109] Far from trying to rein in these declarations, Thomas Friedman jumped in with playground psychology about 'Euro-whining' born of an identity crisis: 'Being weak after being powerful is a terrible thing. It can make you stupid. It can make you reject U.S. policies simply to differentiate yourself from the world's only superpower.'[110]

After France and Germany led an effort in the United Nations and NATO in early February to delay a US-led attack on Iraq, there was a renewed assault on the 'Axis of Weasels'. The *New York Post*'s diatribe from the American Cemetery in Normandy, 'How Dare the French Forget', was not just a tabloid excess;[111] the front page of the *Washington Post* no longer bothered to distinguish between criticism of US foreign policy and a supposed hatred of 'America', using quotations from US legislators and expatriates to headline, 'Sneers from across the Atlantic: Anti-Americanism Moves to W. Europe's Political Mainstream'.[112] Friedman suggested that France should be removed from the Security Council and replaced by India, since 'France is so caught up with its need to differentiate itself from America to feel important [that] it's become silly'.[113] When a French journalist tried to explain Paris' position to Fox News, the presenter interrupted, 'With friends like you, who needs enemies', and took him off the air.[114]

Fortunately, a *Wall Street Journal* editor jumped in with a fig leaf for 'alliance'. Knowing 'that the Schröder–Chirac view of Saddam's threat was not shared by other European leaders … [he] called Rome to get a piece by Prime Minister Berlusconi'. The Italian leader contacted Spain's Prime Minister José Maria Aznar, and the outcome was a letter from eight 'good' European leaders backing the United States. As a grateful William Safire framed the episode, 'Signatories to the new op-ed diplomacy laid it on the line to forgetful French and "ohne mich" [without me] Germans.'[115]

Still, the weak and spineless responses of 'old Europe', by dragging out discussion over US strategy, opened up space for dissent.[116] That space was expanded with continuing revelations of the complexities of US foreign and domestic policy, past and present. An agreement between Central Asian countries to transport oil and gas across northern Afghanistan, and an alleged meeting between Vice President Cheney's staff with Exxon Mobil Corporation, Chevron Texaco Corporation, Conoco Philips and Halliburton over Iraqi oil production after Saddam Hussein's overthrow, were reminders that US intervention might have baser motives than freedom and security.[117] The *Guardian* confirmed that Pentagon discussions with Israeli officials had led to a 'target list for a systematic policy of assassination against those they call terrorists'.[118] The *Washington Post* published an exposé of Rumsfeld's dealings with Saddam Hussein in the 1980s, even though he and the Reagan Administration knew of Iraq's use of chemical weapons.[119] Foreshadowing later manipulations of 'intelligence' by Administration officials seeking war against Iraq, the *Los Angeles Times* reported, 'Senior Bush administration officials are pressuring CIA analysts', who were concluding 'that years of U.N. inspections combined with U.S. and British bombing of selected targets have left Iraq far weaker militarily than in the 1980s', 'to tailor their assessments of the Iraqi threat to help build a case against Saddam Hussein'.[120] (Rumsfeld would go even further, establishing the Office of Special Plans, a separate intelligence unit in the Pentagon, to provide the 'correct' assessments. The OSP reported directly to Paul Wolfwitz, bypassing the CIA and the Pentagon's more cautious Defense Intelligence Agency.)[121]

When European dissent could not be ignored, the possibility of an opposition at home was finally noticed. And when that opposition received attention, a curious notion arose: dissent was not just the preserve of the old, discredited 'Left'.

The human shield convoy to Baghdad might be parodied by opponents as the delusional if not treacherous legacy of 1960s movements, even if that convoy was led by a former US marine who served in the first Gulf War.[122] Dennis Halliday, the former UN Assistant Secretary-General and Head of the UN Humanitarian Program in Iraq, might be suspect because of his years of objection to economic sanctions. It was not so easy to dismiss the concern of General Anthony Zinni, the former Chairman of the Joint Chiefs of Staff ('I don't know what planet [supporters of an attack upon Iraq] are on'; 'Access to energy drives all U.S. policy in the region'),[123] General Norman Schwarzkopf, the commander of Desert Storm's forces, who thought it 'very important for us to wait and see what the inspectors come up with' as he was 'somewhat nervous' at some of Rumsfeld's pronouncements,[124] other veterans and serving officers,[125] or 41 Nobel laureates in science and economics, all former advisers to the US Government.[126] Republican businessmen took out a full-page advertisement in the *Wall Street Journal,* declaring, 'Mr. President, your war on Iraq does not pass the test. It is not a just war,' and urging readers, 'Speak out at your place of worship, at your business, among your friends and relatives.'[127] Even post-9–11 'hawks' such as Richard Butler, the former head of the UN inspection teams in Iraq, drew the line at a US-led assault that did not have the backing of the United Nations.[128]

The challenges were not just internecine quibblings within political-economic-military elites. Polls showed that opposition to military intervention was highest among the 'greatest generation', those who had gone through the Second World War.[129] The Pentagon's Information Awareness Office and its head Admiral John Poindexter were challenged by a counter-operation in which computer specialists created webpages 'posting [Poindexter's] phone number, his home address, his birthday, information about his family, ways to find his Social Security number, and even a satellite photo of his neighborhood'.[130] Joan Didion dissected the 'New American Unilateralism'.[131] Celebrities such as Martin Sheen, Susan Sarandon and Tim Robbins might be savaged as 'lefties' daring to speak on political issues, but even the singer Merle Haggard, who had repelled the hippies and raised the flag with 'Okie from Muskogee', was declaring at concerts, 'In 1960, when I came out of prison as an ex-convict, I had more freedom under parolee supervision than there's available to an average citizen in America right now ... God almighty, what have we done to each other?'[132]

One incident brought protest home to the White House. Early in 2003 Laura Bush, librarian and First Lady, asked a selected group of American poets to visit her to discuss Emily Dickinson, Walt Whitman and Langston Hughes. One of those invited, Sam Hamill, responded by asking others to send anti-war poems. Within days, almost 2,000 poets had responded. The literary gathering was suddenly 'postponed', but on 5 March, Hamill and three other prominent writers presented 15,000 poems to Congress.[133]

Just over a year after 9–11, was America home to a mass movement challenging, rather than endorsing, the rush to power? Sam Smith, the editor of the *Progressive Review*, considered Hitchens' departure from *The Nation* and dared to think so:

> The people who [have] made the difference were not the famous talkers but the little known doers, ordinary people, who in Conrad's phrase, for one brief moment did something out of the ordinary.
>
> They were people who had not studied Marx and Hegel and couldn't tell a Trotskyite from a troll. But they knew, in Pogo's words, when to 'stand on the piano and demand outrage action'.[134]

Smith's assessment might have been rose-tinted; as the *Washington Post*'s ombudsman shyly admitted after yet another failure by his paper to cover a public incident highlighting opposition to US foreign policy, '[There is] a perplexing flaw in coverage that has persisted throughout this long run-up to a controversial war.'[135] Yet for all the efforts of the Bush Administration, often reflected in news coverage, to limit the range of acceptable opinion, the contradictions of its war had finally led to a space for dissent.

8

On the Eve of War: March 2003

On a cloudy February day, for the first time in 16 years, I marched. So did my six-year-old son, bored and cold, and my three-year-old daughter, far more enthusiastic in her chants of '1–2–3–4. We don't want your bloody war.' So did friends and colleagues who had also decided, after much deliberation, that they would protest.

We were not part of the '750,000' estimate – to get to Hyde Park before the speeches ended, we and many others took a road parallel to Piccadilly, where the count was taken. No matter: we knew that we were part of something much, much larger, a cry of defiance that began in Sydney and took in up to three million in Rome, more than a million in Madrid and in Barcelona, 500,000 in Berlin and 400,000 in New York (despite a court order there forbidding any marching). We thought that our opinions finally mattered, that we 'the unheard [had] spoken out'.[1] As Madeleine Bunting put it, 'The very best of Britain was on the city's streets (and for every person marching there were more in sympathy at home); we showed ourselves to be a nation that is at ease with itself, compassionate, multicultural, and tolerant.'[2]

But, just as we were officially absent on the day, so our views were already being written off, not only by Downing Street ('It changes nothing at all. The quicker [the war] is done, the better'), but by our minders in the press.[3] Two weeks before the march, the journalist Julie Burchill had declared, with characteristic modesty, that she would finally 'mention the war'. It was her duty 'to expose the sheer befuddled babyishness of the pro-Saddam apologists' by presenting the arguments that we were supposedly making. We were 'hyperactive brats' chanting, 'It's All about Oil!', but unwilling 'to give up [the] car and central heating and go back to the Dark Ages'. We screamed, 'America's always interfering in other countries!' but, when it

164

did not, we 'derided [it] as selfish and isolationist'. We were retreating into the shell of 'We shouldn't invade any country unless it attacks us!' and finger-pointing, 'Ooo, your friends [namely, George and Tony] smell!'

Having put us in our places, Burchill could declare, 'I'd go so far as to say that my argument's bigger than yours.' Never mind that she hadn't actually made any argument, it was enough to present a crude pastiche of our own complicated, sometimes uncertain, sometimes emotive, thoughts.[4]

Dissecting Burchill's polemic is easy. After all, it is her exaggeration of the crass rather than consideration of substance that puts her column at the front of a weekend supplement. We could be assured that, having broken her silence, she would besiege us with commentary on 'Silly Show-offs against Saddam', explain how 'the disproportionate amount of teenage boys involved in the recent protests' proved that we 'quite like Saddam' and his 'supposed butchness', and berate our call of 'Bring the Soldiers Home' as a selfish attempt to deny them danger and death.[5]

In this case, however, she had laid down a symbolic marker for other 'serious' commentators to follow. The next day David Aaronovitch explained to us, 'Why the Left is Wrong about Saddam'. Unlike Burchill, Aaronovitch was careful to set out a rationale for 'liberal intervention', based on past failures to act in the Rwandan and Bosnian crises and on the necessity for the overthrow of Saddam Hussein. At the same time, however, he offered a variant on Burchill's portrayal of the deluded Left (and reprised Hitchens' post-9–11 targeting) by setting up John Pilger as our representative, 'turning disagreements with him into betrayals of the entire human race'. Pilger/the Left were simplistic, blinded by dogmatism, in contrast to honourable journalists like Aaronovitch ('It isn't like that here [at the *Observer*]').

So, just before we set out for London, Aaronovitch warned us, 'You can march, but you can't hide' from the blood we would have on our hands if Saddam remained in power. And, after up to 2 million of us defied him, he was livid about our 'moment of extraordinary success'. He asked, 'The Kurds, the Iraqis – of whom there are many thousands in this country – where were they?' (There were hundreds on the march; they just 'disappeared' for those who could not accept that any Kurd or Iraqi would oppose Western intervention.) He reduced all of us once more to the old bogeymen like Tony Benn and Harold Pinter, and the canard that we had fallen for 'this parroted "war about oil" stuff'. He married the implication that we were anti-semitic because some were 'wearing stickers bearing the Israeli flag and the words "the fascist state"' to the allegation that 'there's only one fascist state in this equation, and it's the one [you're] effectively marching to save'. To all his questions about the future of Iraq, a future that could lead only to war, he answered for us, 'What do you mean, you don't know?'[6]

A number of *Guardian* readers gave alternative responses to Aaronovitch's jibes – for example, 'Yes, some of the slogans did bother me. Yes, some of the speeches did bother me .... There *were* Iraqis among the marchers .... I did anticipate how [the march] would be interpreted [in Baghdad] and thought long and carefully about going on it ... however, I came to the conclusion that it was so important to do my tiny bit to halt the slide to war that I should march'[7] – but he had moved on. Like Christopher Hitchens, Aaronovitch had valiantly slain us paper dragons to rescue 'America' as well as liberate the Iraqis. Our questions were 'eternal semi-prejudice' and 'pointless ingenuity'; Aaronovitch, with his categorical assurance 'that Bush came to power wanting not to intervene' in other nations, wrote for 'the more sophisticated' who 'Thank the Yank'.[8]

In *The Spectator*, we were 'Marching for Saddam'.[9] In the *Daily Telegraph* we were 'trendies, toffs, students, and men with impressive beards unit[ing] to save Saddam', 'doing Saddam's work for him' with our 'prejudice against Arabs being able to enjoy freedom', arguing in our 'sheer wickedness or naiveté' that 'Hitler is no worse than Churchill'.[10] In *The Times*, we 'could provide cover for terrorists'.[11] In the *Daily Mail*, we were diagnosed by Melanie Phillips as 'suffering from Dianafication', and in the *New York Post* we were a 'religious cult'.[12] Bryan Appleyard's heavyweight analysis decided our concern was 'not about the war at all' but 'about the disench-franchisement of the left .... The luvvies, the unions, the students, and the hairies needed a brave, old-fashioned cause and Saddam handed it to them on a plate.'[13]

Of course, this huffing and puffing was to be expected from the embedded warriors in the media; as the leader writers of the *Guardian* noted, 'Little in British life is so unattractive as the spiteful tantrums of the rightwing elite when denied a kill'.[14] Yet, as Aaronovitch's chiding of erstwhile comrades indicated, it was not just on the screens of Fox News that our march was bankrolled by sinister forces like the 'Workers' World Party', in the pages of the *Daily Telegraph* that we 'were united by a commitment to Marxist thought and practice ... and a belief in world revolution', or in the dream-world of *The Times* that protestors under 18 became cannabis-smoking kids 'legging it' from their teachers.[15] Rod Liddle berated our 'interminably pious wittering' and 'shrieking hysteria'. Michael Ignatieff and Nat Hentoff pondered smugly about 'what [our] support for the Iraqi opposition [would] amount to'.[16] The broadcaster Libby Purves gave us the kindly advice:

If terrorist attacks are – as many believe – a likely and rapid outcome of the war's beginnings, then it is neither patriotic nor prudent to disrupt the running of the country, clog up the streets, coat yourself in ketchup for showy 'die-ins' and generally spread confusion before the terrorists even start.

All of us had become the enemy. Because the march was also backed by the Muslim Association of Britain, Nick Cohen labelled us accomplices of a movement 'which believes the punishment for Muslims who abandon their faith should be death and that Israel should be abolished ... [an association which] refused to condemn the al-Qa'eda killings in Mombasa because Israelis were the target'. Our 'absence of principle is matched only by [our] absence of intelligence', reducing us 'to allying with religious bigots'.[17] Howard Jacobson claimed victim's compensation, pushed into support of war by our supposed militancy:

[The peace movement] put a wall up, forbidding if you weren't already camped on the other side of it, if you didn't take it as a given that Americans were hyenas, or that the world's stockpiles of poisons would go away by wishing them away, or if you believe that only those capable of listening are capable of answering. And thus they left me out there, where I didn't want to be.

Jacobson unmasked us as the real warmongers, 'Is it entirely out of the question that some among the hierarchy of the peaceable never wanted peace at all – but, dreaming of comeuppance, see the war as necessary in the unfolding of history, the 100,000 Osama bin Ladens we've been promised as a consequence being just what the doctor ordered?'[18]

On the eve of military action, we who were campaigning against conflict had somehow become its chief advocates, we who were protesting against the imminence of violence were somehow praying for a multitude of terrorists. Meanwhile, the arguments that we were really making, being inconveniences for advocates of war, were being ignored.

For even the post-9–11 victories had yet to be secured. If the removal of the Taliban secured one long-term American goal, with the World Bank assisting Afghanistan, Pakistan and Turkmenistan in the completion of a $3.2 billion gas pipeline, other objectives proved elusive. Little of the $2 billion disbursed in Afghanistan went into infrastructure or local administration. Ministers had not been paid since June 2002, emergency medical equipment such as incubators was scarce, and classes were held in the shells of destroyed buildings.[19] The United Nations suspended relief operations in parts of the country because of 'generally dangerous conditions', and 'drugs were now a bigger earner for the Afghan economy than overseas aid'.[20] Al-Qa'eda was reactivating training camps in eastern Afghanistan, and the 'fundamentalist warlord' Gulbuddin Hekmatayar, having escaped assassination by the CIA, was calling for attacks on US forces.[21] Amidst declarations of a 'jihad', now broadcast by a mobile radio station, the US military mistook duck hunters for rebel attackers and killed non-combatants with bombs and stray mortar rounds; Afghan prisoners were beaten to death at an American base.[22] The chairman of the Joint Chiefs of Staff conceded, 'We've lost a little momentum there, to be frank'; an operations commander in Afghanistan was franker: 'They are patient, they will try to wear us down over time. It was time that beat the Russians.'[23]

Declarations of post-Taliban freedom and democracy were met by reports that 'those who speak out in Afghanistan have faced intimidation, arbitrary arrest, and violence'. Child abuse, particularly forced sexual relations between men and underage boys, was 'quietly reemerging in some parts of the country'.[24] Hamid Karzai flew to Washington to argue that the planned US attack on Iraq would 'lead to a fall in international support for Afghanistan long before the task of establishing a strong central government, let alone securing peace and reconstructing the shattered country, [was] complete'.[25] (In a meaningful sign of American priorities, Zalmay Khalilzad, the White House envoy to Afghanistan, was redeployed to present Washington's case to Iraqi opposition groups.) The Afghan President's only achievement was public humiliation before the Senate Foreign Relations Committee, which questioned Afghanistan's progress and Karzai's credibility.[26]

US military planners had moved to other deployments in other theatres.[27] The Pentagon pressed for up to 1,000 special operations troops 'in an open-ended mission' against Abu Sayyaf rebels in the Philippines, and military aid and regular troops would supplement US special forces in their intervention against the Revolutionary Armed Forces of Colombia (FARC).[28] Where ground operations were not viable, more drastic plans were being drafted. North Korea's defiant resumption of its nuclear programme was being secretly met with 'a range of military options from surgical cruise missile strikes to sledgehammer bombing, and there [was] even talk of using tactical nuclear weapons to neutralize hardened artillery positions aimed at Seoul, the South Korean capital'. (When Deputy Secretary of State Richard Armitage, nobody's idea of a dove, told Congress he believed in 'a bilateral discussion' with North Korea to seek a solution, an official let David Sanger of the *New York Times* know that the President was 'off-the-wall angry' with Armitage's testimony.)[29] The Administration was discussing 'construction of a new generation of nuclear weapons, including "mini-nukes", "bunker-busters" and neutron bombs designed to destroy chemical or biological agents', with a resumption of nuclear tests and a campaign 'to convince the American public that the new weapons are necessary'.[30]

Meanwhile, Bush's advisers prepared for the use of their current arsenal. Condoleezza Rice promised 'national obliteration' for Iraq if it used weapons of mass destruction, the Army tested the 21,000-pound Massive Ordnance Air Blast, lovingly known as the 'Mother of All Bombs', and a high-power microwave 'death-ray', and an American general in Kuwait acknowledged, 'We have already begun to unwrap our depleted uranium anti-tank shells.'[31] Even as it used Saddam's alleged chemical weapons to justify war, the Administration authorised the use of toxic riot-control agents and tested chemicals such as fentanyl, which killed 117 hostages when used in a Moscow theatre in October 2002, in violation of international conventions.[32]

We were not marching for Saddam but against diplomatic illusions hiding the American strategy, with its projected delivery of 3,000 'precision' bombs and missiles in the first 48 hours of war, for a victory not only to topple Saddam Hussein but to offer essential lessons to the rest of the world. The phrase 'preponderance of power' was never uttered; instead, the public was told in no uncertain terms that 'networks of Iraqi spies [had] set up in UK',[33] that US satellites had 'real killer stuff' showing 'Iraqis ... in full panic' moving suspect equipment and mobile laboratories,[34] that 'Islamic extremists affiliated with al Qaeda took possession of a chemical weapon in Iraq',[35] that 'Iraq could be planning a chemical or biological attack on American cities through the use of remote-controlled "drone" planes',[36] and that 'three giant cargo ships [were] being tracked by US and British intelligence on suspicion that they might be carrying Iraqi weapons of mass destruction'.[37]

We pointed to an American and British diplomacy which included 'gifts' to, threats against and spying on other Security Council members.[38] We noted that Colin Powell's presentation of Iraqi guilt to the United Nations was soon undone by the UN's chief weapons inspector Hans Blix, among others, for the paucity and even distortion of its 'intelligence'. (We added that Powell's report was dependent on more than 40 assertions from unidentified sources, vague graphics and suspect translations of Iraqi communications; much of the Administration's 'intelligence' was coming from its creation, the Iraqi National Congress, which was being paid for the purported information.)[39] Months before it became a 'mainstream' scandal, we echoed the revelation of Mohamed El-Baradei, the head of the International Atomic Energy Agency, that 'evidence linking Iraq to a nuclear weapons program appear[ed] to have been fabricated', including a forged document claiming Iraqi officials had sought uranium in Niger.[40] And we were far from isolated in our objections. CIA officers, through leaks to the press and statements by former personnel, let it be known that 'they had felt pressured to make their intelligence reports on Iraq conform to Bush administration policies', with Dick Cheney in particular sending 'signals, intended or otherwise, that a certain output was desired from [the Agency]'. The reports had 'been cooked to a recipe, and the recipe is high policy', leaving analysts to 'hold their noses' over the outcome. British military intelligence passed information to the BBC which challenged the Saddam–Osama connection.[41] *Newsweek* was given the transcript of the 1995 interrogation of the defector Hussein Kamel al-Majid, Saddam Hussein's son-in-law; far from establishing the extent of Iraqi secret weapons programmes, as the US and Britain had claimed for eight years, Kamel told UN inspectors that all chemical and biological stocks had been destroyed and Iraq's nuclear programme abandoned.[42]

At the time, however, it was essential to the argument for war to treat Powell's allegations as the established 'facts'. This was 'a masterly display by a trusted American' with 'the air of a President'.[43] In contrast, the reports of el-Baradei and Hans Blix on Iraqi progress were explained away as the assertions of 'international civil servants who are desperate to prove that agencies like theirs can be effective'.[44] The United Nations was 'making itself irrelevant in disarming Iraq and will be bypassed'.[45]

(Any flaws and deceptions in Powell's 'evidence' could be superseded by new alarms which justified an invasion of Iraq. There were '"sleeper cells" of Iraqi agents planted [in the US] to strike in the event of war' and a network of spies for 'a wave of sabotage attacks' in Britain. Baghdad's drone planes 'could drop chemicals on troops'. Iraq had 'a new variety of rocket ... to strew bomblets filled with chemical or biological agents over large areas'. 'Saddam tried to kill Laura Bush.')[46]

For, of course, the 'truth' of the US allegations was secondary to their objective: laying the foundation for military action, with or without international sanction.[47] George Bush and Tony Blair confirmed at the start of February the timetable for operations, giving 'UN weapons inspectors and the intelligence agencies as long as six weeks [by 15 March] to persuade a sceptical France and Arab countries to come on board for military action against Iraq'.[48] Paul Wolfowitz had already ordered the CIA to investigate Hans Blix; a 'senior administration official' subsequently explained, 'The inspections have turned out to be a trap .... They have become a false measure of disarmament in the eyes of people. We're not counting on Blix to do much of anything for us.'[49] Undersecretary of State John Bolton told the Russian delegate at the Security Council 'we're going ahead' with or without the Council's approval. Another Council member was assured, 'You are not going to decide whether there is war in Iraq or not .... That decision is ours and we have already made it. It is already final. The only question is whether the Council will go along with it or not.'[50] *Time* magazine gave the game away two days before the first assault on Baghdad:

> Even as it pursued the UN route in the hope of maximizing international support for a war, the Bush team began moving swiftly and without pause to assemble an invasion armada capable of delivering a swift military victory over Saddam's regime. The 'moment of truth' arrived not because of any crisis in the inspection process or any act of provocation by Iraq, but because the invasion force is now ready to fight and the window of optimal weather conditions for a ground war is closing fast. In the end, military logic has determined the timetable of diplomacy, rather than vice versa.[51]

The US pretext of war for the benefit of a 'liberated' Iraqi people was exposed by the revelation that, while the US had spent $2.4 billion moving military forces into the Persian Gulf, it set aside less than $1 million for humanitarian aid after any conflict.[52] (The chief US effort was to ensure that up to $900 million in contracts for rebuilding post-war Iraq went to American companies. One of the recipients of this 'assistance' was a division of Halliburton Corporation, Dick Cheney's former company, which won a multi-million dollar contract to rebuild Iraqi oil wells after a war.)[53]

Still the sceptics gathered, not only in 'the coalition of the unwilling', but within the Anglo-American camp. Tony Blair, facing the challenge of his backbenchers, was confronted not only by his Intelligence Services complaining 'that they [were] being forced to sacrifice their integrity for short-term political gain', but also by a military establishment 'feeling that in order to attack there has to be some kind of aggression in the opposite direction', and by the opposition of former generals, ministers and diplomats, who 'would never have gone within miles of the [anti-war] march in London'.[54] Zbigniew Brzezinski, the National Security Adviser under President Carter, opined, 'We have to ask ourselves, how have we conducted ourselves? We have in effect said to [other countries], "Line up." We have treated them as if they were the Warsaw Pact. The United States issued orders, and they have to follow.'[55] A career State Department official resigned with a public letter to Colin Powell, 'The policies we are now asked to advance are incompatible not only with American values but also with American interests.'[56]

For the campaign to proceed, such disquiet had to be returned to its proper place of a naive and lunatic fringe following devious outsiders. Mick Hume in *The Times* analysed the affliction of 'the anti-war lobby' as 'a fashionable worship of safety-first and fear that doing anything decisive might make things worse'.[57] In the US, George Will found the psychological answer by equating opposition to US foreign policy with anti-semitism: 'Some clarity can be achieved by understanding that America has become for many Europeans what Jews were for centuries.'[58] Thomas Friedman echoed:

There is only one group of Arabs for whom Europeans have consistently spoken out in favor of their liberation – and that is those Arabs living under Israeli occupation, the Palestinians. Those Arabs who have been living under the tyranny of Saddam Hussein or other Arab dictators are of no concern to President Jacques Chirac of France and his fellow travelers. We all know what this is about: the Jewish question.[59]

The limitation of dissent went beyond diatribe. New York City authorities tried to block participants in the global anti-war rallies by refusing a permit to march and attempting to pen in those who gathered on First Avenue. (The quarantine failed, as did the attempt of the British Government to keep marchers out of Hyde Park because of the risk of damage to the grass.) The Dixie Chicks, the best-selling country band, were removed from radio play lists after the lead singer told a London audience, 'We're ashamed the president of the United States' is also a native of Texas.[60] Clear Channel, owning 1,200 radio stations across America (and sponsoring pro-war rallies), allegedly blacklisted anti-war artists such as REM, Lenny Kravitz and Ani DiFranco; 'very prominent' musicians maintained silence rather than risk their careers.[61] The US Government monitored 'foreign' students and scholars with an electronic tracking system.[62] In New Mexico, a chatroom user was detained by city police, accused of making threatening remarks about George Bush after telling another reader that the President was 'out of control'.[63] A man in Albany, New York, was arrested for wearing a 'Give Peace a Chance' T-shirt in a mall (even though he had bought the T-shirt from a shop in that mall); eight activists were arrested in a Maryland mall for handing out anti-war leaflets; a teacher was fired for wearing a shirt emblazoned with a peace sign.[64]

Generally, legal restriction of expression was not necessary, however; the boundaries of the acceptable were established by a political and cultural environment in which the mainstream media served as a gatekeeper for news and comment while serving up Hollywood-produced 'reality' series such as *Profiles from the Front Line*.[65] Dan Rather, the veteran CBS newscaster, summarised:

It starts with a feeling of patriotism within one's self. It carries through with the knowledge that the country as a whole and for all of the right reasons, felt and continues to feel this surge of patriotism within themselves. And one finds one's self saying, 'I know the right question but you know what, this is not exactly the right time to ask it?'

Phil Donahue ventured too far in a talk show and was fired by MSNBC for presenting a 'difficult public face for NBC in a time of war ... a home for the liberal anti-war agenda at the same time that our competitors are waving the flag .... He seems to delight in presenting guests who are anti-war, anti-Bush and skeptical of the administration's motives.'[66] The show was replaced by an expanded version of 'Countdown Iraq', and MSNBC soon featured Michael Savage, who referred to countries with a non-white majority as 'turd world nations' and explained, 'We need racist stereotypes right now of our enemy in order to encourage our warriors to kill the enemy.'[67] Both MSNBC and CNN 'decided to take the coward's road and slant towards the conservative crowd that watch [Rupert Murdoch's] Fox News', which featured conservative commentators like Frank Gafney, the head of the Centre for Security Policy and a close ally of Richard Perle and Donald Rumsfeld, and Ken Adelman, the hardline 'arms control' specialist in the Reagan Administration and a member of Perle's Defense Policy Board. Fox's headline presenter, Bill O'Reilly, announced:

> Once the war against Saddam Hussein begins, we expect every American to support our military, and if you can't do that, just shut up.
>
> Americans, and indeed our foreign allies who actively work against our military once the war is underway, will be considered enemies of the state by me.
>
> Just fair warning to you, Barbra Streisand and others who see the world as you do. I don't want to demonize anyone, but anyone who hurts this country in a time like this, well. Let's just say you will be spotlighted.[68]

This 'self-regulation' was obscured by the myth, disseminated religiously by networks such as Fox and by visionaries such as Barbara Amiel and Andrew Sullivan, that US network news was 'skewed broadly centre-left' and the 'mainstream media are ... chock-a-block with high-minded left-liberals'.[69] (The BBC was an accomplice as 'an undisguised opponent of

American policies', its Arabic Service 'embarking on the same exercise as the controlled press in Arabic dictatorships'.)[70] Meanwhile, the stifling of dissent was often hidden. The major TV networks refused to air anti-war commercials.[71] Dennis Kucinich, Ohio Congressman and Presidential candidate, was vilified by *Washington Post* columnist Richard Cohen for suggesting that the Iraq policy was based on oil; the *Post* refused to print Kucinich's detailed response.[72]

When the first President Bush was booed during a video message to the American Music Awards, ABC dubbed out the catcalls; CBS warned all prospective winners in music's Grammy Awards that they would be taken off air if they mentioned the forthcoming war.[73] NBC told Martin Sheen, 'President Bartlett' of *The West Wing*, that 'his high profile [in protests] could damage the show and called on him to explain his views'; other vocal critics were targeted by the new group 'Citizens Against Celebrity Pundits'.[74] Lou Dobbs, the host of CNN's *Moneyline*, could not tolerate being informed by former Congressman Tom Andrews, now of Win Without War, that 'weapons inspections during the 1990s destroyed more weapons of mass destruction than our entire armed forces were able to destroy in the Gulf War', so he interjected, 'Oh, Tom, Tom, please. If you're going to correct me, correct me on something that deserves it .... Please, if we're going to correct one another, let's keep it to the facts.' Fortunately for Dobbs, his next guest was the heavy metal musician Ted Nugent 'to tell us why war with Iraq in his judgment is necessary'.[75]

(In the most poignant and provocative incident, Bill O'Reilly learned that Jeremy Glick, whose father died in the World Trade Center attack, had signed an anti-war advertisement and asked him to appear on Fox News. Glick maintained his position, so O'Reilly berated him, 'You are mouthing a far left position that is a marginal position in this society .... What upsets me is I don't think your father would be approving of this.' Glick fought back, 'Actually, my father thought that Bush's presidency was illegitimate', and began to critique the history of American involvement with the mujahedin in Afghanistan, leaving O'Reilly to snap, 'I don't want to debate world politics with you .... I don't really care what you think.' When Glick pressed his advantage, 'You evoke 9/11 to rationalize everything from domestic plunder to imperialistic aggression worldwide', O'Reilly ended the interview, 'Man, I hope your mother isn't watching this .... Shut up, shut up .... Cut his mike. I'm not going to dress you down any more, out of respect for your father.')[76]

In February the correspondent Helen Thomas, veteran of eight Presidents, called Bush 'the worst president ever'. In retribution, the Republican Party organised an e-mail campaign lambasting the mainstay of the Washington press corps, who was placed at the back of the room and never allowed to ask another question of the President.[77] Such heavy-handed tactics were rarely necessary, however. CNN's website excised 866 words of Hans Blix's 14 February report to the Security Council, words which just happened to be about Iraqi moves towards compliance and partial refutation of Powell's evidence. The network prepared for the war by instructing reporters that they must submit all copy to officials in Atlanta for script approval.[78]

CNN's measure was an extra precaution. Most journalists, print and broadcast, were 'embedded' with US forces, supported by the US Central Command in Qatar with 'a quarter-million-dollar press briefing room created by a Hollywood set designer ... a media-savvy tool that will help bring the war to life for reporters and the viewers back home'.[79] The catch was that access to information was defined by the 'embedding' with the selected unit and conditional on 'a series of strict prohibitions' on reporting; the effect was to 'essentially cast the journalist into the drama of this war [the US military] are producing'.[80] The independent, prize-winning filmmaker Jon Alpert spent weeks in Baghdad obtaining uncensored, unmonitored footage inside Iraqi homes; no network would screen even an extract from the subsequent documentary, which observed seven American students communicating with seven Iraqi counterparts.[81]

The media was mobilised by the 'us' v. 'them' scenario, not only of the US against Iraq but also of America against 'shameful' allies, reducing dissent to 'anti-Americanism'.[82] The anecdote of a rich Belgian woman telling an American executive '[It was] good that the Americans got hit on Sept. 11. Maybe it taught them a lesson' was extrapolated into 'hating the States is a growth industry across Europe', with Europeans analogous to 'a barbarian ... who mistakes the customs of his tribe for the laws of nature'.[83] The US Ambassador publicly chided his hosts in a speech in Toronto, 'We would be there for Canada, part of our family. That is why so many in the United States are disappointed and upset that Canada is not fully supporting us now.'[84] Spurred by White House adviser Richard Perle, columnists such as George Will ranted about 'the absurdity of [France's] demand to be taken seriously',[85] while Michael Gove wrote a two-page love letter to the US Secretary of Defense: 'If there is a cowboy that Donald Rumsfeld resembles, it is the Gary Cooper of *High Noon*, the sheriff who won't allow the fears of others to prevent him doing what he knows to be right for their protection.'[86]

By March, trans-Atlantic diplomacy had been replaced by farce. In the days before Jacques Chirac's statement that 'there are no grounds for waging war' was distorted into the pretext for war without UN sanction,[87] Secretary of State Powell derided a French proposal for reinforced arms inspectors as a call for more 'Inspector Clouseaus',[88] Speaker of the House Dennis Hastert led calls for restrictions on French exports of bottled water and wine,[89] and a North Carolina fast-food outlet renamed French fries 'Freedom Fries'.[90] (Congressman Bob Ney went further with the consecration of 'Freedom Toast' on Capitol Hill menus, and Congresswoman Ginny Brown-Waite introduced the American Heroes Repatriation Act 2003 to 'allow the families of Second World War dead to dig up their bones [from cemeteries in Normandy] and take them home'.)[91] The US military showed its displeasure with a bunker-busting bomb inscribed 'Fuque the French'.[92] More substantially, the Pentagon began a concerted effort to shift US military bases from Germany to Eastern Europe.[93]

Yet, for all this patrolling of domestic and overseas dissent, the limits of acceptable opinion could no longer be maintained. Senator Robert Byrd declaimed:

What is happening to this country? When did we become a nation which ignores and berates our friends? When did we decide to risk undermining international order by adopting a radical and doctrinaire approach to using our awesome military might? How can we abandon diplomatic efforts when the turmoil in the world cries out for diplomacy?[94]

Canadian Prime Minister Jean Chrétien told President Bush that he was not trusted.[95] In Britain, Joan Smith of the *Independent* wrote, 'If the world has become a more dangerous place since 11 September 2001, it is not solely because of the activities of a bunch of Islamic terrorists', without provoking protest.[96] Simon Jenkins in *The Times*, while accepting there might have to be military action, added, 'I do not then surrender all concern for the scale of violence employed against Iraq', and Philip Stephens of the *Financial Times* warned US officials against their 'new Europe/old Europe' ploy, 'Britain fears U.S. unilateralism every bit as much as France does. Divided over Iraq, Europe is united in its concern to draw a line between American leadership and hegemony.'[97] David Ignatius, a fervent interventionist for 'democracy', complained:

> What's disturbing is that America may soon part company with some of its friends – to pursue goals that are not yet well enough defined to convince most of the world that America is right. How odd that France, the perpetual malcontent, may soon speak for the majority.[98]

Even if 42 per cent of Americans believed Saddam Hussein was behind 9–11, the challenge was no longer to find spirited opposition to war but, 'in the US, to find people who share their leaders' enthusiasm'.[99] The City Council of Los Angeles voted 9–4 for an anti-war resolution, joining more than 100 cities from Chicago to Philadelphia to Detroit. *Washington Post* reporters observed, 'The messages from U.S. embassies around the globe have become urgent and disturbing: Many people in the world increasingly think President Bush is a greater threat to world peace than Iraqi President Saddam Hussein.'[100] Their concern was sustained in the surprise result of an online poll by the European edition of *Time* magazine, 'Which country poses the greatest danger to world peace in 2003 – Iraq, North Korea, or the US?' Of the more than 600,000 votes recorded, the US gathered 87.6 per cent. Even in the 'new Europe', 67–94 per cent of the public opposed their governments' support for US policy.[101]

So some who accepted that the time had arrived for military action took a step back. On 15 February the editors of the *New York Times* had finally accepted war, 'The Security Council doesn't need to sit through more months of inconclusive reports.' Days later, they were beset by worries:

Things could go terribly wrong, very quickly. The war could be brutal and protracted, especially if Mr. Hussein unleashes biological or chemical weapons against Israel or American troops. He may also succeed in setting fire to his oil wells, or disabling those in neighboring countries, crippling the world economy. And if he is destroyed, there is every possibility of a vicious struggle for the lucrative spoils among the disparate clans and ethnic groups in Iraq, drawing in Turkey, Iran and others. In the chaos, the weapons of mass destruction Americans went to war to eliminate could wind up being ferried out of Iraq and sold to the highest terrorist bidder. And just as the American military's presence in Saudi Arabia during the gulf war precipitated the growth of Al Qaeda and Sept. 11, the long-term occupation of Iraq will create resentment in the Muslim world that could lead to more, not less, terrorism.[102]

In early March, the newspaper returned to the defence of diplomacy, 'With the loss of unity, the hawks in Washington will now be pushing hard to bypass further discussion at the Security Council and move directly to combat .... The threat of force, however, should not give way to the use of force until peaceful paths to Iraqi disarmament have been exhausted and the Security Council gives its assent to war.'[103] Even Thomas Friedman made a similar journey, 'Mr. President, before you shake the dice on a legitimate but audacious war, please, shake the dice just once on some courageous diplomacy.'[104]

Such hand-wringing exposed the tensions in US policy which Administration rhetoric about Iraqi transgressions could not hide. As the *Independent* dismissed the alleged cause for action, 'An effectively neutralised Saddam is what we have now .... There is no need for war,' Maureen Dowd offered an alternative explanation:

> The painful parts of Washington history have often been about men trying harder to save face than lives. With or without the fussy Frenchies, we're going to war. For this White House, pulling back when all our forces are poised for battle would be, to use the Bush family's least favorite word, wimpy.[105]

Using geopolitics rather than personality, Paul Krugman, Charles Kupchan, William Pfaff, and Michael Hardt all looked beyond the liberation of Baghdad and saw the broader US strategy, 'Any threats to the uni-polar order must be dismissed or destroyed. Washington's new anti-Europeanism is really an expression of their unilateralist project.'[106]

Of course, this exposure did not check the Administration's draping of 'freedom' and 'democracy' over the quest for a pre-ponderance of power. To the contrary, with 'weapons of mass destruction' challenged as a rationale for war in Iraq, President Bush on 26 February, visiting the American Enterprise Institute that provided so many of his advisers, made a breathtaking leap and turned the liberation of Baghdad into America's gift to the Middle East:

> A new regime in Iraq would serve as a dramatic and inspiring example of freedom for other nations in the region .... Success in Iraq could also begin a new stage for Middle Eastern peace, and set in motion progress towards a truly democratic Palestinian state.[107]

Bush's appeal had some resonance, especially with supportive 'analyses' in the *Washington Post* and *New York Times* extolling his self-belief: 'For Bush, A Sense of History – And Fate'; 'Bush Girds for War in Solitude, but Not in Doubt'.[108] Tony Blair's 'moral case' became the new rationale for an attack, with newspapers shifting from warnings of hidden missiles to stories of torture. Commentators such as Hitchens and Nick Cohen clung to the notion of a 'free' Kurdistan as the postwar model for all Iraq.[109] Johann Hari in the *Independent* assured over and over, 'Democracy in the Islamic world is not a fantasy – it's coming soon. The US is not doing this because of a sudden burst of altruism, but because of a new sense of enlightened self-interest.'[110] William Safire used Bush's rhetoric as a cloak for 'Give Freedom a Chance .... Rather than wring our hands, Americans and our allies are required to gird our loins – that is, to fight to win with the conviction that our cause is just.'[111] Jim Hoagland declared in the *Washington Post*, 'Rapid success in the war in Iraq could change [the attitudes of the Palestinian leadership]. The "Arab street" understands power as only those whose daily survival is threatened by the ruler's caprice can.'[112]

Unfortunately, Bush's proclamation of principle was not exempt from examination. Just below Hari's tribute was Adrian Hamilton's reminder, 'Forget democracy: this is a war for security. Liberation movements are not on Washington's support list.'[113] For José Ramos-Horta's example from East Timor, 'War for Peace? It Worked in My Country', there was Ariel Dorfman's painful conclusion from Chile:

> Heaven help me, I am saying that if I had been given a chance years ago to spare the lives of so many of my dearest friends, given the chance to end my exile and alleviate the grief of millions of my fellow countrymen, I would have rejected it if the price we would have had to pay was clusters of bombs killing the innocent, if the price was years of foreign occupation, if the price was the loss of control over our own destiny. Heaven help me, I am saying that I care more about the future of this sad world than about the future of your unprotected children.[114]

And, against the official rhetoric, there was the caution of the Director of the CIA against making the Iraq war the basis of 'a big domino theory about what happens in the rest of the Arab world'.[115] The State Department concluded in a secret report, 'Political changes conducive to broader and enduring stability throughout the region will be difficult to achieve for a very long time' because of corruption, destruction to Iraqi infrastructure and 'anti-American elements', i.e. Islamist parties who might win any free and fair elections. The title of the report, completed on the same day as the President's speech, summarised, 'Iraq, the Middle East and Change: No Dominoes'.[116]

The devil in Bush's vision was in the detail – or lack of it. The *New York Times* was an immediate nuisance, 'Even under the best of circumstances, the situation in Iraq is likely to be chaotic for years to come. Neither the Israelis nor the Palestinians should have to wait for peace until it is settled'; and the *Guardian* was rude: 'Palestinians should beware of geeks bearing gifts. Mr Bush has talked about a Palestinian state before; but talk is all it amounts to so far.'[117] Ten days later, the Administration confirmed that its proposed 'road map' for negotiations, which had been expected in late January, would not be produced before the resolution of the Iraq crisis.[118] (The 'road map' was suddenly promised once more in mid-March, its primary purpose to give Tony Blair diplomatic armour against an anti-war public and Labour Party backbenchers.)

Even if those inside Iraq were waiting for liberation (and some newspapers and columnists soon pointed out those exiles who were opposed to military action),[119] Iraqi opposition groups had already expressed betrayal at the 'unmitigated disaster' of 'deeply stupid' plans for the US 'to rule the country by military decree', assisted by 'Iraqi quislings palatable to the Arab countries of the Gulf and Saudi Arabia'.[120] Zalmay Khalilzad, Bush's envoy, told Kurdish leaders 'that they would have to give up plans for self-government' and 'accept a large deployment of Turkish troops' in northern Iraq.[121] At a key meeting of opposition groups at the beginning of March, Khalilzad was denounced as a 'bully' as 'the disparate factions [were] left bickering among themselves over their uncertain future'.[122] (Safire was reduced to making up an 'interview from the Great Beyond' with the long-dead Kurdish leader Mustafa Barzani, who assured, 'You'll help us set up our [Iraqi] confederation, organize state and federal elections and courts, repudiate Saddam's corrupt Russian debt, get onstream outside OPEC, block Turkish and Persian mischief, and say goodbye.')[123]

The problematic discovery, if one kept looking, was that Bush's quest for 'democracy' was not a transcendence of the

American quest for 'full-spectrum dominance'; it was integral to it.[124] In his address to the UN in September 2002, Bush had tied regime change in Iraq to the wonders of a 'democratic' Afghanistan and a 'democratic' Palestine and the inspiration of 'reforms throughout the Muslim world'. Significantly, the speech followed comments by Administration allies such as Michael Ledeen that war would 'liberate all the people of the Middle East from tyranny' and 'unleash a tsunami across the Islamic world'. The grandest reminder of the place of 'democracy' in America's global strategy came from no less than Richard Perle, days before Bush's February speech:

> There is tremendous potential to transform the region. If a tyrant like Saddam Hussein can be brought down, others are going to begin to think – they're already thinking. They may begin to act to bring down the tyrants who are afflicting them in pretty much the same way.[125]

The form of that 'freedom' and 'democracy' would be determined by their place within a global system defined for US political, military and economic interests and objectives. Conversely, if those interests were not fulfilled, 'freedom' and 'democracy' would be jeopardised or irrelevant. The endpoint was not only unilateral, with the US-led 'reformist project that seeks to modernize and transform the Arab landscape', but imperial: 'We should not be frightened of being "imperialist". It is the job of the West to plant the seed of liberty in lands now ruled by despots.'[126] Of course, this was cast in the spirit of benevolence, as in Robert Kagan's America saving the world from itself: 'The United States, with all its vast power, remains stuck in history, left to deal with the Saddams and the ayatollahs, the Kim Jong Ils and the Jiang Zemins, leaving the happy benefits to others.'[127] It was the twenty-first-century burden of Michael Ignatieff's very special 'liberalism': 'Multilateral solutions to the world's problems are all very well, but they have no teeth unless America bares its fangs.'[128] Niall Ferguson, the arch-proponent of the British Empire, passed the mantle to America, his new home: '1820s England offers a model for US power today.'[129]

'Freedom' would be brought not only through military intervention, but also 'through the stomach to impose a new political culture on the defeated parties'. International law would be a by-product of American interests: 'The rules may have to evolve, so that which is legitimate is also legal.'[130] (Sixteen eminent academic jurists warned Blair that Washington's 'pre-emptive self-defence' had no basis in international law; after days of silence, Downing Street issued a cobbled justification from the Attorney General.)[131] As Jonathan Schell wrote:

> Democracy is founded on the rule of law, empire on the rule of force. Democracy is a system of self-determination, empire a system of military conquest. The fault lines are already clear, and growing wider every day.[132]

Jonathan Freedland noted in one of the few articles mentioning the Project for a New American Century, 'There will be no place on earth, or the heavens for that matter, where Washington's writ does not run supreme. To that end, a ring of US military bases should surround China, with liberation of the People's Republic considered the ultimate prize. As one enthusiast put it concisely: "After Baghdad, Beijing".'[133] In this quest, however, the Middle East would not be forgotten; as Ignatieff noted, it would be 'the empire's centre of gravity'.[134] Even the most ardent of liberal interventionists, Thomas Friedman, finally threw up his hands in despair when US plans, dedicated to the unilateral quest for dominance, undermined his straightforward notion of exporting 'democracy': 'I feel as if the president is presenting us with a beautiful carved mahogany table – a big, bold, gutsy vision. But if you look underneath, you discover that this table has only one leg. His bold vision on Iraq is not supported by boldness in other areas. And so I am terribly worried that Mr. Bush has told us the right thing to do, but won't be able to do it right.'[135]

The supposed American crusade for freedom had been laid on a struggle over the 'free world' that the US would define and oversee in the new millennium. Justification came through crude renderings such as those of Robert Kagan:

Europe is turning away from power, or to put it a little differently, it is moving beyond power into a self-contained world of laws and rules and transactional negotiation and cooperation .... The United States, meanwhile, remains mired in history, exercising power in the anarchic Hobbesian world where international laws and rules are unreliable and where true security and the defense and promotion of a liberal order still depend on the possession and use of military might.'[136]

While Freedland might advocate, 'Neither a sacrosanct sovereignty, inviolable whatever the circumstances, nor Martini interventionism, a free hand to meddle anytime, anyplace, anywhere .... That will mean rules, and institutions to enforce them',[137] and others might insist on the specific case, 'Mr Blair [must] convince President Bush that a clear mandate from the UN is worth the wait and that the inspectors should be given the time they require',[138] the outcome had been determined. In a conflict which was 'not really about Iraq any longer', but 'about the United States and its role in the world ... [and] the ability of less powerful nations to use the UN as the sole institution that could check the projection of US power',[139] there was no middle ground between internation-alism and the American way.

Inevitably, when this complex, even contradictory, rela-tionship between ideology and power was raised, the challenge was met with the complaint that the deviant Left was refusing the obvious superiority of a US-led campaign. Blair insisted, 'Some of the rhetoric I hear about America is actually more savage than some of the rhetoric I hear about Saddam and the Iraqi regime.'[140] William Shawcross lined up John Pilger and Tony Benn for 'a terrifying moral myopia' that will not acknowledge that 'there are times when the use of force is essential in the pursuit of peace'; Howard Jacobson accused Pilger of 'racism' for his 'perverse loathing, not of the hated other, but of one's hated own'.[141] Conrad Black, publisher of the *Daily Telegraph*, *Sunday Telegraph* and *The Spectator*, came out from behind his publications to assail Russia, China, 'vintage French opportunism', 'misplaced' German 'romantic pacifism' and those with 'bilious envy of the United States', including 'raving, foaming-at-the-mouth Americophobic lunatics' daring to oppose US military might.[142]

The litany was no longer enough, however. As Arundhati Roy wrote, 'To call someone anti-American, indeed, to be anti-American, is not just racist, it's a failure of the imagination. An inability to see the world in terms other than those that the establishment has set out for you: If you don't love us, you hate us. If you're not good, you're evil. If you're not with us, you're with the terrorists.'[143]

Which brings us once more to George Orwell. His fate might not have been firmly lashed to the fortunes of the War on Terror or the War on Iraq; *Nineteen Eighty-Four* was voted the consummate 'English' book by those listening to BBC Radio 4's *Today* programme (although it lost out to Bill Bryson's *Notes from a Small Island* in a World Book Day poll).[144] He might not be the exclusive captive of one side in a political contest; it is still possible to swipe at 'Blairite Britain' as an exemplar of '"Animal Farm" on the corruption of power, "1984" on the manipulation of truth and "Burmese Days" on the corrosive impact of clubby elites' or to condemn the Bush Administration's ill-fated Operation TIPS as an 'Orwellian new initiative' and a step beyond 'George Orwell's "1984"'.[145] Yet Orwell's greatest service in this new millennium, particularly after 9–11, has been as a device to re-establish the superiority of 'objectivity' over one's opponents. Barbara Amiel, the scourge of 'appeasers' such as the BBC and CNN, covered her rant against 'Left-liberalism' with the introduction:

'During the past 20 years,' Orwell wrote, 'the negative, fainéant outlook which has been fashionable among English Left-wingers, the sniggering of the intellectuals at patriotism and physical courage, the persistent effort to chip away English morale and spread a hedonistic, what-do-I-get-out-of-it? attitude to life, has done nothing but harm. It would have been harmful even if we had been living in the squashy League of Nations that these people imagined. In an age of führers and bombing planes, it was a disaster.'[146]

In the *New Yorker*, Louis Menand dared to write, 'There is sometimes a confusion, when people talk about Orwell's writing, between honesty and objectivity. "He said what he believed" and "He told it like it was" refer to different virtues.' He then swiped at Orwell's elevation, by himself and by his followers, above anyone who dared take the debate beyond 'honesty':

> Orwell was against imperialism, fascism, and Stalinism. Excellent. Many people were against them in Orwell's time, and a great many more people have been against them since. The important question, after condemning those things, was what to do about them, and how to understand the implications for the future. On this level, Orwell was almost always wrong.[147]

This was all too much for Leon Wieseltier of *The New Republic*. He rendered Menand's critique as 'the danger ... not in the fading of the concept of objective truth, but in the clinging to the concept of objective truth' before objectively assessing:

> Menand thinks that truth is merely a warrant for terrorism, that objectivity is just an early form of fanaticism, that certainty only kills .... He is indifferent and afraid. His fear is understandable: When one has renounced the inquiry into truth and falsity, certainty must seem terrifying.

Wieseltier, the essayist who had framed thoughtful consideration of 9–11 as 'idiotic',[148] situated his own objectivity in the immediate clash of civilisations, '[For Menand] there is no distinction between a just war and a holy war. What a haul of irony!' (Similarly one assumes that Hitchens' own objectivity was devoid of irony when he criticised, 'Menand had a contrarian itch, the integrity of which is compromised by his failure to read Orwell with attention and by misrepresenting him on this crucial matter of the war.')[149] The shifting of blame was complete: Wieseltier, who had condemned the 'Left' for being appeasers of 'terrorism' and 'fanaticism', passed sentence on Menand for the crime of falsely portraying 'objectivity' as terrorist and fanatical.[150]

On the eve of war, a protester found himself/herself responsible for all evils of the twentieth century, as in Michael Gove's prosecution:

A low throaty guffaw emanates from a cellblock in The Hague. A rasping chuckle breaks the silence in Baghdad. And in a deep corner of Hell there's a chorus of hilarity from ghosts who haven't had anything to celebrate in decades. For Slobodan Milosevic, President Saddam Hussein and the spirits of politburos past, these must be the most delicious of days.[151]

Or there was the burden of the future, as with Michael Kelly's assurance, 'To march against the war is not to give peace a chance. It is to give tyranny a chance. It is to give the Iraqi nuke a chance. It is to give the next terrorist mass murder a chance. It is to march for the furtherance of evil instead of the vanquishing of evil.'[152] It was we rather than the warriors who, according to Prime Minister Blair, must ponder the 'consequences paid in blood'.[153]

There were checkpoints along this path to perdition. William Safire's accusation of 'Yes-Butters' turned into Ferdinand Mount's 'Not-Yetters' or George Will's 'Nay-Sayers'.[154] David Brooks of *The Weekly Standard* declared that any doubters were suffering from a 'certainty crisis'.[155] Rather than confronting the suggestion that war against Iraq was an expression of the 'preponderance of power' sought by US foreign policy, Janet Daley created the Gallic monster: 'Translation: the argument that America was interested in overthrowing Saddam only to get control of Iraq's oil supplies has proved rather embarrassing, since ... as it turned out, oil was at the heart of the motives of the peace party's favourite leader, Jacques Chirac, at least as much as those whom the Left likes to call the "oil men" of the Bush Administration.'[156] Rest assured that, in the end, we would find, 'Oppose America and You Are at War with Yourself': 'Everything [is] very simple. Which side would you like to have nuclear weapons; which states would you trust with them – the United States or the rogue states? Whose side are you on?'[157] (Simon Henderson, 'expert' biographer of Saddam Hussein, reworked the formula for an 'absurd' caller to a BBC Radio 5 phone-in: 'Where would you rather go on your holidays – America or Iraq?')[158]

As the accusers had already set out the dissenters' arguments (or absence of them), there could be no mitigation. Nick

Cohen, despite his own criticism of the War on Terror, could brook no doubters. He posed Harold Pinter as our talisman, put straw man arguments ('War is worse than tyranny', 'It's a war against Islam', 'They couldn't handle freedom', etc.)[159] into our mouths so he could demolish them to pass judgment: 'As the moment of decision arrives, Iraqi democrats and socialists have discovered that their natural allies in the European Left don't want to know them. They must add the shameless Stop the War coalition to the enemies list.'[160] Stephen Pollard cast aside his 'address book [as] the first casualty of war':

> How can I use the word 'friend' to describe such people? .... They wallow in their sense of superiority, but what they wish to protest against, I thank God for. What they consider an affront, I salute. What they regard as a moral outrage, I regard as the only safe way to conduct world affairs. What they stand for, I feel sickened by. This is not about Left versus Right. It is about freedom: those who are willing to protect it, and those who take it for granted.[161]

Johann Hari, Young Journalist of the Year, faced with an even younger generation which was supposed to be apathetic but was now at the forefront of protest, reached for any explanation other than principled opposition: 'We have no positive agenda .... I hear this vague negativism, this lack of hope, every day, wherever people of my age gather ... [It is] a corrosive acid of distrust that is splashed liberally around us.'[162]

What could not be permitted, because it would break down the 'objectivity' of those criticising dissent, was the possibility that there were anti-war arguments beyond delusion or naïveté. Adrian Hamilton's broader call for an 'internationalism' with 'certain principles for the conduct of global behaviour' and development of 'the institutions – the UN, the International Court of Justice and the regional security pacts – to encourage and enforce them' was ignored.[163] Dan Plesch of the Royal United Services Institute challenged 'the idea that we can invade Iraq to bring democracy and freedom' as 'a confidence trick designed to draw western liberals into providing legitimacy for old-fashioned conquest' and called for 'containment with engagement – a strategy that has served us well with Iran, Libya, and even the Soviet Union'; none of the western liberals noticed.[164]

What could never be accepted was the manifesto of Matthew Parris, *The Times* columnist and former Conservative MP, of 'how to be an honest critic of the war'. Parris pondered that Britain and the US might fight banned weapons, might obtain a UN resolution authorising an attack, might succeed with a quick victory welcomed by the Arab world and the Iraqi people. His objection lay beyond these immediate considerations:

> I am not afraid that this war will fail. I am afraid that it will succeed.
>
> I am afraid that it will prove to be the first in an indefinite series of American interventions. I am afraid that it is the beginning of a new empire: an empire that I am afraid Britain may have little choice but to join.[165]

What could not be acknowledged was Freedland's acceptance, after considering the 'pro-war arguments' but finding them 'so painfully thin', after establishing 'a better objection to the new galloping spirit of interventionism is not to the ideal itself but to its likely implementation', that 'those who are opposed to war on Iraq need to show that there is a peaceful way to liberate its people'. There was no consideration of his proposal, building on the ideas of the Oxford Research Group and the Carnegie Endowment for International Peace, for a lifting of sanctions, UN control of the distribution of revenues from oil ('released only if and when the regime made democratic reforms), and 'coercive inspections' for weapons of mass destruction.[166]

None of this could be observed since, as the *Sunday Telegraph* argued, it was imperative to 'Give War a Chance'. Dissent, even the dissent of millions, must be placed on the margins, in the hope that it would simply go away.

Which was the command to which we must not surrender, for 'in the days to come, there [would] be a desperate need for opponents of war to remain engaged – because it is important to work for a more lasting peace in the Middle East, because it is important to care about what happens to those who will suffer, because the war will end and the settlement that follows must be just .... This war may not be in our name, but we bear the responsibility for it nonetheless.'[167]

9

Dissent and 'Liberation'

Two months after we marched in London with more than a million others, the formalities of the military conflict had come and gone. As soon as the first Tomahawks and 'smart bombs' hit Baghdad and the advance troops crossed the Iraq–Kuwait starting line, we were told that we must dutifully mute our concerns and 'should be careful not to overplay their hand' as our 'main effect was to inconvenience fellow citizens'.[1] We were assured that our fears of civilian casualties would be demolished by precision weaponry. As Saddam's statue, if not the real tyrant, toppled in Firdaus Square (in a stage-managed 'spontaneous' demonstration), we were greeted with Ha Ha Ha Redux: 'Grow up. American power is a fact .... From Damascus to Pyongyang, totalitarians everywhere are watching this war with shock and awe.'[2] Fox News' Neil Cavuto celebrated with the message to those 'who opposed the liberation of Iraq', 'You were sickening then, you are sickening now.'[3] William Shawcross trilled, 'The much derided "neocons" in Washington have been shown to be far more correct than all the sneering sophisticates of the EU [European Union].'[4] And the *New York Post* smirked:

> With the coalition of the willing victorious in Iraq, expect a barrage of gloating from those who backed military action. Some of it won't be pretty. Some of it might even be obnoxious. A great deal will be embarrassing to the pre-war naysayers. We wouldn't miss it for the world![5]

There was the homage to martial nobility, as in the elevation of a speech by Lieutenant-Colonel Tim Collins, a British battalion commander, to Shakespearean heights.[6] *The Times* effused about 'Heroes, and Why We Still Need Them' and hailed the SAS as 'ghosts of the desert'; the *Daily Telegraph* 'was struck by the similarities between the British soldiers in Iraq and the pilots of the Battle of Britain'; even the *Guardian* puffed out its English chest, 'The men from Sandhurst are better educated and better at educating than the men from West Point.'[7] Beyond the round-the-clock parade of military experts on American television, a media consultancy firm advised its clients, 'Get the following production pieces in the studio now ... patriotic music that makes you cry salute, get cold chills! Go for the emotion'; MSNBC led the way with its 'America's Bravest' studio wall. The 'Rescue of Jessica Lynch', in which a young, injured, female prisoner of war was freed from a Nasiriyah hospital by US forces, was stage-managed into 'the most heartwarming' television and print spectacular.[8] (In fact, hospital staff had tried to hand over Lynch the previous day, but had been fired on by an American outpost. Iraqi troops had already left; instead, the US 'liberators' handcuffed and interrogated staff, tearing apart the specialist bed – the only one in the hospital – where Lynch had been lying. One hospital administrator was held in an American prison camp for three days.)[9]

In the America of the 'just war', we learned that President Bush had 'the advantage of having a mind that does not flit about much'.[10] Peace could literally be eradicated by Warner Brothers, altering the billboard for its new release *What a Girl Wants*. The female star, posing in a T-shirt emblazoned with the American flag, flashed the V peace sign of the 1960s; on the revised board, the flag remained but the V was gone.[11] The US media, 'from reporters inhaling the exhaust of infantry units to bleary-eyed New York anchors spellbound by squads of generals analysing the data stream', could 'march practically in lock step with the military'.[12] As the President of CBS News explained:

> American journalists are rooting for America to win. You're not going to find a lot of Americans rooting for Iraq. That doesn't mean they're not objective and fair in their reporting.[13]

We were assured that 'Americans are pulling together .... There is greater revulsion at those who are trying to divide the country. There is no tolerance for alienated poses.'[14]

Faced with the shock and awe of vilification and patriotism, we found that 'the not-in-my-name war has turned out to be in our name after all, and it is a profoundly discomfiting experience'.[15] Many gave way, as in Martin Woollacott's abdication, 'Unity is sometimes more important than principle.'[16] Timothy Garton Ash, who had already declared himself 'in defence of the fence',[17] used a conversation with a 'Christian rock' singer in Kansas to shift responsibility for the side-effects of war from its prosecutors to its opponents: 'The Iraq war may be America's crusade, but it's Europe which is closer to the likely Muslim backlash and worse equipped to deal with it.'[18] John Humphrys put himself in Washington's hands: 'We must trust in the determination of the founding fathers to show "a decent respect for the opinions of mankind". First, though, there is a war to be fought.'[19] Michael Walzer offered, 'If there was a real commitment to sustain the little war for as long as necessary, there would be no good reason for the big war.'[20] Henry Porter displayed a faith bordering on naïveté: 'There is one slight ray of hope in all this, and that is the view of Paul Wolfowitz and other conservative hawks in the Pentagon who believe that the best way to defend Western democracy and values is to extend them even to the harshest climates.'[21]

The Bush Administration had triumphed, for the moment, through a fait accompli. Nicholas Kristof sighed, 'We doves simply have to let go of the dispute about getting into this war. It's now a historical question, and the relevant issue, for hawks and doves alike, is how we get out of this war (and how we avoid the next pre-emptive war).'[22] The Liberal Democrats, the largest political party in Britain to challenge the march to battle, took cover, as their leader Charles Kennedy insisted, 'After the event is the time to ask questions about this war. But now is not the time,'[23] and even the *Independent on Sunday*, which had held out against the American crusade for so long, made a tactical retreat, 'This war is wrong, but it is unstoppable. So we must fight for the peace.'[24]

Yet stubbornly, obstinately, millions refused to acquiesce. Thousands of schoolchildren (including Eton's Orwell Society) gathered on British, Swedish, Spanish, Australian, Greek, Belgian and even American streets;[25] 550 writers, illustrators and editors of books for young people opposed a 'war on children'.[26] The Archbishop of Canterbury, Rowan Williams, muted his anti-war statements with an assurance of support for British troops,[27] but the leader of the Catholic Church in England and Wales, Cardinal Cormac Murphy-O'Connor, continued to describe the conflict as 'wrong and evil'.[28] The former President of the Pacific Stock Exchange joined 'Buddhist monks, Catholic priests, nuns, war veterans, students, families of 9/11 victims and average citizens' to sit in the road of San Francisco's financial district. Three days after the start of hostilities, up to 500,000 gathered for the largest wartime marches in British history, 'a very British demonstration, not so much militant as plain shocked, hurt even'.[29] More than 200,000 gathered at the Washington Monument to advance on the White House; another 200,000 protested in New York City; the Palm Springs (California) Vigil For Peace, 'from a 14-year-old boy in red Converse high-tops to men and women who remember Pearl Harbor', maintained its watch.[30] Despite police harassment under the guise of 'anti-terrorist' laws, protestors continued to gather at the RAF base at Fairford, used by American B-52s bombing Iraq.[31] The *Independent on Sunday* soon returned to its immediate concern over Mssrs Bush and Blair, 'They do not know what they are doing or why they are doing it.'[32]

Even though their high profile ensured vilification as well as press attention, some musicians and artists risked their careers. CBS producer Ed Gernon was fired after an interview about his mini-series on Hitler's accession to power strayed too close to contemporary leaders and their societies: 'It basically boils down to an entire nation gripped by fear, who ultimately chose to give up their civil rights and plunged the whole nation into war …. I can't think of a better time to examine this history than now.' ABC responded to Janeane Garofalo's activism by postponing the launch of her situation comedy until early 2004.[33] Still, the Dixie Chicks once more renounced comfortable silence, criticising the President in prime-time television interviews and provocative cover stories, and Susan Sarandon and Tim Robbins would not give up their protest, even when the prominent charity The United Way cancelled Sarandon's appearance at a conference on women's leadership and the Baseball Hall of Fame abandoned a celebration of the film *Bull Durham* and told Sarandon and Robbins, who had starred in it, that they were not welcome in the museum.[34] From Steve Earle to Public Enemy to the West End production 'The Madness of George Dubya', concert tours and plays in Britain turned into public demonstrations.[35]

For the issue was never as simple as 'the war', never to be reduced to 'backing our boys'. The satirist Armando Iannucci made the point for us by going straight:

> The anti-war movement is not the Stop the War Coalition. Instead, it's millions of people with no political or crusading affiliation whatsoever. We do not subscribe to automatic anti-Americanism, we remain unconvinced by wild conspiracy theories about a Western grab for oil and a son's desire to avenge an assassination attempt on his father.
>
> The bulk of us are probably happy to admit that the presence of 250,000 troops around Iraq probably did make the weapons inspectors' job easier.
>
> But then we hit the point of maddening frustration. Why couldn't it go on, why couldn't there be more time, what exactly was the threat, how on earth could Saddam do anything suspect with the eyes of the world on him? And still we feel these questions have not been answered.[36]

The issue was not just 'weapons of mass destruction', real or alleged, and though the words tugged at our emotions, it was not only 'freedom' and 'liberation' for Iraqis. Neil Ascherson voiced our concerns, 'Soon rather than later, [those in control of US policy] will carry forward their programme of pre-emptive attack on "potentially hostile" regimes and strike at another country. If this happens, we enter a century of violence and unpredictable counter-violence.'[37]

We did not need to introduce the complications beyond the call to arms. In their simple aphorisms of the war, 'they' did. We were assured by British Foreign Secretary Jack Straw, who understood us 'as a young participant of peace protests in the 1960s', that 'our intelligence shows that even today, Saddam regards his poisons and diseases ... as active parts of his arsenal of terror',[38] but they never materialised. No matter.

We were reminded by George Bush that, even though we were not fighting Islam, we could be sure the Lord was on our side. As he told US troops a week after the start of the war:

> The liberty we prize is not America's gift to the world, it is God's gift to humanity. We Americans have faith in ourselves, but not in ourselves alone. We do not know – we do not claim to know all the ways of Providence, yet we can trust in them, placing our confidence in the loving God behind all of life, and all of history. May He guide us now. And may God continue to bless the United States of America.[39]

The Anglo-American campaign never came close to meeting this simple rhetorical standard. The 'coalition' might proclaim this 'one of the most unsordid wars in history'.[40] It might wish away the thousands of civilian dead and wounded, shutting them out of American and British living rooms,[41] it might chant over and over about 'the utmost concern to avoid civilian casualties',[42] it might resort to lies to evade responsibility,[43] but with new global broadcasters such as Al-Jazeera (bombed by US planes in Baghdad as in Kabul), Al-Arabiya and Abu Dhabi Television, the bodies of the innocent were on the television screens and the computer terminals of much of the rest of the world.[44] In Baghdad, Suzanne Goldenberg, Andrew Gilligan, Lindsay Hilsum and Robert Fisk broke through the sanitised images of the just war with on-air and front-page accounts putting human features on deaths caused by American bombs and missiles: 'It was an outrage, an obscenity. The severed hand on the metal door, the swamp of blood and mud across the road, the human brains inside a garage, the incinerated, skeletal remains of an Iraqi mother and her three small children in their still-smouldering car.'[45]

Hawkish columnists draped themselves in martial benevolence and turned attack into sacrifice: 'We've been held back by our own scrupulousness. It is safe to say there has never been a conflict in which one belligerent has taken more care not to harm the civilians of the other. And it has already cost us.'[46] It took sharp eyes to notice a bloodier war tucked away at the bottom of stories, as in the comment of an

American officer, 'You try to limit collateral damage, but they want to fight. Now it's just smash-mouth football.'[47]

Depleted uranium and cluster bombs were deployed with quiet admissions and convoluted moral equations such as British Defence Minister Geoff Hoon's assurance that the Iraqi mother of a child killed by such weaponry 'one day ... might' thank British forces.[48] Success consisted of securing oilfields and handing out contracts to US firms for reconstruction,[49] as the combination of a demolished Iraqi infrastructure and the failure to cooperate for a post-Saddam administration and security arrangements left a vacuum filled by looting, murders and local power struggles.

If we peaceniks were guilty of a crime, it was in pointing to these likely by-products of 'victory'. William Raspberry of the *Washington Post* wrote two weeks before the start of war:

Imagine some American viceroy in a postwar Iraq trying to cobble together a government out of warring Shiite and Sunni Muslims, secularists and Islamist theocrats, while holding at bay ambitious Iranians and Turks and damping down the territorial ambitions of independence-minded Kurds. And all this while controlling – largely for our own use, influence and economic benefit – Iraq's huge oil resources.

Steve Richards echoed in London, 'No one has a clue what to do after war. Now that really is frightening.' Fergal Keane, who had positioned himself on the Iraqi border to witness the coming of freedom, wrote candidly:

Overthrowing the president of Iraq by invasion or through a coup has been [the American government's] intention for at least 18 months ... We are so bogged down in the minutiae of the arguments about Iraq that the big picture – the shifting of tectonic plates across the Middle East – is obscured. War is coming. It is what might wait for us afterwards that scares me.[50]

And the initial premise for the war did turn into farce. Daily pronouncements by British and US officials of the discovery of weapons of mass destruction were followed by clarifications, retractions or further lies. The hapless Geoff Hoon dramatically proved that Iraq must have chemical weapons because the 'coalition' has discovered Iraqi protective suits, until it was pointed out that the suits were a precaution against chemical attacks by British and US forces.[51] Kuwait was struck by prohibited 'Scud' missiles which turned out not to be Scuds.[52] The nerve gas ricin in a 'terrorist factory' in Kurdistan never materialised,[53] a 'chemical weapons factory' near Najaf was nothing of the sort,[54] and 'bottles' of white powder dwindled into one innocuous phial.[55] The Euphrates did not have cyanide poured into it, missiles 'with nerve gas' near Hindiyah had no such substance;[56] eleven 'mobile labs' near Baghdad were proclaimed suspicious but soon dropped out of sight.[57] US troops entered the Tuwaitha nuclear site and broke the UN seals on closed facilities, but found no weapons production. Disappointed, they left the area unsecured, and Iraqis stripped the site of containers and equipment tainted by radiation.[58]

President Bush fell back on the justification of 'liberation', but the reception of US and British 'liberators' was uncertain, even hostile, providing embedded reporters with unwelcome black comedy.[59] The 'coalition' forces, often moving into villages in southern Iraq without translators, could not communicate with those whom they were freeing. Iraqis who speak English can be blunt: a British television correspondent was taken aback when a resident criticised Saddam but then, asked about the US President, added, 'Fuck Bush'.[60] A mother in Safran elaborated, 'You ask if we support this war. Let me answer you this way. We have no water, no power and our children are becoming sick.' (A British lieutenant responded, 'They are so ungrateful.')[61] In Baghdad, a doctor treating war casualties said, 'I want to see one of them – those American soldiers. I want to kill one of them';[62] a man standing amidst the dead in a market cried, 'Why does [America] hate the Iraqi people?'[63] A teenager wrote in her diary, 'My father says the American have created this chaos. I think this is part of the plan to destroy our country.'[64] (Attempting to explain why the liberated weren't dancing in the streets, David Aaronovitch tried fear, links with the old regime and the 'Stockholm syndrome' of hostage and captor, before reassuring himself, 'It is one thing ... to be liberated from someone else, but it is quite another to be liberated from yourself.')[65]

'Liberation' brought illness and disease. With the infrastructure for provision of water damaged beyond immediate repair, millions of people had no access to clean supplies in Baghdad and southern Iraq, putting 200,000 children at risk from diarrhoea and promising outbreaks of cholera.[66] Hospitals lacked electricity and basic supplies; premature babies died from lack of oxygen.[67]

'Liberation' brought disorder: 'by minimising the number of troops on the ground, the US ... maximised the chances of a rapid, chaotic descent into post-war mayhem'.[68] The besieged hospitals were stripped of drugs, incubators and heart monitors.[69] The Iraqi National Museum and Iraqi National Library were sacked, and banks looted.[70] The US military, warned by non-governmental organisations and American archaeologists that this would occur, confirmed Washington's priorities by protecting only two major buildings, the Ministry of Oil and the Ministry of Interior with the files of the Iraqi intelligence services.[71]

Far from condemning the looting, the British and US Governments welcomed it as 'a message that the old guard is truly finished'.[72] An observer like Robert Fisk might see 'a civilisation torn to pieces',[73] but Hoon explained in the House of Commons that 'liberation' of items from a 7,000 year-old vase to a ping-pong table was 'redistributing that wealth among the Iraqi people .... I regard such behaviour perhaps as good practice.'[74] A US marine colonel was pragmatic, 'I don't know if they're happy to see us. I think they're happy because they're carting away refrigerators and TVs'; a British military spokesman was blasé, 'Do I look to you like I'm a policeman?'[75] (Meanwhile, Aaronovitch provided more intellectual rationale, 'Is this plundering really so bad?')[76]

Other tensions and contradictions in the 'liberation' quickly arose. The US Government complained vociferously about the display of American prisoners of war on Iraqi television, citing the Geneva Convention, while maintaining that the convention did not apply to those held at Camp X-Ray.[77] In the north of Iraq, thousands of Arabs fled or were forced from their homes by Kurds, and clashes led to dozens of deaths.[78]

A measure of order and basic provision of services were established in towns such as Najaf and parts of Baghdad such as Sadr City (formerly Saddam City), not by the Americans but by de facto authorities led by Shia clerics.[79]

Suddenly the rhetoric of freedom – 'The liberation of Iraq started on July 4, 1776'[80] – wasn't so clear-cut. In Robert Fisk's trenchant summary, 'We bomb. They suffer. Then we turn up and take pictures of their wounded children.'[81] Rare was the consideration such as that of Baroness Nicholson, 'Humanitarians who support the war must face the question: how can it be worth such pain?'[82] Instead, justifications by Ignatieff and Hari bordered on the Vietnam slogan of 'we had to destroy this village in order to save it': 'Sometimes the only way to spread peace is at the barrel of a gun.'[83] Philip Kennicott, possibly with tongue in cheek, reminded readers, 'Sometimes, Jean-Jacques Rousseau said, people must be forced to be free', but Rumsfeld showed no sense in irony in his explanation as 'liberated' cities fell into disorder: 'Freedom's untidy.'[84] Nor did the *Daily Telegraph* with its salute to 'America's Quiet Patriotism'.[85]

(At least Michael Gove was honest in his personal war cry, 'Stop pussyfooting, all that matters is victory', and Niall Ferguson blunt in his rhetorical question, 'If this isn't imperialism, what is?'[86] Meanwhile a CNN anchor stuck to the ideological script, by asking the Iraqi doctor who was treating twelve-year-old Ali Ismail Abbas, the injured symbol of child casualties of US missiles: 'Doctor, does [Ali] understand why this war took place? Has he talked about Operation Iraqi Freedom and the meaning?')[87]

Inevitably, the difficulties of 'liberation' were not associated with US and British operations, but were blamed on those journalists who dared to point out the unexpected problems. Cabinet ministers attacked 'moral equivalents' in the British media, labelling the BBC 'a friend of Baghdad ... trying to rewrite the history of one of the most brutal regimes we have had in the 20th century'.[88] Fisk's confirmation that US missiles, rather than an Iraqi misfire or provocation, were responsible for civilian deaths in Baghdad markets prompted Hoon's declaration to Parliament that the correspondent was a dupe of Saddam Hussein's regime.[89] The *Daily Telegraph*, through its leaders and its columnists, weighed in: 'Of course journalists should always try to hear both sides of the story. But they should also show common sense, and professional pride.'[90]

Pressure on the media went beyond such chides. The English-language website of Al-Jazeera was put out of service, ostensibly by 'private' hackers, and its US-based host 'expelled' the site.[91] Hoon responded to the death of Terry Lloyd, a correspondent for ITV, with a subtle warning to any reporter who was not 'embedded' with the US and British military: 'Having journalists have the protection of our armed forces is good for journalism.'[92] The Pentagon's spokesman in Kuwait also suggested that 'independent' correspondents think twice:

> We are going to control the battle space. Reporters that are not embedded are going to be treated like any other civilian, approached with a certain amount of caution. For many journalists, proving their identity can sometimes be problematic.[93]

In a little-noticed interview with Irish radio just before the war, veteran British reporter Kate Adie claimed that she 'was told by a senior officer in the Pentagon, that if uplinks – that is the television signals out of Baghdad, for example – were detected by any planes … they'd be fired down on. Even if they were journalists'.[94] On 8 April, three of those journalists were killed when US planes dropped bombs on the Baghdad offices of Al-Jazeera and Abu Dhabi television and an American tank fired on the Hotel Palestine, the headquarters for most foreign correspondents.[95]

These complications were only part of the war, however, for Iraq was always a central scene in a far bigger picture 'in which America did not change on 9/11. It only became more itself.'[96] The war wasn't just about oil or revenge for Daddy Bush. It was power, stupid, unilateral, preponderant, superior US power. A power that exposed the shallowness of Nick Cohen's faith in the Pentagon to bequeath 'freedom', of Hari's exhortations to 'side with the Iraqi democrats … and Mr Wolfowitz … to get through this to an honourable, democratic and – at last – peaceful Iraq'.[97] A power with the aim of 'full spectral dominance' that Jacqueline Rose compared to 'the rage of a child when he hits the limits of his powers. Except that unlike the raging child, the US, as the strongest military might in the globe, has the capacity to unleash forces a child can only dream about.'[98]

A United Nations that could not be tailored for the US design had to go since, as William Safire put it, 'Leagues of nations too ponderous to act need realignment into more agile, responsive coalitions.'[99] Charles Krauthammer issued the call, 'You've exposed the United Nations for what it is: the League of Nations, empty, cynical and mendacious. Mr. President ... walk away,' and Richard Perle responded:

> We have made the mistake that people make when they go into a sausage factory: you can never eat sausages again. The UN is a diplomatic sausage factory, and people have seen something that they would rather never see again.[100]

Vice President Cheney echoed that the international institutions 'built to deal with the conflicts of the 20th century ... may not be the right strategies and policies and institutions to deal with the kind of threat we face now.'[101]

The same Tony Blair who insisted 'that in any post-conflict Iraq there is a proper UN mandate for Iraq and the oil goes into a trust fund', who pronounced on 25 March, 'It is important that whatever administration takes over in Iraq has the authority of the United Nations behind it', bowed to US pressure 24 hours later, 'We don't know what the situation is going to be when you get into the post-conflict situation.'[102] The Pentagon clarified that the UN was now 'irrelevant' and moved to prevent Hans Blix's weapons inspectors from returning to Iraq.[103]

French and German Governments that blocked the American way faced more than the threat of 'Freedom Fries', sharp drops in wine sales or Laura Bush's snubbing of the exhibition 'Jefferson's America and Napoleon's France' at the New Orleans Museum of Art.[104] Michael Ledeen of the American Enterprise Institute may have pushed a bit too far, 'We will have to pursue the war against terror far beyond the boundaries of the Middle East, into the heart of Western Europe. And there, as in the Middle East, our greatest weapons are political: the demonstrated desire for freedom of the peoples of the countries that oppose us.'[105] However, in this new American order, the Appeasers and the Axis of Evil had been wedded. Safire brought everything together: 'France, China and Syria all have a common reason for keeping American and British troops out of Iraq: the three nations may not want the world to discover that their nationals have been illicitly supplying Saddam Hussein with materials used in building long-range surface-to-surface missiles.'[106] The *Telegraph* and *Times* sent reporters to Baghdad with instructions to find evidence of French and German collusion with Saddam.[107] When Rupert Murdoch asked Blair if there was anything the *Sun* could do to assist Downing Street, the Prime Minister allegedly replied, 'Step up the attacks on the French.'[108]

There were moments of dark humour. Sony snapped up the term 'Shock and Awe' for a computer game.[109] Richard Perle was confronted by the 1968 student leader Daniel Cohn-Bendit in a Washington debate: 'Recently, your government has been behaving like the Bolsheviks in the Russian revolution.'[110] Perle resigned as chairman of the Defense Policy Board (though he is still a member), not out of penitence but because of conflict-of-interest revelations. Among these were Perle's involvement with a venture capital group, which led to his lobbying for business in Saudi Arabia through international arms dealer Adnan Khashoggi even as the Defense Policy Board prepared for war with Iraq. Perle also held a position with the bankrupt telecommunications company Global Crossing, which was trying to overcome Pentagon opposition to its sale to a Hong Kong billionaire, and with a British firm 'selling advanced computer eavesdropping systems to intelligence agencies around the world', including the US Department of Homeland Security.[111] (Meanwhile, Bush adviser and ultra-hawk James Woolsey continued as a director of the private equity firm Paladin Capital, which made millions after 9–11 by 'invest[ing] in companies with immediate solutions designed to prevent harmful [terrorist] attacks, defend against attacks, cope with the aftermath of attack or disaster and recover from terrorist attacks and other threats to homeland security'. In addition to Perle, eight other members of the Defense Policy Board retained ties to defence companies that won more than $76 billion in contracts in 2001 and 2002.)[112]

The United States and Britain, blocking further UN inspections, moved 1,000 scientists and analysts into Iraq, but still the weapons of mass destruction could not be found.[113] An official in the Bush Administration told ABC News, 'We were not lying. But it was just a matter of emphasis.'[114] The Prime Minister had assured Parliament in September 2002 that such weapons not only existed, but would be 'ready within 45 minutes of an order to use them'; now the *Independent on Sunday* taunted, 'So where are they, Mr Blair?'[115] Russian President Vladimir Putin joined in, embarrassing Blair in a joint press conference in Moscow, 'Where are these arsenals – if they were really there? Maybe [Saddam] is sitting somewhere in a secret bunker with plans to blow all this stuff up at the last minute, threatening hundreds of human lives.'[116] US officials, suspected of the 'crude forgery' which tried to prove Iraqi purchases of uranium from Niger, told the tale that the document 'was originally put in intelligence channels by France'.[117]

For all the black comedy of the search, there was much more to come with the political process after the fall of Saddam. Thomas Friedman, perhaps inadvertently, exposed the nature of US-led 'democracy': 'America broke Iraq; now America owns Iraq.'[118]

Retired American general Jay Garner was appointed 'governor' for the transitional period. For one columnist, 'He [was] the sort of modest, self-deprecating man who makes you think of a more innocent America – a nation of Rotary Clubs and Jimmy Stewart movies and kindly small-town sheriffs.'[119] Perhaps more importantly, he came to the post with recent experience as an executive in the arms industry, supplying missile systems and billion-dollar 'logistical projects' to US special operations units.[120] He paid a visit to Israel, courtesy of the Jewish Institute for National Security Affairs, and was greatly impressed: 'A strong Israel is an asset that American military planners and political leaders can rely on.'[121] His firm was soon helping the Israeli military develop its missile defence.[122]

The American plan was for regional 'proconsuls' and 23 ministries, each headed by an American, with four Iraqi advisers and 'technocrats' selected by Wolfowitz.[123] The 'hawkish former Pentagon aide' Walter Slocombe would head the Ministry of Defence, James Woolsey, the former Director of the CIA, would be Minister of Information, and Zalmay Khalilzad, the former oil company executive and the special envoy to post-Taliban Afghanistan, would also take up a post. Michael Mobbs, colleague of Richard Perle in the Reagan Administration and now the legal consultant to the Pentagon, would be the general overseer of eleven of the ministries.[124]

The American intention was to anoint Ahmed Chalabi, supported by Washington since the first Gulf War and a close friend of the Project for a New American Century and JINSA, as the new Iraqi leader.[125] Chalabi was a risky choice, given that he had left Iraq in 1958 at the age of eleven and had been sentenced in Jordan to 22 years in jail for a $200 million financial scandal, but he had worked with officials such as Cheney and Rumsfeld since the end of the first Bush Adminstration.[126] An intensive campaign in the American and British media churned out fawning profiles and supportive editorials for 'the de Gaulle of Iraq .... His knowledge of medieval Japanese history is exceptional.'[127]

The scheme set up a senior Chalabi aide as liaison officer at US Central Command in Qatar, as Chalabi was airlifted to Nasiriyah in southern Iraq with 700 members of his 'Free Iraqi Forces', trained in Texas and Hungary by the US military.[128] When Saddam fell, the favourite of the Pentagon would be moved into Baghdad to be hailed as the first 'democratic' President. Unfortunately for Chalabi's backers, the intricacies of war and power rewrote the script. The would-be President suffered from a lack of recognition: 'wherever Dr Chalabi goes ... he is met by cries of "Ahmad who?"'[129] FIF units were more interested in setting up profitable enclaves, taking control of the town of Shatrah and 'liberating' Toyota land cruisers in Nasiriyah (losing out on one occasion to a group of Shia clerics);[130] a US sergeant offered the understatement, 'It gives us some heartache that we have to hand over weapons to these Free Iraqi Forces.'[131]

General Garner's first meeting with chosen Iraqis, held at an airbase near the biblical birthplace of Abraham, set the tone

for the future of 'democracy'. As the convocation waited four
hours for President Bush's envoy, Zalmay Khalilzad, journalists
were kept away by FIF 'soldiers' manning wooden barricades
and handed a potted summary of 13 points to establish 'a
federal system' which was 'not imposed from outside'. This was
overshadowed, however, by tens of thousands of Shia marchers
demanding, 'No no no Saddam, no no US'.[132]

Undeterred, the US helped FIF members stage the toppling
of Saddam's statue in Firdaus Square.[133] In Baghdad, Chalabi
was installed in the plush Hunting Club with its high hedges
and well-tended gardens. Guarded by US special operations
forces, he received callers but rarely emerged onto the streets.
His first press conference was conducted to the sounds of
gunfire, as the prospective leader slid back and forth between
declarations that he had no interest in elected office, proclamations in the name of 'his' government, and shadowy
answers about the source of payments to the FIF and his
movement's new flag ('I will not describe it. I will not give
significance to it').[134] Chalabi hurriedly tried to cover himself
with 'revelations' about Saddam Hussein's links to Al-Qa'eda,
while desperate defenders in the US media cried, 'You are not
hearing what you need to know about a man who is neither
an Iraqi puppet for U.S. forces nor a conniving political fortune
hunter taking the Bush administration for a ride.'[135]

While the US staff for reconstruction languished in
beachfront villas and the Kuwait City Hilton, the Pentagon and
State Department were at daggers drawn over American
personnel and the coronation of Chalabi. Donald Rumsfeld,
whose proposal of James Woolsey as 'Minister of Information'
had been blocked, tried to veto eight state nominees.[136] There
were jibes at 'Wolfowitz of Arabia', and James Akins, a former
Ambassador to Saudi Arabia, publicly expressed the sentiments
of many in the State Department, '[Chalabi] has more support
on Capitol Hill than in all Iraq .... There are no serious Arabists
left in the government now; only those who have been telling
the White House what it wants to hear. The dragons have
taken over.'[137]

Wolfowitz proclaimed in exclusive after exclusive interview,
'We don't want it to be an occupation – something that the
coalition imposes on the Iraqis.'[138] Unfortunately, his boss

set out, often on the same page, 'Rumsfeld Urges Interim Government Composed of Exile Leaders'.[139] Once again, the promises of Blair and his ministers – 'Our aim is to move as soon as possible to an Iraq interim authority that will be run by Iraqis .... There will not be foreign nationals running the Iraqi government' – rang hollow.[140]

And while Jay Garner hunkered down in the former Republican Palace behind razor wire and tanks, US troops were stoned in Baghdad streets.[141] Mohammad Mohsen al-Zubaidi, ostensibly an official in Chalabi's Iraqi National Congress, declared himself Mayor of Baghdad and began installing a civil administration. The American leadership initially negotiated with al-Zubaidi, but then declared that it 'alone retain[ed] absolute authority within Iraq' and arrested the 'mayor'.[142] The FIF staged the 'rescue' of looted artefacts, to which the press reacted with a mixture of scepticism and amusement.[143] More entertainment was provided by the Christian missions of Samaritan's Purse, led by Billy Graham's son Franklin, who had labelled Islam 'very evil and wicked', and of the Southern Baptists, training 20,000 members in a Center for Ministry to Muslims.[144] The US and British Governments loudly announced Freedom TV, launched with messages from President Bush and Prime Minister Blair, but while fawning reporters marvelled, the lack of electricity in Baghdad meant few of the intended audience knew that freedom on the airwaves.[145] Unfazed, the American media executive heading Freedom TV explained, 'We won't have the same kind of inflammatory talk television you see on al-Jazeera. It likes to present itself as the CNN of the Middle East, but I think of them more as CNN meets Jerry Springer.'[146] Unfortunately, a far larger audience preferred Al-Alam, the Arabic news channel established by Iran.[147]

The even darker reality behind the black comedy was that, one month after the toppling of Saddam's statue, an inscription on its base urged the Americans, 'All Donne, Go Home.'[148] In Mosul 17 demonstrators were slain when protesting against the occupation of a government building; in Fallujah, US soldiers killed 18 in two days of demonstrations over the American takeover of a school, commanders first denying any firing had taken place and then covering up the incident with claims of snipers and demonstrators 'shooting directly at the soldiers'.[149] The US military were not only failing to provide essential assistance, but were preventing non-governmental organisations such as Save the Children and Oxfam from distributing aid.[150] Explosions in ammunition dumps killed dozens, and more than 80 civilians died in 18 days from cluster bombs which had not exploded on impact.[151] Lack of clean water led to outbreaks of cholera and dysentery.[152] Hospital staff, working without essential supplies and unable to quarantine infectious patients, declared, 'The war has not ended.'[153]

There were some who were profiting from the turmoil, however. Six major American companies, contributors of $3.6 million in campaign funds to the Republican Party, manoeuvred for no-bid contracts from the US Government.[154] The largest beneficiary was Halliburton Corporation, which was allocated a potential income of $7 billion over two years to fight oil fires and provide logistical support to the US occupation.[155] Bechtel, led by George Shultz, Secretary of State in the Reagan Administration and the chairman of the Committee to Liberate Iraq, was handed a $34.6 million contract with the potential of $680 million in 18 months.[156] DynCorp, despite allegations of corruption and criminal behaviour in its work in Bosnia and Colombia, was awarded a multi-million-dollar project to recruit a private police force for the new Iraq.[157]

The Iraqi oil industry was placed in the hands of Philip Carroll, the former President of Shell and chairman of Fluor, one of the 'Big Six' companies handed reconstruction contracts.[158] Plans included a pipeline to Haifa, which would not only provide a guaranteed oil supply but also revenue from transport charges to Israel.[159] Just to establish that oil was not the only interest of the Bush Administration and American companies, Iraqi agriculture was assigned to Dan Amstutz, chief trade negotiator under President Reagan and former chief executive of Cargill, the largest grain exporter in the US.[160]

The irony was that, whatever the immediate profit for individual companies and the longer-term plans for permanent American military bases in Iraq,[161] the political and economic manoeuvring highlighted American vulnerability. Unable to restore order, Washington faced a long-term commitment of 200,000 troops at a cost of $46 billion each year. Paul Wolfowitz might have assured Congress, 'We're dealing with a country that can really finance its own reconstruction relatively soon', but with a bill of up to $105 billion to reconstruct Iraqi infrastructure and with maximum oil production only bringing in $25 billion, 'Iraq's income [had] been spent five or six times over'.[162] The American appeal to other countries to put in money and military units, given pre-war animosities and the potential burdens of any intervention, was met with hesitations and excuses.[163]

So, while all these developments might have been part of what Robert Fisk called 'colonial oppression', they were much more. Far from establishing control, US political and military found itself in a rapidly changing environment after a 'just and unnecessary war'.[164] As a State Department report noted, 'Even if electoral systems were introduced, anti-American feeling runs so strong that they could well elect radical Islamic governments hostile to Washington.'[165] A Department official admitted, 'I don't think anyone took a step backward and asked, "What are we looking for [in a successor regime]?" The focus was on the overthrow of Saddam Hussein.'[166]

The prospect was not just of '100 bin Ladens',[167] but of an emerging Iraqi movement sceptical of, if not hostile to, the United States. Demonstrations, notably a procession of more than a million Shia to Karbala for the holy day of Imam Husayn, turned into manoeuvres for power.[168] With a de facto authority established in the section of Sadr City, nearly 100 clerics gathered in Baghdad to press for an alternative to American occupation. In Karbala itself, the brother of the prominent Shia leader Ayatollah Mohammed Baqr al-Hakim declared that Garner was 'not needed here' as 'Iraqis have the ability to administer and run their own country'.[169] The Iraqi-born cleric Kadhem al-Husseini al-Haeri, still in Tehran, issued a fatwa 'to seize the first possible opportunity to fill the power vacuum in the administration of Iraqi cities'.[170] Such administrations had already been established in Kut and Nasiriyah as well as the holy city of Najaf.[171] Rumsfeld fumed, 'The Iraqi people will do something about it .... If they don't want those people in and those people don't subscribe to the principles that we've set forth ... then they'll stay out, and that's life.'[172]

The Americans tried to stem the alternative tide. Abdul Majid al-Khoei, a London-based cleric, returned to Najaf to forge a new authority, allegedly with $13 million in CIA funds; he was slain by a crowd in the central mosque.[173] Despite the setback, a 'senior administration official' confirmed that the US still wanted 'to find more moderate clerics and move them into positions of influence'. US special forces and intelligence officers were 'identifying [these] friendly clerics in small towns and cities and encouraging them to issue religious edicts, or fatwas, in support of the postwar American administration.'[174] The Shia 'mayor' of Kut was forced out by US Marine commanders supported by low-flying attack helicopters, and American authorities turned to a former Army colonel, who was also a Sunni Muslim, to become the new 'mayor' of Najaf.[175] However, with no US-fostered 'administration' emerging, the protests and the ad hoc Shia administrations were now permanent features of 'liberation'.

The wonder of the American doctrine of 'preponderance of power' was that such instability could contribute to, rather than check, Administration ambitions. General Wesley Clark, the commander of American forces in Kosovo and now a prominent media pundit, captured the essence of revolutionary hubris even as he denied it: 'Take us on? Don't try! And that's not hubris, it's just plain fact.'[176] James Woolsey, advising the Pentagon, declared a Fourth World War, 'a war of freedom against tyranny'.[177] Professors Niall Ferguson and Andrew Bacevich called for imperial honesty: 'It's time to fess up. The surest way to lose an empire is to pretend it's not there.'[178]

Ten days into the War with Iraq, Donald Rumsfeld was threatening military action against Syria for alleged aid to the Iraqi military and against Iran for supporting opposition forces that were not under US command. (Informed of the statement, 'Mr. Bush smiled a moment at the latest example of Mr. Rumsfeld's brazenness .... Then he said one word – "Good" – and went back to work.'[179]) Rumsfeld's ally James Woolsey added a call for 'regime change' since 'the Baathists in Syria and Iraq really are fascist parties ... designed after the Fascist and Communist parties of the 1930s. They look like them. They act like them. They're anti-Semitic like them.'[180] Even Colin Powell, who was supposedly 'taken aback' by the rhetoric, chipped in, 'We're not taking our options off the table.'[181] An administration aide captured the spirit of the US advance: 'Syria should take note [of the fall of Saddam's statue in Baghdad]. I hear there are lots of statues in Damascus too.'[182]

As Saddam fled, Rumsfeld and Wolfowitz stepped up the language of confrontation: 'In recent days the Syrians have been shipping killers into Iraq to try to kill Americans. We don't welcome that.'[183] However, Damascus, after token promises to close the office of three 'terrorist' groups (but not Hezbollah), escaped the full force of Washington's bluster.[184] Condoleezza Rice allegedly vetoed the Pentagon's proposal for cross-border raids, and the Administration settled for economic pressure such as restricting oil revenue through Syrian pipelines. Contingency plans for war against Syria, reviewed on the orders of Rumsfeld, were finally set aside, at least until after the 2004 Presidential election.[185] Instead, for reasons the *Guardian* noted concisely, the unfinished business in Iraq would have to be completed in Iran: 'What is truly novel is the now freely admitted failure of the US to anticipate this Shia resurgence; its feeble efforts to scapegoat Tehran's mullahs; and the embarrassing cluelessness of Jay Garner, the ex-general currently puzzling, glue-pot in hand, over the myriad broken pieces of the Iraqi mosaic.'[186]

Of course, as Donald Macintyre noted, 'Electricity and water will do much more to determine the political direction of Iraq than any number of Iranian agents',[187] but the US built up the spectre of Tehran's deployment of the 'Badr brigade' across the border and of Iranian schemes for 'secretly enriching uranium'.[188] Just before the war on Iraq, the CIA's J. Cofer Black told Congress that the Administration 'looked upon Iran as a serious threat to the United States, as one of, if not the, primary terrorist threat with capabilities to match', and the media were fed 'US intelligence reports' that the Iranian equivalent of the National Security Council had targeted Najaf, Karbala, Basra and Kirkuk as well as Baghdad 'to harass American soldiers once Saddam Hussein's regime fell'.[189] The outcome? Washington, fighting its War on Terror, renewed cooperation with the People's Mujahedin (MKO). The Baghdad-based MKO, which had killed thousands of Iranians in bombings and shootings since 1980, was on the US Government's list of prescribed terrorist organisations. However, after a perfunctory 'attack' on MKO's Iraqi camps, the American military declared a cease-fire and allowed the group to keep its weapons.[190]

Righteous intellectuals mobilised for the new campaign. Michael Ledeen established that Iraq was 'just one battle in a broader war .... It is impossible to win the war on terrorism so long as the regimes in Syria and Iran remain in power', while his fellow expert at the American Enterprise Institute, Richard Perle, assured, 'We will see regime change in Iran without any use of military power by the United States.'[191] The *Daily Telegraph*'s editors were ready to take on every challenge, 'Beyond focusing on the danger of Iran under Ayatollah Khamenei, should not coalition governments be helping those Iranians seeking to break the diktat of corrupt clerics? The same applies, *mutatis mutandis*, to Saudi Arabia and Syria.'[192]

It appeared that the only restraint on Washington would come from within the Government, the Pentagon's foe now the State Department rather than Saddam. As Powell and key subordinates restrained Rumsfeld from military threats against North Korea,[193] Newt Gingrich, the former Republican leader in the House of Representatives and a member of the Defense Policy Board, launched an extraordinary attack in the *Washington Post*. The State Department was 'a broken bureaucracy of red tape and excuses' which, none the less, was engaged in a 'deliberate and systematic effort to undermine the President's policies'; specifically, 'the concept of [Powell] going to Damascus to meet a terrorist-supporting, secret police-wielding dictator [was] ludicrous.'[194] Powell's Deputy Secretary of State Richard Armitage replied, 'It's clear that Mr. Gingrich is off his meds (medications) and out of therapy.'[195]

On the sidelines, the 'liberal interventionists' now flapped helplessly before an Administration recognising no boundaries to such interventions. Johann Hari recoiled at a 'terrifying' Bush, 'a dry alcoholic ... [with] the aggression, the tetchiness, the transference of the addiction to other behaviours, such as fanatical exercise and obsessively acquiring more and more personal power. The thought of the President losing the plot suddenly and drastically is frightening – and not implausible.'[196] Nevertheless, we had no choice but to embrace the menace, 'If [Europeans] eventually want to live on Venus, [they will have to] support the [American] Martians when they constructively rebuild the world around us.'[197] The *Observer* clung to the fantasy that 'Tony Blair has a crucial brokering role ... lean[ing] on his partner across the water and ensur[ing] that Iraq's future is more than a Pax Americana',[198] even as other analysts recognised Blair as 'Rumsfeld's hostage .... The prime minister should harbour no illusion that his well-earned gold medal will protect him from his ruthless new friends when he gets in their way.'[199]

The jeremiads were loudest from an American press which had struck a 'just war' deal with the Bush Administration. Given his ties to the Bush Administration and its strategy, Robert Kagan's call for 'a little self-interested magnanimity' in relations with Europe and the jettisoning of Chalabi could be seen as a quibble over methods rather than ends.[200] Poor Thomas Friedman, however, had to turn the narrative of his alliance with the President's warriors into one of betrayal: 'People who will try to hijack this peace and turn to it their own ends' now included 'ideologues within the Bush Administration.'[201] He was reduced to dismantling his own 'democratic' vision as he penned advice to President Bush from 'Saddam Hussein, in a Baghdad basement': 'If you want to build a self-governing authority here, you had better understand that "shock and awe" is not just for war-making. It's an everyday tool for running this place .... This ain't Norway here, pal. Your powerlessness will scare people here much more than your power.'[202] The *Washington Post*, which had cheered lustily at the start of war, fretted on at least four occasions in a week, 'Postwar Iraq may determine whether the United States regains [international] cooperation – or embarks on a dangerous unilateral course.'[203] With each repetition of concern, it only became clearer that the Administration, having won the acquiescence of the liberal interventionists over the initial attack, was not going to curry their favour over post-war matters.

So the platform for significant 'dissent' was again outside the US, beyond Britain, a challenge highlighted by the crudest American jibes at 'old Europe': 'Memories are being forged right now, and Americans won't forget our friends'.[204] Friedman's grand vision was that, 'if we invest the energy and resources in rebuilding Iraq into a decent, democratising society – about which fair-minded people would say, "America, you did good" – the US–Europe power gap will be more manageable and we will have more partners .... If we build [Iraq], they will come around.'[205] Unfortunately for Friedman, much of Europe as well as the forum of the United Nations was as disposable as democracy in Baghdad. Richard Perle asserted, 'We are left with coalitions of the willing. Far from disparaging them as a threat to a new world order, we should recognise that they are, by default, the best hope for that order, and the true alternative to the anarchy of the abject failure of the UN.'[206] Within the Administration, the strategy was '*non-nein-nyet* ... punish France, ignore Germany, and forgive Russia'.[207] Paris' punishment could include 'limiting French participation in American-sponsored meetings with European allies'.[208]

'Old Europe' was not necessarily going to accept a *non* or even a *nein*. France, Germany, Belgium and Luxembourg went ahead with a meeting for a joint military headquarters.[209] Far from joining a triumphant Anglo-American procession, the British Government risked isolation between two divergent movements. The challenge was laid out from the American neo-conservative Irwin Stelzer ('Blair once saw only one path open to Britain – further integration into Europe in the hope of becoming Europe's man in America. The world has changed: he can no longer have Brussels and Washington, too')[210] to Hugo Young ('Since we can't possibly exist alone – small boat cut adrift by the captain's misjudgement – the European mooring is the one we have to re-establish')[211] to the *Observer* ('It would be a disaster if two camps emerge with an unbridge-able divide about how to approach establishing international order, one led by American conservatives and the other by European internationalists, with Britain caught as piggy-in-the-middle.')[212] Timothy Garton Ash called for 'a new Entente Cordiale',[213] George Monbiot embraced the euro as a strategy for 'those of us who are concerned about American power'[214] and Matthew Parris went beyond Europe to declare, 'The day is coming when the UN must ask whether it is appropriate ... to act as stretcher-bearers for US imperialism – or whether it might be better to rejoin the Rest of the World.'[215]

Conclusion

As Robert Fisk has written, 'The real and frightening story starts now.'[1] It may be the only occasion where he is in accord with neo-conservatives like William Kristol: 'The mission begins in Baghdad, but it does not end there.'[2]

'The new caliphs' are putting out their proclamations.[3] Donald Rumsfeld cannot meet the Iraqi public because of security considerations – unbeknown to the Secretary of Defense, his convoy is fired on three times as he enters Baghdad. He does declare on US-run radio and television, 'Iraq belongs to you .... We will stay as long as necessary to help you [take control] and not a day longer', although he adds testily to journalists, 'I don't know [how long US troops will remain in Iraq] – and it's not knowable.'[4] Richard Perle commands the benevolent authority of the occupier, 'What we have won on the battlefield is the right to establish consistent policies that are for the benefit of the people of Iraq .... It is not as if we are looking for anything for ourselves.'[5]

Tony Blair, his promises that Britain and the US 'don't touch' oil supplies and that the UN would have 'a key role' in post-war Iraq long discarded, tags along as Washington bludgeons the Security Council into sanctioning an 'Iraq Inc.' under a Coalition Provisional Authority.[6] 'Freedom is messy,' a US official aide tells a reporter, 'Everything's going according to plan.'[7] Facing recurrent Iraqi demonstrations, Jay Garner reminds the press, 'We ought to look in a mirror and get proud, and stick out our chests and suck in our bellies and say, "Damn, we're Americans!"'; days later, he and five top aides are replaced in a 'bloodless coup' by L. Paul 'Jerry' Bremer, the State Department's head of counter-terrorism in the 1980s. Barbara Bodine, the 'coordinator' for central Iraq, is abruptly recalled.[8]

The Americans prepare to abandon Ahmed Chalabi,[9] but they have no alternative candidate. So the US Government declares it will name nine Iraqis to form a 'provisional government' by the end of May, only to scrap the plan two weeks later.[10] Bremer imposes stringent rules on the Iraqi media, as the US military seizes 'editorial control' of local television stations with 'predominantly non-factual/ unbalanced news coverage' such as re-broadcasting of Al-Jazeera. The list of 'Prohibited Activities' include items 'calculated to provoke opposition to the CPA or undermine legitimate processes towards self-government'.[11]

There are token advances, such as the naming by the CPA of local councils in Najaf and parts of Baghdad as well as Mosul, where an American general presides throne-like from his chair on the platform,[12] but even British 'success' in Basra is tempered by continuing problems with water, medicine and other public services.[13] As Ayatollah al-Hakim, the Tehran-supported leader of the Supreme Council for the Islamic Revolution in Iraq, returns from exile to a rapturous welcome from hundreds of thousands of Shia supporters, a State Department official exposes Washington's vision of 'self-government': 'The bottom line is we control the purse strings, the appointments, and anything else of political value [in postwar Iraq]. Not just anyone is going to get access to this.' Other White House staff explain that the Shia majority will be checked because 'prior to any referendum, a constitution must be drawn up, an assembly convened, judicial reform enacted – all under the auspices of liberal Iraqis with close ties to the United States'.[14]

The US and British Governments maintain the pretence that they will find weapons of mass destruction, feeding 'exclusives' to reporters such as Judith Miller of the *New York Times*, but the elite search unit, the 75th Expeditionary Task Force, has given up and gone home.[15] President Bush, almost pathetically, insists that two 'mobile labs' are vindication,[16] while the story unfolds of how his Administration, notably the specialist 'intelligence' unit created by Donald Rumsfeld, and the Government fabricated and distorted evidence for their just cause.[17] The CIA becomes the scapegoat for any misleading information, even as Paul Wolfowitz finally exposes to *Vanity Fair* how the Administration manufactured war, 'For bureaucratic reasons we settled on one issue, weapons of mass destruction, because it was the one reason everyone could agree on.'[18] Bush finally resorts to a bizarre revision of history, claiming war occurred only after he 'gave Saddam Hussein a chance to allow the inspectors in and he wouldn't let them'.[19]

The Associated Press finally reports, after a partial search of partial records, that at least 3,240 civilians died in the official 'war'; the complete total is far higher, possibly 10,000.[20] And more are dying every day in 'peace', from violence amongst Iraqis, from shootings by American forces, from the degraded conditions for nutrition, health, sanitation and habitation.[21]

The 'quagmire' looms. Far from demobilising in victory, the homecomings of US forces who have been in the region since September 2002 are postponed indefinitely.[22] The cost of maintaining the 150,000 military personnel is up to $3.9 billion per month,[23] as they progress from shooting looters[24] to mobilising in their thousands in search-and-destroy efforts against 'terrorist training camps'. In the three months after the supposed end of the war, more than 50 US servicemen die and hundreds are injured from shootings, suicide bombings, and rocket-propelled grenades. The GIs compare their experiences with the dystopian film 'Escape from New York', complaining, 'The whole place is bad',[25] while their commanders, maintaining that the cause of the resistance is a shadowy Ba'ath network which has yet to be eliminated, do not dare to admit, or possibly even consider, that the opposition may be widespread.

Partly out of the broader 'vision' that contributed to the showdown with Iraq, partly from the need to ascribe the troubles of occupation to external 'influence' rather than its own failings, the US Government sets up the next showdown using the same pretexts as the previous one. William Kristol sounds the bugle:

> We are in a death struggle with Iran over the future of Iraq .... We must ... take the fight to Iran, with measures ranging from public diplomacy to covert operations. Iran is the tipping point in the war on proliferation, the war on terror, and the effort to reshape the Middle East. If Iran goes pro-Western and anti-terror, positive changes in Syria and Saudi

Arabia will follow much more easily. And the chances for an Israeli-Palestinian settlement will greatly improve.[26]

Meanwhile, the war before the last war lingers in Afghanistan. There is a symbolic 'offensive', launched minutes after the opening salvo against Baghdad, of 1,000 troops hunting in the mountains for opponents of the Afghan Government,[27] then the conflict disappears once more, even though US bombs killed eleven civilians in a single strike,[28] even though the Taliban re-groups to murder a Red Cross worker, assassinate a close ally of President Hamid Karzai and shoot American soldiers,[29] even though the country is effectively divided into a number of zones under the control of different factions, even though 600 clerics call and many villages respond for renewed war against the Americans,[30] even though the US Government sets up yet another showdown with Iran by targeting the Tehran-backed governor of Herat as the chief threat to stability.[31] Karzai begs for assistance and receives little; local leaders take most of Afghanistan's revenue from customs charges.[32] Poppy production is now more than 800 per cent higher than cultivation in 2001 under the Taliban.[33]

Meanwhile, the vaunted 'road map' for an Israeli–Palestinian settlement stutters into publication, with subsequent high-profile deliberations that are long on American publicity and short of results. Meanwhile, Al-Qa'eda is, according to US officials, 'stronger than ever';[34] its cells and local groups kill dozens in attacks in Casablanca and Riyadh. Meanwhile, North Korea declares once more that it will proceed with the development of nuclear weapons while Donald Rumsfeld presses the Bush Administration to 'team up with China to press for the ouster of North Korea's leadership'.[35] Meanwhile, the US Government moves beyond all of these irritants with its long-term vision of security by ending 'restrictions on research of low-yield nuclear weapons', adding funds for development of 'a high-yield nuclear bomb for use against deeply buried targets' and reducing 'the preparation time required for resuming underground nuclear testing'.[36]

Meanwhile, 12,117 prisoners (including juveniles as young as 13) remain in indefinite confinement, without any prospect of charge or trial, in small, brightly-lit cells for up to 24 hours each day, at Camp X-Ray, at the American bases in Bagram, Afghanistan and Diego Garcia in the Indian Ocean, in Belmarsh in Kent, in centres in Egypt, Jordan, Uzbekistan, Syria and Saudi Arabia.[37] The State Department issues a global report criticising other countries for 'torture and physical beatings', prohibition of visits by human rights groups and 'arbitrary arrests and detention', but fails to refer to Guantanamo Bay, US prison camps in Afghanistan or internal 'security' measures.[38] These measures include the proposed Domestic Security Enhancement Act of 2003 which would permit, for the first time in history, secret arrests and the stripping of citizenship from any American who is 'a member of, or provided material support to, a group that the United States has designated as a "terrorist organization"'.[39] Between December 2002 and April 2003, nearly 140,000 immigrants to the US, almost all Muslims, are required to register with the National Security Entry-Exit Registration System. (A total of eleven are 'linked to terrorism'.)[40] Attorney General John Ashcroft rules that 'broad categories of foreigners who arrive in this country illegally can be detained indefinitely without consideration of their individual circumstances if immigration officials say their release would endanger national security'.[41]

Of course, in this new order at home and abroad, marvellous developments might defeat pessimism. The Iraqi 'council', finally named in mid-July, may prove to be more than an 'advisory' fig leaf for the de facto authority of Paul Bremer and the US military (at this point, all but one of the nine rotating 'presidents' are either Kurds or former exiles; the council's 'members work in a largely empty office building, surrounded by US military cordons and coils of barbed wire'.)[42] In a future year, elections may be held; they may even be 'free', with the US accepting a Shia-led Government that may be closer to Tehran than Washington.[43] With the deaths of Uday and Qusay Hussein, if not their father, the attacks against occupation forces may diminish. Restoration of electricity, water and health services, as well as the establishment of an oil industry which brings long-promised revenue to the Iraqi people, may occur, convincing the population that US intentions are to liberate rather than control their nation.

Perhaps officials in the State Department can overturn the dedication of the White House and the Pentagon, the Cheneys, Rumsfelds and, yes, Wolfowitzes, to a 'preponderance of power'. Perhaps the series of unilateral or American-dominated interventions will not continue into Iran or Syria. Perhaps, rather than spurious domino theories for democracy, there will be a return to multilateral efforts from Africa to North Korea and back to Iraq. Perhaps the United Nations, as well as countries like France and Germany, will be treated as necessary partners rather than the all-or-nothing of pawns or adversaries. Perhaps that multilateralism will rethink a War on Terror which will either try, openly in a court of law, detainees or release them.

Or perhaps none of this may happen. For, whatever one's position, a projected certainty of outcome is not the most secure of foundations for argument.[44]

We are beyond 'Right' and 'Left'. In this twenty-first-century configuration of strategy, politics, military forces, economics and 'culture', we are beyond the obsolete labels slapped on capitalism v. socialism, the Cold War of 'Free World' v. Soviet bloc. We are beyond the equation, imposed not by a radical fringe but contrived by a 'mainstream' supporting the US Government, of Right for America, Left against it. A 'Left' embracing Saddam, just like a 'Left' assisting 'Islamic fascism' was always a conjurer's illusion to divert the 'sensible' from interrogations of wider American policies and objectives.

No, dissent never meant wishing dictators well, endorsing oppression, accepting torture and sticking two fingers up at 'America'. Dissent was the recognition, long before the first shots were fired, that 'victory in Iraq will not end the world's distrust of the United States because the Bush administration has made it clear, over and over again, that it doesn't play by the rules'. Dissent was the sentiment that 'tyranny or empire should not be the only two choices offered Iraqis, or the rest of the world'. Dissent was the question, 'Who will [the guns of March] frighten into submission and who will they inspire to hatred of America and its friends?'[45]

We are beyond a devious, deceitful 'Left'. We long ago left behind pun-ridden rants such as Mark Steyn's snipe at Robert Fisk as a 'Saddamite buffoon', hysterical denunciations such as the call of Cal Thomas for a 'Cultural War Crimes Tribunal', spurious equations such as Stephen Pollard's 'Opponents of Military Trials Are Friends of Al-Qaeda'.[46] But we are also beyond the reduction of our opinions and concerns to a 'soft spot for certain tyrants' and a sheepish march behind evil leaders, as in Johan Hari's jeremiad over the alleged treachery of the Labour MP George Galloway:

> If you are one of the mostly decent people who cheered Galloway at the anti-war rally, now is the time to pause and ask yourself, 'What did I do?' .... The day when the left might not even have to be paid by a tyrant – when it might be offering him comfort for *free* – is a day from hell. We are living in that long, sulphur-scented day.[47]

We are even beyond the supposed it's-for-your-own-good advice of Todd Gitlin, as he takes up Andrew Sullivan's claim of our 'rage at reality', adding, 'Helplessness is the main note. Where right-wing resentment is the resentment of the entitled and disappointed, left-wing resentment is the resentment of the forlorn.'[48]

We are beyond a contrived honourable Left which, declaiming the deficiencies and depravities of erstwhile comrades, wraps itself in the Flag. Martin Amis long ago broke any supposed pro-Yank ranks, fearing that the 'unprecedented preponderance of a single power' with a President 'more religious, more theological' to 'feel easier about being intellectually null' leads to 'a kaleidoscope of terrifying eventualities', even if John Lloyd, always a step behind Christopher Hitchens, stormed out of the *New Statesman* with his resignation missive about an anti-war 'Left' which 'has shown itself incapable of thinking through not only the nature of the world as it is today, but also its own claims to be the leading force in making the world better'.[49]

We are beyond the cry of 'anti-Americanism' by learned authorities who, unable or unwilling to grapple with the specifics of politics, economics and military prowess that might provoke criticism, invoke 'a broader hostility to modernity, to the twentieth-century achievement of humanity that America symbolised', hand down quack diagnoses of 'self-loathing' and 'political resistance ... grounded in pure snobbery'.[50] We are beyond the riposte that those who question US foreign policy are 'infantile', 'idiots or scoundrels' who are 'really against liberal democracy', 'nervous nellies' with the 'inability to see the American nation as vulnerable and human'.[51] We are beyond the arrogance of dismissal:

> What explains the anti-American fury, particularly in Europe? Simple. It makes people feel good. It gives them a sense of moral superiority. It doesn't cost them anything. It diverts attention from domestic discontents. It doesn't require hard decisions or hard thinking. It's a convenient moral exhibitionism that, on inspection, is full of delusion, shortsightedness and moral hypocrisy.[52]

We are beyond a 'liberal' simplicity of 'Americans have feelings too' which confuses the desires of other peoples beyond America with the objectives of the US Government: 'I don't like George Bush, but we both believe that the future of freedom in the world depends on US power.'[53]

We are beyond Nick Cohen who, having forgotten that he once wrote, 'The last thing the US wants is democracy in Iraq',[54] now reduces the anti-war movement to Tony Benn, George Galloway, Andrew Murray of the Stop the War Coalition (and, Cohen warns us, the Communist Party of Britain), the Socialist Workers Party and 'the same old scowling faces from the fragments of splinter groups'.[55] We are beyond a Cohen who funnels all history and politics into the supposed betrayal by the 'Left' of US-supported Iraqi freedom. (On the fiftieth anniversary of Stalin's death: 'Just as the greater cause of anti-fascism led decent people to turn a blind eye to Stalin's crimes in the 1930s, so the often silly cause of anti-Americanism leads decent people to turn a blind eye to the plight of the Iraqis.')[56] We are beyond a Cohen whose consideration of Western Muslims is of 'adolescents panting for an answer to their angst'.[57] We are beyond a Cohen who rails that we are 'defeated' because we are not 'on the same side as Bush and Blair'.[58]

We are beyond David Aaronovitch who is caught between a visceral hatred of a France seeking to lead the European

Union as 'a second, better Soviet Union' and a Richard Perle 'masturbating over what he hoped was the grave of the United Nations', who is now reducing the anti-war movement to anti-semitism, 'post-September 11 insecurity', a fear of America born of 'some kind of folk/race memory of the time when GIs came courting our girlfriends with nylons and oral sex, neither of which our boys could offer', and suburban middle classes in 'a state of political priapism, frustrated but up for just about any movement going'.[59] We are beyond an Aaronovitch who wobbles in his certainty, 'Whatever the amount of death and mayhem, it could be years before anyone on either side of the argument can credibly claim vindication', and belatedly warns 'our government', 'Those weapons had better be there somewhere,' but continues to pillory 'Lies and the Left' as embodied (yet again) by George Galloway and John Pilger.[60]

We are beyond Johann Hari when he commands, 'Anti-war movements must never again assume they speak for the people who are about to be bombed', but then, speaking for those people and the rest of us, pronounces, 'The lesson of this conflict: America can be a force for good in the world.'[61] There is no time for our quibbles: 'The looting is ugly, but it's better than torture,' he chastises, before advocating liberation's march with the invasion of North Korea.[62] There is no need for any complication of his certainty: 'Forget the Weapons of Mass Destruction; We Were Still Right to Invade Iraq.'[63]

We are beyond Michael Ignatieff, who has joined the chorus of the new American empire, even as he agonises, 'The choice is not about the company you keep, but between alienating old, but essentially pacifist, friends and appeasing a tyrant.' We are beyond an Ignatieff who dismiss any thoughts, by his friends or any others, about what 'America is or should be' for the simple mantras of 'our safety' and 'the freedom of 25 million people'.[64]

We are beyond Paul Berman, the new champion of 'liberal intervention', the darling of neo-conservatives such as Andrew Sullivan who call for a 'move away … [from] reactionary anti-Americanism towards the true liberal faith'.[65] We are beyond a Berman who throws together Marxism and Islamism, Nazism and Baathism,[66] who uses his profiles of Islamic philosophers to wail, 'Who will defend liberal ideas against the enemies of liberal ideas? Who will defend liberal principles in spite of liberal society's every failure?' We are beyond a Berman who sees the evil 'people of God' abroad but does not recognise them at home.[67]

We are beyond Thomas Friedman who, amid the continuing instability and turmoil in Iraq, fantasises that Iraqis will use 'real resentment for the other Arab regimes, and even towards the Palestinians' to renounce 'Arabism' and provide the break-through in the Israeli–Palestinian crisis. We are beyond a Friedman who then exposes the heart of the fantasy as the desire for an American show of force almost anywhere in the Middle East or Central Asia: 'Saudi Arabia would have been fine; Pakistan would have been fine. We did Iraq because we could.'[68]

We are far beyond Christopher Hitchens. Now he makes headlines with reminiscences not only that he and Bill Clinton shared a girlfriend at Oxford who become 'a very famous radical lesbian', but also that the former President was probably an informant for the CIA.[69] His *Vanity Fair* column becomes a homage to alcohol's contribution to his life and his writing, comparing himself to Hemingway in the process.[70] There is a reprise of his Clinton-era cameo when Sidney Blumenthal refers in his memoir to Hitchens' 1999 'betrayal'.[71] He does a star turn at the Hay Literary Festival, but his contributions to a panel which includes George Monbiot and Ahdaf Soueif are bypassed for his late-night stand-up of 'Lenny Bruce meets Wodehouse' with risqué jokes and the nostalgia of karaoke in North Korea.[72] It is *The Onion*, the satirical on-line magazine, that captures the essence of our moral guide in April 2003 with its fictional headline, 'Christopher Hitchens Forcibly Removed from Trailer Park After Drunken Confrontation with Common-Law Wife'.[73]

For Hitchens' pronouncements on the wars against Iraq and the 'Left' have long ago been reduced to taunts – the 'silly led by the sinister' – to be recycled by the likes of Julie Burchill.[74] The jibes are on a repeating loop: the Left are un-American 'because they know they couldn't make it in America'; 'their prediction and deepest hope was that the black shirts of the [Iraqi] fedayeen were going to win or force a stalemate'.[75] No charge is too grandiose, 'SADDAM: He's Hitler, He is Stalin: Why did we tolerate him for so long?', no dissenting opponent beyond vituperation, 'Each day they dig up dead bodies in personal death camps run by a Caligula dictator and I'm being asked to worry about these fucking fat slags [the Dixie Chicks]!'[76]

Hitchens' analysis has been reduced to a blind faith, despite all evidence to the contrary on the course of US strategy from the end of the Cold War to the present, in Paul Wolfowitz as a crusader for democracy, 'a revolutionary' who is 'making war on the status quo' in the Middle East even if this means 'quarrelling with the Saudis, the Turks, a chunk of the oil lobby here, and part of the American right'.[77] For the contrarian who has converted to this 'revolution', the certainties must remain, irrespective of all contrary indications. Hitchens wrote as early as 25 March, 'The population of Baghdad was making a secret holiday in its heart as those horrible palaces went up in smoke, and this holiday will soon be a public holiday, and if we all keep our nerve we can join the festivities with a fairly clear conscience.'[78] He added a week later, 'You can still meet people who say that there is no "proven" connection between Baghdad and the nexus of international terrorism. You can still meet people, too, who don't think that Iraq has any genocidal weapons.'[79]

And, though the party proved short-lived for the US forces of occupation, though the international terrorists and genocidal weapons did not materialise, there would be no retraction. The future was bright; the future was the Iraqi National Congress: 'Lay Off Chalabi'.[80] The future was yet another contrarian endorsement of the American grand strategy as it moved beyond Iraq to other enemies:

> The overwhelming consensus among inspectors and monitors, including Hans Blix's sidekick Mohammed El Baradei, is now to the effect that Iran's mullahs have indeed been concealing an enriched-uranium program. For good measure, it is a sure thing that they are harboring al-Qaida activists on their territory. Will the 'peace' camp ever admit that Bush was right about this?[81]

Then belatedly, very belatedly, there is a doubt. At the end of May, Hitchens suddenly notices 'that control freaks have taken power' in Iraq. But, because he cannot admit that this was the long-held concern of those he had gleefully maligned, he cannot approach their coherence. He can only stumble and flail, 'It might even be a defense of a kind to say that control-freakery is preferable to factionalism and communal or intercommunal strife. But it's not a very persuasive defense, because there will never be an Iraq that is composed of docile citizens who all see the same things in the same way, and because the dispelling of that very fantasy was part of the point to begin with.'[82]

And so we are beyond 'Orwell'. Of course, tribute is still paid to the national saint. In his centenary year, there are the bookend biographies, the BBC drama posing as a documentary, the sweeping eulogies to Orwell and 'his genius ... his importance for our world, which fails to match his standards of justice and decency in almost every conceivable way'.[83] George is our 'moral force' against unnamed 'orthodoxies ... wearing yet more elaborate disguises', our saviour from the 'great threats' of 'religious totalitarianism and the rise of global plutocracy', 'the most direct and democratic British writer of the twentieth century'.[84]

There is the celebration of mimicry, with the *Independent*'s Paul Vallely retracing Orwell's steps in Wigan, which now has a pier for the tourists, as the BBC asks artist Rachel Whiteread to re-create the 'real' Room 101 in Broadcasting House.[85] There is the celebration of language, as 'Orwellian' is used to label phenomena from London's traffic congestion charge to the operatic production of Margaret Atwood's *The Handmaid's Tale*.[86] There is even the celebration which veers towards melodrama or farce: the *Daily Telegraph*'s 'Cure for TB was Too Late to Save Orwell' and *The Times*' publication of one of the few 'revelations' from the new biographies, 'Orwell Attacked by Jealous Fiancé'.[87]

Inevitably, this is all tied to the mantra of 'What Would George Do?' Geoffrey Wheatcroft verges on pantomime: 'What would Orwell have said about the latest recipient of the Orwell Prize for journalism ... idiosyncratically reactionary columnist and art critic Brian Sewell? ... The only thing we can be sure of is that he would have been as quirky and unpredictable as ever.'[88] Bernard Crick is a grandfatherly confidant: 'E. Blair on T. Blair's Call to Arms ... Bush and Blair adopting Churchillian poses would have turned his tummy.'[89] Thomas

Pynchon gives us the sentimental photograph of Orwell and his adopted son, overcoming the obstacle of George the acerbic, bomb-fearing pessimist, and warbles:

> It is the boy's smile, in any case, that we return to, direct and radiant, proceeding out of an unhesitating faith that the world, at the end of the day, is good, and that human decency, like parental love, can always be taken for granted – a faith so honourable that we can almost imagine Orwell, and perhaps even ourselves, for a moment anyway, swearing to do whatever must be done to keep it from ever being betrayed.[90]

All well and good, but Michael Shelden, in grandiloquent homage to the 'genius ... dedicated contrarian ... hero', inadvertently exposes the devaluation of perpetual reclamation and exaltation: 'In Blair, we have the person whose life belonged only to himself. It is the author who now belongs to the world.'[91] For, if anyone in the world can take hold of 'Orwell', then he is a universal guide not in clarity or consistency but in his political utility.

St George has become the club to beat one's opponents. At his most belligerent, 'Orwell' is used via his 1942 essay on the 'fascifists' to render the Left unworthy of an opinion. Days after the first bombs fell on Baghdad, the *Daily Telegraph* pronounced, on what 'George Orwell once called ... "the peculiar masochism of the English Left": a readiness to side with all manner of villains – the IRA, the Soviet Union, Saddam – provided they are anti-British'.[92] Joann Barkan used the pages of *Dissent* to stifle that concept, twisting those who criticised American foreign policy into Orwell's 'negative nationalists':

> The distinction Orwell makes between nationalism and patriotism might be useful in thinking about the 'blame-America-first' part of the American left. These leftists see only one major problem in the world: the United States with its unlimited power and imperial arrogance .... Coming across the notion of 'negative nationalism' again has been useful for thinking about the blame-America-first leftists

with their obsessiveness, resentments, and ability to shut out inconvenient realities.[93]

From here, it is only a short step to subtler summonings of 'Orwell' in the service of the US or British Governments. Tony Blair invoked in February 2003, a 'foreign policy, robust on defence and committed to global justice. [This idea enables] us to espouse positions that in the past the left had regarded as impossible to reconcile: patriotism and internationalism.'[94]

Of course, 'Orwell' is still up for grabs for the old 'Left'. Both in his recent essays and in his *New Rulers of the World*, John Pilger has portrayed an Orwellian present, with Governments in Washington, London and Canberra deploying a system of control and suppression of other peoples and even some of their own, behind the propaganda of 'freedom'.[95] Yet even this use of the icon risks confusion and self-destruction. George Sciabba wrote confidently in the *Washington Post* that 'Orwell would associate himself with the unsexy democratic left, notably *Dissent* and the *American Prospect*', never pondering that the editor of the former journal, Michael Walzer, had led the call for the 'Left' to support America's 'little wars' in Afghanistan and Iraq.[96] Paul Foot entered 2003 with a warning about the 'doublethink going on now as Oceania (the US and Britain) prepares for war against Iraq' but set limits on fellow dissenters: those who dare criticise George 'hail back to the good old days under comrade Stalin'.[97]

'Bring on the spanners.'
    – Arundhati Roy[98]

There is no need to bury Orwell. That was done more than 50 years ago, in a small country churchyard in Oxfordshire. Instead, it is 'Orwell' that needs to be given the final rites. Despite the inconsistencies, contradictions and outright pettiness of his character assassinations, Orwell can be admired for the power of his writing, for the tenacity with which he held his changing opinions and for certain prescriptions for the social and political issues of his time.

But his time was then, and this is now. Now, with an 'Orwell' not to challenge the State but to support it, to contrive and exalt, in Orwellian fashion, the contrarian who happens to promote the rhetorical and political agenda of that State. Now, with an 'Orwell' to justify, in the guise of 'independent' thought, the suppression of dissent.

When Julian Barnes writes, 'This war was not worth a child's finger',[99] the Orwell of the 1930s, of the Second World War, of the early Cold War cannot respond, except with false or incomplete analogies extracted by others. When Deborah Orr queries, 'If everyone falls into line, who will ask the questions that need asking?',[100] 'Orwell' can be wielded to endorse or dismiss her, but 'he' cannot ask those questions, which should be put to Washington's strategists as well as Baghdad's tyrants, to a prospective 'American' as well as 'Islamic' fundamentalism.[101]

We are beyond 'right' and 'wrong'. Our concerns, objections, alternatives are posed not because we are 'poor fools', 'an auxiliary to dictators and aggressors in trouble' who fear that our opponents are 'smarter and nicer' than us,[102] but because if we do not pose them, resolution occurs by default. We do not know, irrespective of the claims of Christopher Hitchens, Bernard Crick, Michael Walzer, Michael Kelly, the *Daily Telegraph*, or anyone else, what Orwell would 'say' about our current dilemmas. Instead, we have the words of Susan Sontag, who persists despite the attempted use of 'Orwell' to silence her after 11 September 2001:

> It is hard to defy the wisdom of the tribe, the wisdom that values the lives of its members above all others. It will always be unpopular – it will always be deemed unpatriotic – to say that the lives of the members of the other tribe are as valuable as one's own. It is easier to give one's allegiance to those we know, to those we see, to those with whom we are embedded, to those with whom we share – as we may – a community of fear.[103]

Notes

Introduction

1. Edward Said, 'The Public Role of Writers and Intellectuals', *The Nation* (17 September 2001).
2. Peter Davison, *The Complete Works of George Orwell, Volume XX, Our Job is to Make Life Worth Living* (London: Secker and Warburg, 1998), p. 240. The abridged list of suspects and annotations about their characters is on pp. 242–58.
3. The 1941 *Time and Tide* review of Chaplin is quoted in Michael Shelden, *Orwell: The Authorised Biography* (London: Minerva, 1992), p. 354.
4. Davison, *Complete Works of George Orwell*, p. 318. Celia Kirwan (later Goodman), died in October 2002. See her obituary in *The Independent* (25 October 2002).
5. See W. Scott Lucas and C.J. Morris, 'A Very British Crusade: The Information Research Department and the Cold War', in Richard Aldrich (ed.), *British Intelligence, Strategy, and the Cold War* (London: Routledge, 1992).
6. Quoted in Davison, *Complete Works of George Orwell*, p. 319.
7. Ibid., p. 240.
8. See 'Orwell's List', John Ezard, 'Blair's Babe', and Timothy Garton Ash, 'Love, Death, and Treachery', *Guardian* (21 June 2003).
9. 'Knowledge (and Power)', *The Nation* (10 June 2002); 'Evil', *Slate* (31 December 2002).
10. 'Race and Rescue', *Slate* (1 February 2003).
11. George Orwell, 'Why I Write', in *The Collected Essays, Journalism and Letters of George Orwell* (hereafter *CEJL*) (London: Secker and Warburg, 1968), 1, pp. 1–7.
12. Christopher Hitchens, *Letters to a Young Contrarian* (New York: Basic Books, 2001).
13. The quote is from President Truman's Attorney General, Tom Clark, in 1947. See Richard Freedland, *The Truman Doctrine and the Origins of McCarthyism* (New York: Knopf, 1971).
14. See Celestine Bohlen, 'In New War on Terrorism, Words are Weapons, Too', *New York Times* (29 September 2001).
15. George Bush, speech to Congress, reprinted in the *Guardian* (21 September 2001).
16. George Monbiot, 'Gagging the Sceptics', *Guardian* (16 October 2001).

1 Orwell, Policeman of the 'Left

1. D.S. Savage, Alex Comfort and George Woodcock contributions, 'A Controversy', *Partisan Review* (September–October 1942), *CEJL*, Volume 2, pp. 220–6.

2. George Orwell contribution, 'A Controversy', *Partisan Review* (September–October 1942), *CEJL*, Volume 2, pp. 227–30.

3. In a 1944 column Orwell partially recanted: 'We are told that it is only people's objective actions that matter, and their subjective feelings are of no importance. Thus pacifists, by obstructing the war effort, are 'objectively' aiding the Nazis; and therefore the fact that they may be personally hostile to Fascism is irrelevant. I have been guilty of saying this myself more than once.' ('As I Please', *Tribune*, 8 December 1944, in *CEJL*, Volume 3, pp. 288–91). And, in a 1945 'London Letter' in *Partisan Review*, he offered an apology for 'from time to time, spiteful or misleading remarks about individuals. For instance, I particularly regret having said in one letter that Julian Symons "writes in a vaguely Fascist strain" – a quite unjustified statement based on a single article which I probably misunderstood' (*Partisan Review*, Winter 1945, in *CEJL*, Volume 3, pp. 293–9). Orwell, however, never withdrew the specific charge that the pacifist position might assist Fascism. More importantly, his 1944 column did not give up the search for dangerous dissenters, but looked for a more refined approach, one he would take beyond the Second World War into new battles: 'A few pacifists are inwardly pro-Nazi, and extremist left-wing parties will inevitably contain Fascist spies. The important thing is to discover which individuals are honest and which are not.'

4. Review of John Galsworthy's *Glimpses and Reflections*, *New Statesman* (12 March 1938), in *CEJL*, Volume 1, p. 307.

5. Quoted in John Wain, 'In the Thirties', in Miriam Gross (ed.), *The World of George Orwell* (London: Weidenfeld and Nicolson, 1971), p. 83.

6. George Orwell, *The Road to Wigan Pier* (London: Penguin, 1962), p. 130.

7. George Orwell, *The Lion and the Unicorn* (Harmondsworth: Penguin, 1982), p. 112.

8. George Orwell, preface to Ukrainian edition of *Animal Farm*, March 1947, in *CEJL*, Volume 3, p. 402.

9. George Orwell, 'Not Counting Niggers', *Adelphi* (July 1939), in *CEJL*, Volume 1, p. 395.

10. George Orwell, *Tribune* (20 December 1940), quoted in Bernard Crick, *George Orwell: A Life* (Harmondsworth: Penguin, 1982), p. 398.

11. George Orwell, 'London Letter', *Partisan Review* (Fall 1945), in *CEJL*, Volume 3, pp. 393–400.

12. Orwell diary, 31 January–25 March 1936, in *CEJL*, Volume 1, pp. 170–214; *The Road to Wigan Pier*, pp. 11–12 and 16–17.
13. *Nineteen Eighty-Four*, in *The Complete Novels*, p. 836.
14. Ibid., p. 867.
15. 'Marrakech', *New Writing* (Christmas 1939), in *CEJL*, Volume 1, p. 387; Orwell diary, 3 April 1942, *CEJL*, Volume 2, p. 416; 'London Letter', *Partisan Review* (November–December 1942), in *CEJL*, Volume 2, p. 232.
16. Orwell diary, 10 April 1942, in *CEJL*, Volume 2, p. 418.
17. 'On Kipling's Death', *New English Weekly* (23 January 1936), in *CEJL*, Volume 1, p. 159.
18. 'Rudyard Kipling', *Horizon* (February 1942), in *CEJL*, Volume 2, pp. 184–96.
19. *The Road to Wigan Pier*, pp. 17, 21, 31 and 104.
20. Orwell diary, 19 February 1936, in *CEJL*, Volume 1, p. 181.
21. Orwell to Common, 16[?] April 1936, in *CEJL*, Volume I, p. 216.
22. *Tribune* (20 December 1940), quoted in Crick, *Orwell: A Life*, p. 398.
23. 'Notes on Nationalism', *Polemic* (October 1945), in *CEJL*, Volume 3, pp. 361–80.
24. *The Lion and the Unicorn*, p. 93. Orwell set out a shorter version of his argument in two essays written for the 1941 collection *Betrayal of the Left*, edited by Victor Gollancz. Two years later, he asserted in *The English People* that 'there is no revolutionary tradition in England, and even in extremist political parties, it is only the middle-class membership that thinks in revolutionary terms' and 'the outstanding and – by contemporary standards – highly original quality is their habit of not killing one another'. Postponed when the publisher encountered financial problems, *The English People* finally appeared in 1947 as Britain was deciding its political position in the emerging Cold War (*The English People* [London: Collins, 1947], reprinted in *CEJL*, Volume 3, pp. 3 and 30).
25. *The Lion and the Unicorn*, pp. 37 and 41; George Orwell, 'My Country Right or Left', *Folios of New Writing* (Autumn 1940), in *CEJL*, Volume 1, p. 539.
26. Editorial for *Polemic* (May 1946), in *CEJL*, Volume 4, pp. 153–60.
27. *The Lion and the Unicorn*, pp. 104–10.
28. Orwell to Henson, 16 June 1949, in *CEJL*, Volume 4, p. 502.
29. 'London Letter', *Partisan Review* (March–April 1943), in *CEJL*, Volume 2, p. 276.
30. Orwell to Symons, 29 October 1948, in *CEJL*, Volume 4, p. 449–51.
31. 'You and the Atom Bomb', *Tribune* (19 October 1945), in *CEJL*, Volume 4, pp. 6–10.
32. Orwell diary, 15 April 1941, in *CEJL*, Volume 2, p. 395.
33. Review of Oscar Wilde's *The Soul of Man under Socialism*, *Observer* (9 May 1948), in *CEJL*, Volume 4, p. 426.

34. Rayner Heppenstall, *Four Absences* (London: Barrie and Rockcliff, 1960), p. 32.
35. *Keep the Aspidistra Flying*, in *The Complete Novels*, pp. 626–7.
36. Quoted in Crick, *Orwell: A Life*, p. 254.
37. Orwell to Salkeld, 7 May 1935, in Michael Shelden, *Orwell: The Authorised Biography* (London: Minerva, 1992), p. 240.
38. *The Road to Wigan Pier*, pp. 139, 149–52, 156 and 159; Orwell to Common, 5 October 1936, in *CEJL*, Volume 1, p. 233.
39. *The Road to Wigan Pier*, p. 199.
40. Orwell diary, 15 March 1936, in *CEJL*, Volume 1, p. 203.
41. Introduction to *The Road to Wigan Pier* (London: Gollancz, 1937) reprinted in Jeffrey Meyers, *George Orwell: The Critical Heritage* (London: Routledge and Kegan Paul, 1975), pp. 91–9.
42. Quoted in Crick, *Orwell: A Life*, p. 310.
43. Orwell to Common, 19 February 1938, in *CEJL*, Volume 1, p. 303.
44. Orwell to Heppenstall, 31 July 1937, in *CEJL*, Volume 1, p. 279.
45. Letter to the editor of *New English Weekly* (26 May 1938), in *CEJL*, Volume 1, p. 332; Orwell to Spender, 2 April 1938, in *CEJL*, Volume 1, p. 313; *Homage to Catalonia*, pp. 64–5.
46. See the conversation with Chomsky in 'Activism, Anarchism and Power', University of California, 2002, http://globetrotter.berkeley.edu/people2/Chomsky/chomsky-con1.html.
47. Q.D. Leavis, 'The Literary Life Respectable: Mr George Orwell', *Scrutiny* (September 1940), pp. 173–6.
48. 'Inside the Whale', in *CEJL*, Volume 1, p. 516.
49. Orwell to Connolly, 27 April 1938, in *CEJL*, Volume 1, p. 328.
50. 'Inside the Whale', in *CEJL*, Volume 1, pp. 413–60.
51. 'Not Counting Niggers', *Adelphi* (July 1939), in *CEJL*, Volume 1, p. 394.
52. Orwell to Read, 5 March 1939, in *CEJL*, Volume 1, p. 387.
53. *Coming Up for Air*, in *The Complete Novels*, pp. 516–21.
54. Review of Duchess of Atholl's *Searchlight on Spain*, *New English Weekly* (21 July 1938), in *CEJL*, Volume 1, p. 344.
55. *The Lion and the Unicorn*, pp. 41, 49 and 64; 'My Country Right or Left', pp. 535–40.
56. 'In Defence of P.G. Wodehouse', *Windmill* (July 1945), in *CEJL*, Volume 3, p. 341; 'London Letter', *Partisan Review* (March–April 1942), p. 175; Orwell diary, 22 August 1940, in *CEJL*, Volume 2, p. 367.
57. Review of Franz Borkenau's *The Totalitarian Enemy*, *Time and Tide* (4 May 1940), in *CEJL*, Volume 2, p. 24.
58. 'Charles Dickens', in *Inside the Whale* (London: Gollancz, 1940), in *CEJL*, Volume 1, pp. 413–60.
59. *The Lion and the Unicorn*, pp. 104–12.
60. Ibid., p. 37.
61. Ibid., pp. 56–61.

62. Ibid., p. 93.
63. Orwell diary, 25 October 1940, in *CEJL*, Volume 2, p. 377.
64. Orwell diary, 15 April 1941, in *CEJL*, Volume 2, p. 395.
65. Orwell to Heppenstall, 24 August 1943, in *CEJL*, Volume 2, p. 305.
66. 'London Letter', *Partisan Review* (Winter 1945), in *CEJL*, Volume 3, p. 294.
67. 'London Letter', *Partisan Review* (Winter 1945), in *CEJL*, Volume 3, pp. 293–9.
68. 'London Letter', *Partisan Review* (Fall 1945), in *CEJL*, Volume 3, pp. 393–400.
69. 'Literature and the Left', *Tribune* (4 June 1943), in *CEJL*, Volume 2, pp. 292–4.
70. Review of Lionel Fielden's *Beggar My Neighbour*, *Horizon* (September 1943), in *CEJL*, Volume 2, p. 306.
71. 'London Letter', *Partisan Review* (Summer 1945), in *CEJL*, Volume 3, p. 380.
72. Richard Rees, *George Orwell: Fugitive from the Camp of Victory* (London: Secker and Warburg, 1961), p. 88.
73. Preface to the Ukrainian edition of *Animal Farm*, 1947, reprinted at http://orwell.ru/library/novels/Animal_Farm/english/epfc_go.
74. 'Notes on Nationalism', *Polemic* (October 1945), in *CEJL*, Volume 3, pp. 361–80.
75. 'The Prevention of Literature', *Polemic* (March 1946), in *CEJL*, Volume 4, pp. 59–72.
76. 'Politics and the English Language', *Horizon* (April 1946), in *CEJL*, Volume 4, pp. 127–40. It should be noted, for some balance, that Orwell did broaden his scope in this case to consider, as examples of political language as 'the defence of the indefensible', support for continued British rule in India and the dropping of the atomic bomb on Japan, and he emphasised that the effort 'to make lies sound truthful and murder respectable' can be true of 'all political parties, from Conservatives to Anarchists'.
77. Editorial for *Polemic* (May 1946), in *CEJL*, Volume 4, pp. 153–60.
78. 'Why I Write', in *CEJL*, Volume 1, pp. 1–7.
79. Orwell diary, 19 May 1942, *CEJL*, Volume 2, p. 426.
80. George Woodcock, *The Crystal Spirit: A Story of George Orwell* (London: Jonathan Cape, 1967), p. 28.
81. 'Writers and Leviathan', *Politics and Letters* (Summer 1948) and *New Leader* (19 June 1948) in *CEJL*, Volume 4, pp. 407–14.
82. 'As I Please', *Tribune* (8 December 1944), in *CEJL*, Volume 3, pp. 288–91.
83. 'London Letter', *Partisan Review* (Summer 1946), in *CEJL*, Volume 4, pp. 184–91.
84. 'Politics v. Literature: An Examination of Gulliver's Travels', *Polemic* (September–October 1946), in *CEJL*, Volume 4, pp. 205–23.

85. Arthur Schlesinger, Jr., 'The U.S. Communist Party', *Life* (July 1946), p. 84.

86. David Cesarani, *Arthur Koestler: The Homeless Mind* (London: William Heinemann, 1998), pp. 305–10.

87. See Eric Thomas Chester, *Covert Network: Progressives, the International Rescue Committee, and the CIA* (Armonk, NY: M.E. Sharpe, 1995); Frances Stonor Saunders, *Who Paid the Piper?* (London: Granta, 1999); Scott Lucas, *Freedom's War: The US Crusade against the Soviet Union, 1945–1956* (New York: New York University Press, 1999).

88. George Orwell, 'Riding Down from Bangor', *Tribune*, 22 November 1946, in *CEJL*, Volume 1, pp. 313–7.

89. George Orwell, in *CEJL*, Volume 1, pp. 307–8.

90. George Orwell, 'Toward European Unity', *Partisan Review* (July–August 1947), in *CEJL*, Volume 4, pp. 370–5.

91. Quoted in W. Scott Lucas and C.J. Morris, 'A Very British Crusade: The Information Research Department and the Cold War', in Richard Aldrich (ed.), *British Intelligence, Strategy, and the Cold War* (London: Routledge, 1992), pp. 94–5.

92. *Nineteen Eighty-Four*, in *The Complete Novels*, p. 751.

93. Beatrix Campbell, 'Orwell – Paterfamilias or Big Brother?', in Christopher Norris (ed.), *Inside the Myth: Orwell, Views from the Left* (London: Lawrence and Wishart, 1984), p. 135

94. Orwell to Henson, 16 June 1949, in *CEJL*, Volume IV, p. 502.

95. *Nineteen Eighty-Four*, in *The Collected Novels*, p. 773.

96. Fredric Warburg, 'Publisher's Report', December 1948, in Jeffrey Meyers, *George Orwell: The Critical Heritage* (London: Routledge and Kegan Paul, 1975), p. 247.

97. David Hencke and Rob Evans, 'How Big Brothers Used Orwell to Fight the Cold War', *Guardian* (30 June 2000), www.guardian.co.uk/international/story/0,,338230,00.html.

98. Quoted in Les K. Adler and Thomas G. Paterson, 'Red Fascism: The Merger of Nazi Germany and Soviet Russia in the American Image of Totalitarianism, 1930s–1950s', *American Historical Review* (April 1970), pp. 1046–64.

99. *New York Times*, 12 June 1949, reprinted at http://www.angelfire.com/pop/orwell/essay.html.

100. Philip Rahv, *Partisan Review* (July 1949), in Jeffrey Meyers, *George Orwell: The Critical Heritage* (London: Routledge and Kegan Paul, 1975), p. 247.

101. Orwell to Henson, 16 June 1949, in *CEJL*, Volume 4, p. 502.

102. Warburg memorandum, 1948, in Crick, *Orwell: A Life*, p. 567.

103. Irving Howe, 'Orwell and America', in Rob Kroes (ed.), *Nineteen Eighty-Four and the Apocalyptic Imagination in America* (Amsterdam: Free University Press, 1985), p. 30.

104. *Nineteen Eighty-Four*, in *The Complete Novels*, p. 783.

105. Ibid., p. 797.

106. Ibid., p. 784; Mark Crispin Miller quoted in Rob Kroes, 'A Nineteen Eighty-Foreboding: Orwell and the Entropy of Politics', in Kroes (ed.), *Nineteen Eighty-Four and the Apocalyptic Imagination*, p. 86.
107. George Orwell, 'Reflections on Gandhi', *Partisan Review* (January 1949), in *CEJL*, Volume 4, pp. 463–70.
108. Orwell to Koestler, 20 September 1947, in *CEJL*, Volume 4, p. 379.
109. Orwell to Symons, 21 March 1948, in *CEJL*, Volume 4, p. 406.
110. Orwell to Woodstock, 4 January 1948, in *CEJL*, Volume 4, p. 401.
111. Konni Zilliacus and George Orwell letters to *Tribune* (17 January 1947), in *CEJL*, Volume 4, pp. 191–4.

2 The Canonisation of St George

1. George Orwell, 'Lear, Tolstoy, and the Fool', *Polemic* (March 1947).
2. National Security Council Document 68 (NSC 68), 'United States Objectives and Programs for National Security', 14 April 1950, http://www.fas.org/irp/offdocs/nsc-hst/nsc-68.htm.
3. See Frances Stonor Saunders, *Who Paid the Piper?* (London: Granta, 1999); Hilary Spurling, *The Girl from the Fiction Department* (London: Penguin, 2003); Karl Cohen, 'The Cartoon that Came in from the Cold', *Guardian* (7 March 2003).
4. David Hencke and Rob Evans, 'How Big Brothers Used Orwell to Fight the Cold War', *The Guardian* (30 June 2000).
5. Richard Norton-Taylor and Seamus Milne, *Guardian* (11 July 1996); Scott Lucas, *Freedom's War: The US Crusade Against the Soviet Union 1945–56* (New York: New York University Press, 1999), pp. 64–5; Stonor Saunders, *Who Paid the Piper?* pp. 293–301.
6. See Tony Shaw, 'Some Writers are More Equal than Others: George Orwell, the State and Cold War Privilege', *Cold War History* (Summer 2003).
7. C.M. Woodhouse, 'Animal Farm', *Times Literary Supplement* (6 August 1945), pp. xxx–xxxi.
8. Woodhouse was one of the key MI6 personnel involved in the planning and execution of the 1953 overthrow of the Mossadegh government in Iran, which had offended Britain with the nationalisation of the Anglo-Iranian Oil Company. See C.M. Woodhouse, *Something Ventured* (London: Granada, 1982).
9. Julian Symons, '*Tribune's* Obituary', reprinted in Audrey Coppard and Bernard Crick (eds.), *Orwell Remembered* (London: Ariel, 1984), p. 275.
10. Stephen Spender, *World Review* (June 1950), p. 51.
11. George Woodcock, 'Reflections of George Orwell', *Northern Review* (August/September 1953), in Coppard and Crick (eds.), *Orwell Remembered*, pp. 199–234; Richard Peters interview, 9 September 1955, British Broadcasting Corporation, in ibid., p. 90.

12. George Woodcock, *The Crystal Spirit* (London: Jonathan Cape, 1967), p. 7.

13. Tom Hopkinson, *World Review* (June 1950), quoted in Bernard Crick, *George Orwell: A Life* (Harmondsworth: Penguin, 1982), p. 490.

14. Koestler and Pritchett, quoted in David Pryce-Jones, 'Orwell's Reputation', in Miriam Gross (ed.), *The World of George Orwell* (London: Weidenfeld and Nicolson, 1971), p. 150.

15. Lionel Trilling,'George Orwell and the Politics of Truth', in *The Opposing Self* (London: Secker and Warburg, 1955), p. 371.

16. T.R. Fyvel, 'A Writer's Life', *World Review* (June 1950), p. 18.

17. Christopher Hollis, *A Study of George Orwell: The Man and His Works* (London: Hollis and Carter, 1956), p. 208.

18. John Atkins, *George Orwell* (London: Calder and Boyars, 1945), p. 1.

19. Stephen Spender interview, 7 May 1963, reprinted in Coppard and Crick (eds.), *Orwell Remembered*, p. 262.

20. Richard Rees, *George Orwell: Fugitive from the Camp of Victory* (London: Secker and Warburg, 1961), p. 45.

21. Woodcock, *Crystal Spirit*, p. 7.

22. A.L. Morton, *The English Utopia* (London: Laurence and Wishart, 1952), quoted in Crispin Aubrey, 'The Making of 1984', in Crispin Aubrey and Paul Chilton (eds.), *Nineteen Eighty-Four in 1984: Autonomy, Control, and Communication* (London: Comedia, 1983), p. 11.

23. Deutscher, '"1984" – The Mysticism of Cruelty', in *Russia in Transition and Other Essays* (London: Hamish Hamilton, 1957), p. 230.

24. Conor Cruise O'Brien, *Listener* (12 December 1968), pp. 797–8.

25. Raymond Williams, *Orwell* (London: Fontana, 1971), pp. 23 and 26.

26. Crick, *Orwell: A Life*, pp. 17–18.

27. Michael Shelden, *Orwell: The Authorised Biography* (London: Minerva, 1992), p. 10.

28. Ibid., p. 484.

29. Robert Mulvihill, *Reflections on America 1984: An Orwell Symposium* (Athens, GA: University of Georgia Press, 1986), p. 1.

30. Richard Rorty, *Contingency, Irony and Solidarity* (Cambridge: Cambridge University Press, 1989), p. 170.

31. Michael Walzer, *The Company of Critics: Social Criticism and Political Commitment in the Twentieth Century* (London: Halban, 1989), p. 135.

32. Peter Davison, *George Orwell: A Literary Life* (London: Macmillan, 1996), pp. 143–5.

33. Matthew Glazebrook, 'Breakfast in Amerikka: Black Panther Community Programs 1966–1982', unpublished dissertation, University of Birmingham (June 2003).

34. Norman Podhoretz, 'If Orwell were Alive Today, He'd be a Neo-Conservative', *Harper's* (January 1983), quoted in Jonah Raskin, 'George Orwell and the Big Cannibal Critics', *Monthly Review* (May

1983), in *The Chestnut Tree Cafe*, http://www.seas.upenn.edu:8080/~allport/chestnut/cancrtcs.htm.

35. Quoted in Christopher Norris (ed.), *Inside the Myth: Orwell, Views from the Left* (London: Lawrence and Wishart, 1984), p. 16.

36. Bernard Crick, 'Orwell and English Socialism', in Peter Buitenhuis and Ira B. Nadel (eds.), *George Orwell: A Reassessment* (London: Macmillan, 1988), p. 19.

37. Crispin Aubrey, 'The Making of 1984', in Aubrey and Chilton (eds.), *Ninety-Eighty Four in 1984*, p. 13.

38. Christopher Norris, 'Introduction', in Norris (ed.), *Inside the Myth*, p. 7.

39. Deirdre Beddoe, 'Hindrances and Help-Meets: Women in the Writings of George Orwell', in Norris (ed.), *Inside the Myth*, p. 153; Beatrix Campbell, 'Orwell – Paterfamilias or Big Brother?', in ibid., p. 131; Daphne Patai, *The Orwell Mystique* (Amherst: University of Massachusetts Press, 1984).

40. See Geoffrey Wheatcroft, 'Look Right, Look Left, Look Right Again', *New Statesman* (2 April 1999).

41. John Newsinger, *Orwell's Politics* (Basingstoke: Macmillan, 1999), p. 8.

42. John Rossi, 'Orwell and Patriotism', *Contemporary Review* (August 1992), in *The Chestnut Cafe*, http://www. seas.upenn.edu/~allport/chestnut'orwlpatr.htm.

43. John Rodden, 'Orwell and the London Left Intelligentsia', in Graham Holderness et al. (eds.), *George Orwell* (London: Macmillan, 1998), pp. 177–8.

44. Peter Davison, *George Orwell: A Literary Life* (London: Macmillan, 1996), pp. 143–5.

45. Timothy Garton Ash, 'Orwell for Our Time', *The Guardian* (5 May 2001).

46. Jack Straw, 'Blame the Left, Not the British', *The Observer* (15 October 2000).

47. BBC4, *The Talk Show* (24 June 2002), www.bbc.co.uk/bbcfour/talkshow/features/christopher-hitchens-transcript.shtml.

48. Jonathan Freedland, 'We're Watching It', *Guardian* (9 August 2000).

3 Christopher Hitchens: Becoming George

1. Quoted in Elizabeth Wassermann, 'The Power of Facing', *Atlantic Unbound* (23 October 2002), http://www.theatlantic.com/unbound/interviews/int2002–10–23.htm.

2. Christopher Hitchens, *Letters to a Young Contrarian* (New York: Basic Books, 2001), p. 2.

3. Christopher Hitchens, *Orwell's Victory* (London: Allen Lane, 2002), pp. 149–50.

4. *Letters*, pp. 25 and 138.
5. *Orwell's Victory*, p. 3.
6. Ibid., p. vi.
7. Ibid., p. 13.
8. Ibid., p. 98.
9. Ibid., p. 71. Hitchens does offer a one-sentence caveat in the introduction that Orwell's 'shudder generated by homosexuality appears
   to have resisted the process of self-mastery', but adds immediately,
   'And even that "perversion" he often represented as a misfortune
   or deformity created by artificial or cruel conditions; his repugnance
   ... was for the "sin" and not the "sinner"' (*Orwell's Victory*, p. 7).
10. Ibid., pp. 109–10.
11. Ibid., p. 7.
12. Quoted in Edward Lempinen, 'How the Left Became Irrelevant',
    Salon (29 October 2002), http://www.salon.com/news/feature/
    2002/10/29/hitchens/index_np.html.
13. Quoted in Bill Steigerwald, 'Here's Why Orwell Matters', *Pittsburgh
    Tribune-Review* (19 October 2002).
14. Quoted in ibid.
15. *Orwell's Victory*, p. 8. Hitchens does quote Orwell's 1947 statement,
    'A socialist United States of Europe seems to me the only worthwhile
    political objective today', but only to put down the neo-
    conservative Podhoretz. There is no further consideration of
    'Socialism' beyond the sentence (*Orwell's Victory*, p. 72).
16. Ibid., p. 10.
17. Ibid., p. 9.
18. Ibid., p. 150.
19. Ibid., p. 33.
20. Ibid., pp. 26–7 and 29–30.
21. Ibid., p. 30; George Orwell, 'Inside the Whale', in *Inside the Whale*
    (London: Victor Gollancz, 1940), in *CEJL*, Volume 1, pp. 413–60.
22. *Orwell's Victory*, p. 90; 'Hitchens Responds', *AndrewSullivan.com* (29
    October 2002), http://www.andrewsullivan.com/book_club.php?
    book_num=book_club_blog.html.
23. *Orwell's Victory*, pp. 27 and 30–2.
24. Ibid., p. 32.
25. See the chapter on Williams in *Unacknowledged Legislators* (London:
    Verso, 2002). Hitchens gets away with his assault in part because of
    his conflation of Williams' 1971 book on Orwell with the critic's
    later interviews with the editors of *New Left Review*, collected in a
    1979 volume. In the latter, Williams moved from his reading of
    the constructed 'Orwell' into the 'objective' depiction of an 'ex-
    socialist', an assertion that rested uneasily with Orwell's insistence,
    towards the end of his life, that he was still true to the cause. Along
    the way, Williams' admiration of Orwell was replaced with the curt,
    'I must say that I cannot bear much of [his work] now.' This cruder

approach, accentuated by its presentation in interviews rather than in another monograph, gave Hitchens a better footing for his denunciation of Williams' 'contempt of Orwell'. (See Raymond Williams, *Politics and Letters: Interviews with New Left Review* [London: New Left Books, 1979]).

26. *Orwell's Victory*, pp. 35–6.
27. Ibid., pp. 38–9. Hitchens and *Orwell's Victory* were assisted by interviewers who re-presented this image of, in the words of the BBC's Andrew Marr, 'Raymond Williams who was a shameful communist misreader of Orwell' (BBC4, *Talk Show*, 24 June 2002).
28. *Orwell's Victory*, p. 39.
29. Ibid., pp. 111–21.
30. Andy Croft, 'Remembering George Orwell', *Guardian* (25 May 2002).
31. *Letters*, p. xi.
32. Appearance and vanity are recurrent themes of interviews with and presentations of Hitchens. For example, Lynn Barber of the *Observer* wrote an extended love letter to 'Hitch' after a 'five-hour, two-bottle lunch' in which even the waiters 'were in thrall to his charm'. In sharp contrast, David Brock's renunciation of his neo-conservative career in Washington included an encounter with a 'misshapen, unkempt, and seemingly unshowered' Hitchens. Hitchens replied, 'Those who know me will confirm that while I may not be tidy, I am so clean you could eat your dinner off me' (Lynn Barber, 'Look Who's Talking', *Observer* [14 April 2002]; David Brock, *Blinded by the Right: The Conscience of an Ex-Conservative* [New York: Crown, 2002]; Christopher Hitchens, 'The Real David Brock', *The Nation* [27 May 2002]).
33. Occasionally, these alliances survived the post-9–11 invective. Hitchens could lambast Susan Sontag for her appeasement of terrorists but still remember Sontag, on the day of the *fatwa* against Rushdie, 'saying – rather splendidly – Well, it would be contemptible to point out to the president such a small thing as the fact that Mr. Rushdie's wife – an American – had gone into hiding with him; that would be paltry' ('America, Afghanistan, and the Contrarian', Commonwealth Club lecture, San Francisco [17 December 2001], http://www.commonwealthclub.org/archive/01/01-12hitchens-intro.html).
34. Christopher Hitchens, 'Orwell – A Snitch?', *The Nation* (February 1998); Alexander Cockburn, 'Orwell and Koestler', *The Nation* (April 1998).
35. Alexander Cockburn, 'Hitch the Snitch', *Counterpunch*, http://www.counterpunch.com/snitch.html.
36. Maureen Dowd, 'Streetcar Named Betrayal', *New York Times* (24 February 1999).
37. Mark Steyn, 'Sid 'n' Hitch', *National Review* (8 March 1999); Frank Rich, 'The Death Rattles', *New York Times* (10 February 1999).

38. 'Lawmakers Call for Investigation of Blumenthal', CNN.com (7 February 1999), http://edition.cnn.com/ALLPOLITICS/stories/1999/02/07/blumenthal/.

39. 'What Really Happened', *The Nation* (1 March 1999).

40. Meryl Gordon, 'The Boy Can't Help It', *New York Magazine* (26 April 1999).

41. 'Bloody Blundering: Clinton's Cluelessness is Selling out Kosovo', *Salon* (5 April 1999), http://www.salon.com/news/feature/1999/04/05/hitchens/; 'Srebrenica Revisited', *The Nation* (19 April 1999); 'Ethnic Poisoning', *The Nation* (3 May 1999).

42. 'Belgrade Degraded', *The Nation* (17 May 1999).

43. 'Srebrenica Revisited', *The Nation* (19 April 1999).

44. 'Port Huron Piffle', *The Nation* (14 June 1999).

45. Edward Herman, 'Hitchens Degraded', *ZMag* (8 May 1999), http://www.zmag.org/sustainers/content/1999-05/may_8mherman.htm. See also Edward Herman, '"Balance" Sickness at the Nation', *ZMag* (5 June 1999), http://www.zmag.org/sustainers/content/1999-06/june_5herman.htm.

46. 'Port Huron Piffle', *The Nation* (14 June 1999).

47. 'Genocide and the Body-Baggers', *The Nation* (29 November 1999); 'Kosovo on Hold', *The Nation* (17 April 2000); 'Body Count in Kosovo', *The Nation* (11 June 2001).

48. The charge of 'retrospective justification' is made in Chomsky's 'Kosovo in Retrospect', in *A New Generation Draws the Line: Kosovo, East Timor and the Standards of the West* (London: Verso 2001), pp. 94–147.

49. 'Kosovo on Hold', *The Nation* (17 April 2000).

50. 'Democratic Centralism', *The Nation* (6 November 2000).

51. MSNBC, *Hardball with Chris Matthews* (30 October 2000).

52. Panel discussion, 'Regarding Henry Kissinger', National Press Club, Washington, DC (22 February 2001), http://harpers.org/online/kissinger_forum/.

53. Quoted in Tom Ivancie, 'Q&A with Christopher Hitchens', *Doublethink* (6 February 2003), http://www.americasfuture.org/viewBrainwash.cfm?pubid=210.

54. *Letters*, p. 113.

55. Ibid., p. 10

56. *Orwell's Victory*, p. 4. While Hitchens advised vigilance against intellectuals, Right or Left, the only examples of compromised intellectuals he offered were the Webbs and George Bernard Shaw.

57. 'Hitch Redux', *LBO-Talk Archive* (6 March 2002), http://squawk.ca/lbo-talk/0203/0403.html.

58. Quoted in Edward Lempinen, 'How the Left Became Irrelevant', *Salon* (29 October 2002), http://www.salon.com/news/feature/2002/10/29/hitchens/index_np.html.

59. 'Why Orwell Matters', Commonwealth Club lecture, San Francisco (21 October 2002), http://www.commonwealthclub.org/archive/02/02-10hitchens-speech.html.

60. *Orwell's Victory*, p. 9.

61. BBC4, *Talk Show*, 24 June 2002.

62. 'The E-Mails Pour In', *AndrewSullivan.com* (30 October 2002), http://www.andrewsullivan.com/book_club.php?book_num=book_club_blog.html.

63. *Letters*, p. x; 'Your Turn: Readers Write In to Hitch', AndrewSullivan. com (29 October 2002). The importance for Hitchens of discovering a twenty-first-century Orwell embracing the American way was illustrated by David Brooks' exposure in *The Weekly Standard* of the author's limitations: '[Orwell] would matter if he had written about American idealism, America's sense of mission, mass affluence, the triumph of the market mentality, American history, or Pax Americana. But while he seems to have had a general disdain for American culture – and championed, in a vague way, European socialist unity as a way to counterbalance American hegemony – he never turned his full attention to this country and its ideas' ('Orwell and Us', 23 September 2002).

4 9–11

1. 'America, Afghanistan, and the Contrarian', Commonwealth Club lecture, San Francisco (17 December 2001), http://www.commonwealthclub.org/archive/01/01–12hitchens-intro.html.

2. 'We're Still Standing', *Evening Standard* (12 September 2001).

3. 'The Morning After: So is This War?', *Guardian* (13 September 2001); 'On Bush – Cometh the Hour Cometh the Man?', *Mirror* (14 September 2001).

4. Leon Wieseltier, 'Heroes', *The New Republic* (15 October 2001). This was Hitchens' offending paragraph: 'With cellphones still bleeping piteously from under the rubble, it probably seems indecent to most people to ask if the United States has ever done anything to attract such awful hatred. Indeed, the very thought, for the present, is taboo. Some senators and congressmen have spoken of the loathing felt by certain unnamed and sinister elements for the freedom and prosperity of America, as if it were only natural that such a happy and successful country should inspire envy and jealousy. But that is the limit of permissible thought.'

5. 'The Pursuit of Happiness is at an End', *Evening Standard* (19 September 2001).

6. Chomsky's claim was based on an article by the former German Ambassador to the Sudan, who wrote in 2001:

It is difficult to assess how many people in this poor African country died as a consequence of the destruction of the Al-Shifa factory, but several tens of thousands seems a reasonable guess. The factory produced some of the basic medicines on the World Health Organization list, covering 20 to 60 percent of Sudan's market and 100 percent of the market for intravenous liquids. It took more than three months for these products to be replaced with imports. (Werner Daum, 'Universalism and the West', *Harvard International Review* [Summer 2001], http://www.hir. harvard.edu/articles/index.html?id=909).

See also James Astill, 'Strike One', *Guardian* (2 October 2001) on the complete loss of drugs such as those to combat tuberculosis and to prevent the passage of diseases from animals to humans.

7. Noam Chomsky, 'A Quick Reaction', *CounterPunch* (13 September 2001), http://www.counterpunch.org/chomskybomb.html.

8. 'The Chorus and Cassandra', *Grand Street Magazine* (Autumn 1985), reprinted at http://www.abbc.com/aaargh/fran/chomsky/cassandra. html.

9. Ibid.

10. Quoted in Peter Scholtes, 'Road to Baghdad', *City Pages* (20 November 2002), http://www.citypages.com/databank/23/1146/ print10878.asp. Hitchens had also defended Edward Said, another of the Leftist suspects after 9–11, when the Palestinian-born author was accused in 1999 of falsifying his background ('Commentary's Scurrilous Attack on Edward Said', *Salon* [7 September 1999], http:// www.salon.com/news/feature/1999/09/07/said/).

11. Christopher Hitchens, 'Never Trust the Imperialists (Especially When They Turn Pacifist)', *Boston Review* (December 1993–January 1994); Noam Chomsky, 'Humanitarian Intervention', *Boston Review* (February–March 1994). While Chomsky questioned the motives for any involvement by the US Government (although he left open intervention as a 'separate matter'), Hitchens commented, 'It is, in short, going to be very hard to discuss foreign policy in the future if the main thrust of radical and critical argument is purely non-interventionist.'

12. 'Minority Report', *The Nation* (29 November 1999).

13. Noam Chomsky, 'The Single Standard in Kosovo', *The Nation* (3 January 2000).

14. 'Hitchens Replies', *The Nation* (3 January 2000).

15. 'Against Rationalization', *The Nation* (8 October 2001). The article was posted on the website of *The Nation* on 20 September.

16. 'Of Sin, the Left, and Islamic Fascism', *The Nation* (24 September 2001 – website edition), reprinted at http://sixtiessurvivor.org/docs/ hitchens092401.html. Husseini's crime was to venture, 'The fascists like Bin-Laden could not get volunteers to stuff envelopes if Israel

had withdrawn from Jerusalem like it was supposed to – and the US stopped the sanctions and the bombing on Iraq.' In daring to raise the possibility of motive, linked to the Israel–Palestine issue and US policies, for the attacks, Husseini had become a 'self-appointed interpreter for the killers'. Hitchens created an image he would use repeatedly against deviant intellectuals, 'I might, from where I am sitting, be a short walk from a gutted Capitol or a shattered White House. I am quite certain that Husseini and his rabble of sympathizers would still be telling me that my chickens were coming home to roost.'

17. Jonathan Belke, 'Years Later, US Attack on Factory Still Hurts Sudan', *Boston Globe* (22 August 1999); Werner Daum, 'Universalism and the West', *Harvard International Review*, Summer 2001. In contrast, Robert Fisk had alleged that US operations, directly or through Israel, were intended to kill civilians; Hitchens, however, chose not to confront Fisk.

18. 'A Rejoinder to Noam Chomsky', *The Nation* (4 October 2001 – website edition).

19. Noam Chomsky, 'Reply to Hitchens's Rejoinder', *The Nation* (15 October 2001 – website edition).

20. 'America, Afghanistan, and the Contrarian', Commonwealth Club lecture, San Francisco (17 December 2001), http://www.commonwealthclub.org/archive/01/01-12hitchens-intro.html.

21. 'The Fascist Sympathies of the Soft Left', *The Spectator* (29 September 2001).

22. 'Lines on Lord Archer', *Guardian* (26 September 2001).

23. 'Don't Forget Kissinger', *Guardian* (26 September 2001).

24. 'Murder was their only motive', *Guardian* (26 September 2001).

25. 'Artists Appeal for Campaign Against War, not Afghans', *Independent* (20 September 2001).

26. Harold Pinter and John Pilger with reply by Christopher Hitchens, 'Dissenters Put the Record Straight', *Guardian* (28 September 2001).

27. Rhys Southan, 'Free Radical', *Reason* (November 2001), http://reason.com/0111/fe.rs.free.shtml; Elizabeth Wassermann, 'The Power of Facing', *Atlantic Unbound* (23 October 2002), http://www.theatlantic.com/unbound/interviews/int2002-10-23.htm; Lynn Barber, 'Look Who's Talking', *Observer Magazine* (14 April 2002).

28. 'We're Not All Stupid', *Guardian* (3 October 2001); 'From Coast to Coast, America is Filled with … Indifference', *Evening Standard* (10 October 2001).

29. 'Troubling Times for the Washington Hawks', *Guardian* (3 October 2001).

30. Letter from Julie Burchill, *The Spectator* (6 October 2001).

31. Ramesh Ponnuru, 'What We're Not Fighting For', *National Review* (5 November 2001).

32. See 'America, Afghanistan, and the Contrarian', Commonwealth Club Lecture (17 December 2001); 'The Night of the Weak Knees', *Guardian* (5 December 2001).

33. Michael Kelly, 'The Left's Great Divide', *Washington Post* (7 November 2001).

34. 'Ha Ha Ha to the Pacifists', *Guardian* (14 November 2001).

35. Rebecca Traister et al., 'Oliver Stone and Christopher Hitchens Spar over Hollywood's Efforts to be Relevant', *New York Observer* (15 October 2001); 'Stranger in a Stranger Land', *Atlantic Monthly* (December 2001).

36. 'Why Peace Lovers Must Welcome This War', *Mirror* (15 November 2001).

37. 'The Idiocy of a Bombing Pause', *Hamilton Spectator* (16 November 2001).

38. See Christopher Hitchens, 'Letters to a Young Contrarian', *Guardian* (10 November 2001); Tom Carson, 'The Envelope, Please', *Washington Post* (13 November 2001); Irin Carmon, 'You Say You Want a Revolution', *Harvard Crimson* (16 November 2001); Lynne Coady, 'Why the World Needs Christopher Hitchens', *Vancouver Sun* (17 November 2001); Patti Thorn, 'A "Contrarian" is Born in Midcareer', *Rocky Mountain News* (24 November 2001).

39. Gavin Lewis, 'No Laughing Matter', *Guardian* (15 November 2001).

40. George Monbiot, 'Blasting Our Way to Peace', *Guardian* (15 November 2001).

41. Joan Smith, 'Reason is on the Run', *Independent* (18 November 2001).

42. 'A New Tragedy for a Shocked Nation', *Evening Standard* (13 November 2001); 'The Night of the Weak Knees', *Guardian* (5 November 2001); 'Battle Blunders', *Mirror* (6 December 2001).

43. 'In Case Anyone's Forgotten: Torture Doesn't Work', *Guardian* (14 November 2001).

44. Hitchens distorted Chomsky's remarks not only by taking a quote out of context, but by eliding it with ellipsis to give a misleading impression. Chomsky, in fact, was warning about the possibility of famine in Afghanistan over the winter. See 'The New War Against Terror', speech at MIT (18 October 2001), http://www.nadir.org/nadir/initiativ/agp/free/9-11/chomskywar.htm.

45. 'The Ends of War', *The Nation* (17 December 2001).

46. 'Stop the Bombing and Bring Out the Bayonets', *Mirror* (17 January 2002).

47. 'Bush Has Gone Soft on Sharon', *Evening Standard* (28 January 2002); 'Houston We Have a Problem', *Guardian* (5 February 2002); 'America More Serious? You Must Be Joking', *Guardian* (6 March 2002); 'False Spring', *Newsweek* (25 March 2002).

48. 'Your Presence Here is Offensive, Kissinger', *Mirror* (24 April 2002).

49. 'America is Blinded on Human Rights', *Mirror*, 22 January 2002.

50. 'America, Afghanistan, and the Contrarian', Commonwealth Club lecture, San Francisco (17 December 2001), http://www.commonwealthclub.org/archive/01/01-12hitchens-intro.html.

51. 'Hey, I'm Doing My Best', *Observer* (20 January 2003).

52. 'Tsars in Their Eyes', *Guardian* (20 February 2002). According to Hitchens, his stand against Ashcroft was part of the author's post-9–11 embrace of Americanism. Hitchens had intended 'as an act of solidarity' to 'become a U.S. citizen', but he passed up naturalisation when 'the attorney general informed me that if I remained a Green Card holder, I could be arrested and executed without knowing the charges against me, and in secret. So in solidarity with the 20 million other people who have had their habeas corpus taken away, I say you can have my body but my habeas corpus not' ('America, Afghanistan, and the Contrarian', Commonwealth Club lecture. See also 'Battle Blunders', *Mirror* [6 December 2001]).

53. 'Where is this Evil Axis Bush Speaks of?', *Mirror* (26 February 2002).

54. MSNBC, *Hardball with Chris Matthews* (16 January 2002).

55. 'Where is this Evil Axis Bush Speaks of?', *Mirror* (26 February 2002).

56. 'Saddam is the Next US Target', *Evening Standard* (5 March 2002).

57. 'Is it Still a Good Idea?', *Guardian* (20 March 2002).

58. Ibid.

59. 'Does Blair Know What He's Getting Into?', *Guardian* (20 March 2002).

60. 'Boy George', *Mirror* (11 September 2002).

61. 'Has Bush Already Chosen Saddam's Successor?', *Mirror* (15 July 2002); 'Secrecy at Heart of US Terror Case', *Mirror* (30 July 2002); 'Questions America Must Answer', *Mirror* (26 August 2002).

62. 'Knowledge (and Power)', *The Nation* (10 June 2002).

63. 'Saving Islam from Bin Laden', *The* (Melbourne) *Age* (5 September 2002).

64. 'Knowledge (and Power)', *The Nation* (10 June 2002).

65. 'It's A Good Time for War', *Boston Globe* (8 September 2002).

66. 'Hawks in the Dovecote', *Observer* (25 August 2002). In fact, Kissinger's position was far more complex than either Hitchens or many anti-war activists noted. His doubts were more to do with the manner of how the Bush Administration was moving towards war, in particular its failure to secure international support, rather than with military action to remove Saddam Hussein from power. See 'Deposing Saddam Could Backfire', *Washington Post* (12 August 2002).

67. 'White House Itching for War', *Mirror* (18 September 2002).

68. 'We Must Fight Iraq', *Mirror* (25 September 2002).

69. 'The Ballad of Route 66', *Vanity Fair* (November 2002); 'The Maverick Kingdom', *Vanity Fair* (December 2002).

70. Editors, 'Concerning Hitchens', *The Nation* (14 October 2002); Hitchens, quoted in Edward Lempinen, 'How the Left Became

Irrelevant', *Salon* (29 October 2002), http://www.salon.com/ news/feature/2002/10/29/hitchens/index_np.html. The editors highlighted that many responses were 'personal', but the published letters dwelt on the perceived threat from the US Government rather than from 'terrorists'. Readers pointed to 'the fascist foragings of John Ashcroft and the dude who sponsored him, "Shrub"', 'the nation I love, in its fear and rage, stinging itself to death like a scorpion', the 'militaristic response to the crimes of 9/11', and the 'cold war "patriots" who helped to slaughter 3,000 people, and tried to kill me at my desk [at the Pentagon]' ('How 9/11 Changed Our Lives', *The Nation*, 23 September 2002).

71. Atta's supposed meeting with an 'Iraqi intelligence officer', built up by the US for months as proof of Saddam Hussein's link to 9–11, was finally established in October 2002 as an 'unverified report' (James Risen, 'Prague Discounts Iraqi Meeting' and 'How Politics and Rivalries Fed Suspicions of a Meeting', *New York Times*, 21 October 2002; Peter Green, 'Havel Denies Telephoning U.S. on Iraqi Meeting', *New York Times*, 23 October 2002). Hitchens' reference to the 'gang' in Iraq anticipated Washington's later ploy: throughout 2002 and into 2003 before the United Nations, US officials such as Colin Powell would claim Saddam Hussein was supporting Anwar al-Islam, a fundamentalist faction in Kurdistan, despite evidence that was specious at best.

72. 'Taking Sides', *The Nation* (14 October 2002).

73. 'So Long, Fellow Travellers', *Washington Post* (20 October 2002).

74. Noam Chomsky, 'Serbia: Comments on the Milosevic Ouster', *ZMag* (16 October 2000), http://www.zmag.org/chomskyonelec.htm.

75. 'So Long, Fellow Travellers'.

76. Katha Pollitt, 'Subject to Debate', *The Nation* (25 November 2002).

77. Pollitt defended the diverse character of the Washington demonstration against the concern, expressed by David Corn, that it had been hijacked by extremists, by writing, 'I can't tell you how many people I've spoken with who do not recognize in Corn's *LA Weekly* description the DC event they attended.' Hitchens, in reply, altered Pollitt's sentence to give the opposite impression: '"I can't tell you how many people I've spoken with who do not recognize … the DC event they attended." I could have tried to put it better, but I doubt I should have succeeded.'

78. 'The Hitchens–Pollitt Papers', *The Nation* (16 December 2002).

79. Lempinen, 'How the Left Became Irrelevant'; 'Armchair General', *Slate* (11 November 2002); 'Anti-Americanism', *Slate* (27 November 2002); 'Imperialism', *Slate* (10 December 2002); 'Why Orwell Matters' debate (1 October 2002), http://capitalinflux. blogspot.com/2002_10_01_capitalinflux_archive.html#85601104; Margaret Wente, 'The Bad Boy of the Left', Toronto *Globe and Mail* (2 November 2002); 'Why Hitchens Has Left the Left', Toronto *Star* (8 November 2002).

80. National Public Radio, 'Talk of the Nation' (24 October 2002). As for the 'Left', Hitchens gave his summary flogging: 'I do not admire people like Ramsey Clark ... – and the International Action Center, as it calls itself, a front organization for the Workers World Party who, in the name of a sort of pacifism or anti-warism, are actually carrying water for Saddam Hussein, as they did for Slobodan Milosevic, and as they will do tomorrow for Kim Jong Il of North Korea. These are not pacifists or anti-war people at all. They are supporters of the old idea that utopia is brought about by a party-state with a supreme leader where the right of the citizen is to be the property of the government and states that not only carry out but plan attacks on their neighbors, as well as atrocious treatment of their own populations. I am through with that, and I wish there were more people who saw through it. And I'm afraid to say that *The Nation* tries to split the difference, and I thought, well, I'm not interested in splitting this difference any longer.'

81. Quoted in Lempinen, 'How the Left Became Irrelevant'.

82. 'A World is Born', *Newsweek* (30 December 2002).

83. 'The E-Mails Pour In', *AndrewSullivan.com* (30 October 2002), http://www.andrewsullivan.com/book_club.php?book_num=book_club_blog.html.

84. National Public Radio, 'Talk of the Nation' (24 October 2002). Hitchens carried out further linguistic hair-splitting a week later, 'I don't favor an invasion of Iraq. But I favor a confrontation with Saddam Hussein .... I would prefer to call it an intervention against Saddam Hussein.' Quoted in Lempinen, 'How the Left Became Irrelevant'.

85. 'Terrorism', *Slate* (18 November 2002).

86. 'Evil', *Slate* (31 December 2002).

87. '"WMD" and "Inspection"', *Slate* (26 December 2002). Hitchens added in this forthright mood, 'The term "smoking gun" is one of the more ridiculous phrases to have emerged from the recent argument over intervention against Saddam Hussein .... In other words, the demand for a full inspection is another way of calling for a regime change, which for many other reasons is already long overdue' ('Saddam Caught Red-Handed', *Mirror*, 28 January 2003).

88. Quoted in Tom Ivancie, 'Q&A with Christopher Hitchens', *Doublethink* (6 February 2003), http://www.americasfuture.org/viewBrainwash.cfm?pubid=210.

89. PBS, *Now with Bill Moyers* (20 December 2002); 'Drumbeat', *Slate* (24 February 2003).

5 Beyond the Spirit of '68

1. The quotes in subsequent paragraphs can be found in the transcript 'The War on Terrorism: Is There an Alternative?', London Review

of Books discussion panel (15 May 2002), http://www.lrb.co.uk/enduringfreedom/index.php.

2. Michael Berube, 'Ali v. Hitchens: Battle on the Left', *Chronicle of Higher Education* (3 May 2002).

3. BBC Radio 4, *Today* (15 May 2002).

4. Among those spotted by the front doors were Nick Cohen and Francis Wheen.

5. *Letters to a Young Contrarian* (New York: Basic Books, 2001), p. xi.

6. Frank Rich, 'The Death Rattles', *New York Times* (10 February 1999).

7. Joy Press, 'The Belligerati', *Village Voice* (26 October 2001); Kelly Burke, 'Angry Not So Young Man Refuses to Join the Belligerati', *Sydney Morning Herald* (30 May 2002); Tariq Ali, 'The New Empire Loyalists', *Guardian* (16 March 2002).

8. Sunder Katwala, 'Tariq Ali v. Christopher Hitchens: The War of Words', *Observer Worldview Extra* (19 May 2002), http://www.observer.co.uk/worldview/story/0,11581,718494,00.html.

9. 'Letters to a Young Contrarian', *Guardian* (10 November 2001).

10. John Lloyd, 'A Performance on the Barricades', *New Statesman* (7 May 2001).

11. John Lloyd, 'We Can Save the New World Order', *New Statesman* (1 October 2001), 'A Plan for the World', *New Statesman* (22 October 2001), and 'The Whole World in Their Hands', *New Statesman* (12 November 2001).

12. John Lloyd, 'Enter the Red Brigades', *New Statesman* (1 April 2002).

13. John Lloyd, 'How Anti-Americanism Betrays the Left', *Guardian* (17 March 2002).

14. Stephen Robinson, 'Left-wingers Fall out over Claims of Censorship', *Daily Telegraph* (5 March 2002).

15. John Lloyd, 'In Bed with Bush', *New Statesman* (11 March 2002). Lloyd would follow Hitchens in his special redefinition of the 'Left'. He blamed the anti-globalisation movement for the rise of 'far right' movements in Europe. ('The Twilight of the Left', *New Statesman*, 21 January 2002). He warned that the excesses of Europe's 'Left' meant 'anti-European opinion was rife among the "Left" as well as the "Right" in the US', with the result that 'Americans see us as subordinates' (*New Statesman*, 5 August 2002). His admiration of American power led him, in alliance with neo-conservatives in the US, to the moral defence of 'empire' as the framework 'to stop the worst depredations of those tyrants, mass murderers and warlords who prevent people having a decent life' ('The Return of Imperialism', *New Statesman*, 15 April 2002). Inevitably, he advocated an attack on Iraq as 'the left has become ridiculed on the right because of its lack of any concept of evil at all' ('The Case for a Just War', *New Statesman*, 16 September 2002).

16. See Tariq Ali, 'The New Empire Loyalists', *Guardian* (16 March 2002).

17. Salman Rushdie, 'Anti-Americanism Has Taken the World by Storm', *Guardian* (6 February 2002); Salman Rushdie, 'How to Fight and Lose the Moral High Ground', *Guardian* (23 March 2002).

18. Rushdie, 'How to Fight and Lose the Moral High Ground'.

19. Salman Rushdie, 'Yes, This is about Islam', *New York Times* (2 November 2001), and 'No More Fanaticism as Usual', *New York Times* (27 November 2002).

20. Salman Rushdie, 'A Liberal Argument for Regime Change', *Washington Post* (1 November 2002).

21. Salman Rushdie, 'The Altered States of Anti-Americanism', *Guardian* (31 August 2002); Salman Rushdie, 'Ironic if Bush Himself Causes Jihad', *Sydney Morning Herald* (10 September 2002).

22. Martin Amis, 'Fear and Loathing', *Guardian* (18 September 2001).

23. Martin Amis, 'The Voice of the Lonely Crowd', *Guardian* (1 June 2002). Nor would Amis emerge from his resignation in his contribution to the *Daily Telegraph*'s edition on the anniversary of 9–11: 'The towers collapsed, and so did much else, including all notions of America as an island or a fortress or a "gated community". The collateral catastrophe of September 11 is our sudden introduction to a barely recognisable planet, a planet which is not going to leave us alone' ('Window on a Changed World', *Daily Telegraph*, 11 September 2002).

24. John Pilger, 'Martin Amis Represents a Problem', *New Statesman* (17 June 2002). See also Peter Wilby in the *New Statesman* who turned a review of Amis' historical *Koba the Dread* into the jab, 'Like so many of his generation, on the monstrosities of our own age, and our own moral and political challenges, he remains silent' ('The Forward March of History' [2 September 2002]).

25. See Martin Amis, *Koba the Dread: Laughter and the Twenty Million* (New York: Talk Miramax, 2002).

26. Christopher Hitchens, 'Lightness at Midnight', *Atlantic Monthly* (September 2002).

27. Christopher Hitchens, 'Don't. Be. Silly.', *Guardian* (4 September 2002).

28. John Lloyd, 'Show Trial: The Left in the Dock', *New Statesman* (2 September 2002). Lloyd's essay was redeemed by a *double entendre*, presumably unintended: '[The Left] needs a little prick to prompt reflection.' Amis' response to this characterisation is not known.

29. Charles Taylor, '*Koba the Dread*, by Martin Amis', *Salon* (16 July 2002), http://www.salon.com/books/review/2002/07/16/amis/.

30. John Pilger, *New Statesman* (17 September 2001); Tariq Ali, 'Hitchens at War', *Counterpunch* (26 September 2001), reprinted at http://humanities.psydeshow.org/political/tariq-ali.htm.

31. Robert Fisk, 'The Wickedness and Awesome Cruelty of a Crushed and Humiliated People', *Independent* (12 September 2001); Seumas Milne, 'They Can't See Why They Are Hated', *Guardian* (13

September 2001); Rana Kabbani, 'Terror Has Come Home', *Guardian* (13 September 2001).

32. 'In Buildings We Thought Indestructible', and Cristina Odone, 'Why is There No British Equivalent of the American Dream?', *New Statesman* (17 September 2001); Charlotte Raven, 'A Bully with a Bloody Nose is Still a Bully', *Guardian* (18 September 2001).

33. Jonathan Freedland, 'View from the Kitchen Table', *Guardian* (13 September 2001).

34. Frances Stonor Saunders, 'The End of the Open Society', *New Statesman* (17 September 2001); James Meek, 'Killer Germs', *Guardian* (24 September 2001).

35. Dilip Hiro, 'Saudi "Occupation" is Key to Attacks on America', *Observer* (23 September 2001); 'A Bitter Harvest', *The Economist* (15 September 2003).

36. Ahdaf Soueif, 'Our Poor, Our Weak, Our Hungry', *Guardian* (15 September 2001).

37. Fred Halliday, 'No Man is an Island', *Observer* (16 September 2001); Martin Woollacott, 'Don't Inflate the Size of the Enemy to Fit the Crime', *Guardian* (14 September 2001); Jonathan Steele, 'Force is not the Answer', *Guardian* (19 September 2001).

38. Polly Toynbee, 'The Middle Ground is the Second Casualty of This War', and Jon Snow, 'The War against Hatred', *Guardian* (19 September 2001).

39. Edward Said, 'Islam and the West are Inadequate Banners', *Observer* (16 September 2001).

40. Arundhati Roy, 'The Algebra of Infinite Justice', *Guardian* (29 September 2001).

41. Madeleine Bunting, 'A World Apart', *Guardian* (24 September 2001).

42. George Monbiot, 'The Need for Dissent', *Guardian* (18 September 2001).

43. 'This war will be won by diplomacy and intelligence, not just by armed might', *Independent* (22 September 2001); Brenda Maddox, 'Taliban Cannot Wait to Get Shot of its Dangerous Guest', *The Times* (21 September 2001); John Humphrys, 'It's Not Anti-American to See Both Sides of the Argument', *Sunday Times* (23 September 2001); 'So are We Really Sure He's Guilty?', *Daily Mail* (21 September 2001).

44. Quoted in 'How International Strategists see the Crisis Developing', *The Sunday Times* (30 September 2001).

45. John Arlidge, 'BBC Apologises to Envoy for Anti-American Abuse', *Observer* (16 September 2001).

46. '11 September', *London Review of Books* (4 October 2001). Others focused on the personal: Terry Castle was too dispirited ('I feel like an effigy') to return to a book review; Hal Foster bounced back, 'Come delight in the city again, swap stories, argue politics, see a show, have a drink'; Michael Wood dwelt on the pictures of people

jumping from the windows of the World Trade Center: 'Falling from an immense height is the nightmare of many of us, and the thought of choosing this death, of seeing and knowing and refusing a worse death, is surely beyond nightmare.'

47. Ian Buruma, 'They are Free to Speak Their Minds, So Why Don't Western Thinkers Tell the Truth about Tyranny in the Muslim World?', *Guardian* (9 October 2001).

48. Seumas Milne, 'Lurching towards Catastrophe', *Guardian* (11 October 2001); Gary Younge, 'War against the Weak', *Guardian* (1 October 2001); George Monbiot, 'Backyard Terrorism', *Guardian* (30 October 2001); Polly Toynbee, 'Limp Liberals Fail to Protect Their Most Profound Values', *Guardian* (10 October 2001); Jonathan Freedland, 'Wrong Tool for the Job', *Guardian* (31 October 2001).

49. 'The World at War', *Guardian* (8 October 2001).

50. Quoted in 'Is It Still a Good Idea?', *Guardian* (20 March 2002).

51. Paul Peachey, 'Charities under Attack for Humanitarian Pleas', *Independent* (22 October 2001).

52. Quoted in 'Chelsea Takes Offence at Oxford Classmates', *Guardian* (9 November 2001).

53. Robert Fisk, 'What Will the Northern Alliance Do in Our Name Now? I Dread to Think ... ', *Independent* (14 November 2001); Brenda Maddox, 'Allies Cannot Ignore Victors' Excesses', *The Times* (13 November 2001); Chris Stephen, 'Key Afghan Military Players', *Observer* (18 November 2001).

54. Peter Beaumont, 'Tyranny of Veil is Slow to Lift', *Observer* (30 December 2001); Polly Toynbee, 'Was It Worth It?', *Guardian* (13 November 2002).

55. Michael Boyce, 'We Must Win Hearts and Minds as Well as Battles', *Independent* (13 December 2001).

56. David Clark, 'Blair Must Stand up to Bush', *Guardian* (28 November 2001).

57. Ronan Bennett, 'The Return of Internment', *Guardian* (14 November 2001); Nick Cohen, 'Return of the H-Block', *Observer* (18 November 2001).

58. John Sutherland, *Guardian* (January 2002); Glover and *Daily Telegraph* quoted in Hugo Young, 'We Will Not Tolerate the Abuse of War Prisoners', *Guardian* (17 January 2002).

59. Richard Norton-Taylor, 'The War against Terror is Making Villains of Us All', *Guardian* (22 January 2002); Faisal Bodi, 'We Have No Loyalty to This State', *Guardian* (24 January 2002).

60. Andy Beckett, 'Did the Left Lose the War?', *Guardian* (17 January 2002).

61. Quoted in 'Is It Still a Good Idea?', *Guardian* (20 March 2002).

62. Margaret Thatcher, 'Islamism is the New Bolshevism', *Guardian* (12 February 2002).

63. Seumas Milne, 'Can the US Be Defeated?' *Guardian* (14 February 2002); Will Hutton, 'Time to Stop Being America's Lap-Dog', *Observer* (17 February 2002); Nick Cohen, 'Blair's Just a Bush Baby', *Observer* (10 March 2002).

64. Jonathan Freedland, 'Wedded to Another War', *Guardian* (13 March 2002); John O'Farrell, 'The Joys of War', *Guardian* (30 March 2002); Rod Liddle, 'Never Mind Saddam. What about Nuking the Belgians?', *Guardian* (13 March 2002).

65. Mary Riddell, 'Let Go of Dubya's Coat-Tails', *Observer* (3 March 2002). Perhaps most significantly, especially in light of his later support for intervention in Iraq, Cohen identified the roots of a US foreign policy of 'preponderance of power' in the 1992 Defense Policy Guidance drafted by Dick Cheney and Paul Wolfowitz: '[America] won't pull out [of the Persian Gulf] because Washington wants to "discourage" the "advanced industrial nations from challenging our leadership", while maintaining a military dominance capable of 'deterring potential competitors from even aspiring to a larger regional or global role' (Nick Cohen, 'With a Friend Like This ... ', *Observer* (7 April 2002)).

66. See Ian Jack, 'Censors and Sensibilities – An Everyday Tale of Literary Folk', *Guardian* (2 March 2002).

67. 'A World Transformed', *The Times* (9 March 2002).

68. Fred Halliday, 'New World, but the Same Old Disorder', and Abdel Bari Atwan, 'Americans are Masters of Destruction', *Observer* (10 March 2002).

69. BBC1, *Question Time* (11 September 2002).

70. Yasmin Alibhai-Brown, 'Questions from the Anti-War March for Mr Blair', *Independent* (30 September 2002); Euan Ferguson, 'A Big Day Out in Leftistan', *Observer* (29 September 2002).

71. Jonathan Petre, 'Carey "Wary" of Attack on Iraq', *Daily Telegraph* (30 September 2002); Clare Dyer, 'Ousting Saddam Illegal, PM Told', *Guardian* (8 October 2002); John Nichol, 'My Cuttings', *Guardian* (25 November 2002); Jackie Ashley, '"Little Joke" and How It Led to a Sense of Betrayal', *Guardian* (9 September 2002).

72. Woody Harrelson, 'I'm an American Tired of American Lies', *Guardian* (17 October 2002).

73. Julian Borger et al., 'US Hardline on Iraq Leaves Full-Scale Invasion a "Hair-Trigger" Away', *Guardian* (3 October 2002).

74. Correlli Barnett in the *Daily Mail* (25 September 2002); 'There's Nothing New in Blair's Dossier', *Mirror* (25 September 2002); Simon Jenkins, 'This is not a Dossier but an Act of Desperation', *The Times* (25 September 2002); Leader, *Financial Times* (2 October 2002).

75. Jonathan Freedland, 'Bali Proves that America's War on Terror Isn't Working', *Guardian* (15 October 2002); Oliver Burkeman and Ewen MacAskill, 'UN Vote Casts the Die', *Guardian* (9 November 2002).

76. Andrew Sullivan, 'Blair's Courage Makes the Anti-Americans Look Small', *Sunday Times* (19 January 2003); Michael Gove, 'Saddam's Useful Idiots Pollute the British Left', *The Times* (3 December 2002); Bill Emmott, 'Capitalism: Endangered Saviour of the Planet', *Sunday Times* (12 January 2003); Nicholas Lemann, 'Right Hand Woman', *Sunday Telegraph Magazine* (8 December 2002).

77. Bob Woodward, 'Marching off to War', *Sunday Times* (24 November 2002).

78. Polly Toynbee, 'This Great Government', *Guardian* (4 October 2002).

79. Timothy Garton Ash, 'Washington at War', *Guardian* (12 December 2002).

80. 'A Stretching Ocean', *Guardian* (9 November 2002).

81. Jackie Ashley, 'Instead of a Debate over War, There's Been a National Shrug', *Guardian* (23 December 2002).

82. 'If It's War, it Has to be Legitimate', *Observer* (22 December 2002).

83. Quoted in Ian Traynor, 'Experts Whose Verdict Could Start a War: But Can They Stop It?', *Guardian* (23 December 2002).

84. 'Iraq: Why Force May Be Needed', *Observer* (19 January 2003).

85. Nick Cohen, 'How to Stitch up a Terror Suspect', *Observer* (12 January 2003), and 'Saddam Won't Run', *Observer* (5 January 2003).

86. David Aaronovitch, 'The Ultimate Jewish Conspiracy Theory', *Guardian* (15 January 2003), and 'Stand up the Real Lady Bountiful', *Guardian* (21 January 2003).

87. Noam Chomsky, 'Drain the Swamp and There will be No More Mosquitoes', *Guardian* (9 September 2002); Harold Pinter, 'The American Administration is a Bloodthirsty Wild Animal', *Daily Telegraph* (11 December 2002).

88. Quoted in Richard Norton-Taylor, 'A Blindness that Puts Us All in Danger', *Guardian* (23 January 2003).

89. Stephen Bates, 'Archbishop Warns against Conflict', *Guardian* (27 December 2002).

90. Ghada Karmi, 'An Attack on Us All', *Guardian* (28 December 2002); Edward Said, 'When Will We Resist?', *Guardian* (25 January 2003).

91. Polly Toynbee, 'Three Resolutions to Help Blair Win Back Lost Friends', *Guardian* (3 January 2003), and 'The Blair Butterfly Needs to Come Back to Earth', *Guardian* (15 January 2003).

92. Martin Kettle, 'If Tony Blair Will not Speak for England, Then Who Will?', *Guardian* (28 January 2003).

93. Seumas Milne, 'Direct Action May Become a Necessity', *Guardian* (16 January 2003).

94. Burhan Wazir and Martin Bright, 'Anti-War Protests Span the Globe', *Observer* (19 January 2003).

95. Andy McSmith, 'A World against the War', *Independent on Sunday* (19 January 2003).

96. Ann Treneman, 'Peaceniks: The Unlikely Alliance', *The Times* (21 January 2003).

97. Andrew Gumbel, 'A Journey to the Heart of Middle America', *Independent* (28 January 2003); Duncan Campbell, 'We Don't Want a War Either, says Bagdad, California', *Guardian* (18 January 2003).

98. 'Take Time, then Act', and Ferdinand Mount, 'Paris and Berlin: The Axis of Weasel', *Sunday Times* (26 January 2003); Julian Borger, 'Rumsfeld "Offered Help to Saddam"', *Guardian* (31 December 2002); 'Madness in the Making', *Guardian* (11 January 2003); Duncan Campbell, 'US Interrogators Turn to "Torture Lite"', *Guardian* (25 January 2003).

99. 'Stop. Think. Listen'; and Robert Fisk, 'Does Tony have any Idea what the Flies are like that Feed off the Dead?', *Independent on Sunday* (26 January 2003).

100. Richard Sennett, 'This Time, One Country Indivisible', *Guardian* (17 September 2001).

101. Quoted in Peter Preston, 'Armchair Generals vs. "Prada-Meinhof Gang"', *Observer* (23 September 2001).

102. David Aaronovitch, 'Help! There's Been an Outbreak of Pinterism', *Independent* (21 September 2001).

103. Matthew Engel, 'Anti-War Message Blunted', *Guardian* (1 October 2001).

104. Ian Buruma, *Guardian* (28 January 2003).

105. Henry Porter, 'The Triumph of Reason', *Observer* (23 December 2001).

106. Patrick Wintour and Michael White, 'US Response "Changing Left's Hostility"', *Guardian* (29 September 2001); Peter Hain, 'Embrace Global Action', *Guardian* (9 February 2002).

107. Christopher Hitchens, 'Race and Rescue', *Slate* (1 February 2003), http://slate.msn.com/id/2078003/.

108. Quoted in 'Cakewalk', *Salon* (28 March 2003), http://www.salon.com/opinion/feature/2003/03/28/cakewalk/index_np.html.

109. BBC Radio 4, *Any Questions?* (31 January 2003).

6 Our Friends in America

1. CNN International, *International Correspondent* (October 2001).

2. Gustav Niebuhr, 'U.S. "Secular" Groups Set Tone for Terror Attacks, Falwell Says', *New York Times* (14 September 2001); Laurie Goodstein, 'Falwell's Finger-Pointing Inappropriate, Bush Says', *New York Times* (15 September 2001).

3. On the order to shoot down hijacked aircraft, see Bob Woodward, *Bush at War* (New York: Simon and Schuster, 2002), pp. 17–18.

4. Oliver Burkeman, 'Fox on the Run', *Guardian* (25 November 2002).

5. The summary of US press opinion is in 'What the Papers Say', *Guardian* (13 September 2001).

6. Maureen Dowd, 'Old Ruses, New Barbarians', and Paul Krugman, 'What to Do', *New York Times* (19 September 2001).

7. Quoted in Matthew Engel, 'No Room for Dissent as Spirit of Flagwaving Sweeps the Nation', *Guardian* (17 September 2001).

8. 'President Bush's Address on Terrorism Before a Joint Meeting of Congress', *New York Times* (21 September 2001).

9. Susan Sontag, 'First Reactions', *New Yorker* (24 September 2001).

10. Joel Rogers, 'The End of Innocence', *The Nation* (1 October 2001).

11. Katha Pollitt, 'Put Out No Flags', *The Nation* (8 October 2001).

12. Charles Krauthammer, 'Voices of Moral Obtuseness', *Washington Post* (21 September 2001).

13. Gary Younge, 'The Risk Taker', *Guardian* (19 January 2002).

14. Lawrence Kaplan, 'No Choice', *The New Republic* (1 October 2001); Jacob Weisberg, 'Left Behind', *Salon* (4 December 2001), www.slate.msn.com/id/2059328/.

The cruellest sneer at *The New Republic* was that of Leon Wieseltier, who upheld dissent to demolish it once and for all:

> Let us transgress the limit, and throw caution to the winds, and act like genuine intellectuals, and endanger our livelihoods, and risk the loss of friends and lovers, and think impermissible thoughts. To wit: Osama bin Laden is a shy, enigmatic, and cruelly misunderstood individual. There is nothing more urgent in the world than the satisfaction of the Palestinians, and the attacks on New York and Washington would not have happened if Israeli tanks had not spent a few hours in Jenin last month. Capitalism and democracy are the cunning devices of imperialism. The United States has brought mainly misery upon the nations of the earth. Saddam Hussein is an innocent victim of America's surrender to Zionism. Terrorism is a form of political criticism. The use of force against terrorists is not different from the use of force by terrorists. A greater measure of vigilance in America is really a greater measure of racism in America.
>
> It will be plain, I hope, that those propositions are not heroic. They are idiotic. The 'permissibility' of a thought has nothing to do with its truth or its falsity. It has to do only with the vanity of the individual who thinks it. But no matter. America is permissive (which is why America has been attacked). And we are one people. These heroes will have to be defended by those heroes, I mean the actual ones. ('Heroes', 15 October 2001).

15. Quoted in Richard Bernstein, 'Counterpoint to Unity: Dissent', *New York Times* (6 October 2001).

16. American Council of Trustees and Alumni (Jerry L. Martin and Anne D. Neal), 'Defending Civilization: How Our Universities Are Failing America and What Can Be Done About It',

http://www.goacta.org/publications/Reports/acta_american_memory.pdf.

17. Kristine McNeil, 'The War on Academic Freedom', *The Nation* (25 November 2002). In November 2002, the New York *Sun* built on a Campus Watch dossier and quoted Daniel Pipes to highlight Columbia University's offer of a chair to Rashid Khalidi, headlining, 'Pro-Palestinian Professor is Vocal Critic of Israel'. The newspaper reported, 'While Mr. Khalidi is respected among his fellow Middle East scholars, many of whom share his hostility toward Israel, he has also come under attack from other Middle East experts who say he is soft on militant Islam and excuses terrorism' (5 November 2002).

18. In June 2002, graduating seniors at Ohio State University were informed by loudspeaker 'that they would be expelled and arrested if they turned their backs' on Condoleezza Rice, the guest speaker at the commencement ceremony (Associated Press, 14 June 2002).

19. In 'The No Spin Zone', O'Reilly told the head of the American–Arab Anti-Discrimination Committee, questioning the treatment of al-Arian as a 'terrorist', 'With all due respect, Mr. Ibish, you know butkus.' When another guest, in a follow-up interview, challenged O'Reilly's tactics as 'guilt by association', the host responded, 'All right. Cut Mr Vickers' mike [microphone] forever.' [*Fox News*, 2 October 2001 and 15 January 2002]. See also Eric Bohlert, 'The Prime-Time Smearing of Sami al-Arian', *Salon* (19 January 2002), http://www.salon.com/tech/feature/2002/01/19/bubba/; Nicholas Kristof, 'Putting Us to the Test', *New York Times* (1 March 2002).

20. Eric Lichtblau and Judith Miller, 'Indictment Ties U.S. Professor to Terror Group', *New York Times* (21 February 2003).

21. Emily Wax, 'The Consequences of Objection', *Washington Post* (9 December 2001); Matthew Rothschild, 'McCarthyism Watch', *The Progressive* (14 December 2001), http://www.progressive.org/webex/wxmc1214a01.html.

22. George Monbiot, 'The Taliban of the West', *Guardian* (18 December 2001); Julia Scheeres, 'ACLU Acts against Patriot Act', *Wired* (16 October 2002), http://www.wired.com/news/conflict/0,2100, 55838,00.html.

23. Andrew Mandell, 'Puzzling at the Post Office', *Voices in the Wilderness* (24 November 2001), http://www.nonviolence.org/vitw/old_site/WH&P%20Update.html.

24. ABC Television, *Politically Incorrect* (17 September 2001).

25. Ari Fleischer press briefing (26 September 2001), http://www.whitehouse.gov/news/releases/2001/09/20010926-5.html; Walter Kim, 'The End of the Affair', *New York Times* (26 May 2002).

26. 'CNN Chief Claim US Media "Censored" War', *Press Gazette* (15 August 2002), http://www.pressgazette.co.uk/News.aspx?Action=View&ID=43301.

27. Kate Zernicke and Evelyn Nieves, 'New Generation Confronts Notions of War and Peace as Their World Changes', *New York Times* (21 September 2001).

28. Gore Vidal, 'The End of the Affair', *Index on Censorship* (22 November 2001), http://www.indexonline.org/news/202_20020426_vidal. shtml. The essay was published in Italy in a collection of Vidal's work, *La fine della libertà: verso una nuova totalitarianismo.*

29. Richard Bernstein, 'Counterpoint to Unity: Dissent', *New York Times* (6 October 2001); Alexander Star, 'If You Take My Advice … ', *New York Times* (9 December 2001).

30. Edward Rothstein, 'Attacks on U.S. Challenge the Perspectives of Postmodern True Believers', *New York Times* (22 September 2001); Patricia Cohen, 'Response to Attack Splits Arabs in the West', *New York Times* (29 September 2001).

31. See Eric Alterman, 'Affirmative Action Reaction', *The Nation* (1 July 2002).

32. Alessandra Staley, 'Opponents of the War are Scarce on Television', *New York Times Magazine* (9 November 2001).

33. Ed Vulliamy, 'Waving not Drowning', *Observer* (23 September 2001).

34. Thomas Friedman, 'Grapes of Wrath', *New York Times* (12 March 2003).

35. 'Op-Ed Echo Chamber: Little Space for Dissent to the Military Line', *Fairness and Accuracy in Reporting* (2 November 2001), http:// www.fair.org/activism/nyt-wp-opeds.html.

36. Steve Hill, 'Researchers: Magazines Silenced Opposition Voices after September 11', *University Week* (22 August 2002), http://depts. washington.edu/~uweek/archives/2002.08.AUG_22/news_b.html.

37. Cheryl Arvidson, 'Newspaper Editors are Critical of International News Coverage Following 9/11 Terrorist Attacks', *Pew Newswire* (10 June 2002).

38. Matt Wells, 'CNN to Carry Reminders of US Attacks', *Guardian* (1 November 2001). An alternative ending was 'The Pentagon has repeatedly stressed that it is trying to minimise civilian casualties in Afghanistan, even as the Taliban regime continues to harbour terrorists who are connected to the September 11 attacks that claimed thousands of innocent lives in the US.'

39. Richard Bernstein, 'No Sympathy for Terrorists, but Warnings about Overreaction', *New York Times* (6 October 2001). Jonathan Alter, 'Blame America at Your Peril', *Newsweek* (October 2001); Michael Kelly, ' … Pacifist Claptrap', *Washington Post* (26 September 2001).

40. Debra J. Saunders, 'Courage is the Last Casualty', *San Francisco Chronicle* (16 October 2001).

41. Quoted in BBC2, *Newsnight* (16 May 2002), transcript at http://news.bbc.co.uk/hi/english/audiovideo/programmes/ newsnight/archive/newsid_2029000/2029634.stm.

42. Michael Walzer, 'Can There be a Decent Left?', *Dissent* (Spring 2002).

43. Joe Klein, 'It's Interrogation, not Torture', *Guardian* (4 February 2002).

44. Joe Klein, 'France? It's Like 1970s America', *Guardian* (28 May 2002).

45. Thomas Friedman, 'Enough is Enough, It's Time the US Got its Turkey Back', *Guardian* (16 February 2002).

46. Matthew Engel, 'To Complain is to be UnAmerican', *Guardian* (23 January 2002). Kurtz and Thompson quoted in Howard Kurtz, 'War Coverage Takes a Negative Turn', *Washington Post* (17 February 2002).

47. Salim Muwakkil, 'Pipeline Politics Taint US War', *Chicago Tribune* (18 March 2002).

48. Paul Kennedy, 'Has the US Lost its Way?', *Observer* (3 March 2002).

49. Thomas Friedman, 'Enough is Enough, It's Time the US Got its Turkey Back', *Guardian* (16 February 2002).

50. Robert Fisk, 'America "Chasing Phantoms" in Iraq, Says Arms Expert', *Independent* (17 February 2002); Courtland Milloy, 'A Call to Arms: An Enemy of War Against Iraq', *Washington Post* (13 November 2002).

51. Quoted in *West Virginia Gazette* (29 June 2002). Byrd also asked, 'If we expect to kill every terrorist in the world, that's going to keep us going beyond Doomsday. How long can we afford this?' (Quoted in Jonathan Steele, 'A Premature Declaration of Victory', *Guardian*, 12 March 2002).

52. Kucinich speech (17 February 2002), reprinted at http://www.house.gov/kucinich/press/sp-020217-prayer.htm.

53. Cynthia McKinney statement (12 April 2002), reprinted at http://www.ratical.org/co-globalize/CynthiaMcKinney/news/pr020412.htm.

54. Frank Rich, 'The Bush Doctrine, R.I.P.', *New York Times* (13 April 2002).

55. Not in Our Name, 'We Won't Deny our Consciences', and Duncan Campbell, 'US Artists Deny "War without Limit"', *Guardian* (14 June 2002). A subsequent letter opposing the invasion of Iraq was written by faculty at the University of Minnesota, distributed to other institutions, and placed on the web by faculty at MIT. Within five weeks, it had been signed by more than 30,000 people, including 14,000 academics ('Bush has Failed to Make Case for Attack: Academics', *New York Times*, 2 November 2002).

56. Thomas Friedman, 'A Failure to Imagine', *New York Times* (19 May 2002).

57. See Paul Krugman, 'Everyone is Outraged', *New York Times* (2 July 2002).

58. Enron Gave Taliban $Millions', *National Enquirer* (4 March 2002), http://www.nationalenquirer.com/stories/feature.cfm?instanceid=22359.

59. Howard Kurtz, 'As Reporters Seek Details, The Media Climate Shifts', *Washington Post* (17 May 2002).

60. Frank Rich, 'The Jack Welch War Plan', *New York Times* (28 September 2002).

61. Helen Thomas, 'Bush Acting as Imperial President', *Seattle Post-Intelligencer* (3 July 2002).

62. Philip Delves Broughton, 'Bush Jokes as French Leader Airs Criticism', *Daily Telegraph* (27 May 2002). Bush had been angered when the reporter, David Gregory of NBC, asked him and Chirac about 'anti-American' demonstrations in Paris. As he left the podium, he called to Gregory, 'As soon as you get in front of a camera, you start showing off' (Mary McGrory, 'Hesitant Hawks', *Washington Post*, 30 May 2002).

63. 'Bush Hooked by Putin's Fishy Tale', *Reuters* (25 May 2002), reprinted at http://www.philly.com/mld/philly/news/politics/3336746.htm.

64. Dana Milbank, 'The Adventures of Intercontinental Man', *Washington Post* (28 May 2002). As Milbank noted, 'Presumably [Bush] did not mean the literal definition of "securities", which is to turn a commodity into a stock that can be traded – Russian nukes on the Chicago Board of Trade'.

65. CNN, *American Morning* (30 May 2002). Chomsky debated his best-selling book *9–11* with former Reagan Administration 'drug czar' Bill Bennett. Chomsky was invited, however, only after CNN had done an earlier segment on *9–11*, in which Bill Bennett 'discussed' the book with host Paula Zahn. Viewer protests that Chomsky was not present to defend his work led to his belated appearance (*American Morning*, 9 May 2002).

66. 'Striking First', *New York Times* (23 June 2002); Mark Morford, 'Let Us Now Crush Everybody', *San Francisco Chronicle* (12 June 2002).

67. Dick Meyer, 'John Ashcroft: Minister of Fear', *CBS News.com* (12 June 2002).

68. Jonah Goldberg, 'Representative Awful', *National Review Online* (12 April 2002), 'Guilt and Arrogance' (1 May 2002), and 'Blame Islam', *National Review Online* (12 July 2002).

69. Andrew Sullivan, 'America's Left Surrenders Itself to the Giant Sulk', *Sunday Times* (30 March 2002).

70. The Cavuto comment was circulated on the *Guardian Unlimited* talkboards in autumn 2002.

71. Todd Purdum and Patrick Tyler, 'Top Republicans Break with Bush on Iraq Strategy', *New York Times* (16 August 2002); William F. Buckley, 'Saddam Hussein – Man or Mouse?', *Sacromento Bee* (2 August 2002).

72. Charles Kaiser, 'A War of Words', *Guardian* (9 September 2002); Duncan Campbell, 'Bush's Secret Visa Courts after Sept 11 Ruled Illegal', *Guardian* (28 August 2002).

73. Thomas Friedman, 'Bush's Mideast Sand Trap', *New York Times* (21 August 2002).

74. Susan Sontag, 'Real Battles and Empty Metaphors', *New York Times* (10 September 2002).

75. Maureen Dowd, 'Texas on the Tigris', *New York Times* (13 October 2002); William Raspberry, 'Bush's Worst-Case Scenario', *Washington Post* (14 September 2002). See also Molly Ivins on the 2002 National Security Strategy 'No. This is not acceptable. This is not the country we want to be. This is not the world we want to make. The United States of America is still run by its citizens. The govt works for us. Rank imperialism and warmongering are not American traditions or values. We do not need to dominate the world. We want and need to work with other nations. We want to find solutions other than killing people. Not in our name, not with our money, not with our children's blood' ('Just Say No War', *Texas Observer*, 11 October 2002).

76. Simon Schama, 'A Whiff of Dread for the Land of Hope', *New York Times* (15 September 2002).

77. 'Rights and the New Reality', *Los Angeles Times* (8 September 2002).

78. Adam Nagourney, 'Barbra Streisand to Step up for Democrats', *New York Times* (19 September 2002).

79. James Fallows, 'The Fifty-First State?', *The Atlantic* (November 2002).

80. 'A Reckless Rush to War', *The American Prospect* (25 September 2002). Speaking in Britain, Bonnie Greer claimed, 'The dangerous thing that's happening in America that no one talks about is that there's actually a gulag there now. There is a place where people have disappeared. I know people who have vanished. People know people who have vanished. People are afraid to speak out. I've been afraid to say things' (BBC Radio 4, *Broadcasting House*, 8 September 2002).

81. Fareed Zakaria, 'The End of the End of History', *Newsweek* (24 September 2001); Zakaria Friedman quoted in Ed Vulliamy, 'War Plans under Fire as Even Bush Heartland Talks Peace', *Observer* (20 October 2002).

82. Jay Bookman, 'Bush's Real Goal in Iraq: Invasion Would Mark the Next Step Toward an American Empire', *Atlanta Journal-Constitution* (29 September 2002).

83. Joe Klein, 'Democrats Can't Duck This Fundamental Shift in American Policy', *Guardian* (3 October 2002).

84. David Postman, 'McDermott Accuses Bush of Plotting to be Emperor', *Seattle Times* (7 October 2002); 'Church Executive Urges Bush Not to Attack Iraq', *United Methodist News Service* (3 September 2002), http://umns.umc.org/02/sep/384.htm; Ed Vulliamy, 'Iraq War "Unjustifiable", says Bush's Church Head', *Observer* (20 October

2002); Anthony Lewis, 'Bush and Iraq', *New York Review of Books* (7 November 2002). The conservative activist Arianna Huffington joined in the criticism of Bush, 'In this latest rewrite of history, Osama has suddenly lost his beard and grown a mustache, morphing into the Butcher of Baghdad … [The President] can't differentiate between a group of evil ultra-radical Islamic fundamentalists that carried out the Sept. 11 attacks and an evil secular nationalist who, despite the frantic efforts of the Bush administration, has not been directly linked to 9/11' ('The White House on Iraq: We Don't Need No Stinkin' Proof', *Arianna Online*, 30 September 2002, http://www.ariannaonline.com/columns/files/093002.html).

85. Ed Vulliamy, 'War Plans under Fire as Even Bush Heartland Talks Peace', *Observer* (20 October 2002).

86. Greil Marcus, 'Nothing New under the Sun', *First of the Month* (Autumn 2002), http://www.firstofthemonth.org/9_11/9_11_marcus_nothing.html.

87. Todd Gitlin, 'Blaming America First', *Mother Jones* (January/February 2002).

88. Todd Gitlin, 'Who Will Lead?', *Mother Jones* (October 2002).

89. George Packer, 'The Liberal Quandary over Iraq', *New York Times Magazine* (8 December 2002). A reader put Packer and the *New York Times* in their proper places, 'Missing from Packer's article were liberal voices opposed to a so-called war with Iraq: Noam Chomsky, Howard Zinn, Michael Lerner and Cornel West, to name a few. The news media have virtually excluded anti-war voices. Remarkable. Paul Wellstone [the anti-war Senator from Minnesota, who died in October 2002 in a plane crash], we miss you' (Gif Fariello, 'The Liberal Quandary over Iraq', *New York Times Magazine*, 22 December 2002).

90. Michael J. Totten, 'A Liberal's Case for Bush's War', *Front PageMagazine.com* (8 January 2003), URL. See also the critique of Richard Goldstein, 'Leftists Who Love the War Too Much', *Village Voice* (30 October 2002).

91. 'Buoyant Bush Wins Mandate for War', *The Times* (7 November 2002).

92. Danny Schechter, 'War Dances and Media Complaints', *Globalvision News Network* (6 March 2003), reprinted at http://www.alternet.org/story.html?StoryID=15312.

93. 'Knocking on Hussein's Door', *Chicago Tribune* (14 November 2002).

94. 'A Nation Wary of War', *New York Times* (8 October 2002); 'Iraq in the Dock', *New York Times* (10 December 2002).

95. John Hughes, 'How Can the US Not Act on Iraq?', *Christian Science Monitor* (11 December 2002).

96. William Raspberry, 'Questions that Bother and Bewilder', *Washington Post* (30 December 2002). Or, as Jay Bookman of the *Atlanta Journal-*

Constitution, one of the few journalists to consider the long-term strategy of the Bush Administration (see Chapter 7), wrote, 'This war, should it come, is intended to mark the official emergence of the United States as a full-fledged global empire, seizing sole responsibility and authority as planetary policeman' ('An Empire by Any Other Name', 6 October 2002).

97. Thomas Friedman, 'The New Math', *New York Times* (15 January 2003).

98. See Stuart Reid, 'The Odd Coupling', *Guardian* (4 November 2002).

99. Michael Getler, 'Worth More than a One-Liner', *Washington Post* (6 October 2002).

100. Jennifer Barrett, 'Where's the Dissent?', *Newsweek* (16 January 2003 web edition).

101. 'Crowds Cry for Peace in Washington, across U.S., Around the World', Fox News (18 January 2003); 'W Pushes War, but People Push Back', *New York Daily News* (30 January 2003). Other national television networks aired similar reports with a neutrality which had not been present since 9–11.

102. 'Chew on This', *The Stranger.com* (16–22 January 2003), http://www.thestranger.com/2003–01–16/feature2.html.

103. 'Pious Nonsense', *Slate* (10 March 2003), http://slate.msn.com/id/2079860/.

104. PBS, *Now with Bill Moyers* (20 December 2002); CNN, *Lou Dobbs Moneyline* (13 March 2003). Or, as Hitchens assured in the *Mirror*, '[Bush] has intelligence reports which will one day be made public, showing that the "inspectors" have been infiltrated by Saddam' ('Bush is Bored with Iraq Argument', 10 March 2003).

105. The account of Hitchens 'in [a] smalltown outside Seattle' is 'We're Still Standing', *Evening Standard* (13 September 2001). The revised account of Hitchens in Washington, DC, was offered to PBS, *Now with Bill Moyers* (20 December 2002).

106. 'Chew on This', *The Stranger.com* (16–22 January 2003), http://www.thestranger.com/ 2003–01–16/feature2. html.

7 How We Dissent:
On Bushmen and the 'Preponderance of Power'

1. Susan Sontag, 'September 11, 2001', *The New Yorker* (24 September 2001); Mary Beard, '11 September', *London Review of Books* (4 October 2001).

2. 'Bush planned Iraq "regime change" before becoming President', Glasgow *Sunday Herald* (15 September 2002); Project for a New American Century, *Rebuilding America's Defenses: Strategy, Forces, and Resources for a New Century* (September 2000), http://www.newamericancentury.org/RebuildingAmericasDefenses.pdf;

The National Security Strategy of the United States of America, September 2002, http://www.whitehouse.gov/nsc/nss.pdf.; Francis Fitzgerald, 'George Bush and the World', *New York Review of Books* (26 September 2002).

3. Karen DeYoung and Mike Allen, 'Bush Shifts Strategy from Deterrence to Dominance', *Washington Post* (21 September 2002). Thomas Barnett, an adviser to the Pentagon and Professor at the Naval War College, has written at length that 'our next war in the Gulf ... [will] mark a historical tipping point – the moment when Washington takes real ownership of strategic security in the age of globalization' through control of 'the Non-Integrating Gap ... namely the Caribbean Rim, virtually all of Africa, the Balkans, the Caucasus, Central Asia, the Middle East and Southwest Asia, and much of Southeast Asia' ('The Pentagon's New Map', *Esquire*, March 2003, http://www.nwc.navy.mil/newrulesets/ThePentagons NewMap.htm). The editor of *Esquire* magazine effused to readers that the Professor's presentation to his staff 'was amazing and kind of breathtaking. It made each of us feel as though we had a slightly better grip on some of the most frightening issues ever to face our country and the world. I hope it has the same effect on you, making your life a little better.'

4. Excerpts from the 1992 Defense Planning Guidance were published in the *New York Times* of 18 February 1992. The initial document was watered down after it was leaked to the press, provoking criticism inside and outside Washington. The revised version was profiled in the *New York Times* on 24 May 1992.

    Another link between the first and second Bush Administrations was the public testing of the strategy by Zalmay Khalilzad in a book, *From Containment to Global Leadership?: America and the World after the Cold War* (Santa Monica, CA: RAND, 1995). Khalilzad joined Cheney's staff in 1991; ten years later, after a stint as a consultant to the oil company Unocal, he would become the second President Bush's envoy to post-Taliban Afghanistan.

5. William Kristol and Robert Kagan, 'Toward a Neo-Reaganite Foreign Policy', *Foreign Affairs* (July–August 1996); Project for a New American Century, *Rebuilding America's Defenses*.

6. Jay Bookman,'Bush's Real Goal in Iraq: Invasion would Mark the Next Step toward an American Empire', *Atlanta Journal-Constitution* (29 September 2002); Project for a New American Century, *Rebuilding America's Defenses*; Bill Berkowitz, 'Wars of Domestic Destruction', *Working for Change* (26 February 2003), http://www. workingforchange.com/article.cfm?itemid=14559.

7. Jason Vest, 'Turkey, Israel, and the US', *The Nation* (2 September 2002 web issue); Robert Kaiser, 'Bush and Sharon Nearly Identical on Mideast Policy', *Washington Post* (9 February 2003). Eliot Abrams, the hardline anti-Communist involved in the Iran–Contra scandal

in the 1980s, returned to the National Security Council in 2002 to take charge of Middle Eastern affairs. He began replacing 'even-handed' NSC staff with assistants who would take a 'harder pro-Israel stance' (Richard Sale, 'Staff change means Mideast Policy Shift', *United Press International*, 26 February 2003).

8. Jason Vest, 'The Men from JINSA and CSP', *The Nation* (2 September 2002); Jack Shafer, 'The Power Point that Rocked the Pentagon', *Slate* (7 August 2002), http://slate.msn.com/?id=2069119#powerpoint. In the American media the illusion is maintained that Perle is simply a 'private' citizen with some forthright opinions. When interviewed on British programmes, such as BBC's *Newsnight*, his Defense Policy Board role is highlighted, but on CNN he is merely referred to as a 'former Assistant Secretary of Defense' now connected with the American Enterprise Institute. See, for example, CNN's *Lou Dobbs' Moneyline* (24 February 2003).

9. Charles Moore et al., 'You Can Only Defend by Finding Terrorists and Rooting Them Out', *Daily Telegraph* (25 February 2002).

10. Interviews with Colin Powell, Richard Perle, William Kristol and Brent Scowcroft in PBS, *Frontline: The War Behind Closed Doors* (20 February 2003).

11. Project for the New American Century letter to Clinton (26 January 1998), http://www.newamericancentury.org/iraqclintonletter.htm. The letter led to a meeting between Rumsfeld, Wolfowitz, Perle and Clinton's National Security Adviser Sandy Berger, but, Rumsfeld complained, 'Sandy Berger's response had to do with how [the overthrow of Saddam] would look and not with what it meant for our security.' The PNAC turned to Newt Gingrich and Senate Majority Leader Trent Lott for 'force to protect our vital interests in the Gulf – and, if necessary, to help remove Saddam from power ... indicting him as a war criminal' (Project for the New American Century letter to Gingrich and Lott, 29 May 1998, http://www.newamericancentury.org/iraqletter1998.htm).

12. Project for a New American Century, *Rebuilding America's Defenses*.

13. Evan Thomas of *Newsweek*, quoted in Public Broadcasting System, *Frontline: Gunning for Saddam* (8 November 2001).

14. Elaine Sciolino, *New York Times*, quoted in *Gunning for Saddam*; Neil Mackay, 'Official: US oil at the heart of Iraq crisis', Glasgow *Sunday Herald* (6 October 2002). Sciolino summarised the Iraq debate inside the Administration: 'Colin Powell has said over the years that Saddam Hussein is like a toothache, and it recurs from time to time and you just have to live with it. At other times, he's compared Saddam Hussein to a kidney stone that will eventually pass. But he has never said you have to operate and take out the kidney stone.'

15. Dick Cheney, 'Defense Strategy for the 1990s: The Regional Defense Strategy' (January 1993), http://www.naarpr.org/naarpr_Defense.pdf.

16. Roger Cohen, 'Shifts in Europe Pose Prickly Challenge to U.S.', *New York Times* (11 February 2001).

17. William H. Smith, 'Europeans Hardly Fit to Preach to the USA', *USA Today* (15 June 2001).

18. Elizabeth Becker, 'On World Court U.S. Focus Shifts to Shielding Officials', *New York Times* (7 September 2002); 'Bush Withholds Backing of EPA Report on Warming', *Washington Post* (5 June 2002); Peter Slevin, 'U.S. Drops Bid to Strengthen Germ Warfare Accord', *Washington Post* (19 September 2002); Judith Miller, 'Threats and Responses: Chemical Weapons', *New York Times* (12 November 2002); 'U.N.: Defend Civilians in Terror War', *Newsday* (30 July 2002). See Federation of American Scientists, 'US Biodefense Program', http://www.fas.org/bwc/usbiodefense.htm on new secret US biological and chemical projects.

19. Molly Ivins, 'Oily Residue on Cheney's Hands', *Sacramento Bee* (3 September 2002). See also Jeff Gerth and Don Von Natta, 'In Tough Times, a Company Finds Profits in Terror War', *New York Times* (13 July 2002). The ultimate link was the revelation in 'alternative' media that part of the finance for the younger President Bush's entry into the oil business was $50 million provided by the Texan business adviser to Osama bin Laden's eldest brother. Even after 9–11, the link was maintained through the Carlyle Group's handling of investments for the bin Laden family. Robert Scheer, 'Making Money the Bush Way', *Los Angeles Times* (19 February 2002), at http://www.commondreams.org/views02/0219-05.htm.

20. See Dan Brody, *The Iron Triangle: Inside the Secret World of the Carlyle Group* (London: John Wiley, 2003).

21. Larry Chin, 'Unocal and the Afghan Pipeline', *Centre for Research and Globalisation Online Journal* (6 March 2002), http://globalresearch.ca/articles/CHI203A.html; Robert Scheer, 'Bush's Faustian Deal with the Taliban', *Los Angeles Times* (22 May 2001); Camelia Fard and James Ridgway, 'The Accidental Operative', *Village Voice* (6 June 2001).

22. Jean-Charles Brisard and Guillaume Dasquié, *Ben Laden, la Verité interdite* (Paris: Denoël, 2001); Jonathan Steele et al., 'Threat of US Strikes Passed to Taliban Weeks before NY Attack', *Guardian* (22 September 2001). The final meeting between a US official and the Taliban was 2 August when Christina Rocca, the director of Asian Affairs at the State Department, met the Taliban Ambassador in Islamabad. In the 1980s Rocca was at the CIA supervising contacts with Islamist guerrilla groups, including the delivery of Stinger missiles to Afghan mujaheddin. An aide of the Taliban's Foreign Minister, Wakil Ahmed Muttawakil, warned US and UN contacts in July 2001 'that Osama bin Laden was going to launch an attack on the United States'. The aide did not indicate that he had come directly from Muttawakil, however, and the warning was

disregarded. A source told the *Independent*, 'As I recall, I thought he was speaking from his own personal perspective. It was interesting that he was from the Foreign Affairs Ministry, but he gave no indication this was a message he was carrying.' ('Revealed: The Taliban Minister, the US Envoy and the Warning of September 11 that was Ignored', (7 September 2002).

23. Bob Drogin, 'U.S. Tells of Covert Afghan Plans Before 9/11', *Los Angeles Times* (18 May 2002).

24. Stephen Kinzer, 'Today's Silk Road Might Carry Black Gold', *New York Times Week in Review* (17 March 2002); Marjorie Cohn, 'The Deadly Pipeline War: U.S. Afghan Policy Driven by Oil Interests', *Jurist* (7 December 2001), http://www.jurist.law.pitt.edu/forum/forumnew41. php.

25. Jonathan Tepperman, 'Can Mercenaries Protect Hamid Karzai?', *The New Republic* (25 November 2002).

26. Carlotta Gall, 'Afghan Raid Leaves a Trail of Shock, Grief, and Anger', *New York Times* (5 July 2002).

27. 'Faction leader survives CIA assassination attempt', *Sydney Morning Herald* (10 May 2002).

28. Kate Connolly and Rory McCarthy, 'New Film Accuses US of War Crimes', *Guardian* (13 June 2002). See also Ben Nichols, 'Prisoners of War Held in Horrific Conditions in Afghan Jails', *World Socialist Web Site* (27 May 2002), http://www.wsws.org/articles/2002/ may2002/afgh-m27.shtml.

29. Jason Bennetto, 'Massive Post-War Rise in Production of Afghan Opium', *Independent* (26 September 2002).

30. Jonathan Steele, 'Women Lead Protests as Afghan Warlords Muscle in on Power', *Guardian* (13 June 2002); Jennifer Seymour Whitaker, 'Women at Risk in Afghanistan', *Boston Globe* (30 July 2002).

31. Madeleine Bunting, 'This Futile Campaign', *Guardian* (20 May 2002).

32. 'Rumsfeld: Ungrateful World Kicks U.S. Off Rights Panel', *CNN.com* (6 May 2001), http://www.cnn.com/2001/US/05/06/us.rights/index. html.

33. Quoted in Maureen Dowd, 'I Vant to Be Alone', *New York Times* (12 March 2003).

34. 'Bush Says US Will Strike First', *BBC News* (1 June 2002), http://news.bbc.co.uk/1/hi/world/americas/2020813.stm. See Max Boot, 'Doctrine of the "Big Enchilada"', *Washington Post* (14 October 2002). Jonathan Schell, in a devastating critique of 'pre-emption', has noted the break of the second Bush Administration with previous US policy: 'The proposal was never seriously considered by President Truman and, until now, has been rejected by every subsequent President' ('The Case against War', *The Nation*, 3 March 2003).

35. Susan Milligan, 'Critics Fault Rumsfeld for Cutting Oversight of Antimissile Plan', *Boston Globe* (9 March 2002); Duncan Campbell,

'Star Wars Arrives in Alaska Moose Country', *Observer* (16 June 2002).

36. 'US Missile Defence Test Dodges Decoys', *NewScientist.com* (15 October 2002), http://www.newscientist.com/news/news.jsp?id= ns99992924.

37. Juan Forero, 'Administration Shifts Focus on Colombia Aid', *New York Times* (6 February 2002); James Dao, 'Warm Reaction to Bigger Pentagon Budget', *New York Times* (13 February 2002); Julian Borger, 'Pentagon Outlines Plans to Take War on Terror to Georgia', *Guardian* (28 February 2002); Barbara Starr, 'U.S. turns to Africa for al Qaeda' *CNN.com* (18 September 2002), http://www.cnn.com/2002/ US/09/18/alqaeda.starr.otsc/index.html. 'Since September 2001 US forces have built, upgraded or expanded military facilities in Bahrain, Qatar, Kuwait, Saudi Arabia, Oman, Turkey, Bulgaria, Pakistan, Afghanistan, Uzbekistan and Kyrgyzstan; authorized extended training missions or open-ended troop deployments in Djibouti, the Philippines and the former Soviet republic of Georgia; negotiated access to airfields in Kazakhstan; and engaged in major military exercises, involving thousands of US personnel, in Jordan, Kuwait and India. Thousands of tons of military equipment have been added to stockpiles already pre-positioned in Middle Eastern and Persian Gulf states, including Israel, Jordan, Kuwait and Qatar. And discussions are still under way with Yemen about increasing American access to facilities there and establishing an intelligence-gathering installation aimed at monitoring activities in Sudan and Somalia' (William Hartung et al., 'Operation Endless Deployment', *The Nation*, 21 October 2002).

38. 'U.S. Drops Pledge on Nukes', *Washington Times* (22 February 2002).

39. Alexandra Williams and Bob Roberts, 'Bush's Nuclear "Lunacy"', *Mirror* (11 March 2002).

40. Susan Schmidt and Thomas E. Ricks, 'Pentagon Plans Shift in War on Terror', *Washington Post* (18 September 2002); William Arkin, 'The Secret War', *Los Angeles Times* (27 October 2002).

41. Nicholas Lemann, 'The Next World Order', *The New Yorker* (1 April 2002); Steven Wiesman, 'Pre-emption: Idea with a Lineage whose Time has Come', *New York Times* (23 March 2003).

42. Chris Floyd, 'Into the Dark: The Pentagon Plan to Provoke Terrorist Attacks', *Counterpunch* (1 November 2002), http://www. counterpunch.org/floyd1101.html. In the early 1960s the US military drafted Operation Northwoods, in which 'terrorist' acts would be staged in American cities to provoke war with Cuba (David Ruppe, 'Friendly Fire', *ABCNews.com*, http://abcnews.go.com/ sections/us/DailyNews/jointchiefs_010501.html).

43. Mike Allen, 'Bush Asserts That Al Qaeda Has Links to Iraq's Hussein', *Washington Post* (26 September 2002).

44. 'Plans for Iraq Attack Began on 9/11', *CBSNews.com* (4 September 2002), http://www.cbsnews.com/stories/2002/09/04/september11/main520830.shtml.

45. Bob Woodward, *Bush at War* (New York: Simon and Schuster, 2002). See also the comments of Kenneth Pollack, then with the National Security Council staff: 'From the first moments after September 11th, there was a group of people both inside the administration and out who believed that the war on terrorism should target Iraq – in fact, should target Iraq first. They made Saddam Hussein out to be the greatest threat to the United States and the source of all evil, if not in the world, then certainly in the Middle East. And they were pushing very early on to make Iraq the first stop in the war on terrorism' (quoted in *Frontline: The War Behind Closed Doors*).

46. Quoted in *Frontline: The War Behind Closed Doors*.

47. Quoted in *Frontline: Gunning for Saddam*.

48. Project for a New American Century to Bush, 20 September 2001, http://www.newamericancentury.org/Bushletter.

49. Andrew Murray, 'Spinning to War on Iraq', *Guardian* (4 March 2002).

50. Peter Beaumont et al., 'Secret US Plan for Iraq War', *Observer* (2 December 2001).

51. Michael Elliott and James Carney, 'First Stop Iraq', *Time* (31 March 2003).

52. CNN, *Capital Gang* (18 January 2003).

53. Roland Watson, 'The Servant Who Wields Power over Policy from the Shadows', *The Times* (24 March 2003).

54. Project for a New American Century to Bush, 20 September 2001.

55. David Frum, quoted in Julian Borger, 'How I Created the Axis of Evil', *Guardian* (28 January 2003).

56. Eric Schmitt, 'Bush Tells Iran not to Undercut Afghan Leaders', *New York Times* (11 January 2002).

57. Suzanne Goldenberg, 'Global Aid for Kabul, Iranian Arms for Heart', *Guardian* (24 January 2002).

58. CBS, *Face the Nation* (3 February 2002).

59. Neil MacFarquhar, 'Millions in Iran Rally Against U.S.', *New York Times* (12 February 2002).

60. Rob Sabhani on CNN, *Wolf Blitzer Reports* (13 February 2002).

61. 'Inside Iran: A Regime That May Not Be as Secure as it Looks', *The Times* (4 February 2002); Armitage quoted in CBS, 'Hezbollah: "A-Team of Terrorists"', *60 Minutes* (18 April 2003). *The Times* raised the possibility that a name from pre-Revolution days could save Iran, as did the *Wall Street Journal*, 'The man emerging as an important figurehead of the nascent rebellion is none other than the late shah's son, Reza Pahlavi. The 41-year-old former fighter pilot has spent most of his two-decade exile living in obscurity in Maryland. Long-forgotten in Iran, he literally materialized in many Iranian

homes this year from thin air, over satellite-television broadcasts beamed in from Los Angeles. His agenda – nonviolent civil disobedience, secular democracy, separation of mosque and state – is tailor-made for Iran's restive youth, fed up with the constant harassment and petty intrusions of the militia' (Hugh Pope, 'Winds of Change: Iran's Islamic Leaders Face Sudden Unrest since Terror Attacks', *Wall Street Journal*, 5 November 2001).

62. Wes Vernon, 'U.S. Says China, Russia, Cuba, Syria, Libya Abet Terrorism', *Newsmax.com* (7 May 2002), http://205.180.85.40/ w/pc.cgi?mid=17873&sid=9665. Bolton was another example of a 'hawk' who had moved from the network of the PNAC and allied organisations into the Bush Administration, possibly as a balance to and even check upon the 'dovish' Colin Powell (Ian Williams, 'Bush's Hatchet Man in the State Department', *Salon*, 10 May 2002, http://www.salon.com/politics/feature/2002/05/10/bolton/index_ np.html).

63. 'The Top Ten Conservative Idiots (No. 66)', *Democratic Underground* (6 May 2002), http://www.democraticunderground.com/top10/ 02/66.html.

64. Conn Hallinan, 'US Cooking Up a Coup in Venezuela?', *San Francisco Examiner* (28 December 2001); Alan Bock, 'Financing Venezuelan Mischief', *antiwar.com* (30 April 2002), http://www.antiwar.com/ bock/b043002.html.

65. Marcela Sanchez, 'Bush Administration Stumbles again in Venezuela', *Washington Post* (19 December 2002); Alex Bellos, 'Strike Forces Oil Exporting Venezuela to Import Fuel', *Guardian* (28 December 2002); 'Democracy's Last Chance', *Washington Post* (1 March 2003).

66. Paul Knox, 'Rights Trampled in U.S., Report Says', *Common Dreams* (15 August 2002), http://www.commondreams.org/headlines02/ 0815-01.htm.

67. A challenge in a Federal court to the detentions was dismissed on 11 March 2003. See the editorial responses of the *New York Times*, 'Forsaken at Guantanamo' (12 March 2003), and the *Independent*, 'It is Wrong to Deny Prisoners Any Rights' (13 March 2003).

68. Scarlet Pruitt, 'Groups Rally against US Domestic Snooping Powers', *InfoWorld.com* (20 September 2002), http://www.infoworld.com/ articles/hn/xml/02/09/20/020920hnsnoop.xml; Declan McCullough, 'Secret U.S. Court OKs Electronic Spying', *CNET News.com* (18 November 2002), http://news.com.com/2100-1023-966311.html.

69. Dan Eggen and Robert O'Harrow, 'U.S. Steps Up Secret Surveillance', *Washington Post* (24 March 2003).

70. Curt Anderson, 'FBI Has Fleet of Aircraft Helping to Track Suspects in War on Terror', *Associated Press* (14 March 2003).

71. Susan Schmidt and Dan Eggen, 'FBI Given More Latitude', *Washington Post* (30 May 2002); 'FBI Quizzes Libraries on Suspects'

Reading Habits', *Index on Censorship* (27 June 2002), http://www.indexonline.org/indexindex/20020627_unitedstates.shtml; Lawrence Donegan, 'Anger as CIA Homes in on New Target: Library Users', *Observer* (16 March 2003).

72. John Markoff, 'Chief Takes over at Agency to Thwart Attacks on U.S.', *New York Times* (13 February 2002); William Safire, 'You Are a Suspect', *New York Times* (14 November 2002); 'A Snooper's Dream', *New York Times* (18 November 2002).

73. Neil Lewis, 'Court Overturns Limits on Wiretaps to Combat Terror', *New York Times* (19 November 2002).

74. Bill Berkowitz, 'AmeriSnitch', *The Progressive* (24 May 2002); Jeremy Lott, 'Volunteerism Goes Undercover: The Administration's Orwellian New Initiative', *The American Prospect Online* (31 July 2002), http://www.prospect.org/webfeatures/2002/07/lott-j-07-31.html; Nat Hentoff, 'Ashcroft's Master Plan to Spy on Us', *The Village Voice* (2 August 2002).

75. Dave Lindorff, 'When Neighbors Attack!', *Salon* (6 August 2002), http://www.salon.com/news/feature/2002/08/06/tips/index_np.html.

76. 'INS Detentions are a Bust', *Los Angeles Times* (20 December 2002); Mark Engler and Saurav Sarker, 'Ashcroft's Roundup', *The Progressive* (March 2003).

77. 'Bush planned Iraq "regime change" before becoming President', *Glasgow Sunday Herald* (15 September 2002).

78. CNN, *Late Edition* (14 October 2001).

79. 'Muslims Call US "Ruthless, Arrogant"', *CNN.com* (26 February 2002), http://www.cnn.com/2002/US/02/26/gallup.muslims/index.html.

80. Charlotte Beers' address to National Press Club (18 December 2002), http://www.state.gov/r/us/16121.htm.

81. See Scott Lucas and James Boys, 'With Us or against Us: Cultural Projection and US Foreign Policy After 9–11', *49th Parallel* (Spring 2003), http://artsweb.bham.ac.uk/49thparallel/currentissue/coll_lucas.htm.

82. Seymour Hersh, 'The Debate Within', *The New Yorker* (11 March 2002); Franklin Foer, 'Flacks Americana', *The New Republic Online* (20 May 2002), http://www.tnr.com/docprint.mhtml?i=20020520&s=foer052002. In 2002 Rendon's Washington website, with 'a wealth of info about clients, case studies, speeches and bios about key execs' no longer functioned. A Rendon spokesman claimed the site was undergoing a technical re-design. As of spring 2003, it was still inoperative; when it was resurrected, it contained no reference to Rendon's work for the Pentagon beyond the listing of the 'United States Department of Defense' and 'Defense Advanced Research Projects Agency' as clients. (Rendon website, http://www.rendon.com; 'The Best War Money Can Buy: John Rendon and

Iraq', CASI Newsletter, 16 June 2002, http://www.casi.org.uk/discuss/2002/msg00838.html).

83. James Dao and Eric Schmitt, 'Pentagon Readies Efforts to Sway Sentiment Abroad', *New York Times* (19 December 2002). When asked about the relationship about the 'firewall' between her operations and those of the OSI, Beers stumbled close to an admission of the Pentagon's 'misinformation', 'Well, the firewall is really simple. We only tell the truth. And we have every means to evaluate whether what we have in our hands and going out over our various channels is the truth .... As far as I understand, Secretary Rumsfeld made it very clear that he, himself, is only interested in communicating the truth. So I don't think there's any conflict of interest here, but we are very careful in our coordination with the Department of Defense that we are dealing with what we would call only the most overt, transparent programs .... And besides, they are all that really work' (Beers' speech to National Press Club, 18 December 2002).

84. Quoted in STRATFOR Report, Stratfor.com (16 December 2002).

85. 'Secrecy News', *FAS Project on Government Secrecy* (27 November 2002), http://www.fas.org/sgp/news/secrecy/2002/11/112702.html.

86. Chicago Council on Foreign Relations and German Marshall Fund of the United States, 'European Public Opinion and Foreign Policy', *Worldviews 2002* (4 September 2002), http://www.worldviews.org/detailreports/europeanreport/index.htm.

87. Quoted in James Dao, 'Panel Urges U.S. to Revamp Efforts to Promote Image Abroad', *New York Times* (29 July 2002).

88. Council on Foreign Relations, 'Public Diplomacy: A Strategy for Reform' (30 July 2002), http://www.cfr.org/publication.php?id=4683; Julian Borger, 'White House Acts to Shed Arrogant Image', *Guardian* (31 July 2002).

89. Jane Perlez, 'U.S. is Trying to Market Itself to Young, Suspicious Arabs', *New York Times* (16 September 2002); Ewen MacAskill and Brian Whitaker, 'Allies Strive for Arab Hearts and Minds', *Guardian* (30 November 2002).

90. Bush address (20 December 2002), http://www.whitehouse.gov/news/releases/2002/12/20021220-7.html.

91. Pew Research Center, 'What the World Thinks in 2002' (4 December 2002), http://people-press.org/reports/display.php3?ReportID=165.

92. 'Coca Cola Deserts Middle Eastern Base', *BBC News* (2 March 2003), http://news.bbc.co.uk/go/pr/fr/-/1/hi/business/2813025.stm.

93. 'U.S. Propaganda Pitch Halted', CBS News (16 January 2003), http://www.cbsnews.com/stories/2003/01/16/world/main536756.shtml.

94. 'Bush's Muslim Propaganda Chief Quits', *CNN.com* (4 March 2003), http://www.cnn.com/2003/US/03/03/state.resignation/index.html.

95. Anne Kingston, 'Uncle Sam Can't be Sold like Uncle Ben's', (Ontario) *National Post* (25 February 2003).

96. Suzanne Goldenberg, 'CIA Accused of Torture at Bagram Base', *Guardian* (27 December 2002).

97. Donald Kagan, 'Comparing America to Ancient Empires is "Ludicrous"', *Atlanta Journal-Constitution* (6 October 2002).

98. Nicholas Kristof, 'Losses, Before Bullets Fly', *New York Times* (7 March 2003).

99. Glenn Frankel, 'In Britain, War Concern Grows into Resentment of U.S. Power', *Washington Post* (26 January 2003).

100. Victor Davis Hanson, 'Goodbye to Europe?' *Commentary* (October 2002).

101. Jeffrey Gedmin et al., 'Friends? Foes? Disconnected Strangers?', *The American Enterprise Online* (December 2002), http://www.theamericanenterprise.org/taedec02d.htm#osullivan.

102. David Brooks, 'Among the Bourgeoisophobes', *Weekly Standard* (15 April 2002). Other *Weekly Standard* commentators such as George Will, Charles Krauthammer, William Kristol and Fred Barnes have dwelt upon the need for a 'moral' America to correct, lead and even dominate an 'anti-semitic' Europe.

103. Anatole Lieven, 'The Push for War', *London Review of Books* (3 October 2002).

104. Project for a New American Century, *Rebuilding America's Defenses.*

105. Quoted in Steven Erlanger, 'German Joins Europe's Cry that the U.S. Won't Consult', *New York Times* (13 February 2002) and Keith B. Richburg, 'Europe, U.S. Diverging on Key Policy Approaches', *Washington Post* (4 March 2002).

106. David Ignatius, 'Dissing the Dissenters', *Washington Post* (23 August 2002); 'US Advisor Demands Schroeder's Resignation', *Handelsblatt* (1 October 2002). Donald Rumsfeld added, 'I have no comment on the German elections outcome, but I would have to say that the way it was conducted was notably unhelpful.' Charles Krauthammer, the prominent American columnist, told the BBC, 'We can certainly conduct our foreign policy without Germany; I wonder how the Germans will be able to do without the United States and perhaps some of their closer allies in Europe' (BBC Radio 4, *PM*, 23 September 2002).

107. 'Rumsfeld: France, Germany are "Problems" in Iraqi Conflict', *CNN.com* (23 January 2003), http://www.cnn.com/2003/WORLD/meast/01/22/sprj.irq.wrap/index.html.

108. Thom Shanker, 'Rumsfeld Faces Tense Greeting and Anti-War Rallies in Munich', *New York Times* (7 February 2003). Rumsfeld snapped, 'There are three or four countries that have said they won't do anything. I believe Libya, Cuba and Germany are the ones that I have indicated won't help in any respect.' In fact, Germany had promised to provide logistical facilities for American forces (Rupert Cornwell,

'Rumsfeld "Mends Fences" by Lumping Germany with Cuba and Libya in an Axis of Bad Boys', *Independent*, 8 February 2003).

109. Quoted by *United Press International* (4 February 2003). Perle tipped off his declaration of independence from Europe in November in an interview with the *Guardian*: 'Europe has lost its moral compass ... Germany has subsided into a moral numbing pacifism ... I have seen diplomatic manoeuvre, but not moral fibre [from France]' (Edward Pilkington and Ewen MacAskill, 'Europe Lacks Moral Fibre, Says US Hawk', *Guardian*, 13 November 2002).

110. Thomas Friedman, 'Ah, Those Principled Europeans', *New York Times* (2 February 2003). Max Boot of the Council on Foreign Relations wrote of NATO as '[American] satisfaction of extending peace and freedom in an important region – but scant thanks from the Europeans, who have adopted the attitude of a petulant 16-year-old toward his parents' (*International Herald Tribune*, 26 November 2002).

111. *New York Post* (10 February 2003). The paper charged, 'The French were Hiding. Chickening out. Proclaiming, *Vive les wimps!*' By 3 March, it was claiming, 'FRANCE'S AMI SADDAM PUT THE "IRAQ" IN CHIRAC', for 'Saddam's best friend in the West is still doing his bidding, not to mention profiting from his oil.'

112. Glenn Frankel, 'Sneers from across the Atlantic', *Washington Post* (11 February 2003).

113. Thomas Friedman, 'Take France off the Security Council', *Guardian* (11 February 2003).

114. Gary Younge and Jon Henley, 'Wimps, Weasels and Monkeys – The US Media View of "Perfidious France"', *Guardian* (11 February 2003).

115. William Safire, 'And Now: Op-Ed Diplomacy', *New York Times* (3 February 2003).

116. Alexander Chancellor wrote, in contrast to the prevailing American sentiment, 'Let's Hear it for the Germans': 'What could be more reassuring than a peace-loving, war-hating Germany? This is what we spent most of last century praying for; now that we have it, all we do is complain' (*Guardian*, 1 February 2003).

117. Nick Paton Walsh et al., 'US Begins Secret Talks to Secure Iraq's Oilfields', *Guardian* (23 January 2003); Dan Morgan and David B. Ottaway, 'In Iraqi War Scenario, Oil is Key Issue', *Washington Post* (15 September 2002). See also the report commissioned by Vice President Cheney, 'Strategic Energy Policy Challenges for the 21st Century', quoted in Neil Mackay, 'Official: US Oil at the Heart of Iraq Crisis', Glasgow *Sunday Herald* (6 October 2002), and the report by Craig S. Smith, '3 Groups Already Squabbling over Oil-Flush North Iraq Should Hussein be Toppled', *New York Times* (12 September 2002).

118. Tony Geraghty and David Leigh, 'The Name of the Game is Assassination', *Guardian* (19 December 2002).

119. Christopher Dickey et al., 'How Saddam Happened', *Newsweek* (23 September 2002); Michael Dobbs, 'U.S. Had Key Role in Iraqi Buildup', *Washington Post* (30 December 2002). See also National Security Archive summary of the documentary evidence at Joyce Battle (ed.), 'Shaking Hands with Saddam Hussein: The U.S. Tilts toward Iraq, 1980–1984', *National Security Archive*, http://www. nsarchive.org/NSAEBB/NSAEBB82. For revelations on the British role in development of Iraqi chemical plants, see David Leigh, 'The Strange Case of Falluja 2', *Guardian* (6 March 2003). Rumsfeld was also alleged to have profited in 1998 'from a $200 million deal to send the latest nuclear technology – including plenty of terrorist-ready "dirty bomb" material – to the rogue state of North Korea'. According to *Neue Zurcher Zeitung*, Rumsfeld was a director of ABB,the Swiss-based energy technology company arranging the transfer (Chris Floyd, 'Swing Blades', *Moscow Times*, 2 March 2003; Randeep Ramesh, 'The Two Faces of Rumsfeld', *Guardian*, 9 May 2003).

120. Greg Miller and Bob Drogin, 'CIA Feels Heat on Iraq Data', *Los Angeles Times* (11 October 2002); Julian Borger, 'White House "Exaggerating Iraqi Threat"', *Guardian* (9 October 2002).

121. Paul Harris et al., 'US Rivals Turn on Each Other as Weapons Search Draws a Blank', *Observer* (11 May 2003). Months after the subsequent invasion of Iraq, it would be revealed that the CIA had balked at President Bush, in his speech of 7 October setting out the case against Saddam Hussein, using the forged 'evidence' of Iraqi purchase of uranium from Niger. The incident, in combination with CIA Director's George Tenet unacceptably pessimistic testimony to Congress on the possible course of a war with Baghdad, may have spurred Rumsfeld's creation of the Office of Special Plans (Rupert Cornwell, 'CIA Kept Niger Claims out of Bush Speech', *Independent*, 14 July 2003).

122. Paul Harris, '"Human Shields" Head for Iraq', *Observer* (29 December 2002).

123. 'US Envoy Warns Against War', *BBC News* (9 September 2002), http://news.bbc.co.uk/1/hi/world/americas/2245632.stm.

124. Quoted in Thomas Ricks, 'Desert Caution', *Washington Post* (27 January 2003).

125. See Parker Borg, 'The Experts Speak Out', *Center for International Policy's Project on Iraq* (6 November 2002), http://www.ciponline.org/iraq/experts.htm; Call to Conscience to Active Duty Troops and Reservists, 'Statement to the Troops', http://www.oz.net/~vvawai/CtC/.

126. William J. Broad, '41 Nobel Laureates Sign Declaration against a War without International Support', *New York Times* (28 January 2003). See also 'Nobel Laureates against the War', *The Times* (15 February 2003).

127. Published in *Wall Street Journal* (13 January 2003).

128. 'U.S. Guilty of "Shocking Double Standards" on Iraq – Butler', *Reuters* (28 January 2003), reprinted at http://www.commondreams. org/headlines03/0128-02.htm.

129. Johanna Neuman, 'What Would This War Be Good For?', *Los Angeles Times* (18 January 2003).

130. Peter Barnes, 'Tracking John Poindexter', *ABC News.com* (23 December 2002), http://abcnews.go.com/sections/scitech/TechTV/ techtv_trackPoindexter021223.html.

131. Joan Didion, 'War is Bush's Fixed Idea', *Independent on Sunday* (2 February 2003).

132. Quoted in Alexander Cockburn, 'The Anti-War Movement and its Critics', *Counterpunch* (14 November 2002), http://www. counterpunch.org/cockburn1114.html. Neil Young went through a hyper-patriotic phase after 9–11, penning the anthem 'Let's Roll!', but returned to his protesting ways when he was inducted into the Rock and Roll Hall of Fame in March 2003: 'We're having fun tonight, but we're gonna start killing people next week. I feel like I'm in a great gas-guzzling SUV, driven by someone who's drunk as fuck' (Alexis Petridis, 'Sound of Silence', *Guardian*, 14 March 2003).

133. Katha Pollitt, 'Poetry Makes Nothing Happen? Ask Laura Bush', *The Nation* (24 February 2003); Marcus Warren and Sally Pook, 'American Poets in Anti-War Protest', *Daily Telegraph* (6 March 2003). Tony Blair also received 10,000 poems, including verse by Harold Pinter, Benjamin Zephaniah and the Poet Laureate, Andrew Motion.

134. Quoted in Cockburn, 'The Anti-War Movement and its Critics'.

135. Michael Getler, 'Connecting the Blips', *Washington Post* (16 March 2003).

8 On the Eve of War: March 2003

1. Mary Riddell, 'The Great Unheard Finally Speak Out', *Observer* (16 February 2003).

2. Madeleine Bunting, 'We are the People', *Guardian* (17 February 2003). See also Euan Ferguson's passionate account:

There were, of course, the usual suspects – CND, Socialist Workers' Party, the anarchists. But even they looked shocked at the number of their fellow marchers: it is safe to say they had never experienced such a mass of humanity.

There were nuns. Toddlers. Women barristers. The Eton George Orwell Society. Archaeologists Against War. Walthamstow Catholic Church, the Swaffham Women's Choir and Notts County Supporters Say Make Love Not War (And a Home Win against Bristol would be Nice). They won 2–0, by the way. One group of SWP stalwarts were joined, for the first march in any of their histories, by their mothers. There were country folk and lecturers, dentists and poulterers, a hairdresser from Cardiff and a poet from Cheltenham. ('One Million. And Still They Came', *Observer*, 16 February 2003).

3. Ewen MacAskill and Michael White, 'Blair to Defy Anti-War Protests', *Guardian* (17 February 2003).
4. Julie Burchill, 'Why We Should Go to War', *Guardian* (1 February 2003).
5. Julie Burchill, 'Silly Show-offs against Saddam', *Guardian* (1 March 2003), 'The Thrill of the Killer', *Guardian* (5 April 2003), and 'Bringing it All Back Home', *Guardian* (19 April 2003).
6. David Aaronovitch, 'Dear Marcher, Please Answer a Few Questions', *Guardian* (18 February 2003).
7. David Aaronovitch, 'Marchers with Answers Aplenty', *Guardian* (19 February 2003).
8. David Aaronovitch, 'Thank the Yank', *Observer* (9 March 2003).
9. Lloyd Evans, 'What do They Want? Victory for Saddam', *The Spectator* (15 February 2003). The piece, beyond the standard denunciation of demonstrators 'exercising the very freedom they would deny to others', was distinguished by a crude portrayal of Bianca Jagger, another stock villain for pro-war essayists: 'Her accent still bears a melancholy echo of Neeg-uh-ruh-wuh. "These cry sees," she said, "is about oy-eel".'
10. Jenny McCartney, 'Trendies, Toffs, Students, and Men with Impressive Beards Unite to Save Saddam', *Sunday Telegraph* (16 February 2003); David Pryce-Jones, 'The Marchers are Doing Saddam's Work for Him', *Sunday Telegraph* (16 February 2003); Barbara Amiel, 'If This Was a Peace March, Why Did Saddam Get No Stick?', *Daily Telegraph* (17 February 2003).
11. Tom Baldwin, 'Marchers "Could Provide Cover for Terrorists"', *The Times* (14 February 2003).
12. Melanie Phillips, 'The Dianafication of the British Bulldog', *Daily Mail* (17 February 2003); Mark Goldblatt, *New York Post* (10 April 2003), quoted in Michael Hann, 'The British and US Tabloid Reaction', *Guardian* (11 April 2003).
13. Bryan Appleyard, 'A Divided Nation', *Sunday Times* (16 February 2003).
14. 'Message to Baghdad', *Guardian* (19 February 2003).
15. Philip Johnston, 'Anti-War Demos Give Marxists a New Lease of Life', *Daily Telegraph* (21 March 2003); Patience Wheatcroft, 'We Need to Be Frightened if We're to Feel that This is Our War', *The Times* (21 March 2003); Philip Johnston, 'Anti-War Demos Give Marxists a New Lease of Life', *Daily Telegraph* (22 March 2003); Nicholas Hellen, 'Hard Left Drives Protests by School Truants',

Sunday Times (23 March 2003). For the views of teenage activists in Britain, see Libby Brooks, 'Kid Power', *Guardian* (26 April 2003).

16. Michael Ignatieff, 'I Am Iraq', *New York Times Magazine* (23 March 2003); Nat Hentoff, 'Why I Didn't March This Time', *Village Voice* (28 March 2003).

17. Nick Cohen, 'The Left's Unholy Alliance with Religious Bigotry', *Observer* (23 February 2003).

18. Howard Jacobson, 'If You Want Peace, Preach to the Unconverted', *Independent* (5 April 2003).

19. Phil Reeves, 'Living in Poverty and Fear of Abandonment, the Barely Functioning State that Trusted Its Saviours', *Independent* (24 February 2003); Christina Lamb, 'USA Inc to Build a New Iraq but Afghans See the Flaws', *Sunday Times* (23 March 2003).

20. Faisal Islam, 'World Bank Chief Issues Opium Alert', *Observer* (16 March 2003).

21. Rory McCarthy, 'Old Warlord Threatens Afghan Peace', *Guardian* (10 February 2003).

22. Syed Saleem Shahzad, 'Afghanistan: The War Gathers Momentum', *Asia Times Online* (17 February 2003); Duncan Campbell, 'Afghan Prisoners Beaten to Death at US Military Interrogation Base', *Guardian* (7 March 2003).

23. Catherine Philip, 'Hit-and-Run Attacks Keep US Troops on Back Foot', *The Times* (13 February 2003).

24. Institute for War and Peace, 'A Terrible Tradition is Back in Afghanistan', *Guardian* (8 March 2003).

25. Phil Reeves, 'Karzai Pleads with US not to Abandon Afghanistan', *Independent* (28 February 2003).

26. Phil Reeves, 'Fifteen Killed in Attack Blamed on Al-Qa'ida', *Independent* (1 February 2003); Rory McCarthy, 'Taliban Blamed for Deadly Bomb Attack', *Guardian* (1 February 2003). President Bush later called Karzai to apologise about the public 'grilling' by the Senate. Meanwhile, Karzai's chief of staff pleaded in the *New York Times* for assistance for his President's disarmament plan, 'Kabul, once a vibrant and sophisticated capital, is like an armed camp .... The sight of the armed men is enough to deter most Afghans from participating in rebuilding their country.' (Said Tayeb Jawad, 'The Guns of Kabul', *New York Times*, 15 March 2003). On the same day that George Bush issued his final ultimatum to Saddam Hussein, international donors pledged $2 billion in aid to Afghanistan to 'help it counter international terrorism and curtail heroin production' (Fox News, 'Donors Pledge $2B in Aid to Afghanistan', 18 March 2003). None of the promised money had reached Kabul as of August 2003.

27. Thomas Withington, 'America's Forces Patrol the World', *Observer* (6 April 2003).

28. George Monbiot, 'To Crush the Poor', *Guardian* (4 February 2003); Martin McNamara, 'US Considers Intervention in Colombia', *Guardian* (23 February 2003).

29. E.J. Dionne, Jr., 'Heed the Hawks', *Washington Post* (4 March 2003).

30. Julian Borger, 'Pentagon Wants Mini-Nuke Ban Ended', *Guardian* (7 March 2003).

31. John Sutherland, 'Why does the US Want to Attack Iraq?', *Guardian* (17 February 2003); Bob Herbert, 'Bombs and Blood', *New York Times* (13 March 2003); Robert Fisk, 'Hope Fades as the Citizens of Baghdad Begin to See the Appalling Fate Awaiting Them', *Independent* (19 March 2003).

32. Geoffrey Lean and Severin Carrell, 'US Prepares to Use Toxic Gases in Iraq', *Independent on Sunday* (2 March 2003); Alastair Hay, 'Out of the Straitjacket', *Guardian* (12 March 2003); George Monbiot, 'Chemical Hypocrites', *Guardian* (8 April 2003).

33. Jason Burke, 'Network of Iraqi Spies Set Up in UK', *Observer* (16 March 2003).

34. Elaine Monaghan, 'US Satellites "Spot Iraqis Hiding Suspected Arms"', *The Times* (1 February 2003).

35. Ben Russell and Nigel Morris, 'Blair Appeals to Public by Connecting Iraq and Ricin Seized in London', *Independent* (7 February 2003).

36. James Bone and Roland Watson, 'Secret Drone "Part of Iraqi Chemical Warfare Plans"', *The Times* (10 March 2003).

37. 'Cargo Ships "May Contain Iraqi Weapons"', *Guardian* (19 February 2003).

38. On 'incentives' for and pressure upon Security Council members, see Pepe Escobar, 'Coercion in the Name of Democracy', *Asia Times Online* (6 March 2003), http://www.mwaw.org/print.php?sid=2070; 'Small Fry at UN Feel the Heat from US', *Independent on Sunday* (2 March 2003); '"Bribes" Pushing UN Waverers into Support for War', *The Times* (8 March 2003). An American diplomat warned Mexico that refusal to vote for a US resolution could 'stir up feelings' against Mexicans in the United States. President Bush suggested that if Mexico or other countries opposed the US, 'there [would] be a certain sense of discipline' (Paul Krugman, 'Let Them Hate as Long as They Fear', *New York Times*, 7 March 2003). On spying on Security Council members, see Martin Bright, 'Revealed: US Dirty Tricks to Win Vote on Iraq War', *Observer* (2 March 2003); Martin Bright and Ed Vulliamy, 'Bugging Row Prompts UN Investigation', *Observer* (9 March 2003). Meanwhile the Bush administration, without a hint of irony, asked more than 60 countries to find and expel several hundred Iraqi diplomats that the C.I.A. and others have identified as suspected intelligence agents, saying they 'pose a threat to our personnel and installations overseas'. On the lack of American coverage of the story of US espionage, see 'New York Times, Networks Shun U.N. Spying Story', *Fairness and Accuracy in Reporting*

(11 March 2003), http://www.fair.org/activism/un-observer-spying.html; Michael Tomasky, 'Spooky Story', *The American Prospect Online* (12 March 2003), http://www.prospect.org/webfeatures/2003/.

39. Gilbert Cranberg, 'Powell's U.N. Report Apparently Contains False Information', *Des Moines Herald-Tribune* (24 February 2003); Raymond Whitaker, 'Revealed: How the Road to War was Paved with Lies', *Independent on Sunday* (27 April 2003).

40. Anne Penketh, 'Baradei Says US Reports Were False', *Independent* (8 March 2003); Felicity Barringer, 'Forensic Experts Uncovered Forgery on Iraq, an Inspector Says', *New York Times* (9 March 2003). Almost all the media failed to notice that this was not the first time the US had produced false or non-existent 'evidence' on the Iraqi nuclear programme. In early September 2002, President Bush set up the pretext for war by claiming that the International Atomic Energy Agency had documented in 1998 that Iraq was 'six months away' from a nuclear weapon. An IAEA spokesman commented, 'There's never been a report like that issued from this agency' (Joseph Curl, 'Agency Disavows Report on Iraqi Arms', *Washington Times*, 27 September 2002). See also Julian Borger, 'White House "Exaggerating Iraqi Threat"', *Guardian* (9 October 2002). The Niger forgery eventually overtook the earlier embarrassment that a supporting British dossier on Iraq's threat included a section plagiarised, with some distortion for dramatic effect, from an American doctoral thesis (Michael White et al., 'Downing St Admits Blunder on Iraq Dossier', *Guardian*, 8 February 2003).

41. James Risen, 'C.I.A. Analysts Feel Pressure in Preparing Reports', *New York Times* (23 March 2003); 'Ex-CIA Accuse Bush of Manipulating Iraq Evidence', *Associated Press* (14 March 2003); Andrew Buncombe and Marie Woolf, 'Cheney under Pressure to Quit over False War Evidence', *Independent* (16 July 2003).

42. Julian Borger, 'Iraqi Defector's Testimony Confuses Case against Iraq', *Guardian* (1 March 2003).

43. Rupert Cornwell, 'A Masterly Display by a Trusted American', *Independent* (6 February 2003); Bronwen Maddox, 'Powell Has the Air of a President as He Shines Under the Spotlight', *The Times* (6 February 2003). Mary McGrory of the *Washington Post* subsequently apologised to readers for her initial reaction, 'I'm Persuaded': 'I did not make it clear enough that while I believed what Colin Powell told me about Saddam Hussein's poison collection, I was not convinced that war was the answer' ('To My Very Persuasive Readers', *Washington Post*, 6 March 2003).

44. 'Are Inspections Working?', *Washington Post* (11 March 2003).

45. Jim Hoagland, 'Thinking Parochially, Acting Selfishly', *Washington Post* (13 March 2003). Hoagland sneered, 'No speech by George W. Bush could do more damage to the Security Council than the games

that weapons inspector Hans Blix has begun to play with his reports, apparently in an effort to prolong his bureaucracy's tenure and his place in the world spotlight.'

46. Lisa Myers, 'The Hunt for Iraqi "Sleeper Cells"', *MSNBC* (6 March 2003); Jason Burke, 'Network of Iraqi Spies Set Up in UK', *Observer* (16 March 2003); James Bone, 'Iraqi Drone "Could Drop Chemicals on Troops"', *The Times* (8 March 2003); John H. Cushman, Jr. and Stephen Weisman, 'U.S. Says Iraq Retools Rockets for Illicit Uses', *New York Times* (9 March 2003); 'Saddam Tried to Kill Laura Bush', *Sunday Telegraph* (9 March 2003).

47. See 'America Wants War, and All the Rest is Window Dressing', *Independent on Sunday* (16 March 2003).

48. Patrick Wintour and Julian Borger, 'Saddam Gets Six More Weeks', *Guardian* (1 February 2003).

49. Stephen Weisman, 'To White House, Inspector is Now More a Dead End than a Guidepost', *New York Times* (2 March 2003).

50. 'US Officials Say UN Future At Stake in Vote', *Washington Post*, 25 February 2003.

51. Tony Karon, 'Bush Writes His Own History', *Time* (17 March 2003).

52. Kenneth H. Bacon and George Rupp, 'Unready for the Aftermath', *New York Times* (7 March 2003).

53. 'Halliburton wins contract on Iraq oil firefighting', *Reuters* (6 March 2003); Neil King, Jr., 'US is Quietly Soliciting Bids for Rebuilding Postwar Iraq', *Wall Street Journal* (10 March 2003).

54. Peter Beaumont and Gaby Hinsliff, 'The Spies and the Spinner', *Observer* (9 March 2003); Richard Norton-Taylor, 'British Military Leaders Question Mission and Ethics', *Guardian* (5 February 2003).

55. CNN, *Late Edition* (2 March 2003).

56. Felicity Barringer, 'US Diplomat Resigns, Protesting "Our Fervent Pursuit of War"', *New York Times* (27 February 2003).

57. Mick Hume, 'It's Time Time Ran Out', *The Times* (24 February 2003).

58. George Will, 'Europe's Monomania', *Washington Post* (23 February 2003).

59. Thomas Friedman, 'The Gridlock Gang', *New York Times* (26 February 2003).

60. 'Dixie Chicks: Anti-American?', *Guardian* (19 March 2003).

61. Tim Jones, 'Media Giant's Rally Sponsorship Raises Questions', *Chicago Tribune* (19 March 2003); Edward Helmore, 'Storm Hits US Airwaves Over Radio Control', *Observer* (20 April 2003); Interview with Laurie Anderson in Alex O'Connell, 'Escape from New York', *The Times* (29 April 2003). On Clear Channel, see Paul Krugman, 'Channels of Influence', *New York Times* (25 March 2003).

62. One operation which the FBI finally confirmed was surveillance of students and staff at Indiana University ('FBI Acknowledges Mystery Flights', *Associated Press*, 4 March 2003).

63. 'Santa Fe Police Detain Library Patron over Chat-Room Visit', *American Libraries* (24 February 2003).

64. 'Protestors Gather at Crossgates Mall', *WNYT-TV* (Albany, NY) (5 March 2003); 'Man's Anti-war T-Shirt Lands Him in Custody', *Los Angeles Times* (5 March 2003); Maria Allwine, 'Peace Protestors Arrested and Detained in Baltimore Suburb', *Buzz Flash* (4 March 2003), http://www.buzzflash.com/contributors/03/03/04_protest.html; Tim Robbins, 'Our Voices Are Lost in the Tide of Intolerance Sweeping America', *Observer* (20 April 2003).

65. 'In Iraq Crisis, Networks Are Megaphones for Official Views', *Fairness and Accuracy in Reporting* (18 March 2003), http://www.fair.org/activism/iraq-sources-networks.html. *Profiles from the Front Line* was produced by Jerry Bruckheimer (*Top Gun*, *Black Hawk Down*, *Pearl Harbor*) for ABC (Joy Press, 'The Axers of Evil', *Village Voice*, 5–11 March 2003).

66. Doug Henwood, 'Time to Turn TV on Again', *The Times* (25 April 2003).

67. 'GE, Microsoft Bring Bigotry to Life', *Fairness and Accuracy in Reporting* (12 February 2003), http://www.fair.org/activism/msnbc-savage.html.

68. Rick Ellis, 'The Surrender of MSNBC' (25 February 2003), reprinted at *AllYourTV.com*, http://www.allyourtv.com/0203season/news/02252003donahue.html; Bill O'Reilly, 'Talking Points', *Fox News* (26 February 2003). See also Matthew Engel, 'The US is on the Right Wavelength', *Guardian* (4 March 2003).

69. Andrew Sullivan, 'America Turns to the Voices that Tell it Like it is', *Sunday Times* (2 March 2003).

70. Barbara Amiel, 'The BBC Has Become an Open Opponent of America's Policies', *Daily Telegraph* (3 March 2003).

71. See Ben Cohen, 'Wake America From its Bloodless Trance', *AlterNet* (9 March 2003), http://www.alternet.org/story.html?StoryID=15340.

72. Dennis Kucinich, 'Obviously Oil', *AlterNet* (11 March 2003), http://www.alternet.org/story.html?StoryID=15359.

73. Alexis Petridis, 'Sound of Silence', *Guardian Review* (14 March 2003).

74. Martin Sheen, 'A Celebrity, but First a Citizen', *Los Angeles Times* (17 March 2003).

75. CNN, *Lou Dobbs' Moneyline* (26 February 2003). Just before operations against Iraq, Dobbs ended his show with the country musician Darryl Worley, who sang before footage of the collapsing World Trade Center, 'Some people say that with this war, we're just looking for a fight, I say, after 9/11 ... well, that's all right.' See Zoe Heller, 'It's Getting Hard to be Pro-American', *Daily Telegraph* (15 March 2003).

76. FoxNews, *The O'Reilly Factor* (4 February 2003), transcript available at http://www.nosheetsleft.com/misc/transcript.html. O'Reilly learned of Glick from an interview with Not in Our Name's Miles

Solay, who was also dismissed: 'All right, Mr. Solay, we appreciate you coming in but this is disgraceful.'

77. John Bogert, 'Doubting Thomas offers her press veteran's take on state of presidency', (Torrance, CA) *Daily Breeze* (19 January 2003), and 'Bush quote takes Thomas aback, but she's not about to take it back', (Torrance, CA) *Daily Breeze* (24 February 2003); 'Organised Official Republican Party Smear Campaign against Helen Thomas', *Information Clearing House* (February 2003), http://www.informationclearinghouse.info/article1613.htm.

78. 'How CNN Edited Blix's Transcript', *ExtCirc.com* (16 February 2003), http://danken.com/oo/mtorchivoc/000411.shtml#updated; Robert Fisk, 'How the News Will be Censored in this War', *Independent* (25 February 2003).

79. 'Hollywood Designer Creates Military Media Center', *FoxNews.com* (16 March 2003), http://www.foxnews.com/story/0,2933,81191,00.html; Robert Fisk, 'The War of Misinformation Has Begun', *Independent* (16 March 2003); David Charter, 'Movie Men Add Special Effects to Media War', *The Times* (11 March 2003).

80. Professor Robert Thompson, quoted in Todd S. Purdum and Jim Rutenberg, 'Reporters Respond Eagerly to Pentagon Welcome Mat', *New York Times* (23 March 2003). For a subsequent account, from both 'unilateral' and 'embedded' journalists, of how the military controlled reporting, see Jamie Wilson and Lucy Mangan, 'Friend or Foe?', *Guardian* (7 April 2003).

81. Michael Woolf, 'All Fired Up', *Guardian* (24 March 2003).

82. Andrew Buncombe, 'Rumsfeld Condemned for Insulting Germans during Fence-Mending Jaunt into Old Europe', *Independent* (10 February 2003).

83. Glenn Frankel, 'Sneers from across the Atlantic', *Washington Post* (11 February 2003). For *Daily Telegraph* columnist Jenny McCartney, a Belgian waiter correcting a request for 'flat water' to 'still water' became the conclusion, 'In British anti-war circles, any American is regarded with suspicion, until he or she performs a fervent national self-denunciation of the Susan Sarandon variety' ('A Brush with Anti-Americanism', *Sunday Telegraph,* 16 March 2003).

84. Paul Cellucci, 'Canada Has Let Down its Old Friend', *Independent* (27 March 2003).

85. 'Top Bush Aide Savages "Selfish" Chirac', *Guardian* (23 February 2003); George Will, 'The War is On', *Washington Post* (7 March 2003).

86. Michael Gove, 'High Noon for a Lonesome Cowboy', *The Times* (6 March 2003).

87. The US and Britain alleged that Chirac had 'poisoned' the diplomatic process by promising a veto of a second UN resolution 'whatever the circumstances'. In fact, Chirac made clear that the position was '[France] considers *this evening* that there are no

grounds for waging war', and subsequent French statements expressed desire to explore 'all opportunities' for compromise. As the editors of the *Guardian* noted, 'It is dishonest to try to scapegoat France's present, logical and in many ways admirable stance on continued inspections for an avoidable crisis that is essentially one made in America' ('The Gall of France', 15 March 2003). Amidst the drive for war, however, that 'dishonest' representation was the norm in British and American media.

88. NBC, *Meet the Press* (9 February 2003).

89. Customs officials obliged by 'inspecting everything [about French wine] more carefully ...[to] find little flaws on the labels so they can't allow them in' (Wine expert Robert Parker, quoted in London Spy, 'French Wine is Turned away at US Borders', *Daily Telegraph*, 21 March 2003).

90. 'Fried Politics', *CNN.com* (19 February 2003), http://www.cnn.com/2003/US/South/02/19/offbeat.freedom.fries.ap/.

91. 'House Cafeterias Change Names for "French" Fries and "French" Toast', *CNN.com* (11 March 2003), http://www.cnn.com/2003/ALLPOLITICS/03/11/sprj.irq.fries/; Roland Watson et al., 'Americans Turn Fire on Ungrateful Nation', *The Times* (14 March 2003). David Letterman, the talk-show host, joked: 'France wants more evidence. The last time France wanted more evidence, it rolled right through France with a German flag.' Dennis Miller added, 'The only way the French are going in is if we tell them we found truffles in Iraq' (Dominic Rushe, 'US Offensive on the Jokes Front Hides Real Anger', *Sunday Times*, 16 February 2003).

92. Glen Owen, 'Explosive Messages for Every War', *The Times* (14 March 2003).

93. Peter Beaumont et al., 'US to Punish German "Treachery"', *Observer* (16 February 2003); Mark Landler, 'General Tells of Plan to Thin out G.I. Presence in Germany', *New York Times* (4 March 2003).

94. Robert Byrd, 'Why I Weep for My Country', *Observer* (23 March 2003). See also Robert Byrd, 'We Stand Passively Mute', *Guardian* (18 February 2003).

95. Shawn McCarthy, 'You're Not Trusted: PM to U.S.', (Toronto) *Globe and Mail* (21 February 2003).

96. Joan Smith, 'It's about Time the US Got over 9/11', *Independent* (9 February 2003).

97. Simon Jenkins, 'A Lesson in War from Titian and the Medici', *The Times* (21 February 2003); Philip Stephens, 'Bound Together Despite Everything', *Financial Times* (13 February 2003).

98. David Ignatius, 'Translating for the French', *Washington Post* (4 March 2003).

99. Arundhati Roy, 'Mesopotamia. Babylon. The Tigris and Euphrates', *Guardian* (2 April 2003). See also Michael Powell, 'Peace

Correspondent: Democracy Now! Host Amy Goodman is Making Her Voice Heard on Iraq', *Washington Post* (10 March 2003).

100. Glen Kessler and Mike Allen, 'Bush Faces Increasingly Poor Image Overseas', *Washington Post* (24 February 2003).

101. 'Polls Find Europeans Oppose Iraq War', *BBC News* (11 February 2003), http://news.bbc.co.uk/1/hi/world/europe/2747175.stm; Dick Meyer, 'World on Iraq: Shadows of Doubt', *CBSNews*.com (6 March 2003), http://www.cbsnews.com/stories/2003/03/06/opinion/meyer/main543005.shtml

102. 'Disarming Iraq', *New York Times* (15 February 2003).

103. 'The Rush to War', *New York Times* (3 March 2003); 'The Worst Case Scenario Arrives', *New York Times* (6 March 2003).

104. Thomas Friedman, 'Grapes of Wrath', *New York Times* (12 March 2003).

105. Maureen Dowd, 'I Vant to be Alone', *New York Times* (12 March 2003).

106. Michael Hardt, 'A Trap Set for Protestors', *Guardian* (21 February 2003).

107. Bush speech, 'Free Peoples Will Keep the Peace of the World', *New York Times* (27 February 2003). Fittingly, Bush delivered the speech at the American Enterprise Institute, the former 'home' of 20 members of his Administration.

108. Dana Milbank, 'For Bush, A Sense of History – and Fate', *Washington Post* (9 March 2003); Elisabeth Bumiller, 'Bush Girds for War in Solitude, but Not in Doubt', *New York Times* (9 March 2003). One should note the irrepressible Andrew Sullivan who, without a shred of evidence, could join the President, ideology and power in happy union: '[Bush] is merely a vivid representative of a deep and idealistic strain within [US foreign policy]. And history shows that the world has far more to gain from the deployment of that power than by its withdrawal' ('Clinton Talked a Good War – Bush Has to Fight it', *Sunday Times*, 9 March 2003).

109. Nick Cohen, 'The Left isn't Listening', *Observer* (16 February 2003). See the response of Hilary Wainwright, letter to the *Observer* (23 February 2003). For a differing Iraqi view, see Sami Ramadani, 'Whose Interests at Heart?', *Guardian* (18 March 2003).

110. Johann Hari, 'Democracy in the Islamic World is Not a Fantasy – It's Coming Soon', (28 February 2003). See also the leader of the *Daily Telegraph*, 'The planting of the rule of law, plural civil society, the beginnings of democracy will not be easy, but why should anyone insist that the Arab political desert can never bloom?' ('Beyond Debate', 18 March 2003).

111. William Safire, 'Give Freedom a Chance', *New York Times* (6 March 2003).

112. Jim Hoagland, 'A Springboard for Mideast Peace?', *Washington Post* (2 March 2003).

113. Johann Hari, 'Democracy in the Islamic World is Not a Fantasy – It's Coming Soon', and Adrian Hamilton, 'Forget Democracy: This is a War for Security', *Independent* (28 February 2003). Indeed an editor, possibly out of mischief as well as a search for balance, repeatedly undercut Hari's exaltations of liberation with Hamilton's analyses of US policy and the Middle East. Thus 'Stop the War? Try Telling that to the Tyrannised People of Iraq' (7 February 2003) was offset by 'Far from Being a Liberation, the Occupation of Baghdad will be seen as an Exercise in American Power'.

114. José Ramos-Horta, 'War for Peace? It Worked in My Country', *New York Times* (25 February 2003); Ariel Dorfman, 'A Reply to an Iraqi Dissident Urging Invasion', *Independent* (26 February 2003). The State Department circulated the Ramos-Horta essay around the world in its information programmes. It did not do the same with Dorfman's article.

115. Quoted in Sam Tanenhaus, 'The Rise and Fall and Rise of the Domino Theory', *Washington Post* (23 March 2003).

116. Oliver Burkeman, 'Secret Report Throws Doubt on Democracy Hopes', *Guardian* (15 March 2003).

117. 'President Bush's Nation-Building', *New York Times* (27 February 2003); 'Geeks Bearing Gifts', *Guardian* (4 March 2003).

118. Stephen Weisman, 'Bush Freezes Mideast Plan During Crisis in Iraq', *New York Times* (9 March 2003).

119. See, for example, Jonathan Steele, 'Independent Iraqis Oppose Bush's War', *Guardian* (5 March 2003); Donald MacIntyre, 'History Has Honed Iraqi Suspicions of Foreign "Liberation"', *Independent* (5 April 2003); May Abdalla, '"Our Fate is Bleak"', *New Statesman* (14 April 2003).

120. Kanan Makiya, 'Our Hope Betrayed', *Observer* (16 February 2003).

121. Michael Howard and Luke Harding, 'US Troops Deal Alarms Kurds', *Guardian* (10 February 2003); Jason Burke and Luke Harding, 'Kurds in Fear of Turkish Motives', *Observer* (2 March 2003).

122. Agence France-Presse, 'Iraqi Opposition Groups Show Fissures at a Unity Meeting', *New York Times* (2 March 2003). A six-person committee of two Kurds, three Shi'a and one Sunni was finally named by the meeting but the Sunni representative immediately rejected his membership. A last-ditch meeting was held in Ankara in mid-March with senior Kurdish leaders, only days after Turkey banned its own Kurdish parties (Suna Erdem, 'Last-Ditch Talks over Row with Iraqi Kurds', *The Times*, 17 March 2003).

123. William Safire, 'The Kurdish Ghost', *New York Times* (3 March 2003).

124. See George Monbiot, 'A Wilful Blindness', *Guardian* (11 March 2003): 'Those of us who oppose the impending conquest of Iraq must recognise that there's a possibility that, if it goes according to plan, it could improve the lives of many Iraqi people. But to pretend that this battle begins and ends in Iraq requires a wilful denial of

the context in which it occurs. That context is a blunt attempt by the superpower to reshape the world to suit itself.'

125. Quoted in Joseph Cirincione, 'The Shape of the Post-War World', *San Francisco Chronicle* (23 March 2003).

126. Daniel Kruger, 'The Case for Colonialism', *Spectator* (15 March 2003).

127. Robert Kagan, 'Power and Weakness', *Policy Review* (June 2002).

128. Michael Ignatieff, 'The Burden', *New York Times Magazine* (5 January 2003).

129. Niall Ferguson, 'In Praise of Failed Diplomacy', *New York Times* (23 March 2003)

130. Anne-Marie Slaughter, 'Good Reasons for Going around the U.N.', *New York Times* (18 March 2003). See also Jonathan Glover's critique 'Can We Justify Killing the Children of Iraq?', *Guardian* (5 February 2003).

131. Michael White and Patrick Wintour, 'No Case for Iraq Attack Say Lawyers', *Guardian* (7 March 2003); Richard Norton-Taylor, 'Law Unto Themselves', *Guardian* (14 March 2003).

132. Jonathan Schell, 'The Case against War', *The Nation* (3 March 2003).

133. Jonathan Freedland, 'Decisions, Decisions', *Guardian* (26 February 2003).

134. Michael Ignatieff, 'The Burden', *New York Times Magazine* (5 January 2003).

135. Thomas Friedman, 'The Long Bomb', *New York Times* (2 March 2003). Three days later, Friedman added: 'Mr. Bush also has some dangerous blind spots. Every day he asks us to ignore more and more troubling facts, and every day it seems more and more that Mr. Bush has mustered not a coalition of the willing, but rather, as one wag put it, "a coalition of the billing". It is very disturbing that so many of our "allies" have to be bribed or bludgeoned into joining this war' ('Chicken à la Iraq', *New York Times*, 5 March 2003).

136. Quoted in Paul Vallely, 'Paradox and Power: The Philosopher of a World in Turmoil', *Independent* (15 March 2003).

137. Jonathan Freedland, 'If We Are Going to Intervene, There Will Have to Be Rules', *Guardian* (8 March 2003).

138. David Clark, 'Mr Blair is in a State of Confusion over this War', *Independent* (18 February 2003).

139. Editorial, *Newsday* (11 March 2003), quoted in 'It's not about Iraq any Longer', *Guardian* (12 March 2003).

140. Michael White, 'Get Real, Blair Tells European Critics of America', *Guardian* (19 February 2003).

141. William Shawcross, 'Why This Paper is Wrong about Bush and Blair's Stance on Iraq', *Independent on Sunday* (9 February 2003); Howard Jacobson, 'Is it Possible to be an Unconscious Racist?', *Independent* (12 April 2003).

142. Conrad Black, 'Britain is Right to Stick by America', *The Spectator* (15 February 2003).

143. Arundhati Roy, 'Not Again', *Guardian* (27 September 2002). Or, in the blunter words of Richard Dawkins, 'Those of us opposed to the war are sometimes accused of anti-Americanism. I am vigorously pro-American, which is one reason I am anti-Bush' ('Why Should We in Britain Help Bush to Get Re-elected?', *Independent*, 1 March 2003).

144. James Morrison, 'Do They Really Mean Us? Authors Rail at Bizarre Choice of "English" Books', *Independent* (1 March 2003); Nigel Reynolds, 'Self-Loathing is a Way of Life for the English', *Daily Telegraph* (6 March 2003).

145. Philip Bowring, 'Orwell Would Be Shocked', *International Herald Tribune* (18 February 2003); 'Volunteerism Goes Undercover: The Administration's New Orwellian Initiative', *The American Prospect* (31 July 2002).

146. Barbara Amiel, 'Blair's Dilemma', *Daily Telegraph* (17 March 2003).

147. Louis Menand, 'So Misunderstood', *The New Yorker* (27 January 2003).

148. Leon Wieseltier, 'Heroes', *The New Republic* (15 October 2001).

149. Quoted in Tim Rutten, 'Orwell, Right or Wrong?', *Los Angeles Times* (15 February 2003).

150. Leon Wieseltier, 'Aspidistra', *The New Republic* (17 February 2003).

151. Michael Gove, 'Palmerston versus Pirates, Parasites, and Pacifists', *The Times* (11 February 2003).

152. Michael Kelly, 'Immorality on the March', *Washington Post* (19 February 2003).

153. Colin Brown and Francis Elliott, 'Blair Warns Marchers of "Blood on Your Hands"', *Sunday Telegraph* (16 February 2003); Tony Blair, 'The Price of My Conviction', *Observer* (16 February 2003).

154. Ferdinand Mount, 'Not-Yetters Ignore the Price of Inaction', *Sunday Times* (2 March 2003); George Will, 'Addressing the Naysayers', *Washington Post* (19 March 2003).

155. David Brooks, 'The United States is in the Grip of a Certainty Crisis', *The Times* (7 March 2003).

156. Janet Daley, 'America Threatens an Epidemic of Freedom', *Daily Telegraph* (5 March 2003). Daley also put international law beyond meaningful use by dissenters, since it is 'nothing more than corruptly manipulated decisions by the UN Security Council'.

157. Minette Marrin, 'Oppose America and You are at War with Yourself', *Sunday Times* (16 February 2003).

158. BBC Radio Five Live, *Nicky Campbell Morning Phone-In* (7 March 2003).

159. Nick Cohen, 'The Only Way to Peace', *Observer* (2 March 2003).

160. Nick Cohen, 'The Left isn't Listening', *Observer* (16 February 2003).

161. Stephen Pollard, 'My Address Book is the First Casualty of War', *The Times* (18 February 2003). See also Phil Craig's 'My Lefty Friends are Wrong', *The Spectator* (15 February 2003).

162. Johann Hari, 'Smells Like Teen Spirit?', *Independent* (7 March 2003).

163. Adrian Hamilton, 'Yes, There is an Alternative to This Approaching War', *Independent* (14 February 2003).

164. Dan Plesch, 'A Con Trick for Western Liberals', *Guardian* (7 March 2003).

165. Matthew Parris, 'A Dove's Guide: How to Be an Honest Critic of the War', *The Times* (1 February 2003).

166. Jonathan Freedland, 'Catch Me if You Can' (5 February 2003), 'If We Are Going to Intervene, There Will Have to Be Rules' (8 March 2003), and 'What Would You Suggest?' (19 February 2003), *Guardian*. See also Kenneth Cowan, 'So, Have We Forgotten All about Conciliation?', *Independent on Sunday* (16 March 2003) and Hendrik Hertzberg, 'Cakewalk', *New Yorker* (14 April 2003).

167. 'America Wants War, and All the Rest is Window Dressing', *Independent on Sunday* (16 March 2003).

9 Dissent and 'Liberation'

1. 'Democracy and Dissent', *The Times* (21 March 2003).

2. Ferdinand Mount, 'Europe Still Hasn't Learnt the Lesson of US Power', *Sunday Times* (13 April 2003); Charles Krauthammer, 'Killing a Regime, Not a People', *Washington Post* (10 April 2003). See also William Safire, 'Jubilant V-I Day', *New York Times* (10 April 2003).

3. Quoted in Jim Rutenberg, 'Cable's War Coverage Suggests a New "Fox Effect" of Television', *New York Times* (16 April 2003).

4. William Shawcross, *Wall Street Journal* (10 April 2003), quoted in 'April 9 Will Live in Legend', *Guardian* (11 April 2003).

5. Mark Goldblatt, *New York Post* (10 April 2003), quoted in Michael Hann, 'The British and US Tabloid Reaction', *Guardian* (11 April 2003). See also Damian Thompson, 'I Was Right About the War ... and My Ex-Friends Were Wrong', *Daily Telegraph* (19 April 2003). The leader in the *Daily Telegraph* was confident enough to risk the racial imagery of nineteenth-century Empire: 'The more we see, the more we shall know that we were right to invade, and the more the world will want to help the Iraqi people move towards the freedom and peace that our great Anglo-Saxon civilisation takes for granted' ('A Day of Joy for Iraq, a Day of Reckoning for Tyrants', 10 April 2003).

6. 'There are some [enemy] who are alive at this moment who will not be alive shortly. Those who do not wish to go on that journey, we will not send. As for the others, I expect you to rock their world. Wipe them out if that is what they choose' (Tim Collins, 'Tread Lightly in the Historic Land of Iraq', *Independent*, 21 March 2003).

See Stuart Wavell, 'Words that Make Troops Walk above the Ground', *Sunday Times* (23 March 2003).

7. Richard Morrison, 'Heroes: Are They Really So Hard to Find?', *The Times* (24 March 2003); Jonathon Carr-Brown et al., 'SAS Teams are Ghosts of the Desert', *Sunday Times* (23 March 2003); Patrick Bishop, 'Another Mission for the Fighter Boys', *Daily Telegraph* (29 April 2003); Blake Morrison, 'Officer Class', *Guardian* (3 April 2003). After the war, embedded reporter Audrey Gillan offered the highest tribute to British forces: 'They had tattoos, they farted, and their feet certainly smelled, but they were also gentlemen' ('"If You Cop It, Can We have Your Radio?"', *Guardian*, 28 April 2003).

8. Colman McCarthy, 'TV's Military Embeds', *Washington Post* (19 April 2003); Rupert Cornwell and Justin Huggler, 'Anti-War Demonstrators Halt Rush-Hour Traffic in Washington as Arab Protests Continue', *Independent* (29 March 2003); 'War News Gets Better', *New York Times* (3 April 2003). NBC's Ashleigh Banfield dared to admit to an audience at Kansas State University, 'There were horrors that were completely left out of this war .... It was a grand and glorious picture that had a lot of people watching and a lot of advertisers excited about cable TV news. But it wasn't journalism, because I'm not sure Americans are hesitant to do this again – to fight another war, because it looked to them like a courageous and terrific endeavor." (Matt Moline, 'MSNBC's Banfield: Media Filtered Realities of War', *Topeka Capital-Journal*, 24 April 2003).

9. Richard Lloyd Parry, 'So Who Really Did Save Private Jessica?', *The Times* (16 April 2003).

10. David Brooks, 'Rediscovered Optimism Puts the United back into USA', *The Times* (4 April 2003).

11. Andrew Pierce, 'People', *The Times* (4 April 2003).

12. Lucian K. Truscott, 'In This War, News is a Weapon', *New York Times* (25 March 2003).

13. Howard Kurtz, 'In Iraq, Too Much Coverage, or Just Right? Battle Assessment Begins For Saturation Reporting', *Washington Post* (28 April 2003).

14. Brooks, 'Rediscovered Optimism Puts the United back into USA'.

15. Terence Blacker, 'Even We Surrender-Monkeys Are Confused', *Independent* (1 April 2003).

16. Martin Woollacott, 'Unity is Sometimes More Important than Principle', *Guardian* (14 February 2003).

17. Timothy Garton Ash, 'In Defence of the Fence', *Guardian* (6 February 2003).

18. Timothy Garton Ash, 'Islam and Us', *Guardian* (6 March 2003).

19. John Humphrys, 'First Victim of War is UK's Standing Abroad', *Sunday Times* (23 March 2003). Martin Woolacott also gave himself up to Washington, 'Action is Risky, but Turning away Could be Even Riskier', *Guardian* (7 February 2003).

20. Michael Walzer, 'What a Little War in Iraq Could Do', *New York Times* (7 March 2003).

21. Henry Porter, 'Democracy is not in the War Plans', *Observer* (16 March 2003).

22. Nicholas Kristof, 'Hearts and Minds', *New York Times* (28 March 2003).

23. Marie Woolf, 'After the Event is the Time to Ask Questions About this War. But Now is Not the Time', *Independent* (24 March 2003).

24. 'This War is Wrong, but it is Unsupportable. So We Must Fight for the Peace', *Independent on Sunday* (23 March 2003).

25. Ben Hoyle and Dominic Kennedy, 'Thousands Stage School "Breakout" for Day of Protest', and Richard Beeston, 'New Wave of Protesters Takes to World's Street', *The Times* (21 March 2003); John Vidal et al., 'Thousands Take to the Streets in Protest as War Begins', *Guardian* (21 March 2003), and 'School's Out as the Young Rediscover Radical Voice', *Guardian* (22 March 2003).

26. 'Oppose War on Children', *Guardian* (6 February 2003).

27. Williams did revisit his concerns about the process that led to war in 'Weaknesses and Moral Inconsistency Led Us to War', *The Times* (25 March 2003).

28. Stephen Bates, 'Catholic and Anglican Primates Join in Condemnation and Prayer', *Guardian* (24 March 2003).

29. Euan Ferguson, 'Marchers Blow the Whistle for Encore', *Observer* (23 March 2003); Marcus Tanner, '200,000 Marchers Join "Very British Demonstration"', *Independent on Sunday* (23 March 2003); John Vidal and Tania Branigan, 'UK Sees Biggest Wartime Protest', *Guardian* (24 March 2003).

30. '200,000 Protesters Head for White House', *Independent on Sunday* (16 March 2003); Rupert Cornwell and Justin Huggler, 'Anti-War Demonstrators Halt Rush-Hour Traffic in Washington as Arab Protests Continue', *Independent* (29 March 2003); Evelyn Nieves, 'Peace Groups Expand the Fight', *Washington Post* (26 March 2003).

31. Philip Johnston, 'Girl, 11, Searched by Police Under Anti-Terror Laws', *Daily Telegraph* (16 July 2003).

32. 'They Do Not Know What They Are Doing or Why They Are Doing It', *Independent on Sunday* (1 April 2003).

33. Andrew Gumbel, 'Hollywood Revives McCarthyist Climate by Silencing and Sacking War Critics', *Independent* (21 April 2003).

34. Duncan Campbell, '"Dixie Sluts" Fight on with Naked Defiance', *Guardian* (25 April 2003); Tim Robbins, 'Our Voices Are Lost in the Tide of Intolerance Sweeping America', *Observer* (20 April 2003).

35. Martin Bright, 'Sound and Fury', *Guardian* (6 April 2003); Alexis Petridis, 'Public Enemy', *Guardian* (4 April 2003); Michael Billington, 'Drama out of a Crisis', *Guardian* (10 April 2003).

36. Armando Iannucci, 'There's a Perfectly Simple Reason Why the Stop the War Coalition', *Daily Telegraph* (21 March 2003). Iannucci's

response to the call to support our troops also deserves quotation: 'I wish our forces well. It's just that I'd rather they didn't die. Those who do die, die tragically, because such a death is a true waste of life, a life extinguished as a result of a hunch, a political whim in the face of firmer, less violent alternatives' ('I Wish Our Forces Well: I'd Just Rather They Didn't Die Because of a Hunch', *Daily Telegraph*, 28 March 2003). See also his response to the pro-war triumphalists: 'I Suppose You Expect Me to Raise My White Flag and Come out and Surrender?', *Daily Telegraph* (18 April 2003).

37. Neil Ascherson, 'A Fearful War to Remember', *Observer* (6 April 2003).

38. Jack Straw, 'I Joined the Peace Protesters in the Sixties. Believe Me, This is Different', *Independent* (23 February 2003).

39. 'George Bush's Speech to Troops', *Guardian* (26 March 2003). As the historian Jackson Lears noted, 'While a war on terrorism may not need Providence to justify it, a war to transform the Middle East requires a rhetoric as grandiose as its aims. The providentialist outlook fills the bill: it promotes tunnel vision, discourages debate and reduces diplomacy to arm-twisting' ('How a War Became a Crusade', *New York Times*, 11 March 2003).

40. 'A Smart War', *Daily Telegraph* (24 March 2003).

41. Among the graphic images which were not shown were pictures of a ten-year-old child who lost the top of his head, apparently when a cluster bomb was used on Basra. The video footage was the lead item on Al Jazeera news, but the only 'mainstream' reproduction of the photograph in Britain or the US was a thumbnail image in the *Guardian* several days after the incident. On the footage which was never screened, see Ian Burrell, 'Broadcasting Guidelines Row over Clash of Values', *Independent* (24 March 2003).

42. 'Casualties of War', *Daily Telegraph* (2 April 2003). The nature of this supposed care for civilians was highlighted in an incident when a US Marine shot and killed a woman standing next to a man in uniform. He explained later, 'I'm sorry, but the chick got in the way' (John Pilger, 'We See Too Much. We Know Too Much. That's Our Best Defence,' *Independent on Sunday*, 6 April 2003).

43. Robert Fisk had predicted after US missiles hit a Baghdad market, 'I'll bet we are told President Saddam is ultimately responsible for their deaths.' Sure enough, the US military soon claimed, 'It is entirely possible that this may have been, in fact, an Iraqi missile that went up and came down; or, given the behaviour of the regime recently, it might have been a deliberate attack inside the town' (Robert Fisk, 'It was an Outrage, an Obscenity', *Independent*, 27 March 2003. See also Cahal Milmo, 'US Blames Iraqis in War of Words Over Slaughter in Market', *Independent*, 28 March 2003). The cycle was repeated days later after a deadlier missile strike on another

market. See Cahal Milmo, 'Proved: Iraq Marketplace Deaths were Caused by a US Missile', *Independent* (2 April 2003).

44. The first civilian who died was a Jordanian taxi driver killed by a 1,000 lb bomb dropped on an isolated telephone office (Jon Swain, 'I See First Casualty of the Reign of the Selective Bomb Raid', *Sunday Times*, 23 March 2003). This was followed by at least 50 civilian dead in Basra, some from cluster bombs, 22 March; at least 33 Kurds killed by US missile in Khormal, 22 March; five killed in Syria by a stray missile, 24 March; at least 14 killed in a Baghdad market, 26 March; at least 55 dead in a second Baghdad market, 28 March; at least 33 die in Hilla bombing, 1 April; dozens killed at coalition checkpoints; at least 18 dead in Kurdistan 'friendly fire' incident; 100 casualties per hour in Baghdad hospitals; more than 80 slain in a coalition strike at Furat near Baghdad Airport.

     On Al Jazeera's coverage, see Brian Whitaker, 'Al-Jazeera Causes Outcry with Broadcast of Battle Casualties', *Guardian* (24 March 2003).

45. Fisk, 'It was an Outrage, an Obscenity'. See also Suzanne Goldenberg in the *Guardian* (9 April 2003): 'A picture of killing inflicted on a sprawling city – and it grew more unbearable by the minute'.

46. Charles Krauthammer, 'Kofi Annan's Offense', *Washington Post* (28 March 2003).

47. Quoted in Nicholas Kristof, 'Hearts and Minds', *New York Times* (28 March 2003).

48. Richard Norton-Taylor and Owen Bowcott, 'British Use of Cluster Bombs Condemned', *Guardian* (4 April 2003); Paul Waugh and Ben Russell, 'Hoon is "Cruel" for Claims on Cluster Bombs', *Independent* (5 April 2003). For an examination of some of the controversial ordnance used by the 'coalition' in the early part of the war, see Simon Helweg-Larsen, 'Irregular Weapons Used Against Iraq', *ZNet* (7 April 2003), http://www.zmag.org/content/showarticle.cfm?SectionID=15&ItemID=3410.

49. Far from being a surprise, the post-Saddam balance sheet of protecting oil while allowing hospitals, power plants and museums to be ransacked by looters was anticipated in a 23 January exposé in the *Guardian*, 'US Begins Secret Talks to Secure Iraq's Oilfields'. Irwin Stelzer in *The Weekly Standard* outlined the strategy, 'About the best thing the politicians can do is eliminate uncertainty by getting on with the war, winning it quickly, and opening Iraq's oil industry to new investment. That would be a real stimulus package' (quoted in *The Progressive*, March 2003). See also George Trefgarne's conclusion, 'What the Economy Needs is a War', in *Daily Telegraph* (3 March 2003).

50. Steve Richards, 'No One has a Clue What to Do after War. Now That Really is Frightening', *Independent* (9 February 2003); Fergal Keane, 'Whether the United Nations Likes It or Not, America's

Patience is Exhausted', *Independent* (15 February 2003). Two weeks after the first bombs fell, the *New York Times* concluded, 'The United States badly misjudged the Iraqis going into the war, and there seems little reason to hope that we will be much smarter when it comes to nation-building' ('Second-Guessing the War', 2 April 2003).

51. Paul Waugh, 'Hoon Withdraws Claim that Protection Suits are "Proof" of Chemical Weapons', *Independent* (28 March 2003).

52. Raymond Whitaker, 'How the Road to War was Paved with Lies', *Independent* (27 April 2003).

53. Stuart Millar, 'Fog of War Shrouds the Facts', *Guardian* (5 April 2003).

54. Vikram Dodd, 'Report of Arms Factory May be Bogus', *Guardian* (25 March 2003).

55. David Charter, 'False Alarms Dash Hopes of Finding a "Smoking Gun"', *The Times* (5 April 2003).

56. Ibid., and Ewen MacAskill, 'Missile Cache Could Contain Nerve Gas', *Guardian* (8 April 2003).

57. Tim Reid, 'Troops Find "Suspicious Labs" Buried Near Factory', *The Times* (15 April 2003).

58. Ian Traynor, 'US in Row over Nuclear Project', *Guardian* (11 April 2003), and 'Nuclear Looting Alarms UN Watchdog', *Guardian* (14 May 2003); Judith Miller, 'U.S. Experts Find Radioactive Material in Iraq', *New York Times* (4 May 2003).

59. See James Meek, 'Marines Losing the Battle for Hearts and Minds', *Guardian* (25 March 2003).

60. The incident occurred as Sky News covered the 'liberation' of southern Iraq at the end of March.

61. Stewart Payne, 'Troops Find that Aid Buys Little Friendship', *The Times* (2 April 2003).

62. Suzanne Goldenberg, 'Wayward Bombs Bring Marketplace Carnage', *Guardian* (27 March 2003).

63. Anthony Shadid, 'The Whole World Cries', *Washington Post* (29 March 2003).

64. Janine di Giovanni, 'Diary of a Family at War', *The Times* (15 April 2003).

65. David Aaronovitch, 'Guns or Roses', *Observer* (30 March 2003).

66. Justin Huggler, 'Cholera Warning as Red Cross Tries to Restore Clean Water to Basra Residents', *Independent* (26 March 2003); Ewen MacAskill and Burhan Wazir, 'Iraqis Face Water Crisis in Battle Zone', *Guardian* (5 April 2003); Tim Franks, 'Umm Qasr Gets Clean Water – At a Price', *The Times* (5 April 2003); Ian Cobain, 'Cholera Fears Add to Postwar Power Problems', *The Times* (14 April 2003); Ewen MacAskill, 'Three Weeks On, and Still No Water. Now Doctors Fear an Epidemic', *Guardian* (14 April 2003); Owen Bowcott, 'Lack of Fresh Water Threatens Hospitals Swamped by Casualties',

Guardian (8 April 2003); 'The Toll of a War that has Taken Allies to the Gates of Baghdad', *Independent* (5 April 2003).

67. Cahal Milmo and Andrew Buncombe, 'Hospitals Overwhelmed by Waves of Civilian Wounded', *Independent* (9 April 2003); Owen Bowcott, 'Baghdad Hospitals Pushed to the Limit', *Guardian* (9 April 2003); Sandra Laville, 'In an Iraqi Hospital which Ran Out of Oxygen, Hope is in Short Supply', *Daily Telegraph* (14 April 2003).

68. 'Beyond Baghdad', *Guardian* (5 April 2003); Julian Borger, 'Pentagon was Warned over Policing Iraq', *Guardian* (28 May 2003). See also Maureen Dowd's use of Leonard Woolf's injunction that the limit of an imperial administration's aspirations should be to 'prevent people from killing one another or robbing one another, or burning down the camp'. 'History up in Smoke', *New York Times* (16 April 2003).

69. Andrew Buncombe, 'As the Injured Lie Suffering, a Gang of Looters Steals Drugs from Hospital', *Independent* (4 April 2003); Philip Smucker and Michael Smith, 'Hospital Looters Stealing Incubators and Drugs', *Daily Telegraph* (12 April 2003).

70. Andrew Gumbel and David Keys, 'US Blamed for Failure to Stop Sacking of Museum', *Independent* (14 April 2003); Jonathan Steele, 'Museum's Treasures Left to the Mercy of Looters', *Guardian* (14 April 2003); Oliver Burkeman, 'Ancient Archive Lost in Baghdad Library Blaze', *Guardian* (15 April 2003); Paul Martin et al., 'US Army was Told to Protect Looted Museum', *Observer* (20 April 2003); Phil Reeves, 'Baghdad's Banks Stripped as US Soldiers Stand By', *Independent* (19 April 2003).

71. Robert Fisk, 'Americans Defend Two Untouchable Ministries from the Hordes of Looters', *Independent* (14 April 2003).

72. Daniel McGrory, 'UN and Army at Odds as Troops Encourage Looting', *The Times* (6 April 2003).

73. Robert Fisk, 'A Civilisation Torn to Pieces', *Independent on Sunday* (13 April 2003).

74. George Jones, 'Carry on Looting, Hoon Tells Civilians in Basra', *Daily Telegraph* (8 April 2003).

75. James Meek, 'Marines Meet Disorder as Iraqis Cheer, Toot, and Loot', *Guardian* (10 April 2003); R. Jeffrey Smith, 'Law and Order: The Military Doesn't Want to Touch It. Who Will?', *Washington Post* (13 April 2003).

76. David Aaronovitch, 'Is This Plundering Really So Bad?', *Guardian* (15 April 2003).

77. See the *New York Times'* criticism of the Administration in 'Protecting Prisoners of War' (26 March 2003).

78. Eliza Griswold, '20 Die as Kurds and Arabs Clash in Mosul Firefights', *Sunday Times* (13 April 2003); Patrick Cockburn, 'Tensions Boil over Between Kurds and Arabs in North', *Independent* (14 April 2003); C.J. Chivers, 'Groups of Kurds Are Driving Arabs From Northern

Villages', *New York Times* (14 April 2003); Jason Burke, 'Arabs Flee Revenge of the Kurds', *Observer* (20 April 2003); Kim Sengupta, 'Americans Accused of Turning Blind Eye To Killings by Kurds', *Independent* (23 April 2003).

79. James Meek, 'Armed Shia on Streets in First Sign of Power Tussle', *Guardian* (15 April 2003).

80. William Rees-Mogg, 'The Liberation of Iraq Started on July 4, 1776', *The Times* (14 April 2003).

81. Robert Fisk, 'This is the Reality of War. We Bomb. They Suffer', *Independent on Sunday* (23 March 2003).

82. Emma Nicholson, 'A Terrible Victim, but Also Why We Went to War', *The Times* (9 April 2003).

83. Johann Hari, 'Sometimes the Only Way to Spread Peace is at the Barrel of a Gun', *Independent* (26 March 2003).

84. Philip Kennicott, 'Photos Give a Different Perspective on "Operation Freedom"', *Washington Post* (20 March 2003); Andrew Buncombe and John Lichfield, 'A City in Flames, A Nation in Chaos', *Independent* (12 April 2003).

85. 'America's Quiet Patriotism', *Daily Telegraph* (1 April 2003).

86. Michael Gove, 'Stop Pussyfooting, All that Matters is Victory', *The Times* (26 March 2003); Niall Ferguson, 'The Empire That Dare Not Speak its Name', *Sunday Times* (13 April 2003).

87. Sam Jones, ' "Does He Understand Why War Took Place?"', *Guardian* (19 April 2003).

88. Colin Brown and Francis Elliott. 'Labour Chairman Says BBC is Acting Like "Friend of Baghdad"', *Daily Telegraph* (30 March 2003); Matt Wells, 'Blunkett Accuses Media over Reports from "Behind Enemy Lines"', *Guardian* (4 April 2003); Rosemary Bennett, 'BBC Report on Baghdad's Fears Enrages No. 10', *The Times* (12 April 2003).

89. Paul Waugh, 'Hoon: "No Proof that Allied Bombs Hit Marketplace', *Independent* (4 April 2003).

90. 'Where was the BBC News?', *Daily Telegraph* (12 April 2003) and Nigel Farndale, 'The Baghdad Brigade Led Us All Astray', *Sunday Telegraph* (13 April 2003). See also Jack Straw's assertions that the reporting of 24-hour television stations might have led to the loss of the First and Second World Wars (Tom Leonard, 'TV News Could Have Cost World Wars, Says Straw', *Daily Telegraph*, 2 April 2003); and the criticisms of Brian Burridge, the commander of British forces (Rachel Sylvester, '"The UK Media Has Lost the Plot .... It's the Equivalent of Reality TV"', *Daily Telegraph*, 7 April 2003).

91. Dominic Timms, 'Al-Jazeera Websites "Hit by Hackers"', *Guardian* (26 March 2003).

92. John Pilger, 'We See Too Much. We Know Too Much. That's Our Best Defence', *Independent on Sunday* (6 April 2003).

93. Howard Kurtz, 'The Ups and Downs of Unembedded Reporters', *Washington Post* (3 April 2003).

94. RTE Radio 1, *The Sunday Show* (9 March 2003), transcript available at http://www.ccmep.org/2003_articles/Iraq/031003_pentagaon_ threatens_to_kill_inde.htm.

95. Elaine Monaghan et al., 'Arab Fury over Al-Jazeera Death', *The Times* (9 April 2003); Robert Fisk, 'Is There Some Element in the US Military That Wants to Take Out Journalists?', *Independent* (9 April 2003).

96. Robert Kagan, quoted in Paul Vallely, 'Paradox and Power: The Philosopher of a World of Turmoil', *Independent* (15 March 2003).

97. Nick Cohen, 'The Left isn't Listening' *Observer* (16 February 2003); Johann Hari, 'Do You Trust George Bush to Run the War?', *Independent* (21 March 2003). See also Stephen Pollard, 'There is a Conflict in Washington Too', *Independent* (4 April 2003). Once again Hari was sabotaged by *Independent* editors who placed a demolishing column underneath his call to democracy. Mary Dejevsky wrote: 'There is not the slightest hint in the Bush lexicon of a world that might not be transformed into an ideal, Disneyfied America, no recognition that prosperity and American-style freedom might not be the first, or even most precious, conditions desired by Iraqis from their unsought "war of liberation". There is none of the cultural sensitivity at which Bill Clinton excelled, and no room for a reborn Iraq – as Iraq. Just the flat canvas of an American future, with Bluebeard (sorry, "tyrant Saddam") magicked out of his castle and the snow-capped mountains and the sunlit green fields beyond' ('Bush Had Iraq in His Sights Before He Became President', *Independent*, 21 March 2003).

98. Jacqueline Rose, 'We Are All Afraid, but of What, Exactly?', *Guardian* (21 March 2003).

99. William Safire, 'The Asian Front', *New York Times* (3 March 2003).

100. Charles Krauthammer, 'Call the Vote. Walk Away', *Washington Post* (12 March 2003); Perle quoted in Roland Watson et al., 'US Hawks Press Bush to Go to War, UN or Not', *The Times* (13 March 2003). See also Herbert London, 'In Search of an American Foreign Policy', *Fox News* (20 March 2003), http://www.foxnews.com/story/ 0,2933,81573,00.html; Charles Krauthammer, 'Forget Them All, Mr Bush', *Guardian* (26 March 2003).

101. Quoted in Ronald Brownstein, 'Washington on Brink of a New Era', *Los Angeles Times* (18 March 2003).

102. Anton La Guardia, 'Blair Says UN Must Run post-Saddam Iraq to End Oil Row', *Daily Telegraph* (7 March 2003); Bronwen Maddox, 'Blair Bows to US over a Reduced Role for UN', *The Times* (27 March 2003); George Jones et al., 'Blair Plays Down the UN's Role in Rebuilding Iraq', *Daily Telegraph* (27 March 2003).

103. Ed Vulliamy and Kamal Ahmed, 'US Begins the Process of Regime Change', *Observer* (6 April 2003); James Bone, 'Britain Upset by

American Plan to Sideline Blix', *The Times* (14 April 2003). Blair accepted the reduction of the UN to an advisory role even though 57 per cent of the British public supported a UN interim administration and only two per cent a US-led authority (Anthony King, 'Britons Express Grave Doubts over US Role in Post-War Iraq', *Daily Telegraph*, 7 April 2003).

104. Robert J. McCartney, 'French Businesses Say U.S. Boycott is Hurting Them', *Washington Post* (16 April 2003); Marcus Warren, 'Anti-French Feelings Run High in Most Gallic US City', *Daily Telegraph* (2 May 2003).

105. Michael Ledeen, 'A Theory', *National Review Online* (10 March 2003), www.nationalreview.com/ledeen/ledeen031003.asp.

106. William Safire, 'French Connection II', *New York Times* (20 March 2003).

107. David Harrison, 'German Spies Offered Help to Saddam in Run-up to War', *Sunday Telegraph* (20 April 2003); Matthew Campbell, 'Dossier Reveals France Briefed Iraq on US Plans', *Sunday Times* (27 April 2003). The *Telegraph* was also on the lookout for intelligence damning the Labour MP George Galloway, the former arms inspector Scott Ritter, the Russians and the Jordanian Government (which had convicted Ahmad Chalabi on fraud charges) as accomplices of Saddam. See, for example, Inigo Gilmore and Charles Laurence, 'Iraqis Tried to Bribe Scott Ritter with Gold', *Sunday Telegraph* (4 May 2003).

108. Bruce Anderson, 'Our War Leaders Need to Agree on How to Keep France out of the Middle East', *Independent* (7 April 2003).

109. Julia Day, 'Shock and Awe™ – It's Just a Game', *Guardian* (11 April 2003).

110. Alexander Chancellor, 'Why Bush is Just a Bolshevik', *Guardian Weekend* (5 April 2003).

111. Seymour Hersh, 'Why was Richard Perle Meeting with Adnan Khashoggi?', *New Yorker* (17 March 2003); Maureen Dowd, 'Perle's Plunder Blunder', *New York Times* (23 March 2003); David Leigh, 'Pentagon Hawk Linked to UK Intelligence Company', *Guardian* (21 March 2003). Perle subsequently called Seymour Hersh 'the closest thing American journalism has to a terrorist' (CNN, *Late Edition*, 9 March 2003).

112. Antony Barnett and Solomon Hughes, 'Bush Ally Set to Profit from the War on Terror', *Observer* (11 May 2003); André Verlöy and Daniel Politi, 'Advisors of Influence', *Center for Public Integrity* (28 March 2003).

113. Tim Reid and Tom Baldwin, 'Bush Goes it Alone with Iraq Arms Task Force', *The Times* (18 April 2003); John Hooper and Oliver Burkeman, 'US Sends in Its Own Weapons Inspectors', *Guardian* (18 April 2003).

114. Raymond Whitaker, 'Revealed: How the Road to War was Paved with Lies', *Independent on Sunday* (27 April 2003).

115. Bronwen Maddox, 'Reports of Weapons "Greatly Exaggerated"', *The Times* (25 April 2003); 'So Where are They, Mr Blair?', *Independent on Sunday* (20 April 2003).

116. Andrew Grice, 'Putin Snubs Blair by Refusing to Lift Sanctions', *Independent* (30 April 2003).

117. David Ignatius, 'Tipping Points', *Washington Post* (10 April 2003). The charge was repeated in Michael Smith, 'French Secret Service "Kept CIA in the Dark over Iraq and Uranium"', *Daily Telegraph* (14 July 2003).

118. Thomas Friedman, 'Hold Your Applause', *New York Times* (9 April 2003).

119. David Ignatius, 'Groping toward Democracy', *New York Times* (18 April 2003).

120. Paul Foot, 'Jobs for the FDR Boys', *Guardian* (2 April 2003).

121. Quoted in Paul Vallely, 'The US General Waiting to Replace Saddam', *Independent* (5 April 2003).

122. Bob Herbert, 'Spoils of War', *New York Times* (10 April 2003).

123. Douglas Jehl and Jane Perlez, 'Pentagon Sending a Team of Exiles to Help Iraq', *New York Times* (26 April 2003); Douglas Jehl, 'U.S.-Backed Iraqi Exiles Return to Reinvent Nation', *New York Times* (4 May 2003).

124. Brian Whitaker, 'Hawkish Lawyer to Oversee Iraqi Ministries', *Guardian* (4 April 2003).

125. Rupert Cornwell, 'The Saviour of Iraq – Or a Chancer Whose Time Has Come?', *Independent* (12 April 2003).

126. David Leigh and Brian Whitaker, 'Financial Scandal Claims Hang over Leader in Waiting', *Guardian* (14 April 2003).

127. Daniel Johnson, 'Only We Can Get People to Rise up against Regime', *Daily Telegraph* (27 March 2003); 'Help the Iraqi Maquis', *Daily Telegraph* (29 March 2003); Andrew Billen, 'Contender Who Would Unite Iraq but Divide Capitol', *The Times* (11 April 2003); Marie Colvin, 'Chalabi the Challenge Finds His Destiny in a Broken Land', *Sunday Times* (13 April 2003); David Leigh and Brian Whitaker, 'Financial Scandal Claims Hang over Leader in Waiting', *Guardian* (14 April 2003).

128. Rajiv Chandrasekaran, 'Exile Finds Ties to U.S. A Boon and a Barrier', *Washington Post* (27 April 2003). 'Embedded' reporters were blocked by the military from writing about the FIF units as they prepared to enter Iraq (Jonathan Finer, 'Embedded in Iraq: Was It Worth It?', *Washington Post*, 4 May 2003).

129. Richard Lloyd Parry and David Charter, 'Fear Grips Iraqis as Rivals Vie for Power', *The Times* (15 April 2003); Ian Cobain, 'Cholera Fears Add to Postwar Power Problems', *The Times* (14 April 2003).

130. Rupert Cornwell, 'Exiles Backed by Pentagon in Bid for Power', *Independent on Sunday* (13 April 2003); Sandra Laville, 'Iraqis Harbour Deep Suspicion of Exile Leaders', *Daily Telegraph* (15 April 2003).

131. Richard Lloyd Parry, 'US-Sponsored Militia Hunt for Plunder', *The Times* (18 April 2003).

132. Rory McCarthy and Ewen MacAskill, 'Chaos Mars Talks on Iraqi Self-Rule', *Guardian* (16 April 2003); Marc Santora and Patrick E. Tyler, 'Pledge Made to Democracy by Exiles, Sheiks, and Clerics', *New York Times* (16 April 2003).

133. 'Fake "Dancing in the Streets"', (New York) *Indymedia* (10 April 2003), http://nyc.indymedia.org/front.php3?article_id=55384& group=webcast.

134. John Kifner and Craig S. Smith, 'Sunnis and Shiites Unite to Protest U.S. and Hussein', *New York Times* (19 April 2003); Kim Sengupta, 'No Fanfare as Chalabi Returns to Iraq', *Independent* (18 April 2003), and 'Gunfire Interrupts First Press Conference by "Pentagon's Man"', *Independent* (19 April 2003); Jonathan Steele, 'Protesters Pour from the Mosques to Reclaim the Streets for Islam', *Guardian* (19 April 2003).

135. Fox News, *Fox News Sunday* (27 April 2003); Jim Hoagland, 'Return of an Iraqi Exile', *Washington Post* (9 April 2003). Chalabi's linkage of Saddam and Al-Qa'eda merely continued the process that the Iraqi National Congress had set in motion within weeks of 9–11 with 'proof' that the operation 'was conducted by people who were trained by Saddam' (Seymour Hersh, 'Selective Intelligence', *The New Yorker*, 12 May 2003). Meanwhile, fairness demands recognition that the British were having their own problems in Basra, as the sheikh-appointed leader of the province happened to be a former Ba'athist Brigadier General, a fact noted by several hundred stone-throwing protesters (Steven Morris and Richard Norton-Taylor, 'British-Appointed Basra Chief Exposed as Former Ba'athist', *Guardian*, 12 April 2003).

136. Toby Harnden, 'Pentagon Gets Tough in Fight over Post-War Vision of Iraq', *Daily Telegraph* (3 April 2003); Rupert Cornwell, 'Turf War Rages in Washington over Who Will Rule Iraq', *Independent* (5 April 2003); Andrew Gumbel, 'Washington Factions Struggle for Control', *Independent on Sunday* (6 April 2003); Ewen MacAskill and Oliver Burkeman, 'Power Vacuum That Has Taken US by Surprise', *Guardian* (11 April 2003); Dan Morgan, 'Deciding Who Rebuilds Iraq is Fraught with Infighting', *Washington Post* (4 May 2003).

137. Ed Vulliamy and Kamal Ahmed, 'When the Shooting Stops', *Observer* (6 April 2003); David Rose, 'Exile Takes Centre Stage', *Observer* (13 April 2003).

138. Toby Harnden, 'Man Who Set Out to Get Iraq's Mafioso', *Daily Telegraph* (5 April 2003).

139. Toby Harnden, 'Rumsfeld Urges Interim Government Composed of Exile Leaders', *Daily Telegraph* (5 April 2003).
140. Philip Webster, 'Blair Parries MPs' Postwar Worries', *The Times* (3 April 2003).
141. Phil Reeves, 'Iraqis Emulate Palestinians by Stoning Troops', *Independent on Sunday* (27 April 2003).
142. Michael R. Gordon and John Kifner, 'U.S. Warns Iraqis Against Claiming Authority in Void', *New York Times* (24 April 2003); David Ignatius, Bush's Confusion, Baghdad's Mess', *Washington Post* (24 April 2003); Craig Smith, 'Americans Arrest Would-Be Leader of Iraq's Capital', *New York Times* (28 April 2003).
143. Phil Reeves and James Morrison, 'Chalabi's Men Hand "Rescued" Artefacts Back to Museum', *Independent on Sunday* (27 April 2003).
144. Laurie Goodstein, 'Groups Critical of Islam Are Waiting to Aid Iraq', *New York Times* (4 April 2003).
145. Ben Macintyre, 'Tony and George Show has Iraqi Viewers Gripped', *The Times* (11 April 2003).
146. David Sanger and Jim Rutenberg, 'Media Campaign is Intended to Speed End of War', *New York Times* (11 April 2003); Oliver Burkeman, 'Arab World Now Faces Invasion by American TV', *Guardian* (24 April 2003).
147. Sabrine Tavernise, 'Iranian News Channel Makes Inroads in Iraq', *New York Times* (29 April 2003).
148. Ewen MacAskill, 'Baghdad Waits in Fear for Rebuilding to Start', *Guardian* (9 May 2003).
149. David Rohde, 'Marines Again Kill Iraqis in Exchange of Fire in Mosul', *New York Times* (17 April 2003); Ian Fisher, 'U.S. Force Said to Kill 15 During an Anti-American Rally', *New York Times* (30 April 2003). For an exposé challenging the American military's account, see Phil Reeves, 'Iraqi Rage Grows after Fallujah Massacre', *Independent on Sunday* (14 May 2003).
150. Jamie Wilson, 'Charity's Anger as US Halts Aid Plane', *Guardian* (18 April 2003); Rory McCarthy, 'Aid Agencies Say Security Concerns are Holding Them Back', *Guardian* (19 April 2003).
151. Richard Lloyd Parry, 'Children Main Victims of Cluster Bombs', *The Times* (19 April 2003); Scheherezade Faramarzi, 'Unexploded Bombs Hurt Children in Iraq', *Washington Post* (25 April 2003); Michael Howard, 'Fighting is Over but the Deaths Go on', *Guardian* (28 April 2003).
152. Ewen MacAskill, 'Three Weeks On and Still No Water', *Guardian* (14 April 2003); Donald Macintyre, 'Protests over Health Chief as Cholera Hits Basra', *Independent* (8 May 2003); George Wright, 'WHO Warns of Cholera Outbreak', *Guardian* (8 May 2003).
153. Phil Reeves, 'The War Has Not Ended', *Independent* (24 April 2003). See also Morten Rostrup of Médicins Sans Frontières, in Ian Sample,

'"We Had Kids Dying Just Before We Started to Operate"', *Guardian* (8 May 2003).

154. David Teather, 'Jobs for the Boys: The Reconstruction Billions', *Guardian* (15 April 2003). On the Government's handling of reconstruction contracts, see Richard A. Oppel, Jr. et al., 'Who Will Put Iraq Back Together?', *New York Times* (23 March 2003).

155. Elizabeth Becker, 'Details Given on Contract Halliburton was Awarded', *New York Times* (11 April 2003).

156. Elizabeth Becker and Richard Oppel, Jr., 'U.S. Gives Bechtel a Major Contract in Rebuilding Iraq', *New York Times* (18 April 2003).

157. Antony Barnett, 'Scandal-Hit US Firm Wins Key Contracts', *Observer* (13 April 2003).

158. David Teather, 'American to Oversee Iraqi Oil Industry', *Guardian* (26 April 2003).

159. Ed Vulliamy, 'Israel Seeks Pipeline for Iraqi Oil', *Observer* (20 April 2003).

160. Heather Stewart, 'Fury at Agriculture Post for US Businessman', *Guardian* (28 April 2003).

161. Thom Shanker and Eric Schmitt, 'Pentagon Expects Long-Term Access to Four Key Bases in Iraq', *New York Times* (20 April 2003).

162. Joseph Biden and Chuck Hagel, 'Winning the Peace', *Washington Post* (6 April 2003); Bronwen Maddox, 'Mother of All Battles Will Be for Black Gold', *The Times* (8 April 2003), 'Post-Saddam Oil Prize May Be a Tarnished Jewel', *The Times* (11 April 2003), and 'How Much Will US Pay for the Future of Iraq?', *The Times* (16 April 2003).

163. Peter Beaumont et al., 'Painful Rebirth of Iraq after Saddam', *Observer* (13 April 2003).

164. Robert Fisk, 'For the People on the Streets, This is not Liberation but Colonial Oppression', *Independent* (17 April 2003); Geoffrey Wheatcroft, 'Saddam was a Despot. True. This Justifies the War. False', *Guardian* (20 April 2003), using Disraeli's words in 1854 about the Crimean War.

165. Oliver Burkeman, 'Secret Report Throws Doubt on Democracy Hopes', *Independent* (15 March 2003). See also Fergal Keane, 'Does the West Understand How This Hated War is Altering the Arab World?', *Independent* (29 March 2003).

166. Quoted in Glenn Kessler and Dana Priest, 'U.S. Planners Surprised by Strength of Iraqi Shiites', *Washington Post* (23 April 2003).

167. The prediction came from Egypt's Hosni Mubarak (Ian Black and Chris McGreal, 'Conflict Will Create 100 Bin Ladens, Warns Egyptian President', *Guardian*, 1 April 2003).

168. Craig S. Smith, 'Elated Shias, on Pilgrimage, Want U.S. Out', *New York Times* (22 April 2003); Kim Sengupta, 'Pilgrims Threaten Jihad Against American Forces', *Independent* (24 April 2003).

169. Craig S. Smith, 'Iraqi Shiites, Jockeying for Power, Preach an Anti-American Sermon', *New York Times* (20 April 2003); Anthony Shadid, 'Iraqi Shiites Grow Uneasy over U.S. Occupation', *Washington Post* (24 April 2003).

170. Craig S. Smith, 'Cleric in Iran Says Shiites Must Act', *New York Times* (26 April 2003).

171. Kim Sengupta, 'Protesters Call for "Army of Occupation" to Quit Iraq', *Independent* (19 April 2003) and 'Foreigners Who Came to Fight for Saddam Turn Guns on Shias', *Independent on Sunday* (20 April 2003); Jonathan Steele, 'Protesters Pour from the Streets to Reclaim the Streets for Islam', *Guardian* (19 April 2003); Peter Beaumont, 'Revolution City', *Observer* (20 April 2003).

172. John Mintz and Dana Priest, 'Shiite Demands for Control in Iraq Challenge U.S. Plans', *New York Times* (16 April 2003).

173. Richard Beeston, 'Murder at Iraq's Holiest Shrine', *The Times* (11 April 2003).

174. Adel Darwish, 'Returned Exile Rallies Sunnis', *Daily Telegraph* (22 April 2003); Quoted in Glenn Kessler and Dana Priest, 'U.S. Planners Surprised by Strength of Iraqi Shiites', *Washington Post* (23 April 2003); Douglas Jehl and David E. Sanger, 'U.S. Tells Iran not to Interfere in Iraq Efforts', *New York Times* (24 April 2003).

175. 'U.S. General Brings Iraqi City Leaders Together, Says He Is In Charge,' *Fox News*, http://www.foxnews.com/story/0,2933,84592,00.html; 'Iraqi Shi'ites Say Ruling Najaf, Ignore U.S. Troops', *Reuters* (26 April 2003); Jonathan Steele and Vikram Dodd, 'US Arrests Bogus Baghdad Mayor', *Guardian* (28 April 2003).

176. Wesley Clark, 'America's Military Might is Practically Invincible', *The Times* (11 April 2003). The phrase 'revolutionary hubris' is Daniel Cohn-Bendit's, quoted in Alexander Chancellor, 'Why Bush is Just a Bolshevik', *Guardian Weekend* (5 April 2003).

177. James Woolsey, 'Welcome to the Fourth World War', *Guardian* (8 April 2003).

178. Andrew J. Bacevich, 'We Have the Power. Now, How Do We Use It?', *Washington Post* (20 April 2003); Niall Ferguson, 'The Empire Slinks Back', *New York Times* (27 April 2003).

179. David Sanger, 'Viewing the War as a Lesson to the World', *New York Times* (6 April 2003).

180. Peter Slevin, 'U.S. Warns of Interference in Iraq', *Washington Post* (29 March 2003); David Sanger, 'Viewing the War as a Lesson to the World', *New York Times* (6 April 2003); Linda Diebel, 'Ex-CIA Chief Gets Tough on Syria', *Toronto Star* (21 April 2003).

181. Rupert Cornwell, 'Powell Flies out with a Post-War Warning for Syria and Iran', *Independent* (1 April 2003).

182. Toby Harnden, 'US Warns Syria Against Becoming "Pariah"', *Daily Telegraph* (15 April 2003).

183. Walter Pincus, 'Syria Warned Again Not to "Meddle" in Iraq', *Washington Post* (11 April 2003).

184. Steven R. Weisman, 'Praising Syria's President, Powell Also Hints at Sanctions', *New York Times* (5 May 2003).

185. Julian Borger et al., 'Bush Vetoes Syria War Plan', *Guardian* (15 April 2003); Tony Allen-Mills, 'Powell Warns Syria as Hawks Push for Attack', *The Times* (4 May 2003).

186. 'Resurgence of the Shias', *Guardian* (24 April 2003).

187. Donald Macintyre, 'The Shia of Southern Iraq Care More About Electricity than Religious Power', *Independent* (25 April 2003).

188. Phil Reeves, 'Iran's Influence Crosses Border to Fill Vacuum', *Independent* (17 April 2003); Michael R. Gordon, 'U.S. Acts to Limit Influence of Iraq in Iran's Politics', *New York Times* (1 May 2003); Julian Borger and Dan De Luce, 'Iranians Enriching Uranium, US Says', *Guardian* (9 May 2003). Demonstrating the complexity and even contradictions of the US approach towards Iran, the Badr Brigade was the military wing of the Supreme Council for Islamic Revolution in Iraq, one of the opposition groups with whom Washington was supposedly negotiating for the post-war administration of Iraq.

189. Eli J. Lake, 'U.S.: Iran Will Infiltrate 5 Iraqi Cities', *United Press International* (3 April 2003); Douglas Jehl, 'Iran is Said to Send Agents into South Iraq', *New York Times* (23 April 2003).

190. Douglas Jehl and Michael R. Gordon, 'American Forces Reach Cease-Fire with Terror Group', *New York Times* (29 April 2003).

191. Quoted in Maureen Dowd, 'Perle's Plunder Blunder', *New York Times* (23 March 2003); Ronald Brownstein, 'Those who Sought War are Now Pushing Peace', *Los Angeles Times* (17 April 2003).

192. 'Shias after Saddam', *Daily Telegraph* (2 April 2003).

193. Andrew Stephen, 'And Now, the Next American War', *New Statesman* (14 April 2003).

194. Maureen Dowd, 'Chest Banging, Here and There', *New York Times* (23 April 2003); Andrew Sullivan, 'Ominous Fault Lines Open Under Bush's Feet', *Sunday Times* (23 April 2003); Toby Harnden, 'Powell Gives Syria "Final Warning" over Terrorism', *Daily Telegraph* (5 May 2003).

195. 'Armitage Says Gingrich is "Off His Meds and Out of Therapy"', *Reuters* (25 April 2003).

196. Johann Hari, 'Do You Trust George Bush to Run the War?', *Independent* (21 March 2003).

197. Ibid., and 'The Gulf Dividing America and Europe is One of History, Not Just Geography,' *Independent* (12 February 2003). Timothy Garton Ash offered another rationale for cooperation with a well-meaning if misguided Washington, 'America has never been the Great Satan. It has sometimes been the Great Gatsby: "They were careless people, Tom and Daisy – they smashed up things and

creatures and then retreated back into their money or their vast carelessness'" .... One of Britain's jobs as America's best friend ... is to keep reminding Tom and Daisy that they now have promises to keep' ('America on Probation', *Guardian*, 17 April 2003).

198. 'The US Should Welcome Help', *Observer* (13 April 2003).
199. Joe Conason, 'Love Ya Tony', *Guardian* (14 April 2003).
200. Robert Kagan, 'Resisting Superpowerful Temptations', *Washington Post* (9 April 2003).
201. Thomas Friedman, 'Watch Out for Hijackers', *New York Times* (6 April 2003).
202. Thomas Friedman, 'Dear President Bush', *New York Times* (30 April 2003).
203. 'After the War', *Washington Post* (3 April 2003); 'Final Battles', *Washington Post* (6 April 2003); 'A Partnership For Iraq', *Washington Post* (8 April 2003); 'Liberated Baghdad', *Washington Post* (10 April 2003). See also 'Ending the Sanctions', *Washington Post* (22 April 2003).
204. William Safire, 'On Rewarding Friends', *New York Times* (3 April 2003).
205. Thomas Friedman, 'The Western Front', *New York Times* (23 March 2003).
206. Richard Perle, 'Thank God for the Death of the UN', *Guardian* (21 March 2003).
207. Toby Harnden, 'Americans Find Ways to Punish the French', *Daily Telegraph* (25 April 2003). The word 'French' had become Washington's sharpest political insult as, for example, in a White House adviser's comment on Democratic presidential candidate John Kerry, 'He looks French', or the branding of Senators who opposed Bush budget proposals as 'Franco-Republicans'.
208. Elisabeth Bumiller, 'U.S., Angry at French Stance on War, Considers Punishment', *New York Times* (24 April 2003).
209. John Lichfield, 'Chirac Leads New Defence Challenge to US', *Independent* (30 April 2003).
210. Irwin Stelzer, 'So, EU or US, Tony? You are Going to Have to Choose', *The Times* (10 March 2003).
211. Hugo Young, 'We Have Been Set Adrift in the Middle of the Atlantic', *Guardian* (25 March 2003).
212. 'How to Win the Peace', *Observer* (23 March 2003).
213. Timothy Garton Ash, 'Grumpy Old Men', *Guardian* (1 May 2003).
214. George Monbiot, 'The Bottom Dollar', *Guardian* (22 April 2003).
215. Matthew Parris, 'It's Time We All Signed Up for the Rest of the World Team', *The Times* (12 April 2003).

Conclusion

1. Robert Fisk, 'For the People on the Streets, This is not Liberation but Colonial Oppression', *Independent* (17 April 2003).

2. Quoted in Ronald Brownstein, 'Washington on Brink of a New Era', *Los Angeles Times* (18 March 2003).

3. 'The New Caliphs', *Guardian* (10 May 2003).

4. Donald Macintyre, 'Rumsfeld Glories in Triumph as He Praises Troops' War Effort', *Guardian* (1 May 2003); Ben Russell, 'Rumsfeld's Soundbites Take a Back Seat as He Lashes Out at Waiting Journalists', *Independent* (3 May 2003); Vernon Loeb, 'Rumsfeld's Flying Circus', *Washington Post* (3 May 2003).

5. David Corn, 'The Gloating on the (Neocon) Cakewalk', *The Nation* (15 April 2003).

6. David Usborne et al., 'Iraq Inc.: A Joint Venture Built on Broken Promises', *Independent* (10 May 2003).

7. Roger Morris, 'Freedom, American-Style', *Los Angeles Times* (23 April 2003).

8. Eric Schmitt and Elisabeth Bumiller, 'Rumsfeld Visits Two Cities in Iraq, Meeting Troops', *New York Times* (1 May 2003); Ewen MacAskill, 'US Sacks Its Woman in Baghdad', *Guardian* (12 May 2003).

9. Julian Coman and Sean Rayment, 'America Nervous as Militant Cleric's Rallies Attract Mass Support', *Daily Telegraph* (20 April 2003).

10. Jonathan Steele, 'Operation Support Garner', *Guardian* (6 May 2003); Peter Beaumont, 'Plan for Iraq Handover Government Scrapped', *Observer* (18 May 2003).

11. Rohan Jayasakera, 'Gives with One Hand, Takes Away with the Other', *Index on Censorship* (11 June 2003), http://www.indexonline.org/news/20030611_iraq.shtml.

12. Stephen Farrell, 'Mosul's Rivals Unite in Search for Democracy', *The Times* (2 May 2003).

13. Alice Thomson, 'After War, the Terrible Peace in a Land Where Fresh Water and Medicine are in Short Supply', *Daily Telegraph* (19 May 2003); 'Resentment Bubbles as British Troops Try to Restore Order in Basra', *Guardian* (15 July 2003).

14. Donald Macintyre, 'Exiled Cleric Returns Home to Call for Free Islamic State', *Independent on Sunday* (11 May 2003); Stephen Farrell, 'Foreign Forces Must Go, Insists Ayatollah', *The Times* (12 May 2003); Lawrence F. Kaplan, 'Clerical Error', *The New Republic Online* (2 May 2003). The Kaplan article continues: 'That constitution will include clauses designed to impede the rise of illiberal forces – among these, the diffusion of national power along federal lines, detailed arrangements for sharing that power in Baghdad, perhaps a ban on "totalitarian" political parties, and a commitment to regular elections. Those elections, moreover, will be held on a "rolling" basis, beginning at the municipal level and proceeding only slowly toward the Iraqi center. In the meantime, American officials hope an influx of financial and humanitarian assistance will diminish Shia resentments in Iraq's south. And, when elections do come, administration officials predict that a more discrete and

narrowly tailored influx of aid will give liberal forces an advantage. Indeed, as American troops in Baghdad and Kut pry self-appointed Iraqis from power, Special Forces and CIA officers have already fanned out across Iraq's south to bolster and create moderate Shia Voices.'

15. Judith Miller, 'Illicit Arms Kept Till Eve of War, An Iraqi Scientist is Said to Assert', *New York Times* (21 April 2003), and 'Leading Iraqi Scientist Says He Lied to U.N. Inspectors', *New York Times* (27 April 2003); Rory McCarthy,'Weapons Taskforce Leaves in Failure', *Guardian* (12 May 2003). On Judith Miller, see Jack Shafer, 'Deep Miller', *Slate* (21 April 2003), http://slate.msn.com/id/2001771/.

16. Mike Allen, 'Bush: "We Found" Banned Weapons', *Washington Post* (31 May 2003). It was soon established by an official British investigation that the mobile labs were for the 'production of hydrogen to fill artillery balloons' (Peter Beaumont et al., 'Iraqi Mobile Labs Nothing to Do with Germ Warfare, Report Finds', *Observer*, 15 June 2003).

17. Richard Norton-Taylor, 'White House Turns on CIA over Uranium Claim', *Guardian* (12 July 2003). On Rumsfeld's Office of Special Plans, see Julian Borger, 'The Spies Who Pushed for War', *Guardian* (17 July 2003).

18. Quoted in Wolfowitz's interview with Sam Tanenhaus, *Vanity Fair* (July 2003).

19. Quoted in Rupert Cornwell, 'Bush', *Independent* (17 July 2003).

20. Associated Press (Niko Price), reprinted in 'AP, in First Nationwide Tally of Iraqi Civilian War Deaths, Counts at Least 3,240', *Redding* (California) *Record Searchlight* (10 June 2003).

21. Associated Press/Niko Price, reprinted in 'Crime Wave Marks Violent Summer for Iraqi Capital', (Chicago) *Daily Southtown* (10 August 2003).

22. Julian Borger, 'Rumsfeld Expects More Attacks Very Soon', *Guardian* (14 July 2003); Tim Reid, 'We Want Our Husbands Back Now', *The Times* (16 July 2003).

23. The British cost of occupation is £150 million per month with a projected total of more than £5 billion (Richard Norton-Taylor et al., 'Cost of Occupation: £5 Million a Day – Human Cost Extra' *Guardian*, 17 July 2003).

24. Alan Philps, 'Looters "to be Shot on Sight by US Troops"', *Daily Telegraph* (15 May 2003). One American battalion alone killed between 20 and 30 Iraqis in the month after liberation (Andrew Buncombe, 'New Mass Grave Found as Anti-US Sentiment Rises', *Independent on Sunday*, 18 May 2003).

25. David Rohde, 'Green Berets Fight Chaos and Callousness in a City Gone Bad', *New York Times* (14 April 2003).

26. William Kristol, 'The End of the Beginning', *Weekly Standard* (12 May 2003).

27. Phil Reeves, 'US Launches Fresh Afghan Offensive to Bolster Karzai', *Independent* (21 March 2003).

28. Todd Pitman, 'Eleven Afghans Killed after American Bomb Misses its Target', *Guardian* (10 April 2003).

29. April Witt, 'Red Cross Worker Gunned Down in Afghanistan', *Washington Post* (29 March 2003); Zahid Hussein, 'Red Cross Worker Shot by Afghan Militants', *The Times* (29 March 2003); Kathy Gannon, 'Afghan Leader's Key Aide Killed by Taliban Forces', *Independent on Sunday* (6 April 2003). See also Carlotta Gall, 'In Pakistan Border Towns, Taliban Has a Resurgence', *New York Times* (6 May 2003).

30. Phil Reeves, 'Afghan Clerics Call for New Holy War', *Independent* (1 April 2003); April Witt, 'Villagers Join Fight Against U.S., Afghan Forces', *New York Times* (3 April 2003).

31. Lucy Morgan-Edwards, 'Old Warlord Proves Thorn in the Side of Afghan Government', *Sunday Telegraph* (13 April 2003).

32. The hypocrisy of US policy was vividly demonstrated when Assistant Secretary of State Richard Armitage visited Kabul and insisted, 'We can be involved in Afghanistan [as well as Iraq] very heavily, and for the long term.' He presented the national musuem with a check for $100,000; the rest of the millions once promised by the US Government never materialised (Luke Harding, 'US Pledges to Rebuild Afghanistan', *Guardian*, 10 May 2003).

33. Patrick Wintour, 'Britain Losing New Afghan Opium War', *Guardian* (7 August 2003).

34. Richard Norton-Taylor, 'Al-Qaida is Back and Stronger Than Ever', *Guardian* (19 May 2003).

35. Rupert Cornwell, 'North Korea Warns US: We Can Produce Six Atom Bombs', *Independent* (16 July 2003); David Sanger, 'Administration Divided over North Korea', *New York Times* (21 April 2003).

36. Walter Pincus, 'Future of U.S. Nuclear Arsenal Debated', *Washington Post* (4 May 2003).

37. Paul Vallely, 'The Invisible', *Independent* (26 June 2003); Oliver Burkeman, 'Children Held at Guatanamo Bay', *Guardian* (24 April 2003).

38. Andrew Gumbel, 'US Accused of Hypocrisy on Human Rights', *Independent on Sunday* (6 April 2003).

39. Nat Hentoff, 'Ashcroft out of Control', *Village Voice* (5–11 March 2003).

40. Rachel L. Swarns and Christopher Drew, 'Fearful, Angry or Confused, Muslim Immigrants Register', *New York Times* (25 April 2003); Christine Pelisek, 'The List', *LA Weekly* (4–10 July 2003).

41. George Lardner, Jr., 'More Illegal Immigrants Can Be Held', *Washington Post* (25 April 2003).

42. See Rajiv Chandrasekaran, 'Troubles Temper Triumphs in Iraq', *Washington Post* (18 August 2003); Vivienne Walt, 'The Power Beyond Their Grasp', *Washington Post* (17 August 2003).

43. Michael Howard, 'Ruling Council in Symbolic First Step', *Guardian* (14 July 2003); Jamie Wilson, 'Iraqi Elections "in Less than Year"', *Guardian* (1 August 2003).

44. As this book goes to print, the *New York Times* reports, 'In a turbulent 12-hour stretch, a pipeline supplying much of Baghdad's water was blown up this weekend, a huge new fire was set off along an oil pipeline, and a mortar attack on a prison left 6 Iraqis dead and 59 wounded. The attacks raised new concerns that the insurgents who have been singling out American soldiers may be widening their strikes to include civilian targets and economic sabotage' (John Tierney and Robert F. Worth, 'Attacks in Iraq May Be Signals of New Tactics', 18 August 2003). The *Washington Post* headlines, 'U.S. Forces Kill Cameraman', 'Long Road to Recovery for Baghdad Hospitals', 'Afghan Rebels Attack Police; 22 Killed' and 'Iraqi Clerics Unite in Rare Alliance: U.S. Fears Sunni, Shiite Cooperation Will Bolster Resistance'.

45. Paul Krugman, 'Victory Won't End Distrust of Bush', *International Herald Tribune* (19 March 2003); Mark LeVine, '"Bush Wins": The Left's Nightmare Scenario', *AlterNet* (13 March 2003), http://www.alternet.org/story.html?StoryID=15379; Fergal Keane, 'What Mr Bush has in Mind is Nothing Less than the Shaping of the World,' *Independent* (1 February 2003).

46. Mark Steyn, 'The War? That was All over Two Weeks Ago', *Daily Telegraph* (5 April 2003); Cal Thomas, 'False Media Prophets', *Jewish World Review* (15 April 2003); Stephen Pollard, Opponents of Military Trials are Friends of Al-Qaeda', *The Times* (14 July 2003).

47. Richard Cohen, 'Hollywood's Darling, Liberals' Blind Spot', *Washington Post* (8 April 2003); Johann Hari, 'I'd Rather It was Money than Belief that Made George Galloway Support Saddam', *Independent* (23 April 2003). See the response to Hari from Francesca Cryer in *Independent* (25 April 2003): 'Labelling the movement "deranged" because a politician who was part of it might turn out to be crooked is ridiculous.' An equally telling indictment of Hari's definition of the 'Left' is its similarity to the told-you-so chanting of the *Daily Telegraph:* 'It is hard to think of a graver setback to the British anti-war movement. How would you feel if you were one of the many well-meaning peace protesters who had followed Mr Galloway's lead? ... [You] may be reluctant to march in support of this kingdom's enemies in future' ('Saddam's Little Helper', 22 April 2003).

48. Todd Gitlin, 'The War's over, but the Fighting's Getting Worse', *Washington Post* (4 May 2003). Gitlin's advice concluded with an affront to those who not only opposed military conflict with heavy

hearts but sought some alternative to the destruction of the Wars on Terror and Iraq: 'It is not part of the left's frame of mind to offer smart domestic security programs to counter Attorney General John Ashcroft's heavy hand. And perhaps most damaging, the left is not in the habit of proposing a constructive foreign policy.'

49. John Lloyd, 'Why I Can No Longer Write for the *NS*', *New Statesman* (14 April 2003). Lloyd's argument, sneakily, consisted of acceptance of the anti-UN line of the US Government: 'The left's programme now should be to argue in favour of committing resources to those multilateral agencies that work.'

50. Mick Hume, 'And the Oscar for Self Loathing Goes to ... America', *The Times* (24 March 2003); Janet Daley, 'Why the Left Will Never Put its Hands Up', *Daily Telegraph* (9 April 2003).

51. Gavin Esler, 'The Danger of This Infantile Anti-Americanism', *Independent* (15 May 2003); Barbara Amiel, 'Anti-Americans Are Really Against Liberal Democracy', *Daily Telegraph* (12 May 2003); Matthew Hoffman, 'Americans have Feelings Too', *Independent* (2 May 2003). See also George Will, 'Europe's Decline', *Washington Post* (11 April 2003).

52. Robert Samuelson, 'The Gulf of World Opinion', *New York Times* (27 March 2003).

53. Matthew Hoffman, 'Americans have Feelings Too', *Independent* (2 May 2003). See also the telling lament of David Ignatius: 'None of [these problems in post-war Iraq] changes the fact that brave American and British soldiers, and their bold leaders back home, have done a good deed. I hope it will benefit us as much as it has the Iraqis, but I wouldn't count on it' ('A Good Deed', *Washington Post*, 25 April 2003).

54. Nick Cohen, 'The Last Thing the US Wants is Democracy in Iraq', *Observer* (28 July 2002).

55. Nick Cohen, 'Strange Bedfellows', *New Statesman* (7 April 2003) and 'The Lesson the Left Has Never Learnt', *New Statesman* (21 July 2003).

56. Nick Cohen, 'Left in Stalin's Shadow', *Observer* (9 March 2003).

57. Nick Cohen, '"A Kind, Really Nice Boy"', *Observer* (4 May 2003).

58. Nick Cohen, 'The Defeat of the Left', *New Statesman* (5 May 2003).

59. David Aaronovitch, 'United Notions', *Observer* (23 March 2003), 'The Real Reasons So Many Are Marching', *Guardian* (25 March 2003).

60. David Aaronovitch, 'What Would Change My Mind on Iraq?', *Guardian* (1 April 2003), 'Those Weapons had Better Be There ... ', *Guardian* (29 April 2003), and 'Lies and the Left', *Observer* (27 April 2003). See also the response of *Observer* reader Mike Roberts to Aaronovitch in the *Observer* of 4 May 2003.

61. Johann Hari, 'The Lesson of This Conflict: America Can Be a Force for Good in the World', *Independent* (11 April 2003).

62. Johann Hari, 'The Looting is Ugly, but it's Better than Torture', *Independent* (15 April 2003), and 'Now North Korea Must Be Invaded and Liberated, for the Sake of its People', *Independent* (18 April 2003).

63. Johann Hari, 'Forget the Weapons of Mass Destruction, We were Still Right to Invade Iraq', *Independent* (11 July 2003).

64. Michael Ignatieff, 'I am Iraq', *New York Times Magazine* (23 March 2003).

65. Andrew Sullivan, 'Hitler? He's Not Half as Bad as Bush', *Sunday Times* (6 April 2003).

66. See the review by Martin Bright, 'From Left Bank to West Bank', *Observer* (20 April 2003).

67. Paul Berman, 'The Philosopher of Islamic Terror', *New York Times Magazine* (23 March 2003).

68. Thomas Friedman, 'Telling the Truth in Iraq', *New York Times* (17 August 2003); Quoted in Oliver Burkeman, '"Some Things are True Even if George Bush Believes Them"', *Guardian* (5 August 2003).

69. The allegation about the girlfriend was repeated in the *Sunday Times*. Professor Mandy Merck set the record straight: 'Hitchens once asked me, "Did we have a moment?", and I said I recalled a kiss, little thinking he would imagine we were dating partners' ('Mandy, the Mystery Lesbian in Bill's Past', *Sunday Times*, 9 February 2003).

70. Christopher Reed, 'Battle of the Bottle Divides Columnists', *Observer* (2 March 2003).

71. Sidney Blumenthal, 'With Friends Like These ... ', *Guardian* (21 May 2003); Christopher Hitchens, 'Thinking Like an Apparatchik', *Atlantic* (July/August 2003).

72. 'Pass Notes No. 2236: Hay-on-Wye', *Guardian* (26 May 2003).

73. 'Christopher Hitchens Forcibly Removed From Trailer Park after Drunken Confrontation With Common-Law Wife', *The Onion* (23 April 2003).

74. Julie Burchill, 'The Thrill of the Killer', *Guardian Weekend* (5 April 2003).

75. Hitchens lecture, Hay-on-Wye (25 May 2003), http://www.hayfestival.co.uk/2003/DOCS/radio/index.htm; Christopher Hitchens, 'Giving Peace a Chance', *Slate* (9 April 2003), http://slate.msn.com/id/2081326/.

76. Christopher Hitchens, 'He's Hitler, He's Stalin ... Why Did We Tolerate Him for So Long?', *Mirror* (21 March 2003); quoted in Ludovic Hunter-Tilney, 'The Preacher: Christopher Hitchens', *Financial Times* (6 June 2003).

77. Michael Dobbs, 'For Wolfowitz, A Vision May Be Realized', *Washington Post* (7 April 2003). See also Christopher Hitchens, 'Unintended Consequences', *Slate* (17 March 2003), http://slate.msn.com/id/2080237/. Hitchens and others such as Hari mis-

represent Wolfowitz as opposing the regime of Saddam Hussein from the late 1970s in the name of a 'democratic' Iraq. In fact, as *Time* pointed out, Wolfowitz's opposition stemmed from the same notion of US strategic interests and 'preponderance of power' that he promoted in the 1990s and into the twenty-first century: 'In the 1970s [Wolfowitz] advocated bolstering the U.S. military presence in the Persian Gulf to deter Iraq from someday invading Kuwait or Saudi Arabia' ('Bush's Brainiest Hawk', *Time*, 20 January 2003, reprinted at http://www.cnn. com/2003/ALLPOLITICS/01/20/timep.hawk.tm/).

78. Christopher Hitchens, 'We Must Keep Our Nerve', *Mirror* (25 March 2003).

79. Christopher Hitchens, 'Our Troops Must Stay Strong', *Mirror* (2 April 2003).

80. Christopher Hitchens, 'Lay Off Chalabi', *Slate* (24 April 2003), http://slate.msn.com/id/2081968/, and 'Catharsis', *Slate* (13 May 2003), http://slate.msn.com/id/2082871/.

81. Christopher Hitchens, 'The Gullible Mr. Kerry', *Slate* (24 June 2003), http://slate.msn.com/id/2084753/.

82. Christopher Hitchens, 'Provisional Government', *Slate* (28 May 2003), http://slate.msn.com/id/2083643/.

83. John Carey, 'The Invisible Man', *Sunday Times* (18 May 2003).

84. D.J. Taylor, *Orwell* (London: Chatto and Windus, 2003); Gordon Bowker, *George Orwell* (London: Little, Brown, 2003); Paul Foot, 'By George, They've Got It', *Observer* (1 June 2003).

85. Paul Vallely, 'On the Road Again', *Independent* (30 April 2003); Richard Brooks,'Orwell's Room 101 to be Work of Art', *Sunday Times* (23 March 2003).

86. J.G. Ballard quoted in James Morrison, 'Do They Really Mean Us? Authors Rail at Bizarre Choice of "English" Books', *Independent on Sunday* (2 March 2003); Anthony Holden, 'This One's Not a Maid to Treasure', *Observer* (6 April 2003).

87. James Le Fanu, 'Cure for TB was Too Late to Save Orwell', *Daily Telegraph* (6 May 2003); Dalya Alberge, 'Orwell Attacked by Jealous Fiancé', *The Times* (1 April 2003).

88. Geoffrey Wheatcroft, 'Is Sewell an Orwellian Nightmare?', *Guardian* (10 April 2003).

89. Bernard Crick, 'E. Blair on T. Blair's Call to Arms', *Observer* (23 March 2003).

90. Thomas Pynchon, 'The Road to 1984', *Guardian* (3 May 2003).

91. Michael Shelden, 'George the Hero, Eric the Contrary', *Daily Telegraph* (29 April 2003)

92. 'War on the Home Front', *Daily Telegraph* (10 March 2003).

93. Joann Barkan, '"My Mother, Drunk or Sober": George Orwell on Nationalism and Patriotism', *Dissent* (Winter 2003).

94. Tony Blair, 'The Left Should Not Weep if Saddam is Toppled', *Guardian* (10 February 2003).

95. John Pilger, *The New Rulers of the World* (London: Verso, 2003).

96. Sciabba quoted in Matt Welch, 'Velvet President', *Reason Online* (May 2003), http://reason.com/0305/fe.mw.velvet.shtml; Michael Walzer, 'What a Little War in Iraq Could Do', *New York Times* (7 March 2003).

97. Paul Foot, 'Triumph of Doublethink in 2003', *Guardian* (1 January 2003). See also John Newsinger's caricature of Scott Lucas's *Orwell* (London: Haus, 2003) as 'the traditional Stalinist attack on Orwell' ('Orwell Dictionary. The Biographies', *Socialist Review*, July 2003).

98. Arundhati Roy, 'Mesopotamia. Babylon. The Tigris and Euphrates', *Guardian* (2 April 2003).

99. Julian Barnes, 'This War was not Worth a Child's Finger', *Guardian* (11 April 2003).

100. Deborah Orr, 'If Everyone Falls into Line, Who Will Ask the Questions that Need Asking?', *Independent* (1 April 2003).

101. See Madeleine Bunting, 'Intolerant Liberalism', *Guardian* (8 October 2001); Scott Lucas, 'USA OK? Beyond the Practice of (Anti)-American Studies', *49th Parallel* (Summer 2001), http://artsweb.bham.ac.uk/49thparallel/backissues/issue8/FRONTPGE8.HTM.

102. Christopher Hitchens, 'Ha Ha Ha to the Pacifists', *Guardian* (14 November 2001).

103. Susan Sontag, 'The Power of Principle', *Guardian* (26 April 2003).

Index